The Manhattan Family Guide to Private Schools

The Manhattan Family Guide to Private Schools

Victoria Goldman and Catherine Hausman

Published by
Soho Press, Inc.
853 Broadway
New York, NY 10003

Library of Congress Cataloging-in-Publication Data

Goldman, Victoria, 1958–
The Manhattan family guide to private schools / Victoria Goldman
and Catherine Hausman.
p.   cm.
Includes index.
ISBN 1-56947-148-7
1. Private schools—New York (State)—New York—Directories.
2. Manhattan (New York, N.Y.)—Directories. I. Goldman, Victoria,
1958–   . II. Title.
L903.N7H38   1997
371.02'025747'1—dc21   96-52239
                                                              CIP

Third Edition

For Our Children

Acknowledgments

This book could not have been written without the help of many people in the independent school community: the parents, students and alumni who answered our extensive questionnaire and shared their experiences with us; the nursery school directors; heads of schools; admissions and development office personnel; educators and psychologists who offered their expertise and insight. And, of course, our editor, Laura Hruska, for her patience (and red pencil).

Authors' Note

As parents of young children (five between us at the moment), we had already been through the nursery school admissions process and found it daunting. When it came time to make applications for our children to ongoing (elementary or elementary/secondary) schools we again found ourselves overwhelmed by the number of choices and intimidated by the admissions process. We vowed that the next time around, we would know better—little did we know, however, that our research would lead to a multi-year project culminating in three editions of this book, the only guide to independent schools in New York City in which the text is *not* controlled by the schools.

We toured the schools (many of them more than once). We scrutinized brochures, annual reports, handbooks, curriculum guides and student publications. We interviewed admissions directors, heads of schools, educators, IQ test administrators, child psychologists, students, alumni and parents. We sent a letter and questionnaire to all of the heads of schools describing our project. Now, we ask for updated information.

It should not surprise parents that the schools that were most open to our questions are also the most secure about their missions and the new directions in which they are moving, and are the most welcoming to parents in general. While we can understand the reluctance of the schools to disclose the inner workings of their admissions decision-making processes, in the end, many heads of schools, admissions directors and administrators were very generous with their time and advice, and we thank them for their cheerful cooperation.

We hope that the third edition of *The Manhattan Family Guide to Private Schools* will serve the interests of families searching for the best school for their child.

Table of Contents

PRIVATE SCHOOL LOCATOR MAP

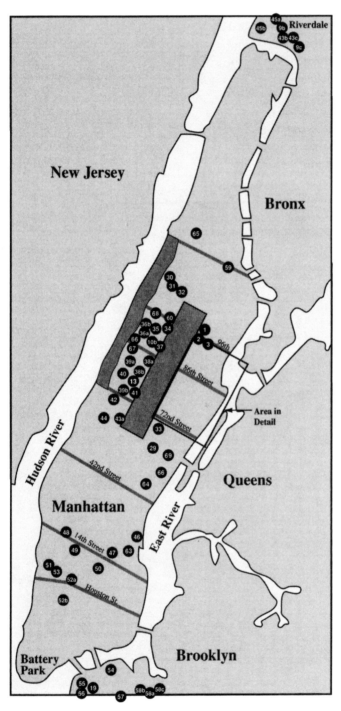

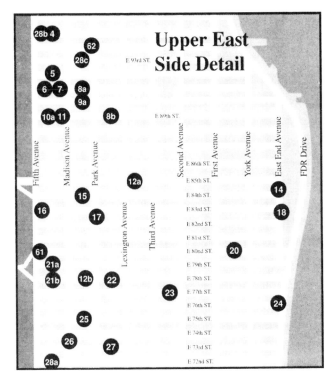

Upper East Side Detail

E 93rd ST.
E 89th ST.
E 86th ST.
E 85th ST.
E 84th ST.
E 83rd ST.
E 82nd ST.
E 81st ST.
E 80nd ST.
E 79th ST.
E 78th ST.
E 77th ST.
E 76th ST.
E 75th ST.
E 74th ST.
E 73rd ST.
E 72nd ST.

Fifth Avenue
Madison Avenue
Park Avenue
Lexington Avenue
Third Avenue
Second Avenue
First Avenue
York Avenue
East End Avenue
FDR Drive

22. The Allen-Stevenson School
23. The Birch Wathen Lenox School
24. The Town School
25. The Hewitt School
26. The Gateway School of New York
27. The Buckley School
28. Lycée Français
    a. N–5th Grade
    b. General Admissions Office 6th–10th Grade
    c. 11th–12th Grade
29. The Browning School
30. St. Hilda's & St. Hugh's School
31. Bank Street School for Children
32. The Cathedral School
33. Rabbi Arthur Schneier Park East Day School
34. Columbia Grammar and Preparatory School
35. Trinity School
36. The Abraham Joshua Heschel School
    a. 3's–5th Grade
    b. 6th–8th Grade
37. The Dwight Anglo-American International Schools
38. The Rodeph Sholom School
    a. N–1st Grade
    b. 2nd–6th Grade

39. The Calhoun School
    a. Lower, Middle, Upper Schools
    b. Lower School
40. Collegiate School
41. Stephen Gaynor School
42. West End Day School
43. The Ethical Culture Fieldston Schools
    a. Ethical Culture School (Midtown)
    b. Fieldston Lower School Bronx, NY
    c. The Fieldston School Bronx, NY
44. Professional Children's School
45. The Riverdale Country School
    a. Upper School Bronx, NY
    b. Lower School Bronx, NY
46. United Nations International School
47. Friends Seminary
48. Corlears School
49. The City & Country School
50. Grace Church School
51. Village Community School
52. a. Little Red School House and
    b. Elisabeth Irwin High School
53. St. Luke's School

54. Brooklyn Friends School Brooklyn, NY
55. The Packer Collegiate Institute Brooklyn, NY
56. Saint Ann's School Brooklyn, NY
57. Polytechnic Preparatory Country Day School Brooklyn, NY
58. The Berkeley Carroll School
    a. Lower School Brooklyn, NY
    b. Elementary School Brooklyn, NY
    c. Middle and Upper School Brooklyn, NY
59. The Children's Storefront
60. Alexander Robertson School
61. Abraham Lincoln School
62. The Gillen Brewer School
63. East Manhattan School for Bright and Gifted Children
64. The Family Schools
65. The Modern School
66. Metropolitan Montessori School
67. The Solomon Schechter School
68. The Studio Elementary School
69. The Geneva School

WHAT'S SO PRIVATE ABOUT PRIVATE SCHOOLS?

INTRODUCTION

The "private"° school admissions season begins the day after Labor Day when New York City parents start to drag their children, barely out of diapers, through four months of touring and testing, then wait in a state of suspended animation until the middle of that bleak wintry day in February or March when a thick or thin envelope arrives in the mail. (Thick envelopes contain a contract; thin, a non-acceptance letter). Parental egos are either elated or deflated, but for those who are disappointed, it's still not too late to go house hunting in Westchester.

There are over seventy independent schools in the New York City area; these include some of the best schools in the nation. There are schools with religious affiliations, schools for children with learning disabilities, Montessori Schools and a Waldorf School: There really is an independent school for everyone, but it just might not be the one you have your heart set on. And though applying to New York City's independent schools has not gotten less stressful over the years, there have been important demographic changes in the city itself that have significantly altered the admissions game.

What Is an Independent School?

All of the member schools of the Independent Schools Admissions Association of Greater New York (ISAAGNY) are not for profit, racially nondiscriminatory, have their own board of trustees, are chartered by the New York State Board of Regents and accredited by the New York State Association of Independent Schools or the Middle-States Association of Colleges and Schools. Independent schools have six basic characteristics: 1) self-governance, 2) self-support, 3) self-defined curriculum, 4) self-selected students, 5) self-selected faculty, 6) small size.°° Private schools, on the other hand, are owned by individuals who may derive profits or incur losses from school operations.°°°

°In New York City most "private" schools are either "independent" (nonprofit) or privately owned and operated for profit. Most of the schools discussed in this book are actually independent schools.

°°*Independent Schools, Independent Thinkers*, edited by Pearl Rock Kane (Jossey-Bass Publishers, San Francisco, 1992), pp. 6–17.

°°°"Independent School Myths and Realities," a newsletter published by NAIS (National Association of Independent Schools), revised March 1994.

3

Teachers in these schools do not need to be certified by the state. They are, however, likely to be experts in their fields, for example, a historian teaching history or a drama department head who is a playwright and director when he's not teaching. Most independent school kindergarten teachers have a master's in early childhood education.

Perhaps the most important difference between independent and public schools is that the formers' "fundamental freedom from state and local governments' regulation has allowed independent schools to develop outside of the ferment that has rocked the public schools."[*] And, of course, public schools do not charge tuition and every child is entitled to placement in such a school (subject to residence requirements and other such prerequisites).

Each school has its own unique character, with a board of trustees that appoints the head of school, who ensures that the school fulfills its educational mission. The headmaster (in conjunction with the development office) assumes the role of CEO and major fund-raiser. Every independent school has its own philosophy of education, its "statement of mission" (the primary aims of the school). This mission statement is always included in the school's literature, but you sometimes have to read between the lines to find it. Each independent school is accountable to its students and their parents; if the parents are not happy with the fulfillment of the school's mission they can remove their children and find another that suits them better. If enough parents do so, the school will fail.

A good reputation is so vital to independent schools that although some myths about a school such as "having the brightest kids" or admitting "only the most terrific families" or "getting the most kids into the top Ivy League colleges" are misleading and often false, they do attract applicants. And some school admissions personnel, perhaps inadvertently, help perpetuate these "positive" myths. The fact is, independent schools are much more mixed than anyone admits. (We found that siblings and legacies were the great equalizers.) As the New York State Association of Independent Schools Guide to Choosing a School states, while SAT scores and college admissions records are "good indicators of the quality of the student body, not necessarily of the school . . . the schools of worth are those whose students, facile or not, are helped to realize their highest potential, develop a lifelong love of learning and forge good character."[**]

[*] *Independent Schools, Independent Thinkers, supra.*
[**] "Choosing a School-A Guide For Parents," a pamphlet published by the New York State Association of Independent Schools (NYSAIS).

The level of work, the pressure, pace of learning and challenge, hours of homework and amount of remedial support provided by the school all contribute to designation as "very selective." The qualities a child needs to get in and stay in one of these schools are strong academic potential, an outgoing nature, aggressiveness, intensity, good self-esteem, independence, maturity and perseverance. A less competitive, more nurturing school would be better for a child with an average IQ, a known learning disability, a very creative or artistic nature or a nonconformist or shy personality. A desire not to subject a child to externally imposed requirements at an early age and a belief in a child's innate abilities, which, given time to flower, will lead him to a happier, more fulfilling life militate against the choice of a highly pressured school experience.

We believe that there truly is a school for your child, but it is not true that if you can pay, your child can go to the school of your choice. The apparent arbitrariness of admissions decisions is hard for "power-house parents" to accept. Said one admissions director: "After all, they got into an Ivy League school, joined the sorority/fraternity of their choice, landed the job of their dreams and they expect the same for their child too." The baby boom echo is making admissions at all levels very competitive. In response, many schools are expanding their lower schools, adding an extra kindergarten or first grade class that will continue up through the school.

In the past few years, schools that give preference to siblings and legacies (descendants of former students) have often had more applicants than places, and have been forced to make some difficult decisions. Your child's year might be a year in which many siblings apply at the school of your choice but take heart: If your child doesn't get into your first-choice school in kindergarten, you might try again in the third grade, by which time attrition will probably have occurred due to divorce and families relocating to other cities and the suburbs, and a place may then be available. (An interesting trend countering suburban flight is that of single, divorced parents moving back into the city with older children to enroll in independent schools.)

Changes in School Services

Gone are the days when women volunteers devoted their time exclusively to serving on school committees, chaperoning field trips and organizing fund-raisers. The two-career family is now the norm (and you are as likely to see a forty-five-year-old father attending the school play or walking afternoon safety patrol as a mother). There is an increased need for after-school, vacation and summer programs, and working parents are happiest if those programs are part of their children's own schools. Most schools now have after-school programs. Caedmon School was the first to introduce "child-minding" until 6:00 P.M. In 1999 Collegiate School started its own after-school program. Girls from the Brearley School can attend The After School Workshop at P.S. 6 until 6 P.M. (Some educators see this as a transfer of surrogate parenting to institutions.) Parents are also scheduling more after-school activities such as sports, music and religious instruction, in addition to playdates, for their children. In future, schools that now have very young students will probably eliminate the younger classes in favor of more extended day programs for older children. Dalton and Friends Seminary dropped their nursery programs because of space needs and also because it was too difficult for them to select two to three year olds who would be right for their ongoing programs.

One outcome of working parents' desire to have their children in school for longer hours is that the Guild of New York Independent Schools agreed to extend the independent school year from 160 days to 170 days (still ten days short of the public school schedule). Schools also agreed to open their doors earlier in the fall, closer to the Labor Day holiday weekend. A handful of schools still give "travel days" on either side of spring break, a vestige of the era in which families routinely packed a trunk for Europe. Now many of these families travel to snow country in Utah or Colorado.

Financial Pressures

The question of the affordability of private school education is becoming more acute as tuition for Manhattan day schools, which doubled in the past decade, continues to rise. Now parents can expect to pay about $14,000 and up for third-grade tuition. In addition, the gap between income generated by tuition and rising operating costs has widened and all schools count upon voluntary giving and annual fundraising revenues. "Schools are under more pressure for outside fundraising from corporate and private sources than at any time in the past," according to an administrator of educational grants at a prestigious foundation. "Capital campaigns seem to come around as often as White Sales these days," says one beleaguered family. We know a couple who received a solicitation letter from their son's school announcing a new capital campaign with a return card enclosed showing a suggested contribution of $10,000. The next day the couple marched into the development office and asked, "Do you expect this much every year?" They were informed that they could pay in monthly installments over a five year period. The pressure to give can be especially intense when the class representative tells you they are hoping for 100% participation. What most parents don't realize is that there is no threshold for annual giving; parents are asked to give whatever they can; contributions within a given class may range from $5.00 to $25,000. Of course only a contribution of $10,000 and above will earn you inclusion in "The Headmaster's Circle": The 90's equivalent of The Social Register.

After the closing of the Fleming School in the middle of an academic year and the merger of two other schools in the late eighties, parents are more likely now to be concerned about the financial health of a prospective school. (However, here's a tip: Do not ask for the annual report until *after* your child has been accepted.) A healthy endowment is important because it can help a school weather hard times, though it shouldn't be the only reason to pick a school. But unless a school has a substantial endowment current parents will be the school's prime source of revenue.

Many parents do not know that tuition covers only about 80 percent of a school's operating expenses and budget, much of this going toward teacher salaries and fringe benefits. Capital improvements, new technology and science labs, and improvements and repairs to existing facilities are necessary to keep the schools competitive. Adding to this pressure is the increased need for tuition assistance of parents whose children are already in the schools.° "A tremendous increase in the amount of money raised by annual giving and capital fund programs over the past decade" has helped schools make ends meet, according to Fred Calder, Executive Director of the New York State Association of Independent Schools. Thus it doesn't hurt to have families who manage charitable foundations in the parent body. As one admissions director confided, "We *are* a business, you know."

There is increased concern about socioeconomic stratification within school populations as many middle and upper middle income families find that they are unable or unwilling to pay approximately $150,000 for thirteen years of private school tuition. Most schools are

°See "Applying for Financial Aid," p. 47, *infra*.

seeing an increase in families with high income levels applying for financial aid. According to Meade Thayer, Director of Financial Aid Services at NAIS, "Families may well have financial need from their perspective, but does the school have the financial aid available to meet the needs of *all* families applying?" Schools are being forced to make tough decisions about which families to support. "The decisions they make illustrate the school's attitude toward socioeconomic diversity and their desire to have it," says Thayer.

Following the national trend towards eliminating junior high schools in favor of middle schools (serving grades 6-8), Community School Districts 2 and 3 on the Upper East and West sides of Manhattan recently decided to end their elementary schools at fifth grade. Beginning in 1995–96, a number of very bright and highly motivated fifth grade public school students began applying to the private schools for entrance at sixth grade. Many of the top private schools are scrambling to make space for them, while at the same time, reserving places for Prep for Prep program graduates who enter at seventh grade. Some schools we surveyed, such as Riverdale Country Day School, the Spence School and Trinity School, told us that because of the way their schools are structured (the lower school is comprised of kindergarten through sixth grade, for instance) and/or because of space restraints, openings in sixth grade at those schools would depend upon natural attrition. Others, including The Brearley School, Horace Mann and the Dalton School said they had already expanded their sixth grades to accommodate public school applicants.

As tuitions climb and the competition for places in the most exclusive schools becomes more intense, the private schools face growing resentment from full-tuition paying families who find that their hard earned tuition dollars are subsidizing increasing numbers of scholarship students. However, NAIS statistics reveal that the numbers of students receiving *full* scholarship is in fact declining. Schools find it is more cost effective to support two families on partial assistance (each paying $6,000 toward tuition, for example) thus achieving a greater diversity of families for the same investment. In another instance of how elementary and secondary private school admissions parallel admissions at the college level, some middle class families of color, Hispanic and Asian families, (all of whom are historically underrepresented in private schools), cognizant of their marketability, find that they are able to shop around for the best deal.

Parents should keep in mind that there is a significant difference between applying for financial assistance at the elementary and secondary levels and applying at the college level where federal assistance is available in addition to institutional assistance. Parents of elementary and secondary school age children also have another viable option—public school. More middle and upper middle class parents are considering select city public schools for a portion of their child's education. Although Hunter Elementary is under the aegis of Hunter College of the City of New York, acceptance to this highly selective tuition-free school is considered as desirable as acceptance to the most prestigious private school. The specialized high schools such as Stuyvesant, Bronx Science and Brooklyn Tech are still magnets for many private school students beginning in ninth grade.

Technology

At one independent school this spring, we watched as the "old" Macintosh 1.1 computers went out the door and the "new" Dell 333 MHz computers came in. To remain competitive and up-to-the-minute, schools are under increasing pressure to spend more of their budget on technology. The National Association of Independent Schools (NAIS) reports that during the 1995–96 school year, NAIS member schools spent $83 million on technology, with an average of $103,277 per school. That figure is certainly much higher today. In addition, many schools are running "computer initiative" capital campaigns to further augment their technology programs. One school hosted a "cybercarnival" to give the school's technology program a boost.

Upgrading hardware, adding high speed connections to the internet and buying the latest CD-ROMS and software is just a part of the expense. The best technology in the world is useless without people; almost every comprehensive independent school now has a Director of Technology. Many schools also find it essential to have a full-time "network administrator" to maintain the system.

And that's not all. A good educational technology program requires trained faculty to integrate all this "stuff" into the curriculum in meaningful ways. Staff training, whether through an outside workshop or an "in-house" technology coordinator, is fundamental—and expensive.

According to one technology seer, the day when "machines are the hand-maiden of cognition in the classroom" is not far off. Students at The Trevor Day School tote Toshiba laptops to and from school in their backpacks and use the computer in every subject class as a "transparent tool"—as they would use pencil and paper. Students at many schools already have access to a school "intranet" or internal web site that allows students to access homework assignments, read school notices, join in school conferences, communicate with faculty and send in their homework via e-mail.

The internet has become a primary research tool and nearly every school library is now on-line. Schools subscribe to several services that allow students to search an extensive database of full-text articles from over 200 periodicals, including *The New York Times* and other major magazines, via the World Wide Web. At The Nightingale-Bamford School, students in a Constitutional Law elective learn how to conduct keyword searches on these Web-based services for information related to their study of a particular amendment. Furthermore, students can use the Web to access legal cases that are currently before the Supreme Court. We found an English teacher at York Prep using the internet to look up the lyrics of Bob Dylan's songs for a course on the Romantic poets. Students in the 8-9's at Manhattan Country School communicate via e-mail with the Zuni Nation in New Mexico.

Desktop publishing gives students "ownership" of the publication process. For instance, The Brearley School offers desktop publishing workshops and an interactive design class for aspiring student editors. We saw tenth graders huddled around a monitor laying out an article for their class publication, *The Pulse*. Students in their own Student Publications Office also produce a literary magazine and the Brearley school yearbook.

At Convent of the Sacred Heart we observed young women in a biology class use special motion, temperature, pH and pressure probes attached to laptop computers to record and graph their laboratory data, allowing them to fine-tune their experiments.

Learning literally "comes alive" when students create multimedia projects using ClarisWorks or Hyperstudio. At The Nightingale-Bamford School students created an interactive tour of a medieval village as part of a third grade social studies unit on the Middle Ages. This "virtual village" was then displayed on a touch-screen computer in the school's lobby. By clicking on different characters, such as "Minstrel Martin" or "Sir William," students could learn about that individual's role in society.

Technology rich schools share the following characteristics: 1) A computer density of fewer than five students per multimedia computer 2) Thirty-eight percent of the technology budget is spent on professional development and ongoing support 3) Annualized technology expenditures per student are between \$180–\$450 per year.*

It is not enough that students acquire basic computing *skills* such as word-processing, computer graphics, desktop publishing, databases and simulation. "Computer literacy means knowing how to use the computer as a tool to help create and think, to manage information, to solve problems, to express ideas and to communicate with others."**

Parents looking at a prospective school should ask:

- Does the school have a Technology Mission Statement?
- How much of the technology budget is devoted to faculty support and training?
- How is technology integrated into all subject areas, not just the obvious ones?

An educational technology consultant suggested parents look at how the computer is used. Does the school use the computer as an "electronic playbook" or as a creative tool involving high level thinking? Do students spend computer time visiting the computer lab to play games such as "Math-blaster" or do they create something of their own using a program such as Microworlds (LOGO)?

In the most developed programs the classroom teacher initiates projects using different applications to solve problems, so students think in new ways. As Michael Smith-Welch, a fifth grade homeroom teacher at Little Red Schoolhouse and Elisabeth Irwin High School told us, "All the hardware in the world can't beat a good curriculum idea." For a unit on the study of ancient civilizations, Smith-Welch created a project that looks at the problems faced by archeologists in the interpretation of artifacts. The project integrates science, math, writing, computer, history and art and culminates in the creation of a classroom museum of artifacts as well as a "computer museum."

Not all students have access to a home computer, and those who do may not have the latest software applications or a connection to the internet. Schools are devising their own solutions to this issue of equity. Some have purchased computers for scholarship students, others are keeping their computer labs open and staffed until late afternoon. Some independent schools bridge the gap by opening the

*Technology Today! A Technology Newsletter for Educators, (A FutureKids publication, volume V, issue 1 Fall, 1996)
**Ibid.

school to public school students on Saturdays. Most NYC public libraries provide internet access free of charge.

Faculty

In addition to the composition of the student body, another essential component in measuring the quality of a school is the calibre of the faculty. Teachers in the independent schools do not have the bargaining power of a union and can be hired and fired at the will of the administration. However, teachers in independent schools do have the ability to design the curriculum and have flexibility in their choice of approach to their subject, books and materials. The advantage for schools is that they can handpick teachers who conform to the school's philosophy and style.

In some cases independent school teachers receive pay parity with public school teachers; in most cases they are paid significantly less. For instance, the head of the English department at an independent school told us that she earns about $10,000 less than her public school counterpart. The exact figures vary from school to school. Heads of schools contend that it is health and other benefits for staff that really eat into the budget. Teacher salaries jumped in the mid-eighties but have stabilized since then. Still, in order to keep the best teachers, schools are under constant pressure to offer faculty inducements such as housing and stipends for study and travel. Many schools have named scholarship funds earmarked for this purpose.

Multiculturalism and Diversity

New York City is the most multicultural city in the country, and many parents and educators believe that its independent schools should reflect that "metropolitan mix" in their student bodies. Despite programs such as Early Steps, a program that promotes diversity at the kindergarten and first grade levels, and Prep for Prep, which prepares talented junior high school students of color for entrance into New York City's independent schools, as well as more abundant scholarship money in the upper schools, the lower schools (K–6) have remained remarkably homogeneous. The so-called "progressive" schools have always been in the vanguard of new thinking, while more "traditional" schools adapt at their own pace, especially regarding the thorny issues of diversity and multiculturalism. Schools such as The Ethical Culture Fieldston Schools, Friends Seminary and United Nations International School have always welcomed a diverse student body. Some of the older, more traditional schools did not always do so but many of these schools now actively recruit students of color. We know of two schools that do not yet give recognition to the Jewish holidays.

During the 1990s the pace of change is likely to become more rapid for two reasons: 1) The changing college admissions profile—in recent years, bright and able students of color have fared particularly well in gaining admissions to the elite Ivy League colleges and universities; since a large part of an independent school's status derives from the number of students they feed to the Ivy League, this trend has inevitably trickled down to kindergarten admissions. 2) Many of New York City's independent schools competed for a lucrative DeWitt Wallace–Reader's Digest Fund Independent School Opportunity Program (ISOP) Grant. To date, thirteen New York City independent schools have received grants of between $200,000 and $400,000 (depending on the size of the school). The large size of the grants was a powerful incentive for change. Most participating schools received scholarship aid for their students of color; others were selected on the basis of their commitment to "increase the representation of faculty of color or create collaborative programs with public schools and other community agencies." Collegiate, Packer Collegiate Institute, Brooklyn Friends and Fieldston created the position of director of multicultural affairs (or diversity). Dalton initiated a public-private school collaboration for the teaching of science and mathematics. ISOP grant money also enabled Dalton to expand a mentoring program for children of color in the school which matches students with professionals within the NYC community. The program extends downward so that these students in turn mentor other students coming up. Nightingale-Bamford established a teaching fund for young alumnae of color, Calhoun set up an Advanced Studies Institute, a three-week summer program for students that focuses on the ways race, class, gender and ethnicity have influenced traditional American values.

The last ISOP grants expired in September of 1998 and currently there are no plans to renew the program. "The legacy of the ISOP program is mixed," said a source close to the program. "Overall the landscape is not significantly different but there are many individual instances of this grant broadening representation of students and faculty of color [in the independent schools]." The ISOP program was successful in jump-starting awareness of diversity issues: "The schools really began to take the issue of diversity seriously; there was the sense of being on-board, or not on-board." Several of the programs established under its aegis will find alternative funding and carry on. Since the grants began to expire the Interschool Faculty Diversity Search Program (see Resources section pp. 470, *infra*.) was initiated to enlarge the pool of talented candidates of color.

A faculty commitment to diversity is important. Diversity training for faculty is on the rise and many independent school teachers spend time at anti-bias retreats and conferences related to these themes. Adah Askew, Chairman of the Faculty Diversity Committee at Dalton, coordinates the student mentoring program there. Each year her high school students visit the traditional Southern black colleges ("where there are role models in every classroom") so that they might consider "The Harvard of the South" for instance, as an alternative to the Ivy League schools. The parent body also influences the pace of change. Many of the independent schools have a parent committee on diversity. Some parents prefer to have their children in a more homogeneous setting and therefore may choose a more "traditional" school.

Students at New York City's independent schools, along with the rest of the nation, are struggling with the issues of race and ethnicity and the meaning of "difference." Active recruiting and competition for children of color makes some educators uneasy, fanning fears of tokenism and concern for the schools' sensitivity to these students' needs once they are enrolled. A former Parents Association president illustrated this attitude by saying "We want to see our kids in a school with a healthy scholarship program, but of course, we will bring *them* up to our level." Support groups for families of color and students of color (some adopted students of color are not from families of color) abound. In addition, many schools now have anti-bias groups, Cultural Awareness Days and clubs such as Students Aware of Multicultural Ethics (S.A.M.E.). There is an Interschool Multicultural Coalition. The New York Diversity Resource Collaborative, comprised of twenty-eight independent schools, sponsors workshops for professionals and job fairs for people of color and provides information about diversity issues through its computer network, Diversity-On-Line. Even in schools with diverse student bodies there are problems. For example, younger children who commute from Upper Manhattan and the boroughs find it difficult to reciprocate playdates. In some instances parents have been mistaken for baby sitters. In the upper grades there are "scholarship cliques" and tensions have been aired in school assemblies or focus groups.

The independent schools, particularly the girls' schools, are also concerned about gender issues. A 1992 study commissioned by the American Association of University Women (AAUW) carried out by the Wellesley College Center for Research on Women, entitled "How Schools Shortchange Girls" documented the subtle gender bias in schools and how girls are steered away from pursuing careers in math, science and technology. The AAUW report showed that young women were not receiving the "same quality or quantity of education as their brothers."[*]

The AAUW issued a new report in 1998 which took a critical look at the value of single-sex education for girls and found no evidence that girls were better off in separate schools: "What the research shows is that separating by sex is not the solution to gender inequity in education. When elements of a good education are present, girls *and* boys succeed." In a press release from the AAUW, Sandy Bernard, president of AAUW says, "No learning environment, single-sex or coed, provides a sure escape from sexism. Sound teacher training is key to reducing sex stereotyping in both the coed and single-sex programs." Ninety-five per cent of America's schoolchildren attend coed public schools. The press release states that there is debate about whether the benefits of some single-sex programs (such as a heightened regard for math and science among girls) derive from factors unique to single-sex programs or factors that promote good education such as small classes and schools, intensive academic curriculum and a disciplined environment. (See also AAUW, infra p. 469).

Some independent schools have special programs to deal with sex bias. For example, the Dalton School has a parent-sponsored committee that reviews sex-equity issues in the school. The Berkeley Carroll School has a faculty sex-equity study group that meets regularly; Manhattan Country School received a five-year "gender equity grant" for $100,000 from a private family foundation in Washington; The Riverdale Country School held a series of parent education evenings on gender issues.

The AAUW Report states, "By the year 2000 two-thirds of the new entrants into the work force will be minorities and women." If these groups are shortchanged now, the future of our country will be compromised. In response, many schools have reevaluated their curricula, either adding or revising courses that include other perspectives including electives such as "Africa in America: an Examination of

[*]*The AAUW Report: How Schools Shortchange Girls*, the AAUW Educational Foundation and the National Education Association, Washington, D.C., 1992 (p. v.).

15

the Literature of the Men and Women Who Shaped Contemporary Black American Culture" and "Reform Movements: The Advent of Feminism, Black History and Civil Rights." Eighth graders at The Allen-Stevenson School study Asian, African and Latin American contributions to Western civilization; eighth graders at The Nightingale-Bamford School study Islamic forms in math and art. Certainly there are still some schools where the DWEM (Dead White European Males) curriculum predominates, and for some parents a classic curriculum in a traditional setting (for example, Chapin, or Trinity) is just fine. That's what freedom of choice is about.

In the early nineties, single-sex, established, traditional schools (many of which have ample endowments) once again became very attractive to many well-to-do parents. Even though both parents might have high-powered careers, these "new traditionalists" are reassured by structured classrooms, the old-fashioned values and a traditional curriculum, as well as the status that acceptance into these schools still confers. But today even the so-called traditional schools are sometimes hard to tell apart from the progressive schools. Some schools have a unique educational philosophy such as Bank Street School for Children, Fieldston Lower School, The Dalton School, The Rudolf Steiner School and The City & Country School; many schools have incorporated what were once considered "progressive" approaches to elementary education into their curricula. Schools are moving away from teacher-directed classrooms and toward encouraging classrooms where collaborative learning is stressed and where different learning styles and different rates of development are accommodated. There is increased integration of subject matter; most elementary programs favor using the experiential or hands-on approach to learning for everything from science to social studies. Parents should be aware that it is in the middle and upper schools that the schools are most different from one another. When they look at a kindergarten they should look at the upper school as well.

Ten years ago, when a concerned mother at an all-girls school brought up the subject of AIDS at a Parents Association Meeting, the other mothers blushed and said, "We don't have to worry about *our* daughters and AIDS." Now nearly every high school provides some form of AIDS education. A group of Interschool students is trying to establish a uniform AIDS curriculum for their schools.

Nearly every independent school addresses environmental issues, and most students participate in some form of environmental study or club that coordinates recycling efforts within the school.

New York City's independent schools are not the ivory towers they once were. Although still exclusionary financially, certain schools are more inclusive in the makeup of their student bodies than they ever have been. When schools renovate, they must now make accommodations for the disabled. But as the former associate director of the Educational Records Bureau reminded us, "Private school education is still a privilege, not an entitlement." The private, independent schools of New York City are still distinguished by their ability to select . . . and exclude.

SELECTING A SCHOOL

Choosing an independent school in New York City is like dating. As one admissions director said, "The chemistry has to be right on both sides." Respect the judgment of the admissions personnel; they really know which children will be successful in their type of program. In making the final decision, a former Parents League president and leader of a toddler group advises, "There should be a commonality between home and school" and in the final decision, "Use your gut feeling. The decision should be 98 percent stomach and heart and 2 percent head." Through it all remember that your child is unique. And be wary of the Trophy Child Syndrome. As David Elkind writes in *Miseducation: Preschoolers at Risk*, "The social pressure on contemporary parents to use their children as symbols of economic surplus and status is powerful, even if parents are not fully aware of it." Misguided parents believe that "a successful child is the ultimate proof of one's own success."[*] As one Director of Admissions advised us, "Consider your *child's* comfort level" when selecting a school.

Factors to consider

1. **Location: City or "Campus"**
   Note that a campus school (located outside of Manhattan) may require busing or other transportation, which can cost up to $2,500 annually. The child attending a school far from his immediate neighborhood spends many hours in travel over the course of his education.

[*]*Miseducation: Preschoolers at Risk*, by David Elkind (Knopf, New York, 1987), p. 78

Parents of young children may choose a campus school so that they can experience a clean outdoor environment for relaxation and recreation daily, and so that, when they are older, they may enjoy grassy playing fields and tree-shaded quads. There is always a late bus to accommodate children enrolled in after-school activities. But for some children there may be better uses for this time. Many adjust with no problem, even in the early years; others find the extra travel draining.

2. **Single Sex or Coed***

In the younger grades, many children do not seem to value friendships with members of the opposite sex. Later, this changes drastically. Parents sometimes prefer a single-sex school where girls may feel more encouraged to be leaders and where their competitive instincts may be less fettered.

3. **Philosophy of School (Educational Practices and Values)**

A school's goals are spelled out in its mission statement. Look at the history of the school, at its founder and his or her philosophy of education. What are the school's traditions? Is the parents' association active and inclusive? Does the school strive for a diverse student body? Are multicultural perspectives included in the curriculum? Are classes formal or informal? When, if at all, does letter/number grading begin? Does the school rank its students? What kinds of awards for achievement are given at the end of the year? Is effort recognized? Is community service required (or incorporated into the curriculum)? Perhaps the most important question parents of a kindergarten applicant can ask is "How is reading taught?" Some schools employ an eclectic method to teach reading, others use a Whole Language–based program (see Glossary, p. 55). Traditional methods usually employ basal readers, workbooks and the teaching of phonetics. Ask your nursery school teacher about your child's learning style to determine what type of learning environment would be best for him or her.

4. **Religious Affiliation**

Is the school presently affiliated with a religious institution? Many schools were founded in church buildings and later became independent entities, although they may retain the name of the church. In some cases, a representative of the church continues to serve on

*Brearley, Browning, Chapin, Collegiate, Dalton, Nightingale-Bamford, Spence and Trinity are members of the coeducational Interschool Program. Students from member schools can participate in after-school activities, academic courses, intramural sports, community service projects and other activities and clubs. Weekend and holiday dances are an adjunct to single-sex schooling.

the board of trustees. Some Jewish schools are associated with a congregation. Is there mandatory prayer or chapel attendance? Which religious holidays are recognized on the school calendar?

5. **Parent Body**

   How well will you fit in? Remember that you have to live with these people for the next eight or more years and their children will form your child's peer group.

6. **Size of School**

   Consider your child's "comfort level." Will he or she fare better in a smaller, more nurturing environment? Are there programs a larger school may be able to offer that will be important to your child's fulfillment?

7. **After-School Programs, Early Bird Programs, Vacation Programs and Child Minding**

   These programs are of particular interest to working parents.

8. **Grade at Which School Ends (sixth, eighth, ninth or twelfth)**

   Pick the school that will be right for your child at the outset. Schools without a high school may put more emphasis on the lower grades and offer more leadership opportunities at an earlier age, such as student council president or editorship of the yearbook. Students say that exposure to the behavior of older adolescents, with the concomitant possibilities of experimentation with sex, drugs and alcohol, is more limited at a school without a high school. On the other hand, a parent may breathe a sigh of relief when his kindergartener begins at a school that continues through twelfth grade. But bear in mind that while the child *may* complete his or her education at this school that is frequently not the case. Further school applications may still lie in wait.

9. **Pace and Expectations of the Academic Program**

   How academic is the kindergarten? Certain New York City schools such as Horace Mann, Dalton, Trinity, Fieldston, Collegiate, Chapin, Brearley and Spence are considered the most demanding of their students and are sometimes categorized as "very selective." However, parents should note that the pace and expectations vary greatly amongst the lower schools at these "top tier" institutions. But a child develops at his or her own pace. Not every child who enters such a school is happy as it becomes more academically demanding; yet many who are not "ready" at the age of five blossom in the later years.

10. **Consider Your Own Family Pattern**

    If your family enjoys ski weekends be aware that some schools require more work on weekends and vacations than others. On the other hand, if your academic expectations are traditional you won't be comfortable waiting until your child *wants* to learn a subject you feel is important.

Feeder Schools

Many New York City parents are concerned about getting their children onto the "Harvard Track"; they believe that if a child is accepted into the right nursery school, then he/she will get into the right ongoing school and will eventually be accepted at a prestigious Ivy League college. A "feeder school" is a nursery school that channels its graduates to a specific ongoing school. Twenty or more years ago, certain schools preselected their applicant bodies. When parents called a nursery school for an application, they would have a "chat" with the admissions director after which an application might or might not be forwarded.

Today, the reality is that each season, certain nursery schools have a large number of applicants to certain ongoing schools. Some are siblings of the students already enrolled, some live nearby, some are following the fashion at that nursery school. And over the years, certain nursery school directors have developed relationships with the admissions directors at the ongoing schools. They can communicate to those schools whether or not certain children would be good candidates for their programs. There is absolutely no guarantee that even at the "right" nursery school, your child will get into your number-one choice ongoing school. An educational consultant and former admissions director told us: "Kindergarten admissions have become terribly arbitrary over the past couple of years."

Even the most traditional schools, which used to take children predominantly from the Upper East Side or Upper West Side, now accept children from all parts of New York City. Admissions directors are having to go farther and farther afield to look at candidates these days. According to Grace Ball, lower school admissions director at The Riverdale Country School, in 1985 there were only eight nurseries "feeding" into Riverdale. In 1993 there were thirty-two, including six in Westchester and two in New Jersey. In a class of forty-four children at Collegiate School, twenty-six different preschool programs are represented. One year, The Chapin School had applicants from sixty nursery schools and enrolled children from twenty.

At nursery schools with a large number of applicants to a particular ongoing school, the director of admissions or a member of the admissions department of an ongoing school will go and observe the applicants in their nursery-school environment. This is an advantage because a child is more relaxed and natural when interacting with his peers in his own familiar classroom. (Some ongoing schools, however, still require that a parent bring the child in for additional testing at the school interview.)

Keep in mind that some ongoing schools have their own nurseries or pre-K programs, most of which were originally set up as a service for the children of alumni. But Friends Seminary and Dalton recently dropped their pre-K programs, and Horace Mann dropped its youngest twos in response to limitations on classroom space and the recognition that it is too difficult to pick a two year old who will ultimately succeed in a demanding academic environment.

The bottom line is, select a nursery school program based on proximity to your home and philosophy and schedule.

THE APPLICATION

Parents of kindergarten applicants should telephone to request school applications soon after Labor Day of the year their child is four years old (applicants to the upper grades can wait a little longer). Applications should be filed no later than the first week of December. Most New York City independent schools have a birthday cutoff date of September 1 (your child must turn five before entering kindergarten). But since the first step in the application process is to make tentative selections of the schools to which you may apply by consulting your nursery school director and other sources, you must start thinking about school earlier than that. Some schools give spring tours.

If your child is in a nursery school program, the director will usually set up a meeting with each family to discuss proposed choices for further schooling. If you need more information than you have been able to obtain about a school or its suitability for your child, you should request a meeting with the director to further discuss ongoing schools.

In early October the Parents League sponsors Independent School Day. Most of the New York City independent schools attend, staff a table and set out their literature. Usually a school's admissions director is there to answer brief questions. Be prepared: It's a little like Macy's at Christmastime. But going, picking up brochures and asking questions will save you a lot of time and phone calls. Some applications are included in the brochures; some schools require a separate phone call to obtain an application.

Try to be organized. We recommend starting a file with each school in a separate folder, to keep track of correspondence and appointments. Have some nice wallet-size photos on hand because some applications require a photograph. (Although one family that sent a nude photo of their toddler to a crusty but prestigious school received an acceptance.)

Type or write your application legibly. The sooner you return your application, the sooner you will get your appointments for tours and/or interviews. It's a good idea to seek an early appointment; in case your child is ill the day of the interview, you will still have time to reschedule.

Some applications, like those for Dalton and Friends, contain essay questions. Read the school catalog very carefully and be familiar with the program before you write your essay. But remember that the essay is about your child, not about your many accomplishments or great expectations. The most difficult part of the entire admissions process can be this essay, as it requires a real knowledge of your child, objectivity and verbal ability.

Don't send anything with the application except a letter(s) of recommendation if requested by the school. And if the school doesn't ask for an essay or photograph, don't send one unless you are a genuinely talented writer or photographer.

Early Notification

If your family is connected to a school (that is, if there is a sibling already enrolled, or if the child is a "legacy") then you are eligible for the Early Notification Program. These families will be notified approximately a month earlier than others not so connected. If your child is accepted and you accept the school, then you are required to withdraw your application to all other schools. You may wait until you have heard from all of the other schools on the regular ISAAGNY reply date, but you are not then guaranteed a place at the school that offered early admission.

A word of advice to parents of boys with spring or summer birthdays: There is a mistaken assumption that these boys are immature. As a result, many parents hold their boys back a year, so that quite a few boys turn seven during the kindergarten year. Discuss with your nursery school director whether or not it would be best to hold your son back. If you think he's ready, trust your instincts.

THE INTERVIEW

After the school receives your application you will be contacted to set up an appointment for your child's interview. Independent schools like to see both parents at tours and parent interviews as a demonstration of their commitment to their child's education. Parents usually meet with the head of school or the director of admissions. The requirements are different for every school so be sure to read the instructions on your admissions packet carefully.

The single-sex schools in particular like to meet with both parents together. At some schools, school personnel only meet parents as members of a tour group. Does this mean they are looking more carefully at the parents at some schools than others? Absolutely. Be prepared to talk in detail about your child. One mother was asked the following sequence of questions at a prestigious school, "When did you wean? When did he walk? When did he talk? Where do you go on weekends?" One admission director simply asks, "Tell me about your daughter."

Nursery school and admissions directors say, "Dress your child comfortably" for the interview. If your child is fussing with his suspenders or playing with her hair it will detract from the interview. Long hair should be pulled back and off the child's face. And keep in the mind the style of the school—that is, whether or not there is a uniform or dress code. For example, when applying to Dalton, Ethical Culture, Riverdale, Friends Seminary, Village Community School or Calhoun, where most of the students will be casually dressed, play clothes are quite acceptable for your child. However, at Buckley, Chapin, St. Bernard's, Spence, Hewitt or Convent of the Sacred Heart, children will be dressed more formally, and your child should be too: boys in a sports jacket or cardigan, collared shirt, slacks and leather shoes; girls in a dress. Parents should also consider the style of the school and dress accordingly.

For kindergarten admissions the interview may be conducted individually or in a group. The interview might be conducted by one of the following: the kindergarten teachers, the head of the lower school or the director of admissions, who will record their observations of your child at play. At some schools your child will be asked to complete specific tasks, or take the school's own age-appropriate test. Children are frequently asked to draw a picture and we found that it does help if he/she can recognize and write his/her name.

You can form an idea about whether or not the school is child-centered during the admissions process, says Grace Ball, director of lower school admissions at The Riverdale Country School. "Who is the admissions director focusing on, you or your child? Is your child addressed by name? Are they really getting down to the child's level? After the interview is over do they give you any feedback about your child? I always give parents a few minutes after the interview," she says.

How to Prepare Your Child

The day or night before your child's interview is enough advance notice to give him or her for preparation. Don't communicate your anxiety to the child. Tell your child as specifically as possible what to expect; for example, if he or she will be accompanying you on a tour or will be joining a group, or will be meeting with a member of the admissions staff alone. The nature of the interview is usually described in the admissions packet but if you are not sure, call the school and ask so that you can prepare your child.

If your child wakes up with a runny nose, looking under the weather, it's a judgment call whether or not to cancel your interview. Some schools are so booked that you might not get another chance. But never miss your appointment without calling the school to notify them!

If you notice during the interview that your child is really feeling and behaving oddly, and later that day the child is diagnosed with a double ear infection, call the school and let them know. They might either invite you back or take it into consideration. These are teachers; they can tell when children are not up to par.

To Bribe or Not to Bribe

Parents who are desperate to get their child to perform well at an important interview may be tempted to use bribes. This can backfire.

According to an early-childhood consultant, if you really want to offer an inducement to cooperate, promise your child quality time, such as playtime in the park with you, lunch with daddy at the office or a visit to grandma's, rather than a material reward like a trip to the toy store or that PEREGO jeep he's always wanted.

What if your child won't separate? We observed a fair amount of leg hanging and weeping at interviews. Please don't feel bad if your child won't go off willingly with a stranger, even though you've explained that it's a teacher. Remember he/she won't be going to kindergarten for another full year! How the school handles the separation is a good indicator of how much independence and maturity will be expected during the following year. For example, at one very selective school we were told if your child doesn't separate easily "it doesn't bode well." At other schools parents were invited to come and sit with their children during the group interview.

You should of course encourage and reassure your child that he or she is able to go with the teacher and that you'll be waiting right there for him or her to come back. The separation at the interview is the most anxiety-producing part of the touring/interviewing process. And don't pay attention to other parents who boast about their child's easy separation. This is only one of many factors, and we know plenty of leg hangers who went on to all of the best schools.

Letters of Recommendation/Thank You Notes

Directors of admissions at nearly every school advised us that letters of recommendation should be written by someone who really knows the family and the child. One admissions director said she could wallpaper her office with letters from celebrities and politicians. The most valuable recommendation comes from a parent of a child already in the school who knows you well. Never send more than two letters. Try to include the letter(s) of recommendation with the application so it can go right into your file. Things can and do get lost in the shuffle. Always keep a copy on hand just in case.

If you know a trustee at the school, now may be the moment to let him know you have an applicant, but be advised that if your child is accepted at that school you are morally obliged to enroll the child there. You have asked for a favor and it would be rude to act otherwise.

After your interview, admissions directors agree that a thank you note is nice. "I keep it in the file; it never makes or breaks a decision; when we look back, after the child is in, it shows that this is a nice parent and we were right," says Grace Ball, Director of Lower School Admissions at Riverdale Country School. But one admissions director said she was already inundated with mail and didn't want any more! If *you* receive a nice note from a school after the interview don't necessarily think the school is recruiting your child. The Spence School sends handwritten thank you postcards to *everyone* who looks at the school, even if they don't apply.

THE ERB

The Educational Records Bureau
220 East 42nd Street (The Daily News Building)
Suite 100
(near Second Avenue)
New York, NY 10017
(212) 672-9800, FAX (212) 370-4096

Sharon Spotnitz, Program Director
Mrs. Lucille S. Porter, Associate Director

If your child is applying for admission to an independent school, he or she will be asked to take the "ERB's". In fact, ERB is not the title of the admissions exam. It stands for the Educational Records Bureau, a national, nonprofit agency that serves approximately 1,250 independent and public schools nationally and internationally, which administers and interprets different types of tests for children from preschool all the way through high school. The ERB employs forty psychologists (examiners) during the admissions season. According to the ERB: "All of the examiners are at least Masters' level school or clinical psychologists, many of them are doctoral level candidates, and some are Ph.D's. They are all experienced examiners. The ERB has been under contract with ISAAGNY (Independent Schools Admissions Association of Greater New York) for over thirty years. For New York City independent schools, the ERB administers a collection of tests that sound like kitchen appliance attachments: the WPPSI-R (revised) for preschool through first grade; the WISC-III for grades two, three, four, and five; and the ISEE for applicants to grades six through twelve. Beginning in September 1999, the ISEE will be administered in three levels. The lower level: entrance to grades five and six, the middle level: entrance to grades seven and eight, and the upper level: entrance to grades nine through twelve. Practice questions are included in the back of the student guide. The ISEE takes approximately three hours. The ERB tests on the premises of approximately forty nursery schools. Tests are also administered at the ERB's offices, as well as at other locations throughout Manhattan. The cost of the WPPSI-R is $200. (There is an ISAAGNY Fee Waiver Program for students requiring financial aid.)

If you are considering applying to Hunter Elementary or a New York City public school program for gifted and talented you'll have to go to an approved testing service for Stanford-Binet testing (approximately $125). (See Programs for Gifted Students, pages 450, *infra.*)

Having a central testing agency administering one test to all children was intended to "eliminate repetitive testing and thus minimize the strain on children and parents." Prior to the selection of the ERB, parents used to take their children for formal testing at each school to which they applied. However, many schools still require up to an hour of their own "informal testing," so you can still expect your child to be thoroughly scrutinized everywhere he or she goes. It seems to parents that it is the strain on the schools that has mostly been alleviated since they can now see many more than one child at a time.

At some nursery schools, says one parent, "the fall semester of the four-year-old group is like 'Stanley Kaplan' for the ERB." The students get worksheets for practicing matching skills, copying geometric shapes and tracking mazes. They are drilled in their colors, taught to write their names and play with parquetry blocks (for spatial relations). Some children even bring *Weekly Readers* home to work on.

The all-important question facing anxious parents is whether and how much to prepare (or coach) their child for intelligence testing. Administrators at the ERB, say emphatically, "Don't do it!" If your child has been coached, it invariably leaks out. The tester is looking for how spontaneous the child is in responding to a question never heard before, and for his problem-solving strategy as well as level of information. One four year old walked into the tester's office and blurted, "I forgot it all!"

The WPPSI-R determines strengths and weaknesses and where along the developmental scale a child falls. The head of a primary school described the ERB to touring parents as "a measuring stick against which all the children stand." The WPPSI-R was not devised as an admissions test, and a national sampling, not an independent school norm, is the measuring standard. It is an evaluation of the child's development in language and visual/motor skills. It is a snapshot of the child's development taken on one day.

Children are compared with others their age; there is no advantage in holding off testing with the idea that "they will know more." In fact, they are expected to do more as they become older; in some cases the younger child may have a slight edge. Also, the later in the year it is, the more likely it is your child may have a cold or other illness. In fact, ERB introduced the option of spring testing in 1992. If your nursery school director thinks your child is ready "and your child is four years old by May 1st and, will separate readily" the spring might be better.

Parents are sent a copy of the confidential ERB report. (See sample report on pages 32–33.) You can discuss the results with your nursery school director.

The WPPSI-R is composed of five verbal and five nonverbal (or performance) sections. Children *do not* have to read or write to take this test.

Verbal

Information: Breadth of general knowledge; alertness to environment; learning ability.

Comprehension: Commonsense judgment; social awareness; ability to evaluate in light of past experience.

Arithmetic: Ability to concentrate; skill in counting; ability to reason with numbers.

Vocabulary: Word knowledge; expressive skills; quality of thought processes; language background and development.

Similarities: Ability to perceive relationships between things and ideas; ability to generalize; maturity and logical thinking.

Performance

Object Assembly: Perceptual organization; recognition of part-whole relationships; visual-motor speed and accuracy.

Geometric Design: Visual memory; spatial visualization; development of fine motor control.

Block Design: Ability to perceive and analyze patterns; spatial visualization; visual-motor coordination.

Mazes: Planning ability; visual-motor speed and accuracy; ability to follow directions and work independently; level of impulsivity.

Picture Completion: Ability to differentiate essential from non-essential details; recognition of part-whole relationships; visual alertness.

It is common belief that some of the very selective schools have a fixed cutoff score below which they will not admit a candidate. This is simply not true. Admissions directors have said, "You wouldn't believe some of the scores we have here," and we know some children with astronomical scores who were not admitted. But some schools are more likely to take an "at-risk child" (with very scattered scores) than others.

Some directors of admission place more weight on the narrative portion of the test (the second page of the ERB report), which describes the child's test-taking behavior. One admissions director told us, "It's a personality thing."

The parent must fill out a form requesting that the test results be sent to the ongoing schools to which the parent has applied. There is a $3 additional charge for each school in excess of five. Be sure to follow up with the schools to make sure they received the results.

In sum, says an ERB administrator, "Have faith in your own child. You know him or her better than anybody else does. In the vast majority of cases your child will look on paper exactly like he or she is."

And remember, ERB reports are just one piece of your child's admissions application. Your child's interview, the evaluation form from your present school and the application are all given serious consideration.

How to Prepare Your Child

Don't say he or she is going to play games or be in a room with other children. Do tell your child, "You are going to work with someone like a teacher who wants to see the kinds of things you know. There'll be some new things and you'll get a chance to learn."

If the test is administered in a participating school, the teacher or director will usually do this for you, presenting the test as enjoyable "special work." You might reinforce this gently beforehand if your child raises questions—but be light and casual.

You may use the same explanation if you are bringing your child to ERB. Explain that he or she will do "special work" with someone like a teacher who is eager to see what 4, 5, or 6 year olds are able to do. Let your child know that you will be in the waiting room with other parents.

If the child is reluctant to separate from you, have your spouse or a caregiver bring him or her.

ERB will not test a child who is unhappy or reluctant. The anticipation of a pleasant experience is the best preparation for being tested.

Retesting

"Schools, either nursery or ongoing, will know if a given test isn't reflective of their observations of the child, and if they determine it is necessary they can request a retest," says an administrator. Retesting is usually done at the request of the ongoing school. (But, of course, results of both tests will be under consideration by the school(s) to which application is being made.) It is rarely requested.

Educational Records Bureau
220 East 42th Street
New York, NY 10017
(212) 672-9800

11/21/98

Student:	Test Date: 10/18/98	Test: WPPSI-R
School:	Birth Date: 03/14/98	Examiner:
Entering: K Sex: F	Age: 4 yrs 7 mo 4 days	Reviewer: _____

The Verbal subtests measure verbal comprehension and reflect skill in reasoning with words, learning verbal material, and processing verbal information. The Performance subtests measure perceptual organization and reflect skill in nonverbal reasoning, using visual images in thinking, and processing visual information.

Verbal Subtests

PR:			1	2	5	9	16	25	37	50	63	75	84	91	95	98	99		
SS:	1	2	3	4	5	6	7	8	9	10	11	12	13	14	15	16	17	18	19

	SS
Information	15
Comprehension	11
Arithmetic	12
Vocabulary	13
Similarities	13

Performance Subtests

PR:			1	2	5	9	16	25	37	50	63	75	84	91	95	98	99		
SS:	1	2	3	4	5	6	7	8	9	10	11	12	13	14	15	16	17	18	19

	SS
Object Assembly	11
Geometric Design	11
Block Design	12
Mazes	11
Picture Completion	14

Percentile Rank (PR) is a number from 1 to 99 that shows how the student's test score compares to test scores earned by children of the same age in the U.S. general population. For example, a subtest scaled score (SS) of 11 has an equivalent percentile rank of 63, which means that the student performed as well as or better than 63 percent of a representative sample of children at that age level.

Scaled Scores that exceed the 75th percentile indicate strengths, whereas scores below the 25th percentile indicate weaknesses. Scaled scores on just one or two subtests ordinarily describe a child less reliably than the sum of the five scaled scores (Verbal or Performance). Please be aware that the sum of all ten scaled scores is not an IQ score. Also note that an overall percentile rank cannot be obtained by averaging the percentiles for the subtests.

Users of this report are reminded that test results need to be weighed in light of information gained from school records, parents and teachers, and student interviews.

Report Format Copyright © 1997 Educational Records Bureau

Student: Examiner:
Date of Birth: Date of Test:

Information on test-taking behavior frequently illuminates inconsistencies in the test performance and aids in judging how accurately the test results describe the student's abilities.

Comfort Level/Self-Confidence:
_____ a sweet, verbal child, easily interacted with the examiner, chatting about his calico cat named Carrot. Throughout the evaluation he was involved in tasks, appeared comfortable, was responsive and displayed excellent effort.

Understanding of Test Directions/Tasks:
Listened to directions and carefully observed all demonstrations. Easily understood what was being asked of him and followed through with purpose.

Language Skills:
Very verbal, easily expressed thoughts. Responses were direct and to the point. General language skills are very well developed. Vocabulary was very good and sentences were complex and filled with description.

Visual-Motor Skills:
Confidently reproduced simple geometric designs. _____ used his right hand; pencil grasp and control were good. Visual-motor integration is nicely developed. Materials were easily manipulated.

Work Traits/Motivation:
Attention and cooperation were very good. Motivated, able to persevere as items increased in difficulty. Responses were thoughtful. Used nice trial-and-error approach on difficult items, which then helped him to understand the more complex block patterns.

Contributing factors:
_____ really enjoyed discovering missing parts of familiar objects (picture completion) and worked with facility, determination and perseverance as items increased in difficulty, clearly enjoying the challenge. Was somewhat uncomfortable with the pictorial part of the similarities subtest and guessed at some of the items. However, when asked to verbalize relationships he had no difficulty, and responses were direct and to the point.

Overall Impressions:
_____ is an independent, verbal child who was comfortable with the examiner and the activities. He took great pleasure in his performance and it was a pleasure to work with him. Both verbal and nonverbal skills are extremely well developed at this time.

Test Preparation

The authors believe that tutoring 4 year olds for ERB testing is futile; however, many New York City parents do have their older children tutored, either privately or in a group, for the ISEE (Independent School Entrance Exam for grades 6-12), the Hunter High School Entrance Exam (7th grade), the SSAT, the Specialized High Schools Exam (Stuyvesant, Bronx Science, Brooklyn Tech) and the SAT.

Candidates should begin to review and refresh their knowledge several months preceding the exam using either a review book and/or a suitable tutor or review class. At the very least, students should look at the sample questions included in the registration materials.

Ideally, tutoring should boost a child's confidence in his/her abilities, familiarize the student with the kind of questions he will find on the test (multiple choice or essay type), teach test taking strategies and hone essay writing skills. It should be preparation that enables students to go into the testing situation thinking, "Hey, I know this stuff, I can do my best." Cramming for any exam the week or two before only results in a sleep-deprived and anxious candidate. Make sure your child has a good night's sleep and something to eat/drink before the test, and because most of these tests are over two hours long, bring a drink and a snack that doesn't make crumbs.

The best way to find a tutor is through word-of-mouth, or though inquiries at the child's present school. In some cases the city offers review courses such as The Math/Science Institute (see pp. 460 *infra.*) National test preparation companies such as Princeton Review and Stanley Kaplan have offices in Manhattan. Parents have recommended the following resources to us; rates vary widely so be sure to ask how much it will cost before you sign up!

S & S PREP, Alan Silver (914) 634-3128, S&S PREP's large group review for the Hunter High School exam is offered at Wagner Middle School, 226 East 76th Street.

School Skills, Inc. (212) 861-5083, Dianne Karlstein DeVizcaino, "Mrs. D." 210 East 73rd Street. Maybe it's the warheads and pretzels she keeps on her desk, or her twenty-five years experience in teaching, but many children we know enjoy going to "Mrs. D." In demand for ERB and Hunter test preparation, Mrs. D. also provides basic skills review, particularly essay writing.

Advantage Testing, (212) 744-8800, 300 East 85th Street. Individual tutoring in your home, Manhattan only. SSAT, ISEE and SAT specialists.

DO'S AND DON'TS

Do

1) The week after Labor Day start to make a list of schools in which you are interested. Call these schools for a brochure and application.

2) Give your nursery school director the school report form from the admissions packet. Note: Some schools send this form directly to the nursery school once they have received your completed application.

3) By early October, make sure that you have requested the required admissions testing from the Educational Records Bureau; promptly fill out the form and return it to the ERB with your check.

4) Read the brochure before your tour and interview.

5) Call ASAP if you are going to miss an appointment, whether for a group tour or your child's interview.

6) Pose thoughtful, not provocative, questions, that show you've really read the material and know the school. Know at what grade the school ends.

7) Say something nice about the school during the parent interview.

8) Ask whom you might contact if you have any additional questions during the admissions process. Being able to call a parent in the school is very helpful.

9) Call the ERB to make sure your child's test scores have been sent to all of the schools to which you have applied, and call each school in early January to make sure your file is complete. The file should contain: 1) your completed application, 2) letters of reference if requested, 3) school report from your nursery school, 4) results of ERB testing.

10) Use discretion when discussing ERB testing results and acceptances. We've seen feelings get hurt and friendships ruined by boasting.

11) If you genuinely have a first-choice school, let your nursery school director know and let the school know (in writing from you or a parent in the school who knows you). But realize that if you are accepted, your child is morally obliged to attend.

12) Do use pull if you have it *before* completing the application

process. Don't wait until after your child is rejected; negative decisions are rarely changed. But use discretion.

13) If you are totally bewildered use an advisory service. Nursery school directors have their preferences as does the Parents League.

14) After admissions decisions have been made, call or write every school at which you have been wait-listed to let them know: 1) that you are still very interested or 2) that you have accepted a place elsewhere.

15) Revisit the school after your child has been accepted, and sit in on classes if you need more information before making a decision.

16) Ask for a copy of the school's annual report only after your child has been accepted.

17) Recognize that you have the right to call a school and (politely) find out why your child was not accepted.

18) Realize that kindergarten is a transition year, and reevaluate your choice of schools every three to five years.

19) Be a supportive parent, try to see your child realistically, know his strengths and weaknesses, be his advocate.

20) Remember that there is no such thing as a perfect parent, a perfect child *or* a perfect school.

21) Realize that you don't know how good a school really is until you have a problem.

Don't

1) Pick a school because your husband's law partner and/or your best friend send their children there.

2) Coach your child for the ERB (WPPSI-R).

3) Be late or miss an appointment without calling.

4) Send a personal essay or any more recommendations than the school requests.

5) Ask for special treatment during the admissions process. Even celebrities have to take the group tour.

6) Ask them to convince you why you should send your child to their school.

7) Stand out on the tour by asking too many questions or taking notes as if you were writing an article or a book.

8) Brag about your achievements.

9) Offer money to or otherwise try to bribe the admissions director.
10) Think that you can change the basic style of the school.
11) Tell a school that it's your first choice unless you intend to enroll your child there.
12) Make the elitist assumption that all students of color are on scholarship.
13) Select a school solely on the basis of how many children get into Ivy League colleges. Do look at the range of schools to which students are accepted.
14) Forget that you're an applicant, not a supplicant.

THICK OR THIN

Admissions decisions are usually made by committee (although the Director of Admissions acts alone at some schools.) The members of these committees vary from school to school. At some schools someone from the development office sits in, and sometimes parents of students are on these committees. There is usually a core group of children comprising siblings and legacies who are definite admissions and the committee tries to put together a balanced class around this core. Schools want a balance of personalities as well; they don't want all leaders or followers. If it is a coed school they need an equal number of boys and girls. So your chances vary from year to year depending on what kind of sibling year it is, or for unpredictable reasons. For example, in 1996–97 at Riverdale Country School, more applications were received than in any previous year, "over five hundred for approximately seventy spots," according to the Director of Lower School Admissions. So a rejection one year might well have been an acceptance the following year. Never take it as a judgment of your child.

Do admissions directors talk? The independent school world is small; admissions directors go to lunch and phone calls go back and forth during the admissions process. Usually, they will not talk about specific families. They will discuss whether the "pool" is up or down for girls or boys this year and so forth. But somehow, if you tell each school that it is your first choice, it will get around. So don't say it unless you mean it.

The yield figure is a mathematical formula, different at each school, which attempts to predict the number of children who, having been accepted to the school, will actually enroll. Anyone whose child is in an over-enrolled kindergarten class knows that this is an inexact method.

There are three elements that make up your child's file:

1) **ERB Testing Results**
2) **The Nursery School Report**

A confidential report (parents never see it) that discusses your child in depth: his growth, maturity, strengths and weaknesses over the past (three) years as well as information about the family such as how supportive the parents are, how promptly they pay tuition, if they have donor potential and so on. Nursery school directors have to be honest in this report; as a former Parents League president put it: "Report plus rapport equals respect." An honest report plus a relationship between the nursery school director and the director of admissions at the ongoing school equals respect for the nursery school director's recommendation. Admissions directors know how to read between the lines of these reports and the notation "Call me for additional information" implies there is more to the story than what's written on the page. An early-childhood consultant told us that "for an unconnected family without significant means, it's essential that your nursery school director have an established relationship with the admissions director at the ongoing school and be able to really go to bat for you." It certainly can't hurt to be active and involved in your nursery school, and if you're unsure whether to give time or money, give both.

3) **Child's Interview**

An admissions director who's been in the business for twenty-seven years says, "I never read a file until I meet the child." The child's profile should fit together like a jigsaw puzzle, says a representative from Ethical Culture admissions. "The nursery school report should correspond to behavior in the interview, the ERB reaffirms both. If a piece doesn't make sense, then we have to look further."

If you've got three out of three you're accepted (provided there's room), and a contract will usually be included with the acceptance letter (thick envelope). Two out of three and you might be accepted or wait-listed. One out of three is usually a nonacceptance (thin envelope containing only a nonacceptance letter). This is not gospel; there are mitigating factors and if the child is outstanding in some way that might outweigh one of the other factors.

What They're Looking For

Schools are looking for readiness, a term in dispute but basically a quality measured by strong academic potential (the mastery of certain skills and tasks such as ability to count to twenty, recognize the alphabet, draw geometric shapes, and so on), and socialization skills (ability to share and get along with others, form an appropriate relationship with the teacher, work independently and show "maturity"). In the past kindergarten might be a child's first school experience, but today most children have been in a preschool program for two to three years and prior to that, countless "Mommy and Me" classes. "Kindergarten has become an experience for which children need to be ready when they arrive."[*] However, this does *not* mean that parents should teach their preschoolers to read. There are some children who will learn to read before kindergarten (you know who they are because parents of such children will invariably boast about their "little geniuses"). However, educators stress that the majority of children are ready for formal reading instruction in first grade or when they are approximately six and a half years old. Admissions directors do not expect candidates for kindergarten to read, nor should you.

A good evaluation of a child, in the words of one nursery school director, is "Verbal, curious, good self-esteem, ability to concentrate, not fidgety, has enough to give to others." Then there is an intangible measurement dubbed "the likability factor" by an early-childhood consultant we know. We'd all like to think our children have it—it's a personality thing.

ADVISORY SERVICES

Aside from this book and the director of your nursery school, there are other useful resources in Manhattan to help you select the right independent school for your family. Keep in mind that the best source of

[*]*Kindergarten, It Isn't What It Used to Be*, by Susan Golant and Mitch Golant, Ph.D. (Lowell House, Los Angeles, 1990).

information is the school itself. Ask if the school you are interested in has spring tours. Perhaps you can rule out a school or take a second look in the fall when you apply. Once the fall admissions process gets rolling you will usually not be able to take a second look until your child is accepted to the school. Advisory services (or educational consultants) help parents approach the independent school admissions process in an organized manner and provide reassurance and advice to apprehensive parents.

All except two of the services listed below require a fee.

1. THE PARENTS LEAGUE OF NEW YORK, INC., 115 East 82nd Street, New York, NY 10028 (212) 737-7385, Patricia Girardi, Executive Director

    The Parents League was founded in 1913 and is a nonprofit organization of parents and independent schools. Annual membership fee: $50. The Parents League offers a School Advisory Service for member parents who need advice about the process of applying to schools and information about the schools. Please call for an appointment. The advisors are volunteers who are trained in-house.

    The Parents League distributes the *New York Independent Schools Directory*, published by the Independent Schools Admissions Association of Greater New York (ISAAGNY). Parents League members can purchase the book for an additional $15.00 at the office, $17.00 by mail. Non-members can also purchase this publication. *Please be aware that the entries in this book are written by the schools themselves.*

    The Parents League sponsors Independent School Day, held in the fall, at which parents can pick up printed material, including brochures and applications, from various city independent schools; representatives from the independent schools are available to answer *brief* questions. Be prepared for a mob scene, but it will save you countless phone calls.

    The Parents League sponsors a Forum on Admissions, at which admissions directors from five or six independent schools speak and then answer questions from the audience about the admissions process. It offers a summer advisory service and a special education advisory service. You must be a member of the Parents League to participate.

2. JOAN MILLER ADVISORY, 4 East 88th Street, New York, NY 10128, (212) 876-6314

Joan Miller, a former teacher and admissions director, offers a more personal approach. Ms. Miller meets with parents in the privacy of her home or yours. Specializing in nursery school and kindergarten admissions, Ms. Miller helps parents through the application and admissions process step by step. The fee is $100 for nursery, $200 for kindergarten and above.

3. LOIS BERMAN, Ph.D., 177 East 87th Street, Suite 502, New York, NY 10128, (212) 722-0250

Dr. Berman was the psychologist at Trinity School for seventeen years and has worked with many independent school families. Dr. Berman advises families on choosing the right independent school for their child (as well as those considering a change of schools). As a licensed psychologist, Dr. Berman can also administer a psychoeducational evaluation to children with suspected learning disabilities.

4. LANA F. MORROW, Ph.D., 1160 Fifth Avenue, Suite 109, New York, NY 10029, (212) 426-1117, Fax (212) 426-0612, e-mail: lanafm@earthlink.net

Dr. Morrow administers neuropsychological evaluations and remediates children who have learning disabilities. She advises families as to which independent school will be best suited for their child.

5. VIRGINIA J. BUSH & ASSOCIATES, 444 East 86th Street, New York, NY 10028 (212) 772-3244

Since 1975, Mrs. Bush has been advising families on school and college options.

6. EDUCATIONAL DIRECTIONS, Jane Ellen Weltz, 360 East 72nd Street, New York, NY 10021, (212) 879-0287

Ms. Weltz, a nursery school teacher, has been advising parents about school admissions from nursery to high school for over ten years. Ms. Weltz offers support, reassurance and encouragement for children who may need it.

7. SCHOOLS & YOU, Sarah D. Meredith, 328 Flatbush Avenue, Suite 372, Brooklyn, NY 11238, (718) 230-8971, website: http://users.freewwweb.com/~schoolsandyou

Ms. Meredith provides information and consultations on school choices from kindergarten through eighth grade for both public and private schools. She will consult at your home or workplace. Resource materials accompany every consultation.

8. HOWARD GREENE & ASSOCIATES, The Educational Consulting Center, Inc., 39A East 72nd Street, New York, NY 10021, (212) 737-8866

   The Educational Consulting Center was founded in 1969 by Howard Greene, former admissions counselor at Princeton University. Known for their college admissions counseling, Howard Greene & Associates will also advise parents about elementary and secondary independent schools. There is a range of fees.

9. SCHOOL CONSULTANTS ON PRIVATE EDUCATION (SCOPE), 309 East 87th Street, New York, NY 10128, (212) 534-6531, or 1-888-214-6590 (toll free), e-mail address, camps4u@aol.com.

   Director Elaine Vipler, M.S.Ed., is the director of SCOPE, an advisory service that helps families select appropriate school and summer programs for their children.

10. THE INDEPENDENT EDUCATIONAL CONSULTANTS ASSOCIATION, 4085 Chain Bridge Road, Suite 401, Fairfax, VA 22030 (703) 591-4850 or 1 800-808-IECA (4322)

    The Independent Educational Consultants Association will send a directory of listings in the New York City area, free of charge.

11. GREENBERG EDUCATIONAL GROUP INC., 315 Central Park West Suite 3W, New York, N.Y. 10025, (212) 787-6800

    Greenberg Educational Group, run by a Fieldston School alumnus Eric Greenberg, provides test preparation, tutoring and educational advising.

MULTICULTURAL/SCHOLARSHIP PROGRAMS

A Better Chance

City College
North Academic Center 3-208
West 138th Street & Convent Avenue
New York, NY 10031
(212) 926-0315 FAX (212) 694-1332

National Office
419 Boylston Street
Boston, MA 02116-3301
(617) 421-0950 FAX (617) 421-0965

Founded in 1963 by twenty-three independent schools in the Northeast, A Better Chance, Inc. (ABC) is the oldest national, nonprofit academic talent-search organization for minority secondary school students. The membership comprises 193 independent day and boarding schools. Students are recruited and admitted to these schools on the basis of high academic achievement and personal initiative. The majority of students apply in the eighth or ninth grade. Applicants must take the SSAT. Financial aid is provided by the member schools. ABC provides ongoing counseling and support. ABC has an Affiliated Colleges Program of over seventy-five colleges and universities that have demonstrated a commitment to increase their minority enrollment.

The Albert G. Oliver Program

44 West 28th Street
New York, NY 10001
(212) 889-0244 FAX (212) 889-4978

Mr. Donn O'Brian, Chairman

The Albert G. Oliver Program, named after an outstanding New York City educator, is a nonprofit organization founded in the 1980s to help talented black and Hispanic youngsters gain access to the city's independent schools at the high school level. The brochure says "A

43

primary goal of the Oliver Program is to nurture the hearts of these gifted young people so they develop a sense of caring, love and responsibility that will make a positive impact on the lives of others." The Albert G. Oliver Program is unique in offering a mandatory community service program (40 hours per year) and a guaranteed paying summer jobs program. Each year up to fifty black and Hispanic students are placed in independent day and boarding schools that offer strong support services including financial assistance. Oliver graduates attend many Ivy League colleges and top universities.

Member Day Schools:

Brooklyn Friends School
The Dalton School
Elisabeth Irwin High School
The Fieldston School
Friends Seminary
Horace Mann School

The Nightingale-Bamford School
The Packer Collegiate Institute
The Riverdale Country School
Trevor Day School
Trinity School

Early Steps
540 East 76th Street
New York, NY 10021
(212) 288-9684 FAX (212) 288-0461

Ms. Jacqueline Y. Pelzer, Executive Director
Ms. Kim Muñoz Bolano, Associate Director

Early Steps is a membership organization that was created in August 1986 to increase the number of students of color in city independent day schools at the kindergarten and first grade levels. Early Steps was an outgrowth of an Independent Schools Admissions Association of Greater New York (ISAAGNY) Minority Affairs Committee study that identified the need for schools to pool resources for the recruitment of younger students of color.

Early Steps provides counseling and referral services for families of color looking for and enrolled in city independent schools. Financial aid is available but families should be prepared to pay a portion of the tuition. Some families pay full tuition.

Prep for Prep
328 West 71st Street
New York, NY 10023
(212) 579-1390 FAX (212) 579-1443

Mr. Gary Simons, Executive Director

The Prep for Prep program is a nonprofit educational organization founded in 1978 by Gary Simons. Some of the original group of Prep for Prep students attended Trinity School. Today, Prep for Prep identifies academically talented students from minority group backgrounds, provides fourteen months of intensive academic preparation and places these students in leading city independent schools and boarding schools with scholarships that are based on financial need and academic performance. The program is highly selective and rigorous; in a typical year, approximately 3,500 qualified students applied, but only 156 fifth graders were admitted into Prep for Prep (day school placement) and sixty seventh graders into Prep 9 (boarding school placement). Once enrolled, students are provided with ongoing counseling and leadership development opportunities until high school graduation. The Prep for Prep community includes over 2,000 students and alumni.

The New York Diversity Resource Collaborative
Brooklyn Heights Montessori School
185 Court Street
Brooklyn, NY 11201
(718) 852-3964 FAX (718) 852-1164

Susan Hinkle, Director
Mercy Rodriguez, Executive Assistant

The Diversity Resource Collaborative is composed of member schools from the independent school community. According to their brochure, the DRC is dedicated to the promotion of diversity in school curriculum, faculty and student body: "The Collaborative is committed to embracing and disseminating those multicultural resources that are unique and special to this area, to making use of the area's diversity and to demonstrating the immediacy of multiculturalism in the greater New York area." The DRC addresses issues relating to race and ethnicity, gender, physical differences, sexual orientation, religion and class. The DRC is funded by grants from the Citizen's Committee for New York City, Inc., strengthening neighborhood assets program, Chase Manhattan Bank, and the Boston Foundation. Funding to establish the DRC was provided by the DeWitt Wallace-Reader's Digest Fund and the Booth Ferris Foundation.

The DRC sponsors workshops and conferences for professionals, and is the cosponsor of the People of Color Job Fair and is conducting a research study "to give clarity to the current status of diversity and multicultural education in our schools."

Information related to diversity issues in the independent schools is available through Diversity-On-Line, a website. (See also "Interschool Faculty Diversity Search," pp. 470, *infra.*)

Member Schools:

The Allen-Stevenson School
Bank Street School for Children
The Berkeley Carroll School
Brick Church School
Brooklyn Heights Montessori School
The Caedmon School
The City & Country School
The Episcopal School
The Ethical Culture Fieldston School
Friends Seminary
Grace Church School
Horace Mann School
Little Red School House and Elisabeth Irwin High School

Manhattan Country School
Marymount School of New York
The Masters School
The Packer Collegiate Institute
Pomfret School
Poughkeepsie School
Professional Children's School
The Rudolf Steiner School
Saint David's School
St. Luke's School
St. Thomas Choir School
The Spence School
Stevens Cooperative School
The Trevor Day School
Trinity School

APPLYING FOR FINANCIAL AID

The rigorous process of qualifying for private school tuition assistance makes kindergarten admissions look easy. After your child has been accepted to an independent school, or if your child is already enrolled in an independent school and you are requesting tuition assistance (such needs may arise because of a divorce or the loss of a spouse's job) your first step is to contact the financial aid administrator in your child's school. The financial aid officer will give you a Parent Financial Statement or PFS which you must complete. Be forewarned that the PFS asks applicants to list all of their assets and expenses, including their country house, boats, family car(s) club memberships, lessons, summer camp, and vacations. The completed form must be returned to the SSS-The School and Student Service for Financial Aid in Princeton, New Jersey. The SSS, an affiliate of the National Association of Independent Schools, is a nationwide service that assists independent schools in processing scholarship applications. The SSS is administered by the Educational Testing Service (ETS).* Parents are usually asked to submit a copy of *both* parents' W-2 forms and the previous year's joint or separate Federal Income Tax returns in support of their application. If there are no young children at home, the SSS will impute an income for a non-working parent.

In processing the PFS the SSS uses national guidelines set for independent schools; families who live in one state might be applying for financial aid from a prep school which is located in another state. A copy of the PFS is then sent back to the school with a recommendation from the SSS of how much tuition that particular family can afford to pay. The school then recalculates; some use specific software for this purpose, taking into account the cost of living in Manhattan.** The final decision rests with the school. Most schools have a scholarship committee which reviews each application and then makes "lifestyle recommendations to the family" as one administrator put it. It is up to each family to decide the financial sacrifices or lifestyle changes it is willing to make. Some families start out on financial aid and eventually become full-tuition paying families and vice versa. Some families choose to "live on peanut butter" and make other sacrifices, others will consider a move to the suburbs, or begin to look at public school options.

*See ETS under "Resources," p.467, *infra.*
** In 1996 NAIS raised the cost of living index in New York City from 1.32 to 2.283 which means that it is 228% more expensive to live in NYC than the national average.

47

TRANSPORTATION

Once your child has been accepted into school, whether public or private, your next consideration is how to get him or her to school and back each day, safely and conveniently. If they live nearby, many parents walk their children to and from school. Those who live further away must rely on a bus service. There are three types of bus service, one is free and public, two are private and require a fee. Depending on the size of your child's school, you might have a limited choice of transportation services. Some parents combine services, depending on their needs.

1. ATLANTIC EXPRESS SERVICE: (A/E or yellow school bus service):

    Administered through the office of pupil transportation within the Board of Education, (718) 784-3313.

    Atlantic Express has an excellent safety record and is free to public school students within the district who attend a gifted or magnet program school, and private school students attending participating schools. Students must apply through their own school. To qualify, students in kindergarten through second grade must live $\frac{1}{2}$ mile or more from school. Students in third through sixth grades must live 1 mile or more from school. In early September, the school provides students with a list of designated bus stops (usually along the avenues) and times for pick-up and drop-off. Students using A/E bus service *do not* receive a bus pass for use on city buses. Middle and high school students are provided with subway and bus passes.

2. PRIVATE VAN SERVICE: The private schools contract with a van service (such as Selby, Street Smart or A&S) which provides door-to-door pickup and drop off at specific times. This service is the most convenient and also the most costly. Roundtrip with Selby in 1998–99 cost approximately $2,050.00, one-way, $1,385.00

3. SCHOOL VAN: Various private schools run their own van service which usually picks up and drops off at designated bus stops. The cost is less than for private van service.

    Students attending a regularly scheduled after-school program one or more times a week often arrange with their school for private van service for dropoff to these activities.

SOCIAL ORGANIZATIONS

Boys and girls who attend the traditional single sex schools have limited social contact with the opposite sex. This is somewhat ameliorated by coed theater and musical productions, interschool classes and activities. But what could be more fitting for the offspring of the socially prominent than charity dances for the pubescent set to introduce them not only to each other but to philanthropy as well? Miniature charity balls, sponsored by organizations such as Yorkville Common Pantry and Goddard Riverside Community Center, are usually held at one of the private schools and the money raised benefits a variety of local causes. These dances for young men and women attending Manhattan's exclusive schools are a quaint but benign form of organized dating for many 11 and 12 year olds as well as a time for parents to enjoy their last vestige of social control because before they know it their teenager will be "moshing" at the downtown clubs.

The "White Glove" social organizations listed below are traditionally "by invitation only." However, you no longer need the proper pedigree to participate; after all, good manners are for everyone.

The Barclay Classes are headquartered in Westfield, New Jersey, (908) 232–8370. For almost 70 years, the Barclay Series has offered classes to children (grades 2 and up) in the social graces, proper party attire and ballroom dancing. The classes meet once or twice weekly. Spit and polish is the order of the day and young ladies wear white gloves until sixth grade. There are real parties twice a year, usually with a theme. Children enjoy the classes because refreshments are served and prizes are awarded. You must write to the Barclay Series to request an invitation if one has not already been sent. There is a waiting list for girls and boys. There is a sibling policy as well.

Dancing lessons offered by **The Knickerbocker Cotillion** begin in fourth grade and children must be invited to attend; unlike the Barclay Series, The Knickerbocker Cotillion is a not-for-profit organization, an older and some say, more exclusive group. Mrs. Jacques Nordeman, the group's coordinator, who also serves as co-director of admissions at the St. Bernard's School, says that from time to time she forwards applications to those who call; however, it is the organization's policy to refrain from publicity.

The Knickerbocker Greys: Contact: Rosemarie Connell, (212) 585-1881. Once upon a time children from Manhattan's best families bought their school uniforms at Alex Taylor and their other clothes at

Best & Company; the girls took dancing classes at Mrs. DeRhams' Dancing School at the Colony Club or if you were Jewish, at Viola Wolfe's, while their brothers drilled with the Knickerbocker Greys at the 67th Street Armory. Originally linked with Patriotic and Historical Societies such as the National Society of Colonial Dames and the Society of Mayflower Descendants this organization appeals to any child who simply likes history and tin soldiers. Since 1881 the Knickerbocker Greys has offered boys (and now girls) ages 6–16 the opportunity to participate in parades, reviews and civic ceremonies in New York City. (Remember when you had to join the Girl Scouts just to march in the Memorial Day parade?) The Greys is not a military organization but they use precision drill and the "pomp and circumstance of beautiful old uniforms." Meetings are held twice a week, attendance is required only one of the two days.

GLOSSARY

Alternative Forms of Testing: Testing that is not standardized, but rather a measure of an individual child's capabilities and progress relative to himself, not to other children. The most popular trend in alternative testing is portfolio assessment: A child will select his best work from the whole semester or year, and submit this work instead of taking a standardized test. This gives the child's judges the ability to gauge the child's progress over the course of the term, and gives them a fuller picture of the child's abilities, rather than a brief snapshot from a test taken on one particular day.

Child-Centered Program: A program in which learning in the classroom is facilitated by the teacher and directed by the students. Activities require active learning and motivation on the part of the student; the teacher does not lecture to a passive class. The phrase "child-centered program" is also used to describe a program in which a child is presented with age-appropriate, meaningful curricula.

Chicago Math: Chicago Math is a program developed at the University of Chicago that teaches children to reason logically, see mathematical patterns and relationships, and understand the usefulness of math in everyday life. Manipulatives, math games and literature are woven into the curriculum to develop abstract mathematical thinking while reinforcing computational concepts.

Classic Curriculum: Featured in traditional schools. A classic curriculum always includes Shakespeare, Virgil and the Greeks. The goal is "a cultured mind nourished by the humanist tradition."

Collaborative Learning: In a classroom that subscribes to collaborative learning, the students work in groups. It is assumed an individual student will be motivated to work because he or she will feel responsible to the group, that a student will learn to clarify his thinking through the need to articulate and debate his ideas within the group, and further, that he will learn new ways of thinking when he analyzes the ideas of other group members.

Cum Laude Society: The Cum Laude Society is an honor society modeled on Phi Beta Kappa, which has member chapters in several New York City independent high schools. The purpose of the Cum Laude Society is the encouragement and recognition of academic excellence. Many chapters (particularly at schools that no longer rank students or do not give grades) make selections by such criteria as character, honor and integrity. New York City independent schools with member chapters and year of induction are: Berkeley Carroll School, Brooklyn, 1989; Collegiate School, 1922; Horace Mann School, 1951; Packer Collegiate Institute, Brooklyn, 1976; Poly Prep Country Day School, Brooklyn, 1908; The Riverdale Country School, Bronx, 1922; Trinity School, 1934.

D'Nealian Handwriting Method: Using the D'Nealian method young children are taught to form print letters with loops and rounded angles so that the transition to cursive writing later on is easier and more natural.

Departmentalization: When students leave their homeroom classroom to go to specialists for different subjects.

Different Learning Styles: This phrase refers to the idea that students learn in different ways, and under different conditions. Some students learn best from reading in a quiet room; other students learn best when engaged in debate. Teachers who subscribe to this theory will try to provide experiences that will accommodate different kinds of learners.

Experiential Learning: Learning through hands-on activities and first-hand experiences.

Fisher-Landau Program: A multimillion-dollar grant program endowed by philanthropist Emily Fisher-Landau to identify and give support to young children with learning problems. The original grant was made to The Dalton School and the Collegiate School. Fisher-Landau specialists conduct workshops and consult at other independent schools.

Integrated Curriculum: A curriculum organized around a central theme. All areas of study (reading, writing, math, science, social studies, art and music) are used to investigate this theme. In this way, the children learn process and content within a unified context. "Core curriculum" is a term that is often used synonymously.

Interage, Mixed-Age or Flexible Class Grouping: Classes that are not grouped according to calendar age. There might be a two-year age span within the class composed of children with "a diversity of achievement, capacity, talent and style, but who have enough intellectual and social congruence to work well together" (Bank Street School for Children brochure).

International Baccalaureate: The I.B. is an internationally recognized curriculum and examination. The I.B. diploma is required for admission to many foreign universities. The I.B. program is administered from Geneva, Switzerland, and taught in over four hundred secondary schools in thirty-eight countries. It is a rigorous and demanding program; students must master a minimum of six subjects and demonstrate the ability to think clearly and communicate effectively. Many colleges and universities in the United States offer advanced placement and/or a year of college credit for superior performance on the I.B. The United Nations International School, Lycée Français and The Dwight/Anglo-American International Schools, all in Manhattan, offer an I.B. program.

Interschool: A consortium of eight New York City independent schools—Brearley, Chapin, Nightingale-Bamford, Spence (girls' schools); Browning and Collegiate (boys' schools); Dalton and Trinity (coed schools)—which share academic, extracurricular and administrative components.

Invented Spelling: What we all do when we try to spell a word: We make an educated guess. The use of this method allows children the freedom to write the words they may not know how to spell, instead of "dumbing down" their writing to avoid making mistakes. Invented spelling is used in a classroom for rough drafts; students must use the correct spellings of words for final copies.

ISAAGNY: Acronym for the Independent Schools Admissions Association of Greater New York. Composed of admissions directors and heads of early childhood programs, ISAAGNY was founded in 1965 in order to simplify and coordinate admissions procedures among independent schools in the New York Metropolitan area. It is now composed of 150 member schools. ISAAGNY contracted with the Educational Records Bureau to administer uniform admissions testing. ISAAGNY also developed a uniform school report form and sets common notification and reply dates.

Kwanzaa: A seven-day African-American cultural holiday similar to traditional African harvest festivals. Kwanzaa means "first fruits" in Swahili. Kwanzaa coincides with the celebration of Chanukah and Christmas.

Learning Disability, Learning Disorder (LD or Learning Difference): The term currently used to describe a handicap that is neurological in origin, which interferes with a person's ability to store, process or produce information. The impairment can be quite subtle and may go undetected throughout life. The primary characteristic of a learning disability is a significant difference between overall intelligence and achievement in some areas according to the National Center for Learning Disabilities. If you or a school suspects that your child has a learning problem, your child will probably be asked to get a four-hour psychoeducational evaluation.

Montessori Method of Education: Based on Dr. Maria Montessori's scientific observations of the behavior of young children who were orphaned, disadvantaged or, for other reasons, institutionalized. The Montessori approach encourages active, self-directed learning in a non-competitive environment. The Montessori classroom features multi-aged, multi-graded heterogenous groups and is based on the principle of freedom within limits. Children are free to work at their own pace with materials they have chosen, either alone or with others. Individual mastery is balanced with small group collaboration within the whole group community. The teacher relies on his or her observations of the children to determine which new activities and materials he may introduce to an individual child or to a small or large group. Several NYC Montessori schools use an "eclectic" or "modified" approach, a comfort to those who think "pure" Montessori is doctrinaire or rigid.

Multiculturalism: In the classroom, multiculturalism introduces subjects and authors that are not typically considered a part of the Western cultural canon. It is a theory of inclusion that allows many cultures a place in the curriculum, with the aim of increasing respect and understanding for the diverse populations of the world.

Multiple Intelligences: Intelligence is not restricted to a score on an I.Q. test but can encompass many areas of life. Some people may excel in music, some in leadership. These are not necessarily testable qualities, but they are forms of intelligence nonetheless.

People of Color (Children of Color): An inclusive term of respect agreed upon by the National Association of Independent Schools' Committee on Diversity for people usually described as non-white ethnic minorities, including: African-Americans, Latinos, Asian-Americans, Native Americans, Pacific Islanders and natives of Alaska.

Progressive vs. Traditional School: These terms are in disrepute these days. Many of the traditional schools have incorporated elements of progressive education into their elementary school classrooms. Progressive schools remain in the vanguard in their use of innovative educational practices. A traditional classroom may have a teacher at the front of the room lecturing to students sitting in rows; children are grouped homogeneously by ability level and generally work on the same material at the same time. A progressive school is more likely to have an informal or seminar-style classroom with more discussion and is one in which children work in small groups independently. We found that traditional schools tend to be the older, established single-sex schools, which have a Latin motto, concentrate on the Western or classical canon, have a dress code or uniform, a handbell choir and "quaint" traditions.

Revolving Loan: At a school without a significant endowment parents are asked to give an interest-free loan to the school, refundable when the student graduates or leaves for any reason.

Whole Language: A practical body of ideas about education that originated in New Zealand with the seminal work of Sylvia Ashton-Warner. The connections between reading, writing and speaking are made complete in the Whole Language classroom. Students in a Whole Language classroom read literature (not basal readers) and write stories, plays and poems (instead of filling out workbooks). A Whole Language classroom uses an integrated curriculum, so learning centers around one subject. In this way, students learn both process (the mechanics of learning, like long division) and content (long division is used to answer a question about the subject under study) simultaneously. Learning becomes relevant to the student, and ceases to be an abstraction. There is some controversy surrounding Whole Language. Some educators would like to see more of the "old-fashioned methods," particularly an emphasis on phonics, included in any Whole Language program, and on drills for matters that must be remembered and reproduced quickly and accurately (such as multiplication tables, spelling, grammar).

Writing Across the Curriculum: Teachers who believe in writing across the curriculum will not confine writing to language arts; instead they will provide writing experiences throughout the curriculum. This will help students refine their writing and will demonstrate that writing can serve a variety of purposes and is used in many disciplines.

Writing Process or Writers' Workshop: The teaching of writing in which students are taught to discover what they think about the topic in question and to clarify those thoughts through the process of writing, editing, rewriting and publishing: 1) drafting (brain drain), 2) revising (sloppy copy), 3) editing (neat sheet), 4) finalizing (final fame). Grammar, usage and spelling are taught within the context of the individual student's writing needs rather than in isolation.

THE SCHOOLS

The Abraham Joshua Heschel School

(Nursery–5th grade)
270 West 89th Street
New York, NY 10024
(212) 595-7087

(6th–8th grade)
314 West 91st Street
New York, NY 10024

Coed
Accessible

Ms. Roanna Shorofsky, Director
Ms. Marsha Feris, Director of Admissions

Birthday Cutoff   Children entering nursery school must be 3 by August 31
Children entering kindergarten must be 5 by August 31

Enrollment   Total enrollment: 450
Nursery 3's places: 25
Kindergarten places: 12–16
Graduating class 1998: 39

Tuition Range 1998–1999 $9,300 to $14,500, nursery 3's–8th grade
Additional fees: for student activities and supplies, are approximately $330 to $550
Capital fund contribution: $750

After-School Program   Heschel After-School Program: until 5:30 P.M.; creative and recreational activities; an additional payment is required

———

The Heschel School was founded in 1980 by a group of Jewish educators and laymen. Named for Rabbi Abraham Joshua Heschel, a prominent scholar, philosopher and colleague of Martin Luther King, the school is not affiliated with a synagogue. The student body is composed of a broad spectrum of families from unaffiliated reform to

59

modern orthodox. "Heschel is a Jewish school as opposed to a religious school," we were told. The school has a "holistic, child-centered approach." Girls participate fully in all aspects of the school.

Interest in Heschel is increasing because, one parent surmised, "Heschel is the answer to the current quest for spiritual renewal without being doctrinaire or rigid." Heschel is committed to Jewish ethics and values. There are social action projects on every level throughout the year. For instance, Pre-K children participated in the Common Cents penny harvest for the homeless; seventh graders collected blankets and brought them to Hale House.

Parents: A parent told us: "Heschel has a very West Side feeling even to a West Sider." According to her, "There are many professionals and lots of academics with Ph.D's.—the type who subscribe to *Tikkun* magazine. Some of the men are bearded and some of the women have Julia-Louis Dreyfus hair." But as Heschel's popularity continues to grow, "You can expect to see more suits and soignée blondes," she said. Admissions looks for the child who is "bright, inquiring and verbal, who can contribute to the Heschel community." There is no dress code except for the yarmulke (or baseball cap) which must be worn during meals and Judaic studies. One parent described the typical student: "She wears hightops, leggings and a cool T-shirt from Mexico."

Program: The Heschel School is rigorous and structured. Each class has two teachers all the way through eighth grade which is unique. Classes often break into many small groups. Formal Hebrew and Judaic studies begin in first grade. Heschel's dual curriculum is composed of Jewish history, culture, and Hebrew language integrated with secular studies. There is no other formal foreign language requirement. "The Jewish and secular curricula are intertwined in an organic and relevant way," parents say. Although quite different in personality, Dov Lerea, Head of Jewish Studies, and Judith Tumin, Head of General Studies, are guiding forces at Heschel. Experiential learning is stressed: Students might map out the campaign for the battle of Sinai. There is an emphasis on creativity and the arts through cooking, drama and art: A scribal artist came in to work with fifth and sixth graders on an illuminated manuscript project.

The Middle School is housed in a fully renovated brownstone on 91st Street between West End Avenue and Riverside Drive. In addition to classrooms, the Middle School building has a library, computer room, science lab, greenhouse, chapel, gym, music room, art room and lunch room.

There are no prizes given out at graduation. The theme for commencement, "Journeys," is derived from the Hebrew "Prayer for Journeyers." After an opening homily and reflections by a member of the staff, students read selections from their poetry journals; choral selections weave the pieces together.

Graduates attend a variety of New York City independent schools (Riverdale, Dalton and Fieldston are popular), select public schools, and Jewish high schools.

The Abraham Lincoln School For Boys
The Abraham Lincoln School For Girls

12 East 79th Street
New York, NY 10021
(212) 744-7300, FAX (212) 744-5876

Nursery–8th grade
partially accessible

Mr. Howard Schott, Headmaster
Mrs. Barbara Solowey, Headmistress
Mrs. Regina Flecha, Director of Admissions

Birthday Cutoff   Children entering nursery school must be 3 years old by October 31
Children entering kindergarten must be 4 years, 6 months by September 1

Enrollment   85 students through 5th grade

Grades   Anecdotal reports for kindergarten through 3rd grade
Letter grades start in 4th grade

Tuition Range 1998–1999 $7,000 (Nursery) through $8,000 (5th grade)
There is a $900 lunch fee

Financial Aid/Scholarship   20% of the student body receives some form of aid

After-School Program   None on the premises. Some children attend the after-school program at P.S. 6

Summer Program   Two week June Nursery School Program

The Abraham Lincoln School opened its doors with one class of 16 first graders in Fall 1994 and will eventually grow, with the addition of a grade each year, through eighth grade. The choice of name reflects a recognition of "the needs and traditions of America" according to the school's literature. The school building is an elegant landmark limestone townhouse which houses The School of Practical Philosophy in the evening. According to the headmaster, "Academics alone will not produce men and women who can lead happy and useful lives. A finely developed intellect needs to be balanced by a heart educated in the virtues."

Like The Ark Nursery School, now under its aegis, The Abraham Lincoln School is closely connected to The School of Practical Philosophy (a non-profit organization chartered by the Board of Regents of the State of New York). According to the brochure, The School of Practical Philosophy "draws upon the timeless teachings of both Western and Eastern traditions to discover the unifying principles that underlie human existence. The emphasis is on the practical application of these teachings."

The teachers at the Abraham Lincoln School are all members of the School of Practical Philosophy: "All teachers have attended the School's teachers group for many years studying both teaching and their particular subject."

Many subjects are taught in separate boys and girls classes in the belief that boys and girls learn better when taught separately.

The daily schedule includes such traditional subjects as reading, writing, mathematics, science and history as well non-traditional areas: philosophy, scripture, and Sanskrit (the oldest extant language known to man and a model for the study of language in general.) The development of strong language skills is emphasized, with particular care given to the clear development of speech. Students examine the universal themes and principles found in the world's great philosophic and religious traditions in weekly philosophy classes. At age ten, students have the option of being introduced to the practice of meditation.

Central Park is used for recreation and exercise. A vegetarian lunch is provided.

The Alexander Robertson School
3 West 95th Street
New York, NY 10025
(212) 663-6441

Coed
Pre-1st–6th grade
Not accessible

Rev. Leslie Merlin, Head of School
Ms. Barbara Winn, Director of Admissions

Birthday Cutoff   Children entering pre-first must be 5 by September 15

Enrollment   Total enrollment: 60
Pre-1st places: 8
1st grade places: 6
Graduating class 1997–1998: 6

Grades   Semester system
Letter grades begin in 4th grade

Tuition Range 1998–1999 $7,300
Additional fees

Financial Aid/Scholarship   Limited

Endowment   N/A

After-School Program   A variety of creative and recreational activities from 3:00 P.M. until 4:30 P.M.; extended day care available to 5:30 P.M. Monday through Thursday open to Alexander Robertson students only; a separate fee is required

Summer Program   None

Founded in 1789, The Alexander Robertson School is one of the oldest coeducational schools in the city. The school is named for its founder, a prosperous Scottish businessman and member of the

64

Second Presbyterian Church. Among the original students were immigrants and freed slaves. Although the Alexander Robertson School is still owned and operated by the Second Presbyterian Church, it is nonsectarian "while strongly espousing Judeo-Christian values and traditions. In 1998 the Reverend Leslie Merlin became Head of School. The Reverend Merlin was Associate Pastor of The Brick Presbyterian Church for eighteen years, and as such was closely associated with the Brick Church School. She taught in the U.S. and abroad before entering Princeton Seminary, where she received her Master of Divinity degree in 1976.

The student body represents the diversity of the surrounding neighborhood. The ERB is required for entering students. The style of the school is traditional and structured. The program follows a logical sequence through all grades with emphasis on basic skills and study habits.

The pre-first class focuses on socialization, exploration of the neighborhood and world, and beginning academic foundations. Reading through phonics is emphasized in first grade, with greater proficiency encouraged in second grade. Basic math skills are taught using traditional methods and manipulatives, progressing through the grades to mastery of sixth and seventh grade concepts. Creative and critical thinking and writing skills are introduced and cultivated in the middle grades leading to clear, concise, expository writing, including reports in social studies and science in the upper grades. ARS's art program has earned awards for its students both locally and nationally. The music program includes movement, instruments (glockenspiels, recorders), theory, introduction to the classics and vocal training. All students spend time in the computer lab. French is offered in second grade. Students bring their own lunch. Central Park is used for recreation and science study.

The Allen-Stevenson School

132 East 78th Street
New York, NY 10021
(212) 288-6710, FAX (212) 288-6802

All boys
Kindergarten–8th/9th grade
Not accessible

Mr. David R. Trower, Headmaster
Ms. Ronnie R. Jankoff, Director of Admissions

Uniform   Lower school: Allen-Stevenson polo shirt with emblem, pants (no jeans), sneakers allowed kindergarten–3, no sneakers grades 4–9
Middle and upper schools: blazer, dress shirts, tie and pants (no jeans)

Birthday Cutoff   Children entering kindergarten must be 5 by September 1
Children entering 1st grade must be 6 by September 1

Enrollment   Total enrollment: 370
Kindergarten places: approximately 36–42
Graduating class size: approximately 22–25

Grades   Semester system in the lower school
Trimester system in the middle and upper schools
Lower school students receive anecdotal reports and checklists
Letter grades begin in 5th grade
Departmentalization begins in 6th grade
Practice exam given in 6th grade
First final exam given in 7th grade

Tuition Range 1998–1999 $17,950 to $19,750, kindergarten–9th grade
All fees are included in the tuition
An alternative payment plan is offered through the Key Tuition Plan

Financial Aid/Scholarship   Approximately 12%–14% of the student body receive some form of aid
$700,000 available

Endowment   Approximately $7.5 million

Diversity   14 Prep for Prep students as of fall 1998
Multicultural Committee for parents
Multicultural elements are incorporated into the curriculum at all levels

Homework   Kindergarten: none
1st–3rd: 15–30 minutes
4th–6th: 1 to 1$^1/_2$ hours
7th–9th: 2$^1/_2$ to 3 hours

After-School Program   Alligator Soup: open to A-S students only, with selected classes offered to Nightingale-Bamford students; kindergarten through 6th graders, 3:30–5:00 P.M., fall, winter and spring; a variety of creative and recreational activities; an additional payment is required
Middle school and upper school intramural program
Junior varsity and varsity sports

Summer Program   June Club: A 2-week sports and trip program open to A-S students and siblings from other schools; last 2 weeks in June. The 6-week summer day camp program is for kindergarten through 3rd grades. Second and 3rd graders may participate in either June Club or Summer Day Camp. The camp program offers a variety of creative and recreational activities; an additional payment is required.

————

The Allen-Stevenson School was founded in 1883 by Mr. Francis Bellows Allen, who was later joined by Mr. Robert Alston Stevenson as administrative head of the school. Allen-Stevenson was originally located in a brownstone next door to The Chapin School on East 57th Street. During this time, a group of A-S boys once climbed across the roof of the building and into the proper girls' school next door and were severely punished. Perhaps to avoid unnecessary temptation, in

1924 the A-S school moved uptown to its present location on East 78th Street. In the 1920s A-S boys would roller skate and roll hoops to school whereas now they rollerblade. A-S is a traditional school with an emphasis on hands-on learning within a structured setting. A-S has always had an emphasis on physical hardiness, music and language arts. Parents say that A-S graduates are very well-rounded and well-mannered.

Allen-Stevenson is located on the Upper East Side. It has a neighborhood school character; parents say the school provides a small and warm community. A-S recently annexed the Brinckerhoff carriage house next door. The new facility increased A-S's physical plant by one-third, adding a new skylit, full-court gymnasium, art and shop facilities, computer lab, two new classrooms and music space. The lunchroom and lobby were also recently renovated.

Getting in: The number of applications to A-S has increased over the past few years resulting in a much more competitive admissions process. After an application has been filed, parents tour the school with a parent tour guide. Parents meet individually with the director of admissions, then parents are invited back with their sons for a small group visit (six to eight boys). While the boys are busy in a classroom with members of the admissions staff, parents are invited to the library to watch a video about the school and to talk with the headmaster and the head of the lower school. The visit lasts about one hour. The school maintains an active wait list and there is a sibling and legacy policy, but admission is not automatic. The most important criteria for admission is a good fit between the school, the boy and the family.

Parents: Parents are very comfortable at A-S. One parent described it as "an open, warm environment, a wonderful place." She described the parent body as "low key, with a lot of professional people." Another parent said, "It's a normal cross-section of independent school families." Annual class cocktail parties are held in the fall at parents' apartments. Fund-raising events include a Holiday Raffle, Book Fair and spring fund-raiser. There are annual holiday and spring concerts. New parents are invited to an evening reception at the school to meet the lower school teachers and administrators. The school has no religious affiliation.

Program: Headmaster David Trower, who came from the Collegiate School, is credited with revising and updating the curriculum and attracting good faculty. Parents say, "Mr. Trower's door is always open and he goes out of his way to know you and your son," "He shakes every parent's and boy's hand." In a recent issue of *The Lamp-*

lighter Mr. Trower is quoted on the tone of Allen-Stevenson: "Our strong academic expectations of the boys are set within a nurturing context. This combination makes Allen-Stevenson unique." The board president, Ron Rolfe, an alumnus, is quoted as saying A-S is "a progressive school with a terrific curriculum and great teachers . . . there is a creativity that abounds."

Allen-Stevenson has a very strong music program and boasts one of the finest elementary school orchestra programs in New York City. All students learn to sing and read music. The Middle School Chorus has sung on the White House Ellipse.

The Artist-in-Residence Program during Book Fair Week at A-S features an artist or writer with a specialty. One year while the kindergarten boys worked with a paper maker, older boys made beautiful bound-book covers. Artwork frequently coordinates with other subjects. For instance, second graders studying dinosaurs in science visit the Museum of Natural History and create their own dinosaurs in art class, and in shop class the boys design carts for the annual Dinosaur Parade. The shop program is extensive and combines art and math skills. Beginning in seventh grade students select an elective arts course during the three weekly "creative" periods.

Public speaking and the dramatic arts are also important at A-S. Upper school boys participate in the annual public speaking contest. Every year there is a middle school play with a student cast and crew. The popular fifth through ninth grade annual Gilbert and Sullivan production often includes faculty in cameo roles or chorus. A classic American play is produced by seventh graders. Girls from the Nightingale-Bamford School play the female roles in the annual upper school Shakespeare production as well as the sixth grade and seventh grade plays.

At A-S technology is used to enhance teaching and learning. Boys are taught how, when and why to use computer systems beginning in kindergarten and technological tools are appropriately used by teachers and students in every grade as aids for thinking, producing and presenting work in all areas of the curriculum.

The lower school at A-S is composed of grades kindergarten through third. Parents say that the lower school has a non-pressured approach to learning. The teachers employ an eclectic array of materials to teach basic concepts and skills. Reading, writing and math skills are taught in small, fluid groups. There are computers in all of the classrooms. In addition to their classroom teachers, boys interact regularly with a science specialist, art and music teachers, computer teachers and the Physical Education staff. Artwork displayed throughout the school reflects A-S's commitment to the integration of the art into the overall curriculum. At the first of many science fairs, lower school boys participate in "The Invention Convention," an exercise in problem solving. One boy solved the problem of soap sinking in the bathtub (he inserted a cork), another solved the problem of the spoon sinking into the sauce pot with a magnetic spoon holder. Seventh through ninth graders participate in the annual Science Fair while fourth through sixth graders have their own Science Festival each winter.

Middle school at A-S is composed of grades fourth through sixth. The boys now wear navy blue blazers with the school emblem on the pocket, a dress shirt and tie. Toward the end of third grade, the boys are invited by the fourth grade to a special "tie ceremony" where they are taught how to knot a tie.

The goal of the middle school program is to develop a student's abilities and self-confidence so that he can begin to take more responsibility for his own learning. Critical thinking is emphasized in English. Science instruction encourages investigation, observation and interpretation of information. In mathematics boys now explore conceptualization, problem solving and logical interpretation of math facts. Fourth graders study map skills and geography as it applies to explorers and exploration as well as current events. The fifth grade history program covers The "Ancients": Near East, Egypt, Greece and Rome integrating art, music and literature. Sixth graders begin the study of American history which continues into seventh grade. The school library is completely computerized with CD-ROM, microfiche and on-line access. Middle and Upper School boys use the computer for writing and research. The Learning Resource Center offers support to students needing extra help in acquiring study skills and strategies as well as enrichment at all levels.

The level of work becomes more demanding in the Upper School (grades seven through nine) as the boys prepare for secondary school admissions. Critical reading of both classical and contemporary literature is emphasized. The boys also complete large "theme projects" such as "Facing History," an inter-disciplinary program dealing with the social implications of the Holocaust. The history curriculum incorporates geography and covers the study of the U.S. and the world.

Upper School mathematics covers the study of algebra, geometry and introductory trigonometry. The science curriculum is designed to develop scientifically literate, independent researchers who are ecologically aware and informed about global issues. Weekly labs provide hands-on experience in life science, physical science and biology.

Foreign language is introduced in sixth grade with a choice between French or Spanish. Latin is added in eighth grade. The Arts are taught by professional artists and musicians. Art and music courses are required through seventh grade; afterward they are offered as electives.

In keeping with the longstanding emphasis on physical hardiness at A-S, there is ample opportunity for exercise. Boys in lower school go to Central Park for "field" three times a week. There is gym on the other days. "A certain level of fitness is expected," said one parent. Another parent said, "The A-S boys are sports-minded but it's not a jock school." A-S offers ice hockey at Chelsea Piers and swimming at the Asphalt Green Aquatic Center. Team sports begin in middle school. Upper school boys go to Randalls Island four times a week in the spring and fall. School colors are blue and gold. One of Allen-Stevenson's big rivals is The Buckley School, just down the avenue.

Allen-Stevenson has traditional lower school weekly assemblies that feature a variety of guest speakers, class performances, poetry readings and so forth. At middle and upper school weekly "morning meetings" a member of the faculty will discuss subjects of concern to the A-S community. Topics have included the AIDS epidemic, community service projects and alternatives to watching television.

Project Charlie, the anti-drug program, begins in first grade. Education about health issues is part of the curriculum in grades seventh through ninth, including AIDS prevention. Seventh through ninth graders attend an advisory period once a week to discuss a variety of issues.

Boys participate in special projects in community service throughout their years at A-S. Ninth graders hold Community Service Week and are required to perform twenty hours of community service.

Extracurricular activities in the upper school include: orchestra, theatre, yearbook, chorus, photography, painting, woodworking, printmaking, newspaper and student council. (Music rehearsals are scheduled so that they don't interfere with other extracurricular activities.)

Special privileges for ninth graders include overnight trips, the use of the seminar room and permission to leave school for lunch once a week.

There are numerous awards in recognition of excellence at A-S. The Anthony G. Couloucoundis Memorial Award is presented to a sixth grader for "scholastic excellence; all-around participation in athletics, the arts and community service and above all, the gift of friendship." Other awards distributed on Prize Day include the Alumni Medal, DAR Medal, an athletic award, the Charles E. Horman Award for Independence of Spirit and for Citizenship as well as awards in many of the academic disciplines, creative writing, public speaking, Latin, music, shop, art and drama. Closing ceremonies are held in the upper gym.

Graduates attend boarding schools and a variety of New York City independent secondary schools.

Traditions   Founders' Day, Grandparents' Day, Mother's Day Lunch, Father/Son Breakfast, Father/Son Dinner, Holiday Concert and Bazaar, Spring Concert, Headmaster for a Day, Dinosaur Parade, Field Day, Science Fair, Book Fair, Arts Festival, middle and upper school picnic, annual Gilbert and Sullivan production, annual Shakespeare play, Young Alumni Day

Publications   Alumni publication: *The Lamplighter*
Lower school literary magazine: *Rabbit Pie*
Middle school literary magazine: *What We Write*
Upper school literary magazine: *Pages*
Newspaper: *The Allen-Stevenson Weekly*
Yearbook: *The Unicorn*

Community Service Requirement   Special projects in middle and upper school; 20 hours in 9th grade; 9th grade Community Service Week

Hangout   The steps outside school

Bank Street School For Children

610 West 112th Street
New York, NY 10025
(212) 875-4420 (main number)
(212) 875-4433 (admissions), FAX (212) 875-4454

Coed
3's–13's (interage groupings)
Accessible

Mr. Reuel Jordan, Dean of Children's Programs
Ms. Betsy Hall, Director of Admissions

Uniform   None

Birthday Cutoff   December 31

Enrollment   Total enrollment: 430 in 1998–1999
Nursery 3's places: 16
4/5's places: 22–35
Graduating class size: approximately 40–44

Grades   Semester system
No letter or numerical grades
Bi-yearly parent conferences and reports
Departmentalization begins in the 10/11's (beginning of upper school)
No formal exams or testing but there are "curriculum tests"

Tuition Range 1998–1999 $13,600 to $15,500, 3's–13's
There is a small additional fee for food and materials
Tuition payment plan available

Financial Aid/Scholarship   Approximately 33% of the student body receive some form of aid

Endowment   Amount N/A; replenished annually through fund-raising

Diversity   Multicultural Committee of parents and teachers
2 Prep for Prep students enrolled as of Fall 1998

Homework   6/7's, 7/8's: 30–45 minutes
8/9's: 45 minutes–1 hour
9/10's: 1 hour
10/11's, 11/12's: 1½–2 hours
12/13's, 13/14's: 2–2½ hours
There are group and individual assignments

After-School Program   Bank Street After-School Program: for children ages 4 and up; 3:15–6:00 P.M.; five days a week
Children 5 years and older have a variety of activities to choose from including: sports, art, violin, woodworking, puppetmaking, theater, judo, flute and quilt making
An extended day program of supervised play is available from 4:30 P.M. until 6:00 P.M.
School vacation program: Bank Street operates a full day program of activities for children age 4 and older
These programs require an additional payment

Summer Program   Bank Street Summer Camp: during the last weeks of June and the month of July

———

The Bank Street School, a demonstration school for children, is part of the prestigious Bank Street College of Education which also includes an independent Graduate School of Education, a Division of Continuing Education and a Publications Group. The Bank Street School uses the "developmental interaction" approach to education, which is based on the views of visionary educator Lucy Sprague Mitchell.

Lucy Sprague Mitchell, the founder of the Bureau of Educational Experiments (which later became Bank Street) was part of a group of educators in the 1920s who believed that children learn best "when they are involved in the process of learning, in a developmentally appropriate environment." Concurrent with this philosophy is the belief that children construct meaning out of interaction with the world—they learn best from direct experience. Mitchell's vision of the "classroom as a community" was very different from the nineteenth-century "factory worker model" for schools. Today at Bank Street these elements of "progressive" education are put into practice with a diverse group of children, backed up with a dedicated and highly skilled staff.

Lucy Sprague Mitchell also believed that when children learn to be members of classroom groups that work together and care about each other's welfare, this lesson will extend to caring about the welfare of the society in which we live. The Bank Street College of Education was involved in designing the Civil Rights Act of 1965 and the Head Start and Follow Through Programs.

Getting in: Parents should call for the dates of the fall open houses and register for one. At the open house we attended in early November, the school's spacious auditorium was packed. Parents are shown a video that illustrates the philosophy of the school. This video was unique—not a public-relations tool but a real snapshot of classroom life. A tour of the school is given after the open house and parents sit in on classes as part of the admissions process. If you then decide that this school would be right for your family call for an application. The WPPSI-R is not required for admission to the lower school but ERB testing is required for admission to the upper school. Parents bring their child to Bank Street for a small group interview (approximately four to five children); separation is handled gently and a parent can stay with the child during the interview. Parents also can observe two classrooms for about ten to fifteen minutes. The final step in the process is the parent interview in which there is an exchange of information. The interviewer will share what she observed about your child. Parents might be asked "What are you looking for in the next twelve years?" In addition to a diverse student body, the brochure says the school "seeks children who give evidence of becoming adventurous learners and who will use the school experience well." An admissions committee of eight staff members makes the final decision.

Parents: Parents describe the atmosphere at Bank Street as informal: "Everyone is on a first-name basis." Many professors from nearby Barnard College and Columbia University send their children to Bank Street. Although one parent said, "There's more money at Bank Street now than there was before," Bank Street is committed to a diverse student body and 33 percent of the student body receive some form of financial aid. Parents are welcome everywhere in the school. "In lower school you might see ten parents listening in at morning meeting or going out on the deck," a mother told us. The cafeteria is the gathering place for parents in the morning. Potluck breakfasts and dinners are held. Parents often serve on committees or task forces; for example, in the 1995–1996 school year a parent-staffed task force examined the music curriculum. Parent education is an important component of Bank Street. One year a teacher conducted a series of evening classes for parents about how math was being taught to their children. Parents say that the administration is always "looking, questioning, improving" the school.

The Parents Association consists of four elected officers and a president and vice-president for each division (lower, middle and upper). In addition, the class parents meet with the dean of children's programs. There are a number of fund-raising activities undertaken in an effort to boost teacher's salaries. Since holidays are not celebrated at Bank Street, the Bank Street Revels are an eagerly anticipated community celebration. Each year a central theme is chosen for the revel (a celebration of the winter solstice). One year it was "fire." The whole school gets involved by writing skits, creating scenery and costumes, and performing. Tickets are usually sold out for this three-night event. There is also a Fall Fair and Auction.

Program: The program at Bank Street requires a lot of student initiative but the teachers are there to back students up. "They have an amazing amount of energy for the children," a parent said. Graduate students from the Bank Street College of Education provide extra manpower within the classrooms. There are two teachers in every classroom until fifth grade. One-third of the teachers at Bank Street are men. A typical 4/5's classroom of twenty-one children has a head teacher (who holds a master's degree), a full-time assistant, one or two graduate assistants, lots of blocks, a live rabbit *and* a worm house recycling pot.

The teachers at Bank Street "lead from behind" rather than lecturing in front of the classroom. They are actively involved with the students, guiding them in their choices. "The teaching is always adapted to the child's style, that's what they pride themselves on," a parent told us. Teachers are encouraged to derive much of the curriculum from student interests and from the students' cultures or environments.

The lower school is composed of ages three through six. Flexible or mixed-age groupings are used throughout Bank Street. In addition to the 3's, there are two 4/5's classrooms and two 5/6's classrooms. There is typically a two-year age span within the classroom groupings. Smaller groups are formed for reading and math. Activities are geared to the appropriate developmental level of the child. For instance, "pre-operational" thinkers are not pushed to master a task that will come naturally at age seven, eight or nine. The brochure says "the creation of meaning is the central task of childhood." In practice, children make sense out of concrete experience using concrete materials. (Bank Street students were among the first to use the Cuisenaire rods, unifix cubes and pattern blocks that have become standard materials used to teach math in many elementary school classrooms.) These are noisy, productive classrooms—there is the time and space for exploration, and a forty-five minute "block-time" is built into each day. There is, however, an underlying structure. Each day begins with a meeting at which students exchange ideas and learn to listen to each other. All of the students have classroom "jobs" that they take very seriously. Parents say students learn organizational skills right from the beginning.

The daily schedule written on the blackboard usually includes reading, writing, math, music, movement, gym time and recess and Spanish exposure. (By sixth grade students choose Spanish or French.) The youngest children play on the deck for forty-five minutes each day. Older students use Riverside Park. In the lower school, movement, gymnastics and imaginative improvisation are all part of the physical education program. Students ten and older participate in interschool teams in soccer, basketball and softball.

The writing program includes Whole Language (teaching of reading from a literature-based program) and involves all areas associated with language: listening, speaking and writing. (The Bank Street Readers were the first multiracial readers geared to young children growing up in an urban environment.) Recently, a 4/5's class visited the Bank Street Bookstore and then made their own bookstore in the classroom that they ran for one week as a real store (using pretend money). They sold library books and homemade books and ordered books by telephone. Other classes and parents came in. The money they made was donated to a charity.

The middle school at Bank Street comprises ages six through ten. Students leave the classroom for woodworking, art, music and gym. The class often breaks into half groups; one-half of the class will go to computer lab while the other half does math in the classroom. In these years, students make the connection between the use of the concrete materials (Cuisenaire rods, unifix cubes and blocks) and the use of symbols.

In science students conduct experiments with natural and synthetic matter; they learn about simple machines. They examine hermit crabs and salamanders, and they experiment with the Nile Delta Stream table.

By third grade the students break into student-led reading response groups in which four to five students read the same book and discuss it. Parents say, "At Bank Street the children's opinions are really valued." By the 7/8's "they're picking magnificent books to read by themselves." Students write and revise their own work with their peers acting as gentle "critics." Using the computer the students then "publish" their work, which becomes part of the classroom library. There are two computer labs with Macintosh computers and students begin writing on the computer in the 7/8's. Parents say there is a lot of independent reading and writing under the watchful eye of the teacher(s). Because of the low student-teacher ratio, learning difficulties are recognized quickly and a reading specialist works with children in the classroom.

Field trips are often integrated into the writing program. All students write in notebooks every day.

Beginning with the 6's, students visit the art studio and woodworking shop. Students are introduced to many media including: sculpture, weaving, batiking and printmaking. Art is frequently integrated into the curriculum. Murals are done in collective groups—we saw an impressive "Egyptian" collaborative mural.

In the lower school the social studies curriculum expands from the study of neighborhood and community to the study of how people work in New York City.

Middle schoolers completed a core study of the Hudson River. A class of 6/7's studied buildings around the city and the students created their own neighborhood complete with video store, pizza shop, and grocery store, all made from wooden crates which they painted and furnished. This "crate city" was then peopled with handmade puppets.

A group of 7/8's studying the evolution of Central Park learned about the original design of the park, talked with the present day parks commissioner, and drew their own maps. The unit culminated in the creation of a huge papier-mâché model of Central Park displayed in the school's lobby.

The music program is multicultural and the Orff method is used. The 7/8's learn to play the recorder. There are instrumental ensembles and chorus in the middle and upper school.

The upper school is composed of ages ten through thirteen. In the upper school the classroom teacher is a homeroom advisor and subject teacher. There is a core curriculum (organized around themes) in English language and literature and social studies. The 11/12's produce a musical in theatre; students also write and produce their own plays based upon themes learned in social studies. Students leave the classroom for specialists in math and science and beginning at age eleven for foreign language as well. Abstract ideas are explored through role playing in the upper school: Students might conduct a mock Senate debate on the president's economic package. In social studies, students examine Europe and Africa in the Middle Ages. Algebra I is taught in the eighth grade. The 11/12's have the option to attend their parent-teacher conference.

The 13's may leave the school building for lunch only. The 13's also participate in the annual four-day trip to Washington, D.C. One student writing in *The Bank Street Bugle* reflected on "our debt to the Greeks" after her Washington trip. The *Bugle* is an impressive school publication; it is thoughtful, incisive and honest.

Bank Street graduates attend a variety of independent day schools (Fieldston and Dalton are popular choices) and New York City public schools.

Traditions   Fall Fair, potluck dinners and breakfasts, theatre party, parents' fund-raiser dance, Tuesday morning meetings, overnight class trips (beginning with the 8/9's), Washington, D.C., trip for 13's, Revels (celebration of the winter solstice), 13's play/musical, Spring Concert, alumni reunions.

Publications   Newspaper: *The Bugle*
Newsletter: *Bank Notes*
Yearbook
Bank Street News Bulletin
Various publications of Bank Street College

Community Service Requirement   None; the 11/12's have a community service project within the school

Hangouts   Pizza Town (between 112th and 113th Streets), Coronet Pizza, New Nacho, Columbia Bagel (students often bring back sandwiches to eat in the cafeteria)

The Berkeley Carroll School

Lower Division (Pre-Kindergarten)
712 Carroll Street
Brooklyn, NY 11215
(718) 965-4166
(718) 638-4993
Elementary Division (Grades 1–4)
701 Carroll Street
Brooklyn, NY 11215
(718) 638-1703

Middle and Upper Divisions (Grades 5–12)
181 Lincoln Place
Brooklyn, NY 11217
(718) 789-6060, FAX (718) 398-3640
website: www.berkeleycarroll.org

Coed
Pre-Kindergarten–12th grade
Not accessible, Lower and Elementary Divisions
Accessible for 5th–12th grade

Dr. Bongsoon Zubay, Headmistress
Mr. Christopher Teare, Director/Upper School
Mr. Henry Trevor, Director/Middle School
Ms. Alison Lankenau, Director/Elementary School
Ms. Angela Apuzzi, Director/Lower School
Ms. Judith Valdez, Director/Extended Day Programs
Ms. Dolores Toolan, Director of Admissions for Lower and
Elementary Division
Mr. Andrew Webster, Director of Admissions for Middle and Upper
Division

Uniform   None

Birthday Cutoff   Children entering kindergarten should be 5 by
September 30 but readiness is key

Enrollment   Total enrollment: 750
Pre-K places: 40
Kindergarten places: 15

1st grade places: 10
6th grade places: 10
9th grade places: 10–15
Graduating class size 1998: 43
1999: 50

Grades   Trimester system, Pre-K through 12.
In all grades, extensive narrative written reports twice a year, as well as family conferences. Beginning in 8th grade, students accompany parents at conferences.
Letter grades and Honor Roll begin in 6th grade
Departmentalization in English, History and Math begins in 5th grade
Required foreign language study begins in 5th grade
First final exam begins in 8th grade

Tuition Range 1998–1999 $6,700 to $15,600, Pre-K–12th grade
Lunch fee for grades 5-11: $720

Financial Aid/Scholarship   Approximately 25% of the student body receives some form of aid

Endowment $1.5 million

Diversity   14 Prep for Prep students as of fall 1998
Early Steps participant
Seeking Educational and Diversity Program: A reading and discussion group for faculty and parents
Perspectives on Diversity Committee of Parent Association: Sponsors cultural activities
Faculty Study Group on Equity & Diversity: Advises the school on ways to insure student gender equity in all disciplines, as well as multicultural studies; vigorous recruitment of faculty applicants of color

Homework   Kindergarten: Begins in the spring with "think about" assignments one night per week
1st: Twice a week, 15–30 minutes
2nd–4th: nightly, Monday–Thursday, 30–60 minutes, lengthening as age increases.
4th: all assignments are given at the beginning of the week to

facilitate longer-range planning. Longer term projects are added
5th/6th: 1½ hours per night
7th/8th: 2–2½ hours per night
9th/12th: 3 hours per night

After-School Program   Extended day program and early morning
(7:30 A.M.) for Berkeley Carroll students only: for Lower and Elementary Divisions, from 3:00 P.M. until 6:00 P.M. A variety of academic, creative and recreational activities; an additional payment
is required
Interscholastic and intramural athletic competition for Grades
5–12
Music and voice instruction available

Summer Program   The Berkeley Carroll Summer Programs run
through mid-August and are open to students from other schools;
an additional payment is required for all summer programs
Summer Day Camp: for Pre-K–4th graders; a variety of creative and recreational activities including swimming trips and
weekly BBQ
Creative Arts Camp: for 8–14 year olds; a variety of creative and
recreational activities with an emphasis on the performing and
visual arts

The Berkeley Institute, named in honor of Bishop George
Berkeley, was founded in 1886. Bishop Berkeley envisioned a white
glove school in which the classics were taught along with the arts. One
hundred and ten years later the Bishop's vision is only a tintype
memory. In 1982 the institute merged with the Carroll Street School,
a growing Montessori-based elementary school. In 1994, The
Berkeley Carroll School was one of four independent schools in the
NYC area to be designated a Blue Ribbon School by the U.S. Department of Education.

Tucked away in the heart of Brownstone Brooklyn, within walking
distance of the Brooklyn Botanic Garden, the Brooklyn Museum and
Prospect Park, the Berkeley Carroll School's four coed divisions are
housed on two campuses only four blocks apart. "Class Links"
programs provide opportunities for the youngest toddlers to mingle
with senior students, for activities such as crafting pottery or a walk in
the park.

A capital campaign completed in 1992 nearly doubled the space of the Lincoln Place (middle and upper school) campus and the award-winning classroom complex also houses administrative offices, a student commons, and floor-through Visual Arts Center. In 1994 a new Media Center was added. Another campaign for a new athletic center is underway.

As Head of the School for over 15 years, Dr. Bongsoon Zubay has been cited by several local organizations such as the Park Slope Civic Council for her many contributions to Brooklyn. In addition to her administrative responsibilities, Dr. Zubay also oversees curriculum development, and recently implemented Cracker-Barrel sessions in all divisions at which parents may raise issues of concern.

Getting in: Parents can attend one of the many open houses that are offered in the Fall which include a tour of the school and Q and A sessions with current parents. To accommodate Manhattan families, open houses are also held in downtown Brooklyn and Manhattan. The school's Parent Ambassador program links prospective families with other BC parents in their neighborhood.

All Lower and Elementary applicants are tested and interviewed on site by Admissions Director Dolores Toolan. Applicants to first grade are given the WPPSI-R. Second and third grade applicants take the WISC-3. Candidates for grade 4 and above must be tested by the ERB. Berkeley Carroll looks for students who are a good match for the program, "A child who is bright and motivated and demonstrates an interest in learning and doing." Middle and Upper School Admissions Director Andrew Webster told us: "Every student we enroll brings distinctive strengths so that students may excel in all areas—academics, the arts and athletics."

Parents: Parents automatically become members of the Parent Association. The PA sponsors parenting workshops and a speakers bureau to which two speakers are invited each year. Recent guests include Terry Anderson, Anna Quindlen, Terry McMillan and Jonathan Kozol. Parents are also welcome to assist in the classroom, serve on committees, volunteer at the library, and accompany children on trips. At BC parents have a real voice in how their school is run because they serve on the school's 25 member Board of Trustees where they comprise the majority of members. But Dr. Zubay is quick to note that the school is "not a parent co-op." The Administration remains firmly in charge of academic direction, class placement and faculty appointments.

Parents who are also authors (and there are quite a few) sign their latest books at the two PA book fairs. Parents created the elementary divisions Law Day, helping students stage mock trials at one of which the appropriate sentence for the Wolf in Little Red Riding Hood was adjudicated. Parents also organize and participate in Career Day at which students have the opportunity to create architectural models, write legal briefs and so on. Parents are involved in the social life of the school from planning a year end trip for graduating seniors to organizing the fifth grade bowling party.

Program: Active hands-on learning is the credo of the Berkeley Carroll School and there is an emphasis on writing, both expository and creative. In a pre-school classroom you might see several children stroking the ears of the class rabbit while charting its growth with pencil and paper. Others will be working independently on a classic Montessori activity such as fitting cylindrical shapes into self-correcting slots or might be gathered around the head teacher, mastering the "M" sound by carefully tracing the shape of a sand-paper letter. "The operative word in our division is 'Discover,' " says lower school division head Angela Apuzzi. Apuzzi recently implemented a full physical education program for the kindergarten.

Reading activities begin in kindergarten in a self-paced instructional setting. Many learning styles are accommodated; worksheets are available for those children who gravitate to them. Phonics and whole-language approaches are used to teach reading and all children work one-on-one with the Head Teacher. To complete a book is more than an exercise in pronouncing the words: children master vocabulary and answer reading comprehension questions after which they are "given" the book as part of their personal "library." By the end of the year, some six-year-olds have acquired a library of 12 books or more, testament to their diligent efforts.

The elementary school at BC is housed within a single building, away from the distractions of both very young and much older children. There is a weekly assembly program. Elementary students receive a solid grounding in the basics through an integrated approach to learning. A first-grade unit on "community" might include activities related to the history of the school, and include field trips to several social service organizations. Second grade students studying Native-American cultures might play Inuit games in physical education. Third graders studying China make Chinese puppets. Parents praise Miss Maxine Barnett, a third grade teacher, for her "incredible ability to reach all children, whether it's a child in the middle, lower or upper portion of the class. She excels with every child." According to tradition, fourth graders studying the history of the American experience in the Westward Expansion, transform their classroom into a 19th century schoolroom for Caddie Woodlawn Day.

The teaching of writing begins with journals in first grade and progresses through the elementary school to include the use of dialogue, appropriate punctuation and grammar skills. In science, lower school students study the life cycle of myriad creatures, make life-sized models of the human body complete with all the internal organs, and create papier-mâché models of the solar system.

Field trips are an integral part of the curriculum beginning in pre-school with visits to pumpkin farms and to dramatic performances. Starting in fifth grade all students take a full-week trip away from the BC campus. Fifth-graders journey to Nature's Classroom in Rhode Island for an adventure in team-building, scientific exploration and dramatic play.

After-school programs in music includes instruction in virtually all instruments and voice. Older children can select from a large variety of mini-courses including: cooking, quilting, chess, puppet-making, fencing, and gardening. Lower and Elementary divisions participate year-round in the nationally recognized Hands-on-Science program.

The Middle School program at BC "recognizes that children are going through major developmental hurdles. We watch and guide children in every aspect of this development." In fifth grade students have three teachers for the five major subjects, with English/history and science/math taught as core subjects. Mandatory foreign language, either French or Spanish is added. By sixth grade, students are grouped according to skill level in foreign language and math. English and history are still taught as a "core" subject. By seventh grade, the curriculum is entirely departmentalized. Subjects are explored in depth and often involve multi-week projects. Sixth graders for example, stage a December Aztec Day, during which one classroom is turned into a marketplace and another becomes a temple. Visitors meet Montezuma and Cortez as well as a priestess who explains the unusual 20-month calendar. Eighth graders use a study of Robinson Crusoe to discuss use of natural resources. During a symposium on tropical rain forest supervision, students play the roles of farmer, rubber tapper, eco-tourism developers, miners and environmentalists, all struggling to co-exist. Historical novels supplement the curriculum. All eighth graders take a full-year geography course.

The fifth grade writing curriculum stresses the conventional five paragraph essay. Middle School students gradually master expository and creative writing. At all grade levels, revision is a major component of the writing process and there is extensive peer and teacher review. The foundation of the Middle School math curriculum is mastery of the basics with an emphasis on creative problem solving, such as finding the most efficient route for a city sanitation crew. Advanced students finish algebra by the end of eighth-grade—some more quickly than others. Seventh graders study tessellations and their relationship to Islamic art. Pi Day (not coincidentally on 3/14 of each year) allows students to derive an approximation of pi using a "human" circle chain.

Science courses in the Middle Division begin with general science in fifth grade, life science in sixth, physical science in seventh and earth science in eighth grade with lab work at the core of each year's curriculum. There are several computer labs at BC. All campuses are hooked up to the Internet and the school's e-mail system allows for virtual links among teachers and between teachers and parents. The libraries at the Elementary School and One Lincoln Place are fully automated and use CD-ROMs.

In the Upper Division students model calculus derivatives on state-of-the-art calculators and computers. In 1996 the Upper Division science curricula were redesigned to put greater emphasis on biochemistry in the mandatory biology course. As a result, physics is taught in ninth grade, chemistry in tenth, and biology in the junior year. More than three quarters of the students take AP courses.

Choice within structure best summarizes the Upper Division at BC and students have several options in arts and athletics. A highly motivated student might play varsity baseball in the afternoon and sing in the choir at night. From ninth through twelfth grades, students take five core academic courses: history, science, English, math and foreign language. They also enroll in two rotating semester electives. (Fifteen electives are offered in everything from chamber orchestra and jazz band to photography and ceramics.) There are often multiple ways of meeting the course requirements—some more rigorous, others explore an interesting aspect of a familiar subject. For instance, juniors may opt for AP American History or select a course on Democracy in America or American Social and Cultural History.

Freshmen take a three period a week mandatory writing course in addition to English class. Sophomores must enroll in a twice-weekly health course; juniors and seniors have a mandatory college counseling requirement. All seniors participate in an internship program to explore an area of professional interest. The school helps them with placement and contacts; internships range from finance and medicine to photography, music, fashion and advertising. Foreign exchange opportunities are available for those who prefer a more far-flung experience. Each spring students from a school outside Paris spend two weeks with Berkeley Carroll tenth graders. BC students make a return trip to France. A companion program with a Spanish institution is another option. BCS is the first independent day school in the metropolitan area to host a small group of international students who will be enrolled for a full year at the school and live with BC families.

Athletics are an important part of the program at BC but this is not your typical "jock" school. In the Elementary and Middle divisions, Berkeley Carroll has won first place for four of the past five years in the independent schools judo championship. In the Middle Division, interscholastic teams are fielded in coed soccer, coed track, cross country, girls volleyball, and there are strong boys' and girls' basketball teams. The girls' softball team posted undefeated seasons in recent years. Berkeley Carroll's varsity baseball team won the Baseball League of Independent Schools championship for two of the past three years.

Community service starts in the preschool years with food drives for Thanksgiving. Older children devise their own community service projects. By the time students reach the age of 18 they are volunteering in soup kitchens, geriatric centers or on park clean-up crews. Upper schoolers are required to perform 50 hours of community service but many graduate with more than 200 hours.

Popular College Choices   Amherst, Vassar, Brown, Yale, Harvard, SUNY/Binghamton, Johns Hopkins, Oberlin, Skidmore, Tufts, Swarthmore, Georgetown

Traditions   All-School Theme Write In (recent topics include gender differences, justice and fairness, and leadership), Arch Day, Lower Division Spring Festival, Thanksgiving Sharing Assembly, Holiday Candle Lighting Ceremony, Middle and Upper Division Prize Day, Parent Association Speakers Bureau, Halloween Party, Sesame Place Trip and Annual Auction

Publications   Lower school quarterly creative-writing compendium: *Explorations*

Newspaper: *Blotter*
Literary magazine: *Reflections*
Yearbook: *The Lion*

Community Service Requirement   50 hours minimum for Upper
Division students

Hangout   Ozzie's Coffee Bar, Roma's Pizza, Prospect Park playing
fields

The Birch Wathen Lenox School
210 East 77th Street
New York, NY 10021
(212) 861-0404, FAX (212) 879-3388

Coed
Kindergarten–12th grade
Accessible

Mr. Frank J. Carnabuci, Headmaster
Ms. Nancy M. King, Director of Admissions

Birthday Cutoff   No specific cutoff; most children entering kindergarten have turned 5 by the beginning of school

Enrollment   Total enrollment: 350
Kindergarten places: 25–30
Graduating class 1998: 25

Grades   Semester system in the lower school
Trimester system in the middle and upper schools
Letter grades begin in 6th grade
Departmentalization begins in 6th grade

Tuition Range 1998–1999 $14,863 to $18,191, kindergarten–12th grade
Additional fees: for trips, books, lunch, P.A. dues, and activity fees are approximately $1,100. Lunch program ($990) is optional for 11th and 12th graders; there is a 12th-grade graduation fee of $585

Financial Aid/Scholarship   25% of the student body receive some form of aid

Endowment $4 million

After-School Program   Open to Birch Wathen Lenox students only; a variety of creative and recreational activities until 4:30 P.M. or 5:30 P.M. daily; an additional payment is required
Junior varsity and varsity teams

Summer Program   June Program: a variety of creative and recreational activities and field trips; an additional fee is required

---

In 1991, the Birch Wathen Lenox School was created by the merger of two established schools: The Lenox School (founded 1916) and The Birch Wathen School (founded 1921). The sale of the former Birch Wathen and Lenox School buildings created a substantial endowment enabling the school to weather the transition. Headmaster Frank Carnabuci, who had been the assistant head at The Dalton School for eleven years, brings administrative skills and enthusiasm to the job. Parents say he knows every student by name and has implemented interesting new programs such as the Russian exchange, Japanese instruction, a swim team, and the overseas study program.

The ERB is required for admission to the school. Parents tour and return on a separate date with their child for an interview.

The Birch Wathen Lenox school is a traditional school with a nurturing atmosphere. A uniform is worn by students until sixth grade.

Birch Wathen Lenox enrolled three students from Prep for Prep in 1998.

Birch Wathen Lenox's strength is the ability to individualize the curriculum to fit the child. The student to teacher ratio is very small. Parents say, "Nobody falls through the cracks." Specialists work with tutors and parents to resolve learning difficulties. French language and culture are introduced in fourth grade.

Popular College Choices   Princeton, Dartmouth, Cornell, Columbia, Connecticut College, Emory, Harvard, Washington University, RISD

The Brearley School

610 East 83rd Street
New York, NY 10028
(212) 744-8582

All girls
Kindergarten–12th grade
Accessible–elevator

Dr. Priscilla M. Winn Barlow, Head of School
Mrs. Jeanne Dickinson, Administrative Assistant to the Head
Mrs. Elizabeth Manley Murray, Director of Admissions

Uniform   Lower school: navy blue jumper, socks can be any color, sneakers permitted but no clogs or boots
Middle school: wrap-around navy-blue skirt, shirt or blouse (with sleeves), shoes or sneakers
Upper school: none

Birthday Cutoff   Girls entering kindergarten must have reached their 4th birthday on or before October 1 of the year in which they apply

Enrollment   Total enrollment: 650
Kindergarten places: 50
Graduating class size: approximately 40–45

Grades   Semester system
Kindergarten: two-parent conferences
Classes I–III: fall parent conference; spring anecdotal report
Class IV: fall parent conference; midyear and spring anecdotal reports with grades
Classes V–XII: marks are given in every subject with comments and suggestions
Departmentalization in science, music, physical education, library and art begins in lower school; math departmentalization begins in class IV
Exams: below class VII, classroom tests are informal and marks are averaged with the term's work; once-a-year examinations begin in class VII and are held in March

Tuition Range   1998–1999 $15,900 to $16,200, K–12th grade
Additional fees: books, supplies, trips, food, physical education, approximately $1,800 ($435 to $2,125, K–12th grade)

Financial Aid   Available to all who qualify

Endowment   Market value as of June 30, 1997: $40,714,126

Diversity   35 Prep for Prep students enrolled as of fall 1998
Students of color advised by faculty member of color who helps to facilitate the middle and upper school health and ethics curriculum. A math teacher of color serves as advisor to lower school families of color
Schoolwide diversity committee; parent diversity forum

Homework   Lower school families are expected to read aloud with their children from kindergarten on; when girls have learned how to read they are expected to spend $^1/_2$ hour per night reading, as well as being read to
Classes II and III: weekly spelling assignments, math facts and puzzles, 20–30 minutes, plus nightly reading
Class IV: 30 minutes on weekdays, 60 minutes over the weekend, plus nightly reading
Class V: 60 minutes daily, 90 minutes over the weekend
Class VI: $1^1/_2$ hours daily
Classes VII and VIII: $1^1/_2$–2 hours
Classes IX–XII: four 50-minute assignments daily

After-School Programs   Afternoon program: "Play & Crafts" for kindergarten through class IV; various Friday afternoon activities until 2:30 P.M. or 3:30 P.M.; an additional payment is required
Classes VII and VIII participate in a variety of activities with boys from the Collegiate School. (see page 163 *infra.*) Class VIII (second semester) and class IX (all year) participate in a required afternoon discussion group once a week
Competition in 13 interscholastic sports, some beginning in middle school

Summer Program   SummerStart, for children grades K–6; 2 weeks in June; creative and recreational activities for an additional fee; open to children in the community
Basketball Camp for grades 5–12 held at the new field house

Brearley was founded by Harvard and Oxford-educated Samuel A. Brearley, Jr. so that girls could receive an education comparable to that offered at the independent boys' schools. Brearley opened its doors in 1884, originally serving many of New York's socially prominent families, including the daughters of the German Jewish upper class. The enrollment has since broadened to include students from a diverse range of families. Many Brearley families exhibit a decidedly intellectual bent. Since 1930 the school has had only four heads: Millicent Carey McIntosh (who later became Barnard's first president), Jean Fair Mitchell, head of school for twenty-eight years and Evelyn J. Halpert, a Brearley alumna, who succeeded Miss Mitchell in 1975.

Jean Fair Mitchell, Brearley's legendary Head of School for 28 years, died in 1998. She guided the school from the late forties through the turbulent sixties and early seventies. Miss Mitchell is remembered by Mrs. Taliaferro, the present Academic Dean of the School as "A Head of School in the old style, intellectually alive, ethically unambiguous, and devoted to the creed of plain living and high thinking." Her memory was honored by the school in a special ceremony.

In 1997, Mrs. Halpert retired and Dr. Priscilla M. Winn Barlow became the tenth head of the school. British born Dr. Winn Barlow earned a Ph.D. in Zoology from the University of Liverpool and spent a Fulbright year at Rutgers. She was most recently Head of Havergal College in Toronto, a girls' prep school known as the Brearley of Canada. Her sense of humor and warmth already permeate the school. In a recent issue of *The Brearley Update* Dr. Winn Barlow described the skills women will need for success in the next century: "They're really all thinking skills. Analysis, creativity, risk-taking, leadership; they've got to know how to run something, solve problems, ask the right questions, communicate both in writing and speaking . . . They should also be extremely comfortable with technology."

Sequestered from the hustle and bustle of the city, Brearley's red brick building on East 83rd Street overlooks the East River. Two floors were recently added providing 10 percent more space. In September 1997 Brearley inaugurated a new 12,000 square foot Field House on East 87th Street, a short walk from the school. From the windows of the hushed library in the school building on East 83rd Street, you can watch the yachts and barges slip through the waves. Although at first sight Brearley might appear staid, when the girls are bustling through the halls or speaking forthrightly in class, informality reigns. At a recent Parents Association fund-raiser, a prominent author who is a parent at the school described Brearley as "an intensely democratic elitist school." Here girls receive a superb education in an environment characterized by intellectual rigor, tolerance and social activism. Aside from the uniform, how do you know a Brearley girl? "She's the one on the cross-town bus with a big book under her arm, looking slightly disheveled because she's too busy thinking of something arcane and intellectual," says one alumna. Another parent characterized the school as being "like my kindergartner's indestructible Brearley tunic: sturdy, practical, and essential. It might come home encrusted with, flour, paint, or papier-mâché but it washes clean and ready to go the next day." Brearley is not, as rumored, all work and no play. Frivolity prevails at the annual family fun nights (which are organized according to grade). Brearley girls are just as well bred as "the green and yellow 'ladies' down the street at Chapin," and also strong, brainy, confident, poised and prepared. "These aren't shrinking violets; everyone has a distinct personality," says a parent of the girls in her daughter's kindergarten class.

Getting in: Brearley's catalog is a very understated, small white book, whose only decoration is the Brearley school motto, "By Truth and Toil" emblazoned on the front cover. Applications must be filed by December 1 for lower school and December 15 for middle and upper school. It is not imperative to apply before you tour the school, but one parent advised that you make your tour appointment by early October. And both parents should come. Tours for middle and upper school applicants are given by middle and upper school students. Parents of lower school applicants are given tours by admissions office personnel or by parents who work for the admissions office. One prospective parent said, "It looks like a school: wide hallways, bright classrooms and everything is up to date and spotless." After your tour you meet with the admissions director, Elizabeth Manley Murray, who has expanded the schedule to make sure there is ample time for conversation with parents. Parents are asked to "describe your daughter." Brearley attracts and enrolls candidates from a broad base; in a recent year the kindergarten class came from 28 different nursery programs. What are they looking for? "Eagerness to learn, a sense of curiosity and the willingness to take a risk in the classroom," says Murray. She adds, "We don't expect the girls to come to us as finished products. It is our happy task to nurture them in their individual development."

During the child's visit, the school looks for the beginnings of critical thinking skills and at how the child approaches a challenge. "Above all," says Murray, "we want to be sure that students can take full and joyous advantage of all that Brearley has to offer."

Interview appointments for applicants are made from October until early February, and a very helpful letter is sent prior to the interview to describe the process in detail. When you arrive with your daughter there are children's books in the waiting room (no squirm test here) and the children go into a classroom with age-appropriate materials. Children might be asked to play a game, tell a story, complete a puzzle or draw a picture while chatting with a teacher. The parents retire to a room with the head of the lower school, giving them an opportunity to learn more about the school. One parent inferred, "They are also looking at the parents." Brearley's admissions decisions are "need blind," and based solely on the merit of the individual candidate. Financial aid is available beginning in kindergarten and there are no "arbitrary cutoff levels." Preference is given to siblings and legacies, but they are not automatically accepted. There is a wait list.

After gaining admission to Brearley, parents are invited to a meeting to discuss the next year's program. They are asked to jot down any questions they might have on the back of an R.S.V.P. form. In May there is a late-afternoon school visit for the incoming girls and their parents.

Parents: The parent body at Brearley, according to one former teacher and alumna, is eclectic, including but not limited to the following types: "Wealthy Park and Fifth Avenue WASPs, Jewish intellectuals, a small arty group of eccentrics and families of color." One East Sider said "There are many families from the West Side which is a pain for playdates." There is an active parents' organization and a parents' newsletter.

The parents association benefits at Brearley are more like an evening at Elaine's. "An Evening With American Essayists," was the theme one recent year, featuring David Halberstam, Jules Feiffer, Calvin Trillin, Russell Baker and Anna Quindlen. The 1996 PA benefit, "Brearley Meets the Press," was held at City Center where some 1,000 Brearley alumnae, parents and friends joined honorary host and past parent Walter Cronkite and a panel of media luminaries (several of whom have daughters in the school) for a close-up look at press coverage of the 1996 presidential contest. In 1998 the Parents Association held a family-oriented CyberCarnival at the Javits Center to benefit the school's computer and technology program. Since 1997, the Parents Association has sponsored an annual Festival of Cultures for Brearley families, students, faculty and friends, celebrating the richness and variety of the cultures represented in the school community; it is an extremely popular event.

Over the years, Brearley has made connections to the families of the girls. "They know a tremendous amount about each girl, but they don't intrude, they feel that the school isn't a parent," said a former teacher. Beginning in lower school, the girls learn to be their own advocates in social and academic matters, parents say. A parent said she was surprised "at how tremendously observant and psychologically astute the teachers and administration are about each girl."

Program: The Brearley kindergarten has fifteen to eighteen girls in each of three classrooms. Separation is handled gradually. Beginning in 1992–1993 the kindergarten day was extended to 2:00 P.M. Monday through Thursday, with early dismissal at 12:30 on Fridays. Kindergarten girls have specialist teachers for library, music, science, dance and physical education. In music they start with Orff instruments and recorder; in class IV girls are introduced to a stringed instrument and hand bells. Lower school girls sing together at Assembly and at Last Day. Although not "academic" in the traditional sense, the kindergarten year at Brearley is rich with creative learning experiences incorporating art and crafts and nature (quilting, weaving, papier-mâché, hatching chicks, butterflies and so forth.) One of the three kindergarten classes studied breads from around the world, made flour from wheat stalks, baked bread and sold bread from their classroom "bakery." In another kindergarten class each girl had a chance to bring Paddington Bear (and his knapsack with pj's and toothbrush) home overnight along with a journal in which they recorded his every experience. During the year the girls get to know each other as they meet in half groups for gymnastics, PE, music, or play with balls, bikes and wagons on "the pier" or playroof and in Carl Schurz Park.

Formal academics begin in class I and II. In class I reading is taught in small groups. One parent said the atmosphere is more relaxed than at some of the other very selective schools and "There is free time in the morning to visit other grades and classrooms." The aim of these early years, according to the brochure, is to help each girl to "form good work habits and to encourage her to be adventurous, responsible and kind." Emphasis is on cooperation, not competition.

One parent said girls get the sense that "everyone is good at something and the school fosters a sense of security and independence."

In classes II and III homework includes a "math puzzle of the week" and some spelling words as homework. Starting in class IV homogeneous math groups are formed but there is movement between groups and the girls all learn the same material, albeit at a different pace. The subject of math tracking is a sensitive one with some parents.

Lower school girls have their own science lab where members of the science department oversee a hands-on approach: To study aerodynamics girls make parachutes and paper helicopters. One of the strengths of Brearley is that all of the faculty teach across the grades so they get to know the girls as they grow.

French and Spanish begin in class V and can be continued through the upper school. One parent said, "When a girl is able, foreign language arts courses are offered; when a girl needs extra help, skills courses are offered." Latin is required in Classes VII and VIII and there are also introductory classes in modern languages offered at Class VII for entering students.

The curriculum in the lower school is integrated with close coordination between the subjects. Frequently, English readings are related to topics in history and geography. One parent gave an example: "For a unit on China they studied the music, language, history, culture, customs, arts and foods of that country. The walls of the lower school were lined with all things Chinese."

Middle school at Brearley consists of class V through class VIII. A quaint tradition at Brearley is the stuffed animal mascot for each class handed down from class XII to the upcoming class V. (This is not to be confused with the official Brearley mascot, the beaver.) By class VI all subjects are fully departmentalized. Attention is still paid to individual learning styles, placement and pace. The coordination of subject matter continues. In sixth grade English the girls study Greek mythology while in history they are studying Greek and Roman history. In sixth and seventh grades, the work load increases. A parent said, "By seventh grade expectations are high and the girls are well aware of their strengths and weaknesses." The parent of a seventh grader said that "reading selections are two years ahead of other schools, and high-level, sophisticated written work is required. Papers are returned with many red lines, sometimes with comments as long as the paper, but their work is the better for it."

In class VII the girls are reading Dickens and Shakespeare and studying European history from the fall of Rome to the late seventeenth century. In the spring term they perform a Gilbert and Sullivan operetta. Drama, music and studio art classes are held once a week.

Girls in class VI take human biology, in which they study all the systems of the body including reproductive, as well as nutrition, drugs, alcohol and cigarette use. Health issues are addressed again in class VIII to fulfill the New York state requirement. Discussion group sessions are held for classes VII through IX. Students also take a one-semester community service course in class IX, and volunteer in school or in the community throughout their upper school years.

Teams in gymnastics, volleyball, soccer, softball, basketball, swimming, track and lacrosse are formed at this point. The Wednesday sports program includes yoga, jazz dance, ice skating and roller blading.

The high school: The catalog says that Brearley students need sixteen credits to graduate but most leave with twenty or more. Students have about four to five frees (free periods) a week. Homework now averages four lessons a day of fifty minutes to one hour each. Formal testing begins in class VII.

Advanced Placement (AP) exams are usually given in fourteen subjects but there are no AP, or honors courses as such. Math is required through Algebra II though most girls go on to Calculus, and students must take two upper school lab science courses. Those with proficiency in science can participate in the Columbia Science Honors Program and choose from five science courses in classes XI and XII.

As an example of how the spirit of intellectual inquiry thrives at Brearley, a 1996 spring science project presented a challenge: "Identify a problem in the community and use science and technology to solve it." Two seventeen-year-old Brearley juniors focusing on the transmission of HIV by the sharing of infected hypodermic syringes, designed a non-reusable syringe. The Brearley students triumphed over 470 other student team projects at the NYNEX Science and Technology Awards in Boston and each girl was awarded a $15,000 scholarship and they became eligible for $250,000 in seed money to develop this invention.

The computer is considered a tool to enhance learning, enabling ninth graders to analyze election results from far-flung countries before the last ballots are cast, for instance. There is no computer science requirement as such, but keyboard proficiency is expected by eighth grade and computer use is an on-going component of lower, middle and upper school math, science, history and language classes. In 1998–99 "Design of Interactive Multimedia" was added to the XI/XII curriculum. Greek courses are offered as part of a Brearley/Chapin exchange.

Class IX English again focuses on the classics: Jane Austen and Shakespeare. All students take modern history, a course in the history and geography of three areas chosen from a group that includes Africa, Central America, the Middle East and Vietnam. In class X students take "American Literature From the Puritans to the Moderns" and "American History From 1607." Their studies culminate in a trip to Washington, D.C.

In classes XI and XII there is a winter requirement of Sophocles' Theban tragedies and Shakespeare's *King Lear*. Spring electives in English are determined by student interest, but even when given a choice, Brearley girls don't seem to stray too far from the classics. Past choices include: Dostoyevsky, modern British fiction and Milton's *Paradise Lost*. More recent electives have been African-American fiction and Virginia Woolf. History electives in class XI and XII include: "Comparative Political Systems," "History of China and Japan," "Political and Social Philosophy," and "Modern European History." (In the seventies Brearley taught an interdisciplinary course for classes XI and XII on nuclear issues and nuclear disarmament.) At town meetings held throughout the year, the students discuss issues of concern, which might range from homework to the balance between arts and athletics.

Students can take art, music or drama throughout the middle and upper school. Class VII performs an annual Gilbert & Sullivan operetta and upper school students perform in plays and in an annual coeducational musical comedy production (*Gypsy* in 1997, *Pippin* in 1998).

For students requiring special help there is the Reading and Testing Department. A faculty advisor system began in the upper school in 1990. All students have a homeroom teacher.

Seniors have other options in the spring. They can choose independent study—for example an extracurricular project, job or internship. A recent project was a student generated production of *The Belle of Amherst*. Girls are also encouraged throughout the upper school to do volunteer work. One opportunity is "Bridges to Learning": a highly successful student-run effort that organizes five or six Saturday programs in the Spring for students from P.S. 102 who come to Brearley for a day of arts, crafts, carpentry, computer and other activities. In addition, there are numerous drives throughout the year at Brearley, including the Annual Mitten Drive in which mittens are bought and strung across the lobby and donated to a shelter. Brearley supported and raised funds for the Asphalt Green AquaCenter.

There are opportunities to nurture the adventurous spirit of the Brearley girl. In addition to Mountain Day, a trip held for classes V through XII at Bear Mountain, class XI girls may spend a semester at the Mountain School program of Milton Academy in Vermont, or attend the Maine Coast Semester program of the Chewonki Foundation. They can apply to spend a term at the John F. Kennedy Schule in Berlin or at the American International School in Vienna, a program arranged by Ambassador Ronald Lauder. Another option is to spend the spring at the College Cevenol in Le Chambon, France. Students may also apply to study for a year in France or Spain under the School Year Abroad Program. In 1997–98 two additional foreign exchanges were added: one for Class VIII students with a school in Toronto and another in which Brearley has been selected as one of three schools to participate in an exchange program sponsored by the Japan Society. Numerous scholarships for study and travel abroad are awarded at graduation to girls in the upper school.

Academic pressure is a fact of life at Brearley. An alumna said, "Girls rank themselves, the school doesn't." Another feels that "the girls know who they are and their energies are channeled in a constructive way." But "sometimes teachers don't check with one another to see how much work each has given," says one parent. One year a history test was rescheduled from Monday to Tuesday because of a school-sponsored ski trip when several parents called to say that the girls couldn't be expected to do all their homework (six hours) *and* study for a Monday test. Several initiatives were begun in 1997–98 by Dr. Winn Barlow and the faculty to evaluate the homework load and coordinate efforts throughout the school to ensure that the Brearley experience is as Dr. Winn Barlow says, "challenging, manageable and fulfilling."

"There are some girls who buckled under the pressure," says an alumna. "Because most are so smart, there's not much of a range and you lose perspective on how smart you really are; because you're judging yourself against impossible standards."

Course titles don't tell you everything. One alumna said that "there is an international excitement to classes, especially English and history. All subjects are thought through; there is no automatic conservatism. Courses are infused with political liberalism and teachers are sensitive to ethnic issues and awareness." Politically correct terms at

100

Brearley are de rigueur. There was a student government initiative in 1993 to broaden the curriculum to include more multicultural perspectives. There is an advisor for students of color and one for lower school families of color.

Students at Brearley are aware of gender issues, and most girls are appreciative of the manifold benefits of single-sex education. In one first grade class a mother who is a pilot for American Airlines came in to talk about her nontraditional occupation. At Brearley's 1992 Parents' Association benefit columnist Anna Quindlen explained why she will send her own daughters to girls' schools: "Because each day when they walk into class they see a smart woman at the front of the room and, on each side a smart girl, and that means that never in their lives will they be able to believe any of the nonsense about all the things girls can't do." The school's emphasis on the written word is evidenced by the thick Bibliography of Alumnae Authors.

Two hotly debated topics in recent years were diversity and leadership. Differences of opinion are respected at Brearley. There is a certain leveling of class differences at Brearley because of the emphasis on intellectual achievement. "Brearley girls never want to appear too rich, too social or too fancy. There's an inverse snobbism," says an alumna.

There is recognition that Brearley girls need to have more fun. As one parent said, "It's not a party school; your socializing is postponed for another time." The school arranges some activities with the opposite sex. Friday night dances start in eighth grade. Girls in classes VII and VIII can participate in the Friday Afternoon Program of coed activities with Collegiate boys. Activities include community service, photography, drama, mixed doubles ping pong and intramural games. Coeducational activities for the upper school students include drama department productions, joint chorus concerts with a boys' school near Philadelphia, and events planned by various student clubs. There is a junior/senior prom (held at the Plaza in 1997 and at 24 Fifth Avenue in 1998) to which girls can ask boys.

Student government is called Self-Government. Two girls form a team and they run for the positions of co-presidents.

There are at least fifteen school clubs, some for class V and up, some only for classes VII through XII. The Service Committee organizes toy, book and mitten drives, and sponsors a child. The Tech Club builds sets for plays. Other popular clubs include the Model U.N., Asian Awareness and Harvard Model Congress. The Music Appreciation Club provides tickets to musical events in the city at reduced cost. The Brearley Environmental Committee is an active organization that is spearheading student involvement in the N.Y.C. Department of Sanitation's WasteLe$$ program in which Brearley was one of three schools invited to participate. The students have performed a vital role in data collection.

Brearley has a solid AIDS curriculum, beginning in fifth grade, focusing on awareness and education. Many Brearley students participated in the AIDS Walk and many others were sponsors. There is an AIDS Awareness Society.

Outstanding sports teams are tennis, cross country and the gymnastics team, which recently was undefeated for the season and won the AAIS championship. Soccer and track teams have captured AAIS championships five years in a row and the lacrosse team (a new sport) won its first AAIS championship in Spring 1998.

There is praise for an extraordinary faculty. A building was recently purchased on East 77th Street for faculty housing. Appreciation for the gifted faculty is evident from the numerous (fifteen) chairs and faculty awards provided. The Jean Fair Mitchell Fund for faculty development has provided enrichment opportunities for faculty. The Class of 1992 Faculty Award Fund (recipients nominated by the senior class) was made in recognition of "the extraordinary commitment of the Brearley faculty to their students and to the entire Brearley community." At the end of the year the students write thank-you notes to their teachers. As Dr. Winn Barlow notes, "Brearley has a faculty that is one of the most competent and caring I've known. They enable our students to be challenged in a safe and supportive environment which is where learning occurs best, especially for young women."

Since Brearley's Centennial in 1984 the school's program has benefitted from major improvements to the Science facilities, libraries, and other teaching spaces, as well as the construction in 1994 of two new floors at the top of the school building and the construction of a new field house. The school has continued its emphasis on providing a rigorous classical education while continually reviewing its academic and extracurricular offerings to keep them relevant. "Brearley's strong curriculum," says Winn Barlow, "provides a firm anchor from which to prepare our students for the future with great confidence."

Brearley makes use of many graceful euphemisms as noted by the co-presidents of the self-government in their "Last Days" speech: "We don't have AP courses—our courses are just impossible. We don't wear underwear—we wear bloomers. We don't get 91's—we get Very

Good minus minus plus slash good plus plus minuses. And we don't graduate—we Last Day Exercise." White dresses are worn at Last Day. There are school prizes in all subjects and scholarships for study and travel. Students are recognized for community service work, and artwork from each class is placed in the school's permanent Kunz Collection.

In the late nineteenth century when college choices for women were extremely limited, Brearley prepared girls almost exclusively for Bryn Mawr College. Since then, Brearley has been very successful over the years in matching its students with excellent colleges and universities. Mrs. Joan Gardiner became the college advisor in 1993.

Does Brearley churn out a yearly crop of super women? Mrs. Halpert says that the school's objective is to "turn out young women who will be good citizens in a democratic society . . . whether successful by the standards of our society or not. It would be wrong, I think, to suggest that we want everybody who leaves this school to be a leader or a powerful person. We want all our students to leave this school happier and stronger because of the experiences they've had here and what they've learned."

Legacies say, "I'm Brearley born and Brearley bred"; "Alumnae gatherings are so exciting, there's never a boring person"; "College was disappointing after Brearley." An alumna writes in the summer bulletin of her years at Brearley: "A superb classical education and a permanent love of learning." From the Last Day speech of 1992 by the co-heads of Self-Government: "This school puts the life of the mind above all else." The process of learning is lifelong and many Brearley girls become distinguished scholars and professionals. A recent alumna now heads The Ford Foundation.

Popular College Choices   Harvard/Radcliffe, Brown, Amherst, Yale, University of Chicago/Stanford University

Traditions   "The best food of all the independent schools," Field Day, Mountain Day, Father-Daughter Holiday Program, Junior and Senior Prom, seventh-grade Gilbert and Sullivan production, eighth-grade carnival with a surprise theme, Book Fair, Brearley General Store, Lower School Family Nights, Last Day Exercises

Publications   Student Newspaper: *The Zephyr*
Class X Newspaper: *The Pulse*
Literary Magazine: *The Beaver*

103

Parents' Association Newsletter: *The Brearley Bulletin, Brearley Update*

Community Service Requirement A one-semester community service course for ninth graders; Brearley's coordinator of community service helps students to secure a year-long community service commitment with various social service agencies

Hangouts The Mansion (a diner at 86th and York), libraries

Brooklyn Friends School

375 Pearl Street
Brooklyn, NY 11201
(718) 852-1029, FAX: (718) 643-4868
e-mail: bfs@brooklynfriends.org
website: www.brooklynfriends.org

Coed
Toddler–12th grade
Not accessible

Dr. James P. Handlin, Head of School
Ms. Sara Soll, Director of Admissions, Preschool
Ms. Jennifer Knies, Director of Admissions, Lower and Middle
School
Ms. Danae Oratowski, Director of Admissions, Upper School

Birthday Cutoff Children entering kindergarten must be 5 by
December 31

Enrollment Total enrollment: 540
Kindergarten places: approximately 15
Graduating class size: 35

Tuition Range 1998–1999 Preschool–12th grade $6,250 to
$15,400
Additional fees: $400 for books and supplies
An optional hot lunch is available for an additional charge

After-School Program Quality Day Care Program beginning at
15 mos, open to Brooklyn Friends families; For older students, a
variety of creative and recreational activities are offered from 3:00
to 6:00 P.M.; an additional payment is required
Friends After Three Program: For Middle School students offers
workshops in computers, the arts, language, drama and sports
Spring and winter vacation programs available subject to demand;
an additional payment is required
Additional program: the Family Center Program at Brooklyn
Friends School is a full-day, 11-month program with flexible

hours for infants from 15 months to 2.9 years old
Clubs, sports, private music instruction

Summer Program   Summer camp: From mid-June through Mid-August. Activities for the younger children include arts, crafts, sports, trips and swimming; middle schoolers can attend Summer Arts Program or Academic Skills enrichment camp. Open to children from other schools; an additional payment is required

———

Brooklyn Friends School is a Quaker college preparatory school founded in 1867 by the Brooklyn Meeting of the Society of Friends. The school is housed in a seven-story art deco building. When you enter through the brass doors you are greeted by lobby displays of student work, from digital photos to paper mâché. In addition to classrooms, four science labs and two libraries, the school boasts a darkroom, music, art, sculpting, ceramics and dance studios, a woodshop, three computer labs, a video production and editing room, two gyms, a roof top playground and a 300 seat theater. The style of the school is informal and there is no dress code.

Getting in: Open house tours give prospective applicants a chance to meet parents and faculty. A personal interview is required for all applicants. Screening by a member of the admissions staff is required for applicants to preschool through fifth grade. The ISEE is required for application to sixth through twelfth grades. One-third of the student body receives some form of financial assistance.

The school is guided by the ideals of tolerance, equality and non-violence. Although Quaker traditions permeate the school parents say that the school is not in the least sectarian. "It manages to provide an enriching academic experience while fostering the sense that there is not a dichotomy between the secular and spiritual aspects of our lives." Students meet in silence for weekly Quaker Meeting and courses in ethics and social justice are offered in the upper school. Brooklyn Friends enrolled five Prep for Prep students in 1998.

Head of School: Dr. James Handlin, Ed.D, known to the school community as "Jim," is also a published poet who one year joined students for a poetry reading at a local cafe. Parents say he takes a hands-on approach to running the school, greeting parents in the morning and visiting classrooms spontaneously.

Parents: The parents at Brooklyn Friends are an eclectic mix of artists, office workers, lawyers, educators, physicians and Wall Street professionals who share a philosophical commitment. According to one parent: "We looked for a private school that reflected and fostered our moral values, where the students were aware of their advantages but were not elitist." The parents play an important role in the school as class parents, library volunteers, and as members of the PTA they engage in fundraising and community building.

Program: Experiential learning is emphasized throughout. All classes are actively engaged in creating, hypothesizing and building. The pre-school curriculum is based on the idea of play as "the work of young children" and fosters independence and the development of language and self-expression through the arts, dance and music. In the Lower School (K–4) students work to develop and increase basic skills as well as taking part in art, dance, music, library and physical education. Computer science, woodworking and Japanese language and culture are also part of the lower school program.

Fifth and sixth graders stay in the classroom for reading, language arts, and social studies. They see specialists for science, math and foreign language. Latin instruction begins in fifth grade; students can select from Spanish, French or Latin thereafter. Seventh and eighth grades are fully departmentalized. The humanities program includes ancient history, the Middle Ages, the Renaissance and the Age of Exploration and American history. Environmental studies and discussions of new technologies enrich the traditional science curriculum. The school has a newly expanded the math department and several new computer labs.

Upper schoolers (grades 9–12) take four years of English, foreign language, social studies, mathematics, and physical education; three years of science and art; one each of computer literacy and application, and ethics. Computers are integrated into the classroom curriculum from the lower school through upper school. The school recently installed a T1 line for internet access throughout the building. In addition to classroom computers, students have access to six computer labs with Dell Optiplex systems. Upper schoolers edit, write and explore scientific and mathematical formulas through a number of software programs. Brooklyn Friends has a web site that is up and running.

The math department offers Calculus AB and BC and electives in engineering, programming, applications and robotics, statistics, architecture, and geometry. There are AP's in biology, chemistry and physics. Humanities course offerings include: American literature, Japanese literature, and Latin American Studies. The arts program is outstanding and includes painting, sculpture, ceramics, woodshop, video production, music and drama. All seniors take part in six week internships in hospitals, community organizations, engineering firms, law offices and so on, depending on their career interests.

Two-thirds of the high school students play on a sports team. For a relatively small school, the teams are quite successful. BFS recently won the volleyball league championships and a New York State Independent School Soccer Championship title. Athletics are seen as an opportunity to build skills and develop good sportsmanship; despite their recent successes, BFS is not a "jock" school; sports are seen as an opportunity to do one's best.

From second grade through the upper school, students take overnight trips to develop peer leadership skills, for academic study and for personal growth. In recent years, students participated in environmental studies on Cape Cod, astronomy explorations in Frost Valley, White House tours in Washington, D.C., rock climbing at Camp Vacamas, language and cultural trips to Italy, Mexico, France, Canada and Puerto Rico.

Popular College Choices   Barnard, Brown, Clark, Colgate, Connecticut College, Haverford, Wesleyan, NYU, Sarah Lawrence, Swarthmore, University of Pennsylvania, University of Rochester, Trinity, Vassar and Yale

Traditions: Fallfest, Holiday Crafts Fair, Dance Concert, Turkey Trot, All School Art Show, International Dinner, Middle School Sports Night, Drama Productions, Sports Dinner

Publications   Pre/Lower School Poetry Magazine; Middle School Poetry Magazine; Middle School Newsletter; Upper School Literary Magazine; Yearbook; School Newsletter

Community Service Requirement: All students take part in community service from pre-school through upper school. Upper schoolers are required to complete 70 hours of community service in order to fulfill graduation requirements

The Brooklyn Heights Montessori School

185 Court Street
Brooklyn, NY 11201
(718) 858-5100, FAX (718) 858-0500

Coed
Pre-Kindergarten–8th Grade
Accessible

Ms. Marcia Gardère, Head of School
Ms. Susanne Peebles, Director of Preschool Admissions
Ms. Maggy Sears, Elementary and Middle School Division Director
Ms. Sonia Nachuk, Director of the Little Room

Birthday cutoff   For 2's Program child must be 2 by September 1 in
year of entry

Enrollment   Total enrollment: 290
Pre-K and kindergarten places: 150
Grades 1–3: 48
Grades 4–6: 48
Grades 7 and 8: 48
Little Room: 33
Little Room Kindergarten: 10

Tuition Range   1998-99 $7,100–12,600 Preschool–8th Grade
Kindergarten: $10,500
Elementary: $12,300–12,600

Financial Aid/Scholarship   8% of the preschool budget is allotted
for scholarships
12% of the elementary school budget is allotted for scholarships
The Little Room is primarily funded by the Board of Education

Endowment   None

After-school Program   A variety of recreational and creative activities are offered including: origami, French, dance, soccer and
more; additional payment is required.

109

Summer Program   The summer program includes trips and arts and sports activities; an additional payment is required

———

The Brooklyn Heights Montessori School opened its doors on October 1, 1965 with twenty children attending the one-room school in the First Presbyterian Church on Henry Street in Brooklyn Heights. Since then the school has expanded and moved to the Cobble Hill section of Brooklyn. The school recently completed an award winning 32,000 square foot expansion, which includes not only spacious light-filled classrooms, but also a library and gymnasium.

Getting In: Parents are invited for personal tours of the school and a personal interview is required of all applicants. For the Preschool program, parents visit the school and children come for an evaluation. Lower Elementary students come for an interview and informal testing. Upper Elementary applicants come for an interview and must submit ERB scores.

Program: There are currently three divisions of BHMS: the Preschool, the Elementary and Middle School Program and the Little Room.

All learning at BHMS is designed to happen within the Montessori model of mixed-age classrooms which are carefully prepared environments organized to offer children a wide range of experience and to facilitate the growth of their skills and confidence. Independent work, depth of study, critical thinking, respect for and understanding of others, are all emphasized by a supportive and developmentally oriented staff at all age levels.

In the Preschool and Kindergarten classrooms the environment is supportive. The educational philosophy and the teaching materials developed by Maria Montessori provide the underlying structure for the program. The BHMS faculty is concerned with the overall growth of each child, so teachers regard social, physical and emotional development as going hand in hand with intellectual growth.

In the Elementary and Middle School Programs, students are taught reading and science as part of an interdisciplinary curriculum based on global studies. Goals for math include development of a deep understanding of mathematical concepts as well as basic skills for problem solving. Students leave the classroom for specialized instruction in Spanish, art, music, physical education and dance. Community service is part of the program for all older elementary students.

The Little Room is a special educational program (preschool through kindergarten) which serves children with speech and learning difficulties. Housed in its own space at BHMS, the Little Room shares much of the Montessori educational philosophy and practices. Integral to the Little Room is a unique mainstreaming program (the oldest in the city for preschoolers) which has been extremely successful in helping students move on to "typical" class placements.

The Browning School
52 East 62nd Street
New York, NY 10021
(212)838-6280, FAX (212) 355-5602

All boys
Kindergarten–12th grade
Not accessible

Dr. Stephen M. Clement, III, Headmaster
Ms. Jackie Casey, Director of Admissions

Uniform Dress code for all grades (coat and tie with an option of turtleneck shirts in the lower school)

Birthday Cutoff Boys entering kindergarten must be 5 by September 1

Enrollment Total enrollment: 340
Kindergarten places: 28
Graduating class 1998: 26
12 Prep for Prep students as of Fall 1998

Grades Semester system
Letter grades begin in 4th grade
Departmentalization begins in 7th grade
Interim report and semester report each term

Tuition Range 1998–1999 $14,787 to $17,053, kindergarten–12th grade
Additional fees: for books and lunch and PE uniforms approximately $1,500
Tuition payment plan available

Financial Aid/Scholarship Approximately 15% of the student body receives some form of aid

Endowment N/A

Homework Kindergarten: approximately 10 minutes each night
Lower School: increases to 1 hour each night

Middle School: about 2 hours each night
Upper School: about 3 hours each night

After-School Program   The Browning After-School Encore Program offers a wide variety of creative and recreational activities for boys in grades one through six until 5:00 P.M.; an additional payment is required
The Browning Sports Club (Intramurals)
Junior varsity and varsity athletic competition

Summer Program   There is a three week recreational program available for the lower school in June

––––––––

The Browning School was founded with five boys as a college preparatory school in 1888 by John A. Browning. It is a traditional school, at one time very socially exclusive in its student body. Today, Browning boys are culled from a more diverse population but they still mind their manners—a group recently went to tea at the Macklowe Hotel. In 1998, Browning enrolled five Prep for Prep students. Parents say Browning offers a nurturing, supportive environment. There is a formal dress code and every morning Browning boys are greeted with a handshake. ERBs are required for admission. Parents tour the school and interview at the same appointment. Middle and upper school candidates return to Browning for a half day visit. Browning has a large sibling population and there is a Brothers' Breakfast each year.

Browning is composed of three divisions: lower school (kindergarten through fourth), middle school (fifth through eighth) and upper school (ninth through twelfth). Foreign language begins in fifth grade with a choice of French or Spanish. Latin is offered in seventh and eighth grades. There is an annual Shakespeare play and public speaking contest. Browning fields strong teams in soccer, cross country, basketball, baseball and tennis. Field Day is a popular annual event.

Browning is a member of Interschool and beginning in fifth grade Browning boys participate in a variety of activities with a number of girls' schools including joint assemblies, dramatic productions and a prom.

College advising begins in Form IV (grade 10) and Forms V and VI (grades 11 and 12) take an annual trip to visit a broad selection of colleges and universities. Personalized guidance enables each student to maximize his college potential.

Hot lunch is served daily in "Ruby's kitchen"—the school cafeteria.

Browning recently completed a $1.5 million renovation to create a new library, two new science labs and more office space.

Popular College Choices   Vassar College, Vanderbilt University, Stanford University, Skidmore College, Harvard University, Boston University

The Buckley School

113 East 73rd Street
New York, NY 10021
(212) 535-8787

All boys
Kindergarten–8th/9th grade
Not accessible

Mr. Brian R. Walsh, Headmaster
Mrs. Jo Ann E. Lynch, Director of Admissions

Uniform   Beginners (kindergarten): prescribed knit blue or white
Buckley polo shirt, pants (no jeans), leather shoes, no sneakers
Grades I–IX: jacket, tie, slacks and leather shoes

Birthday Cutoff   Children entering kindergarten must be 5 by September 1

Enrollment   Total enrollment: approximately 350
Kindergarten places: 40
8th grade graduating class size: approximately 18; more than half
will attend New York City independent day schools, the rest will
attend boarding schools
9th grade graduating class size: approximately 15–17; most will
attend boarding schools

Grades   Trimester system
Kindergarten through 3rd grade students receive anecdotal
reports and checklists
Letter grades begin in 4th grade (3 times a year)
Departmentalization begins in 6th grade
First final exam given in 7th grade

Tuition Range 1998–1999 $15,300 to $16,400, kindergarten–9th
grade
Additional fees: for textbooks, classroom supplies, athletic fees,
publications, lunch and snack, approximately $2,100
Fee for class IX out-of-town field trips approximately $580

Financial Aid/Scholarship   10% of the student body receive some form of aid

$450,000 in financial aid was awarded in 1997–1998

Endowment   Capital fund valued at $13.5 million (as of January 1998)

Diversity   12 Prep for Prep students as of Fall 1998

Homework   Beginners: none

Class I: approximately 20 minutes, weekly spelling tests

Class II: approximately 1/2 hour

Class III: 45 minutes–1 hour

Class IV: approximately 1 1/2 hours

Class V: approximately 2 hours

Classes VI and VII: 2 1/2–3 hours

Classes VIII and IX: 3–4 hours

After-School Program   Classes I through IX: required after-school sports at Ward's Island, fall and spring

During winter term required after-school sports in the Hubball Building

Interscholastic athletic competition in the Manhattan Private School League

Friday Afternoon Lower School Gymnastics Club and Middle and Upper School Basketball Club

Saturday Sports Club (10 A.M.–12 P.M. in the Buckley gym)

Vacation Club (10 A.M.–12 P.M. in the Buckley gym)

Summer Program   The Buckley June Program; 2 weeks in June: swimming, computers, arts and crafts, games and sports at Buckley and Ward's Island; an additional payment is required

---

Founded in 1913 by educator B. Lord Buckley, historically The Buckley School has groomed the sons of New York's captains of industry (including a few Vanderbilts, Rockefellers and their latter-day counterparts) as well as the progeny of prominent politicians (mostly but not exclusively Republican) for the elite boarding schools. Today, "leadership, citizenship and academic excellence" are still valued at The Buckley School, which is traditional in every sense of the word, but the student body now includes children culled from a variety of socioeconomic backgrounds—more than a few from neighborhoods far beyond the tony Upper East Side. While most of the current graduates still go on to schools like Groton and Deerfield, many of the boys now attend New York City independent day schools.

Some elements of the past remain: Buckley still has "travel days" on either side of the spring vacation, a formal tea complete with finger sandwiches is served at Exhibition Day, the male teachers and athletic instructors are addressed as "Sir" and women classroom teachers (who do not wear slacks) are addressed as either Miss or Mrs. (never Ms.). The boys are served by the kitchen staff family-style (the rumored white-gloved waiters are merely an apparition of days gone by). Dole won a 1996 student election by a comfortable margin.

The Buckley School is far removed from the turmoil rocking the public schools. Prospective parents who have toured Buckley are impressed by the sense of clarity and order. Lower School Director Mrs. Sonja Robinson says, "Clear goals make clear kids." The emphasis on a classic curriculum, the strict dress code and unabashed respect for God and country have tremendous appeal to nineties parents dubbed "the new traditionalists." Applications to The Buckley School have been at record levels in recent years.

Is there a typical Buckley boy? Parents say: "A boy who is very interested in sports, very smart, follows directions." But athletic ability and blond hair are not a prerequisite for admission, and we know many boys with a creative bent who managed to find their niche here. What is most important is that the boy will be able to handle the work, because by fourth and fifth grades the curriculum is demanding. Buckley boys are well rounded: Touring parents might see boys with their ties tucked into their smocks painting in the airy art room with classical music playing in the background. First graders recite poetry, lower school boys perform in the annual rhythm band assembly, all classes put on a class play (Buckley's drama program is outstanding). Unfortunately, parents don't tour Ward's Island, where the extensive outdoor afternoon sports program (fall and spring) harnesses the boys' more aggressive instincts.

Getting in: An important criterion is "a match in values between school and home." Although many of the boys (including legacies and siblings) still hail from nursery schools like Park Avenue Christian, Madison Presbyterian and Episcopal, the kindergarten class is composed of boys from many different nursery programs.

Admissions at Buckley consists of four components. After the application is received comes 1) the tour, which is led by the director of admissions, the assistant headmaster or the lower school head, 2) the parents' interview with the director of admissions and the headmaster, 3) the applicant's group interview and 4) the ERB and nursery school report. Decisions are made on the basis of the group interview, observation at the child's preschool, ERB and school report. Both parents are requested to attend the interviews with the director of admissions and the headmaster; they will accommodate scheduling difficulties and meet with the parents separately, if necessary. Letters of recommendation from Buckley parents who know the family are welcome. The group interview is about one hour long (during which the boys are observed playing a variety of "games"), after which the boys stop by Mr. Walsh's office for a Tootsie Pop. One mother said her son enjoyed the experience so much he drew a picture of himself going to Buckley while at his Trinity interview.

What are they looking for? According to Jo Ann Lynch, director of admissions, a boy with "a love of learning, good self-esteem, not a little old man, rather, a naive but curious child who is fun to be with." They are also looking at how the boy socializes in a group. According to Mrs. Robinson the ERB is "a measuring stick against which all the boys stand." And of course, they also look at the family. There is a sibling and legacy policy (some boys' grandfathers attended Buckley); however, the school will not automatically admit a child who they feel would not do well there. Buckley does maintain a wait list.

Patrician Brian Walsh has been headmaster at The Buckley School for over a decade. Parents say, "His goals and ideas are clear and specific. This helps parents and offers them support." "Mr. Walsh visits every classroom weekly, all the boys know him, he is at every function from the Teddy Bear Picnic to the Father-Son Overnight." Another parent said, "He really knows my son—he even writes personal blurbs on his report card." Mr. Walsh is an eloquent proponent of single-sex education. When asked the perennial question, "What is the advantage of an all-boys school?" Mr. Walsh replies, "Aside from the obvious advantage of not having to compete with girls who mature at a faster rate in the early years, boys will sing, speak French, pour themselves into their art and let themselves go on stage in ways that never happen with girls in coed elementary schools."

Mr. Walsh is credited with making Buckley a "kinder, gentler place" than it was in past decades. When Mr. Walsh came to Buckley, boys were still being ranked academically and middle school boys received pins for the highest grade point average. Middle school pins are now given largely for effort. It is acknowledged that Buckley boys are very competitive, but the belief is that this competitiveness can be positive (and a great motivator) if used appropriately. The highest awards at graduation exercises are for character, not the highest G.P.A. Of course, any school is only as good as its teachers, and at Buckley there is tremendous respect for teachers and teaching. Approximately 80 percent of tuition goes toward teachers' salaries and benefits (some of the highest among teachers in city independent schools). Teachers undergo an annual self-evaluation as well as a formal evaluation by the headmaster.

Parents: Mr. Walsh started the first Buckley Parents' Committee (in 1982) for the purpose of "service and communication." There is only one officer—the president. Class representatives are selected by the homeroom teachers and division directors. The Parents' Committee meets once a month, in a closed meeting, and the minutes are distributed to all parents. Parents praise the Buckley mothers, who are "time givers to benefit the school, a cohesive group of women working towards a common goal." School benefits are well organized and well staffed.

The tone at Buckley is definitely formal and very Upper East Side. The "Mortimer's crowd" says one parent. (The staff is reputed to be more liberal than the parent body.) The parents are Wall Street bankers, lawyers and doctors, with a sprinkling of writers and business people. But as one parent said, "It's a cosmopolitan mix of French, Chinese, Japanese, African-American, Jewish and Muslim." Another parent had a different perspective: "Boring, old money, coupon clipping . . . they are more dressed in the morning than Brearley parents are in the evening." Parents dress for all school events (don't even think about wearing blue jeans). The class cocktail party is usually held in a parent's elegant Upper East Side apartment.

The school has no formal religious affiliation—Christmas and Chanukah songs are sung at the Beginners' Christmas party. The nativity play for classes I and II is an annual event, and after the pledge of allegiance, everyone recites the Lord's Prayer at assemblies. However, families of many faiths are comfortable here; the commonality seems to be a basic conservatism.

Traditions are important at Buckley. The used clothing sale and preview party, where parents can purchase gently worn Brooks Brothers pants and blazers for their sons, is a popular event. The Father-Son Overnight (kindergarten through ninth grade) is an annual rite, and the Fathers' Committee selects the Saturday night entertainment. The boys have a marvelous time playing tennis, fishing, throwing a football with Dad (substitute dads are available). One father recalls his first overnight when bedded down in his tent well after midnight, he heard a group of fathers singing "Kumbaya" around a distant campfire. Older boys attend the annual Father-Son Adventure Dinner, which features an explorer or adventurer as speaker. In addition, the annual Father-Son Day at Shea or Yankee Stadium and family skating party help to bond the Buckley community.

Programs: Buckley's main facility consists of two fully renovated connected buildings on East 73rd and East 74th Streets. The adjacent townhouse was purchased in 1996. It has been completely rebuilt to provide additional classroom space for small group instruction and technology. It will also house some of the facilities now in the 74th Street building to be renovated for additional classroom space. In addition, a new Assembly Room with a balcony has been constructed providing more seating space and doubling the stage area of the old facility. The Hubball Building, two blocks away, named for James M. Hubball, headmaster for thirty-two years, houses three full-size gymnasiums plus the two beginners' classrooms. Parents like the fact that the beginners have their own little world, although they travel to "Big Buckley" for Friday assemblies each week. There is a Big Brother Program to help integrate the boys into Big Buckley. Lower school boys write "fan mail" to boys in other grades after watching them perform in a school production.

The lower school at Buckley is composed of kindergarten through grade three. Each year the two classes are reshuffled so the boys relate to different friends. "Kindergarten at Buckley is a gentle transition into grade school," parents say. Mondays and Fridays are short days, so there is time for play dates and for just settling in. "Except for a few leftover nursery school cliques, friendships seem to shift weekly in the kindergarten year," said one parent. The Friday afternoon gymnastics and basketball clubs (for an additional charge) are "more social than athletic" and most of the boys attend. Boys who want to learn gymnastics routines can attend afternoon sessions at the school beginning in first grade. After school several boys attend art classes at the Metropolitan Museum of Art, others go to religious school, take Chinese, piano or karate, and if they haven't had enough sports already, some lower school boys attend the Cavaliers after-school sports program.

The beginners' classroom is traditional, with block and LEGO corners, listening center, library corner and an adjoining outdoor play roof. On three extended days (until 2:45 P.M.), the boys alternate among gym, creative movement and cooking, and science and library. The kindergarten day is organized but not overly structured. Parents say, "They are really tuned into the rates at which little boys develop. Throughout Buckley the boys are challenged, but they are given the skills to meet those challenges." Kindergartners end the year with the Teddy Bear Picnic, to which boys bring their favorite stuffed bear (or other well-worn animal).

Beginning in first grade boys wear a jacket and tie to school, changing into their "Buckley blues" for after-school sports each day. The day is structured and the boys leave the classroom for art, crafts, music, science and library. First through third graders go to the science lab twice a week. There is a recess in the mornings and in the afternoon an hour of sports. Project Charlie is an anti-drug program in the lower school that fosters good self-esteem and responsible decision-making.

Each boy is challenged, basic skills are taught in small groups and there is never the expectation that all the boys are going to be doing the same thing at the same time. Homework is given to teach study skills and responsibility. Parents say that "by third grade the pace is quicker, there is serious traditional work, a certain amount of maturity is expected." Third grade boys know how to use the library, and also have access to the New York Society Library on East 79th Street.

The emphasis at Buckley has always been, and remains, on a "sound traditional curriculum." The Buckley School brochure is notable for its brevity regarding the yearly curriculum, but there is more here than meets the eye. Social studies in the lower school incorporates multicultural viewpoints. Boys learn to work in collaborative groups as well as individually. There are workbooks that reinforce reading, math and handwriting skills. Journal writing begins in kindergarten and first graders write daily. Formal reading instruction begins in first grade—boys break into reading groups based on ability. There is a lot of movement between these groups. Lower School Head Mrs. Sonja Robinson explains that the reading program is literature based and includes the teaching of phonics. (Buckley has not been quick to jump on the Whole Language bandwagon.) Buckley is quick to identify learning problems before a boy's self-esteem is affected. The Skills and Language Arts Program (SLA) provides support where needed. There is a learning specialist for each division of the school. Cathy Bose, a popular teacher "who really taught the boys how to think," is now the lower school math specialist and she is introducing new methods of teaching using manipulatives and a hands-on approach.

There is a computer in the kindergarten classrooms that is used for games. Boys in the lower school "publish" their own books using the computer and there is a lower school literary magazine that is a desktop publication.

Computer in classes I and II is mainly for math and reading games. Formal computer instruction begins in third grade with "Microworlds." LEGO LOGO (designing LEGO constructions and making them "work" with the computer) is very popular. In recognition of the fact that in the near future the older boys will probably be completing most of their homework and writing assignments on the computer, a computer enhancement project is under way at the school. In a third grade geography pilot program Macintosh laptops were used to create state itineraries. The library was automated in 1997, and a T1 line was installed for a school network in 1998. All classes are wired for the Internet.

Throughout the lower school art is frequently integrated into the curriculum. For a unit on the Middle Ages kindergarten boys went to the Arms and Armor Exhibit at the Met and to the Cathedral of St. John the Divine to see and sketch Gothic architecture. Kindergartners make stick puppets and papier-mâché masks. First graders study the cultures of ancient Mexico and Japan. They study Mayan culture, make their own pottery, pictographs, patterns and illustrated stories. (One drawing had the caption "I am going to sacrifice you"). After visiting the Brooklyn Botanic Garden, one class designed their own Japanese gardens. The Japan unit culminates in a visit to the Urasenke Center for a traditional tea ceremony. Second graders make papier-mâché skyscrapers, study immigration and make a map of Manhattan.

The range of the art program at Buckley is visible on Exhibition Day. Works range from terra-cotta dinosaurs to seascapes inspired by Monet, from jungles à la Rousseau to multimedia sculptures and computer projects. There are collaborative murals and freedom quilts. The older boys make actual-size self-portraits of what they would like to be when they grow up: professional basketball player, botanist, illustrator, writer, ski racer, lawyer. In crafts the boys make smooth polished wooden bowls, letter openers and muskets.

Middle school at Buckley is composed of fourth grade through sixth grade. Fourth graders enter through the 74th Street door and on the first day mothers must say goodbye downstairs as their sons find their own classrooms. Homework requires more sophisticated thinking and time, parents say (between forty-five minutes and two hours). There are more long-term assignments. Letter grades begin in this year. Boys choose a book for their book report (one self-described nonconformist told us he chose Stephen King's *Nightshift*). The boys study the ancient world and write research reports. They have their own Olympic games. French and Spanish are offered; Latin is required beginning in seventh grade.

The fifth graders study the Middle Ages, culminating in a Medieval Feast. The boys dress in period costumes, speak Old English and make banners and shields. One parent said by fifth grade the work is more interesting and there is more discussion than in the lower school. Middle schoolers study earth science, physical science and human systems (including reproductive).

Buckley takes athletics seriously and offers a highly organized, competitive sports program. Blue championship banners line the walls of the Hubball Building and the trophy case is full. The brochure says: "Physical fitness and skill development are emphasized." Per von Scheele, the director of athletics at Buckley for over twenty years, rollerblades to school and leads ski trips to Italy during spring vacation. In fall and spring the boys travel to Ward's Island for field sports. Beginning in fourth grade boys have weekly tryouts for the Strength Club, the Super Strength Club or Gladiators in "recognition of achievement of athletic strength at a level several years beyond a boy's grade level." Those who qualify get a T-shirt. By seventh grade afternoon sports are seventy-five minutes long and one mother told us "the boys come home around 5:00 P.M., do a load of work and go to bed." Not every boy needs to be a jock but the boy who is totally uninterested in athletics will not be happy here (although the boys do receive an effort grade in athletics on their report cards). Boys who love to compete and are talented will thrive. Buckley gym birthday parties are popular and parents must book them about a year in advance.

There are middle school intramural leagues and beginning in seventh grade there are Varsity A and B teams. All boys must participate in one sport each trimester. In fifth grade the boys begin playing football. The Buckley Blue Demons are a source of tremendous pride and school spirit, they score on almost every possession and have been league champions for over thirteen consecutive years. In addition to football, Buckley has championship teams in soccer, wrestling, gymnastics, baseball, lacrosse, and track and field. At the end of each season awards are given out recognizing outstanding individual and team achievement. Class champions are named for classes four and up.

At the middle school closing assembly pins are awarded for achievement in the areas of French, athletics, English composition and positive attitude. The Gold Founder's Pin is awarded for the student who made the greatest progress during middle school, and the George Lane Nichols Award is given for "courage, loyalty, helpfulness and reliability."

The upper school at Buckley consists of grades seven through nine. In classes VII and VIII boys read *The Iliad*, tackle algebra and geometry, hone their lab skills and study American history. They continue their study of French and Latin. During the spring term seventh grade boys write a 2,000-plus-word research paper on a topic of their choice in American history (subject to teacher's approval). Classroom discussions in the upper school become increasingly animated. In eighth grade the boys read more classics: Dickens, *Julius Caesar, To Kill a Mockingbird*; they complete another spring research paper and study modern European history up to the Franco-Prussian War.

According to the handbook, ninth grade "readings are chosen for their relevance to the student's developing sense of ethics and justice." They read *Catcher in the Rye, Cry the Beloved Country* and more Shakespeare. There is a weekly debating period. Boys study Euclidean geometry, physics and modern European history through the present. Ninth graders take trips to Boston and Washington, D.C. (where the boys visit the Lincoln and Jefferson Memorials and Arlington National Cemetery, as well as the Holocaust Museum). Ninth graders complete a major research paper during the fall term.

The annual class play, a tradition at Buckley, starts in kindergarten. The boys soon become very comfortable onstage. Every boy participates in making scenery and has a small speaking part. First graders perform in the nativity play and a poetry recital. The annual class plays become more sophisticated in the middle and upper schools; many of these productions offer a contemporary twist on the classics, for example: "A New York Yankee in King Arthur's Court" or "Sherlock Meets the Phantom." For the spring operetta, girls from one of the independent girls' schools often play the female roles. In the annual Jack Woodruff Public Memorial Speaking Contest for seventh and eighth graders boys must go through four rounds speaking from four to five minutes on controversial current issues. Recent topics have included the rise of democracy in Russia, educational vouchers and immigration restrictions. The boys are judged on delivery and content.

Ninth graders take a year-long class in debating and engage in a formal debate before the student body. There are two classes in the upper school on current issues as well as a leadership class taught by

Mr. Walsh. The boys also take a useful CPR and first aid course. Ninth graders can drop one language and take only five academic courses. They have the privilege of leaving school for lunch on Wednesdays during winter term so that they can use local libraries to work on their term papers.

The student council for grades four through nine is elected by popular vote, with some officers appointed by faculty. Other extracurricular activities include the popular Glee Club, which gives three concerts a year including an operetta and an annual Middle School operetta. (Some years boys go behind the scenes at the Met.) Boys can elect to work on the literary magazine *The Dawn* (named by Mr. Buckley after *The Salutation of the Dawn*, from the Sanskrit), the upper school newspaper *The Shield* or join the Environmental Club. Community service activities vary from year to year and there is no hourly requirement.

At upper school closing exercises the Gold Pin is awarded for academic achievement. There is a first and second honor roll, a student athlete award, as well as individual awards in most subject areas. The Harrison S. Kravis Award is given by the Lewis Eisenberg family in recognition of "progress, citizenship, participation in school activities, generosity of spirit." Four major athletic awards, most of them emphasizing character, effort and sportsmanship, are given.

Every graduating Buckley boy carves his own wooden plaque, which is affixed to the school walls. On her tour one parent noticed that in the sixties the plaques featured the occasional *Playboy* Bunny or peace sign, but by the late seventies returned once again to traditional subjects like sailboats, horses, guns, golf clubs, and shields. Nineties plaques show more diverse interests.

Buckley boys have good manners, excel at sports and speak well in public. Parents say that they are well prepared for the most rigorous secondary schools in the nation: "Buckley is prepping our son for life, with high standards in many ways," an alumnus parent says. Whereas a decade ago nearly every Buckley boy went to boarding school, now almost half go to New York City–area day schools. Deerfield, Hotchkiss and Groton lead the recent boarding school choices; Horace Mann, Collegiate and Trinity are popular day school choices.

Traditions Friday assemblies, Father-Son Overnight at Camp Sloane in Lakeville, Connecticut, Father-Son Beginners' Breakfast, Father-Son Adventure Dinner, A Day at Yankee Stadium, Grandparents' Day, Book Fair, Buckley Skating Party, fifth grade

Medieval Feast, Rhythm Band Assembly, Spring Exhibition and Tea, Glee Club operetta, Field Day, nativity play, Holiday Concert, Annual Jack Woodruff Memorial Public Speaking Contest, senior class trips to Boston and Washington, D.C., Fathers' Committee softball game vs. class IX graduates, used clothing and book sale and preview party, Theatre Benefit, alumni party

Publications   Lower school literary magazine: *A World of Stories*
Literary magazine: *The Dawn* (since 1926)
Upper school newspaper: *The Shield*
Yearbook: *Horizons*
Annual report
School and alumni news: *The Buckley Letter*

Community Service Requirement   No hourly requirement; past activities have included volunteering at a food pantry, Clown Care Unit at New York Hospital, annual Central Park cleanup, Ronald McDonald House

Hangouts   The Buckley Gym, EJ's Luncheonette, Duane Reade

The Caedmon School

416 East 80th Street
New York, NY 10021
(212) 879-2296, FAX (212) 879-0627
website: www.caedmonschool.org

Coed
Nursery 2's–6th grade
Not accessible

Carol Gose DeVine, Head of School
Moreen McGurk, Co-Director of Admissions
Mary Ann Winograd, Co-Director of Admissions

Birthday Cutoff   Children entering the beginners' group must be
2½ by September 1
Children entering kindergarten must be 5 by November 1

Enrollment   Total enrollment: 180
Nursery 3's places: 35–40, largest point of entry
Kindergarten places: 5–8
Graduating class 1998: 10

Grades   Semester system
No letter grades; detailed anecdotal reports 2 times a year and
portfolio conference once a year in Elementary; three conferences and one anecdotal report in Early Program (3–5 year olds)
Departmentalization begins in 5th grade

Tuition Range 1998–1999 $6,700 to $12,000, nursery–6th grade

Financial Aid/Scholarship   11% of the student body receive some
form of aid

Endowment   None (yet)

Diversity   20% students of color

Homework   First grade, 20 minutes written work plus reading.
Homework increases as children get older

After-School Program An additional fee is required for all Caedmon after-school programs; open to Caedmon students only. Child minding is available Monday through Friday until 6:00 P.M. The after-school program for 4's–6th grade Monday through Thursday from 3:30 P.M. to 5:30 P.M.; a variety of creative and athletic activities
Clubs for 1st–6th graders meet every Wednesday until 5:30 P.M.
Afterschool instrumental music program: private lessons in piano, classical guitar, violin and flute are available Monday–Friday

Summary Program None

The Caedmon School was founded in 1962 by a group of parents interested in the philosophy of Maria Montessori; Caedmon offers a "modified Montessori" program. The school is housed in a five-story building and classrooms are bright and airy. The outside courtyard, sheltered from the street, has a safety surface playground. There is a large lunchroom with a full kitchen, which serves hot lunch to everyone.

Head of School Carol DeVine points out that Caedmon differs from the classical Montessori mold in the Early Program because "Caedmon utilizes and provides materials for fantasy play and there is an emphasis on group work and relaxed socialization amongst the children. There are many more differences in the elementary program, especially in the materials used."

An "attitude of compassion," community service, multicultural respect and acceptance are woven into Caedmon's curriculum. Ms. DeVine stresses that ". . . we teach the child, not just the curriculum." Twenty-five percent of the student body is international; many parents work at the U.N. missions. One parent said, "My husband is with the U.N.; we move constantly and coming to New York City was overwhelming. Caedmon became an oasis for our whole family." Parents say that Caedmon is "warm and accommodating; they are very responsive to children's differing rates of development." There is praise for an "experienced, superb teaching staff" and for the "creative, well thought out homework assignments." Caedmon has expanded enrollment in the lower grades; the school population is somewhat smaller in the upper grades. A number of students leave for the gifted and talented programs at nearby public schools.

Getting in: The school has a fall admissions procedure but does not have an application deadline. Applications are processed in the order in which they are received. The application fee is $40.00. Parents are welcome to attend one of the two evening Open Houses held in the fall, or they can attend a morning group tour. After the application is reviewed, a date is arranged for the child to visit the school. Children are seen individually, although parents can join their child in the classroom if separation is difficult. One parent said that the focus is on the child, not the accomplishments of the parents.

Parents: Caedmon parents range from artists to investment bankers. The Board of Trustees has seventeen members and five spaces are reserved for parents with children enrolled in the school. The Parents' Auxiliary is close knit and dedicated. The P.A. hosts a "Back to School" night at the beginning of the year to introduce parents to their children's teachers and provide an opportunity for new parents to meet each other. An auction fund-raiser is held in March every year. A wine-tasting party for international parents is held in the fall and another in the spring for in-coming parents. Early morning "Coffee and curriculum" workshops are held throughout the year. Parents are encouraged to talk to their child's teacher either directly or on the phone. Formal conferences are held three times each year.

Program: Classes are small and the overall student/teacher ratio is 8:1. The atmosphere is academic but nurturing. The Early Program is composed of children two and a half to five-years-old and the Elementary Program is from "transition" (a.k.a. Kindergarten) through sixth grade. Specialists work closely with classroom teachers balancing the curriculum with science, French, library/research skills, computer, music, art, gym and community service projects.

The Early Program, for three to five-year-olds, utilizes mixed-age classrooms and children frequently work together in small groups. The modified Montessori approach emphasizes Montessori materials and activities but also encourages creativity. Children on a full-day schedule have lunch and a nap. The afternoon activities include visits to the science room and library.

Kindergarten is known as "transition" because of the "in-between" stage of this age group. Transition prepares five-year-olds for the more teacher-directed and academic demands of Caedmon's Elementary Program. "The teacher really understands that my five-year-old is both a playful child and a budding student," observed one parent.

The Elementary Program is composed of first through sixth grades and offers an integrated curriculum. For example, a social studies class was studying immigration and the students' countries of origin. The music teacher, a former Broadway actor and choreographer, wrote a play along with his class called *Making Tracks in America* with jazz and blues music taken from eighteenth century African-American spirituals and other American musical traditions. In art class, the students created various immigration scenes for the set.

Math is also integrated with other subject matter. Every year, during National Mathematics Month, the entire staff puts together a special all-day math event for the children. A different theme is selected each year with a variety of activities that demonstrate the practical applications of math.

Computer skills begin in Transition (kindergarten) and the children have access to computers in the computer lab, library and every classroom.

Art and Music at Caedmon are exceptionally strong. Artwork by Caedmon students has been exhibited in the Monmouth County Museum (New Jersey), the Manhattan Children's Museum, WNET Channel 13 Student Arts Festival, WNET Channel 13 Student Arts International Exchange, and many other places. Original musical productions are put on twice a year; children from kindergarten through sixth grade participate.

Popular Secondary School Choices: Brearley, Browning, Birch Wathen Lenox, Calhoun, Chapin, Collegiate, Columbia Grammar & Preparatory School, Convent of the Sacred Heart, Dalton, Dwight, Hewitt, Manhattan Country School, Marymount, New York City Museum School, Park East Middle School, Riverdale, St. David's, Salk School of Science, Trevor Day School, UNIS, York Prep

Traditions: Caedmon Meeting (weekly meeting of entire Elementary community), student musicales, Back to School Night, Elementary apple-picking trip, all-school picnic in Central Park, all-school Thanksgiving feast and the Thanksgiving Book, Caedmon Chorus holiday performance at Lord & Taylor, Holiday Assembly, international parent wine tasting party, fundraising auction, Grandparent/Special Friend Day, Parent breakfasts, Mathland, upper level overnight trip, annual spring trip to Jones Beach (Elementary), annual spring park day and picnic (Early Program), and new parent cocktail party.

Community Service: Community service is an integral parent of the curriculum in fifth and sixth grades. Students explore issues related to their community service projects through interdisciplinary thematic units of study.

The Calhoun School

Robert L. Beir Lower School
160 West 74th Street
New York, NY 10023
(212) 721-0990 (main number)
(212) 875-9678 (admissions)
FAX **(212) 721-2025**

(2nd grade–12th Grade)
433 West End Avenue
New York, NY 10024
(212) 877-1700 (main number)
(212) 724-2308 (admissions)
FAX **(212) 877-2450**
website: www.calhoun.org

Coed
Nursery–12th Grade
Not accessible at 160 West 74th Street;
Accessible at 433 West End Avenue

Mr. Steven J. Nelson, Head of School
Ms. Nancy Sherman, Director of Admissions
Ms. Karen J. Booth, Director of Lower School Admissions

Uniform   None

Birthday Cutoff   Children entering nursery 3's must be 3 by September 1
Children entering kindergarten must be 5 by September 1

Enrollment   Total enrollment: 500
Nursery 3's places: 46, largest point of entry
Kindergarten places: 12
Graduating class 1998: 31

Grades   Semester system
Letter and number grades begin in 8th grade
Modified departmentalization begins in 2nd grade (2nd through
4th graders move in homeroom or "cluster" groups to specialists

132

in science, the arts and physical education.) Full departmentalization begins in 7th grade
Timing of first midterm or final exam varies

Tuition Range   1998–1999 $11,900 to $18,500 nursery–12th grade
(includes lunch for 2nd through 12th grades and all materials and
books)
Additional fees: for trips (5th–9th grades range from $80–$375)
Tuition plans of 10 monthly payments can be arranged

Financial Aid/Scholarship   20% to 25% of the student body
receive financial aid

Endowment   N/A

Diversity   8 Prep for Prep students enrolled as of fall 1998; membership in Early Steps and Faculty Diversity Search; SEED
(Seeking Educational Equity and Diversity through inclusive curriculum) former participant: this is a national project involving
public and private schools throughout the world to foster gender
and multicultural equity in education
In 1993 Calhoun was awarded a $408,750 DeWitt Wallace–
Reader's Digest Fund Independent School Opportunity Program
Grant for developing and expanding programs supporting gender
and multicultural equity.
In 1996–98 DeWitt Wallace grant funds were directed to conflict
resolution training through Educators for Social Responsibility
and the addition of an intern of color to the staff

Homework   Nursery–1st grade: none
2nd–4th: approximately 15–45 minutes
5th–8th: 1–3 hours
9th–12th: approximately 2–4 hours

After-School Program   Calhoun ASP: a variety of classes offered
each school day in both buildings to Pre–K4's–4th grades from
school closing hours until 4:45 P.M., with an extended care option
available at the 81st street building until 6 P.M.; activities include
karate, science, computer, woodworking, cooking; an additional
payment is required
ASP also offers courses for adults including driver's education and

CPR Springdays: a full-day program for children ages 4s–1st grade; half-day for 2nd–4th grade, offered during spring recess

Summer Program Junedays: a half-day camp program for Pre-K 4's–1st graders, designed to fill the gap between the end of school and beginning of summer vacation
Summercare: a day camp program for children ages 3–7, directed and staffed by members of the Calhoun School faculty; from the last week in June through the first week in August

---

Founded in 1896 as an all-girls school, Calhoun was renamed in 1924 for Head of School Mary Edwards Calhoun and became completely coeducational in 1971. Calhoun has always been a forward-looking institution known for its innovative curriculum, individualized attention and small class size. Within each division of the school, there are few walls or doors and no rows of desks, but rather areas assigned to each discipline. Although the tone is informal, there is a strong underlying academic structure. Parents say, "Calhoun prepares students well for college because they have learned how to be independent thinkers and achievers."

Calhoun has two locations: Since 1989, preschool through first grade have been housed in the Robert L. Beir Building on West 74th street. Since 1975 grades two through twelve have been located in a modern building at West 81st Street and West End Avenue. The school is organized into four divisions, each with its own director.

Parents have a high regard for the teaching staff at Calhoun. Parents describe Calhoun as a community consisting of administrators, teachers, children and parents. Teachers and administrators are called by their first names. Under the inspired leadership of Dr. Neen Hunt, a gifted educator and former head of school, Calhoun attracted a dedicated and caring staff, some of whom have developed its innovative award-winning curriculum. Faculty incentives such as the Professional Development Program, a grant from the Edward Ford Foundation and the Faculty Enrichment Grant allow teachers at Calhoun to continue to grow and learn. Dr. Hunt stepped down in 1993 and Mrs. Mariana S. Leighton, with twenty-five prior years of administrative experience in NYC independent schools, became the head of school. Mrs. Leighton says, "Calhoun teaches students how to live in a community as participating, thoughtful and responsible individuals." Parents say, "At Calhoun children see good values that are reinforced by example." Mrs. Leighton retired at the end of the 1997–98 school year. Her successor, Steven J. Nelson, comes to Calhoun with experience in a variety of private school and college settings. In describing his philosophy, Mr. Nelson says, "We need to think about education in America in a new way . . . We should identify and nurture the rich mix of intelligences that accompany each child through the schoolhouse door. We should value the abstract painting as much as we value the calculation of compound interest."

Getting in: Parents interested in learning more about Calhoun can attend an open house in the fall before applying. The application fee is $40. There are some short essay questions on the application, such as "Briefly describe your child's personality . . . any special gifts or talents?" The school views the ERB as just one component used to evaluate the match between the child and the school. Calhoun selects students with a broad range of interests and talents who have the potential to be focused and self-motivated and the intelligence necessary to meet the demands of their program. A kindergarten applicant's classroom visit is low-keyed, its aim is to get a sense of the child's personality and interests and to assess facility with basic skills and concepts. Parents meet with admissions personnel to see if Calhoun's philosophy and parental expectations for their child's education are compatible. The preschool program is very popular and the largest point of entry. There are some spaces each year for new four year olds, and space also opens up at the kindergarten level. Calhoun maintains a strong sibling policy.

Parents: Socially, Calhoun is low-key. The primary focus is always on the child, not the parent or social scene. Calhoun counts on parents to be active in their child's educational life, and the school in turn is very supportive of parents. There are frequent conferences, and parents are invited to call or visit when they need to. Annual Parents Association activities include the Lower School Halloween Fest and Book Sale at Barnes & Noble, the PA Spring Carnival, an evening lecture series. Some of the more informal events for parents include Wednesday evening volleyball games and theatre parties, some of which, like *The Nutcracker*, are for families. Many parents say they feel a connection to Calhoun even after their children have graduated, and they continue to attend school events.

Program: At the Robert L. Beir Lower School building (preschool through first grade), classrooms are bright and airy. As in the 81st Street building, and in keeping with Calhoun's educational philosophy and complementary physical space arrangement, there are few walls, fewer doors and table groupings replace the traditional desks in rows. A strong, cohesive team of teachers collaborate to create an impressive curriculum which fully integrates art, music, drama, science, computers, and physical education. The collaborative, interactive model of education is stressed, and learning is noncompetitive at Calhoun. Lower school Director Kathleen Clinesmith has worked with young children for many years and is a strong proponent of Calhoun's collaborative learning philosophy.

Separation is handled gently on an individual basis: All children have a homeroom "cluster" area and a primary or "cluster" teacher; they travel from this cluster area to other rooms and specialists for certain subjects, depending on their grade level. Children in kindergarten and first grade have language arts, math, science, social studies, block building, cooking, art, music, shop, library, computer, drama, physical education and creative movement. Children take recess on the terrace or go to the park each day. Parents say, "Creativity and socialization and the three R's are all stressed in the lower school." Discipline is recognized as an inner process that is developed with the aid of adults. Calhoun teachers are sensitive to the differing rates of social and emotional development in children. A parent said, "Many are creative kids who march to their own tune."

An eclectic approach to teaching reading is employed, making use of Whole Language, phonics, and skill-based instruction techniques. In addition, an innovative program integrates children's creative writing and music. First graders, whose classrooms are on the top two floors of the Beir building, continue to gain spelling skills while given the freedom to use invented spelling. Throughout the school year, first through fourth graders proudly publish their own original books and research papers, handbound and illustrated by the author, with all spelling corrected. First graders continue to follow a curriculum stressing hands-on learning, problem-solving and teamwork. Students begin a year-long study of Central Park. Weekly visits to the park provide experiences which are further developed back in the classroom, including detailed topographical maps of the park, observational drawings of its plants, animals, statues and structures, and classification of the various leaves and rocks that are collected.

Second through twelfth grades are located in the West End Avenue and 81st Street building, where each of the three divisions has its own floor. Second through fourth graders (the elementary school at 81st Street) are divided by grade level into groups or clusters of twelve or thirteen students, and assigned an advisor. They travel as a cluster, to other classroom and activity areas within the school. (Calhoun's cluster advisory system changes somewhat in the middle and upper schools, where clusters are formed across the grades and students follow increasingly individualized schedules.)

Joyce Blyn, Elementary School Director, has more than twenty years of experience as a teacher and administrator. She views learning as a lifetime experience and the school's job to keep children motivated and provide them with the tools they will need to move on to higher levels of education.

Once again an eclectic approach is used to improve reading skills. Small reading groups are the norm. A reading specialist and a part-time learning consultant are on staff. Students engage in creative and journal writing and learn the writing process. Research writing skills are introduced in first grade and developed further in successive grades. In third grade students complete a paper on a chosen topic. (By the end of the eighth grade, students are expected to have strong skills in research writing. They choose topics and write individual formal thesis papers.)

Math skills in mechanics and abstract thinking are taught in creative hands-on classes in which students participate fully, even writing their own math work problem books to share with other math students. Homework assignments reinforce skills as well as challenge students. Critical thinking and problem solving encourage divergent thinking.

Calhoun has a reputation for individualized attention. Parents say there is always an appropriate level of challenge. If a student needs enrichment in a certain area a mentor will be found or the school will tailor a special program for the child. Similarly, if there is a special problem Calhoun will find a solution. One mother whose child had a specific difficulty told us, "The school worked together with us as a team. My child was never looked down upon, never viewed as needing remediation; it was handled so that the child did not feel bad about herself." Another parent with a child whose reading level in kindergarten was at least three years above that of his classmates spoke of the expert and sensitive way in which that child was always challenged and excited by the work he was given while never having to be isolated from his peers.

The interdisciplinary approach, according to Mrs. Leighton, "allows students to look at a subject from many different perspectives. We strive for a depth of understanding." The ultimate goal is "to develop students who are lifelong learners, lovers of language, able users of language and active inquirers." Though present in the earlier grade levels, Calhoun's interdisciplinary approach is most clearly obvious, beginning at the elementary level, when the lower school literature is integrated with social studies, science and other subjects. The artful interweaving of different subjects into a cohesive whole is the hallmark of the program, evident at each grade level.

Second graders learn about the settlement of Manhattan through a special project with the New York Historical Society. Multicultural contributions of early settlers are demonstrated through literature, art, music and cooking. In their study of Africa, third graders read and write their own fables and folktales. They do research on African animals, create fabric art, masks and pottery, and build a model African village. As they read *Coming to the Americas as a Slave*, *Letters from Rifka*, *All of a Kind Family* and *African American Folktales*, fourth graders learn why we are called "a nation of immigrants." Children enjoy modeling the designs and pottery of Native Americas and preparing and eating Pilgrim recipes. Dramatic presentations, trips to the Tenement Museum and to Ellis Island, guest speakers and the creation of a mural depicting contributions of numerous immigrant groups both past and present are but some of the year's highlights.

The middle school at Calhoun is composed of grades five through eight. The integrated English and social studies curriculum for fifth and sixth graders was developed by two Calhoun teachers and won recognition from the National Conference of Teachers of English. "Tapping Our Roots" and "Stories Old and New" represent the two-year cycle in which students examine the roots of Western civilization and read the literature of different ethnic groups, including Greek, Roman, Egyptian and Islamic. The course description says "Students discover similar motifs, plot devices and types of characters that reappear in old and new literature, no matter what its cultural origin." Units are enhanced by related activities: art, music, drama, library assignments and/or computer study. For instance, the art program, complementing English and social studies curricula, structures projects in stained glass and illumination (5th/6th grade medieval studies) and impressionistic landscapes (7th grade European history).

Eighth graders write a formal thesis. Each part of the research process is graded, and after the finished product is presented, further revision may be done. An alumna at Stanford University says that papers at college are easier than those at Calhoun. The middle school math curriculum is viewed as a process that extends over the four years of the division. At the eighth grade level, homogeneous or ability grouping begins. Advanced math students are given first year algebra. Two math/science teachers at Calhoun have won recognition: middle/upper school science teacher John Roeder, who has been at Calhoun for twenty-five years, won the National Tandy Technology Scholar award for excellence in science teaching. Middle school math teacher Phil Bender earns praise for his innovative conceptual math program. One project in applied math involves baseball statistics; another uses a trip to the Bronx Zoo as an opportunity to collect and process data. Each year a number of Calhoun students are accepted to the specialized math and science public high schools (see pp. 459–462 *infra*).

Foreign language study is introduced in sixth grade with one semester each of French and Spanish. The program begins officially in seventh grade with a choice between the two languages, and continues through advanced literature, conversation courses and AP courses.

Calhoun's computer program spans all grade levels. In the lower school, students use graphics and word processing programs, in addition to educational games which reinforce math, language, and problem solving skills. Elementary school students (grades 2–4) use the computer as a tool to enhance the curriculum in all subject areas. Children create their own multimedia projects and interactive programs, using HyperStudio and Microworlds (Logo programming) By the end of fourth grade all children complete a keyboarding program. All fifth and sixth graders continue with keyboarding, application software and Logo programming. Sixth graders are introduced to PhotoShop. Projects, including multimedia presentations, remain integrated with the interdisciplinary social studies/English curriculum. Seventh graders learn Excel and advanced programming skills with Lego Logo Robotics. All eighth graders complete a basic upper school course, which includes word processing, database, spreadsheet, desktop publishing and image scanning. Upper school students can choose from many advanced electives including multimedia programming, desktop publishing and designing and creating Web pages. Several Calhoun upper school students have parlayed their computer expertise into well-paying summer jobs.

The Upper School at Calhoun consists of grades nine through twelve. Parents describe the upper school student body at Calhoun as diverse; students with different strengths and interests as well as different backgrounds make up the relatively small class.

Robert Schaecher, Upper School Director, has been at Calhoun for twenty years. Formerly he was director of the Community Service Program, and coordinator of the selective Peer Leadership Program and

Life Skills Program, which he developed. As part of the Peer Leadership Program at Calhoun, eleventh and twelfth graders help ninth graders adjust to school life. Activities range from escorting them around on orientation day to leading discussions in the weekly life-skills course. Ninth graders and peer leaders also attend a two-day overnight in late September.

The cluster advisory system continues in the upper school. Parents find that it is an excellent and easy way to keep communication open and consistent. Beginning in the middle school and continuing through the senior year students are scheduled once a week to meet individually with their cluster advisors. For graduation, 21 credits are required, including three in science, one-half in computer science and three in foreign language. There are, in addition, the following non-credit requirements: four years of physical education and sixty hours of community service.

Classes are mostly discussion-based seminars. Parents say it is impossible for students to be lost in the shuffle because classes are small (an average of fifteen per class), and students are always active participants. Parents praised the exceptional English and social studies departments.

A Senior Masterworks Program allows students to design their own projects for half or one credit in the subject of their choice, culminating in an oral or written presentation or performance before a Masterworks Committee. Sample projects have included play directing, a personal family history of the Holocaust, a collection of short stories, a sculpture, a dance demonstration/performance and vocal recital.

Calhoun participates in the Network of Complementary Schools, which offers a three-week exchange program for students as well as faculty at other innovative schools throughout the United States and Canada. For example, students may attend a school on a Navajo reservation in Arizona, an arts program in Interlochen, Michigan, or Oklahoma, an outdoor survival program in the Colorado mountains, or they can study architecture in a San Francisco school. Through Network, select students are also given the opportunity to attend a Multicultural Leadership Workshop in Toronto. In the past, Calhoun has been host to students from the Navajo reservation, from Seattle, Washington and from a small rural town in Kansas. While on an exchange visit at a school in San Francisco, an upper school English teacher developed a curriculum in Latino literature, now used at Calhoun.

Upper school students have a student lounge and, from tenth

grade on, may leave school during a free period or during lunch. An active Student Government Executive Council is made up of class officers from each class and the elected president, vice-president, secretary and treasurer. The student government has, among its many activities, sponsored students at the AIDS Dance-a-thon.

The MCC or Multicultural Committee organizes assemblies and discussions on cross-cultural issues. The school also has an environmental concerns club: SAFE; the Umbrella Club, where political and philosophical issues are discussed, and a film club. Calhoun also has a very successful Forensics team whose members compete at the state and national levels each year in solo/duet acting, debating or public-speaking formats.

There are two upper school drama productions each year held in the auditorium at the Robert L. Beir building. Café Calhoun, sponsored by student government, is a showcase for upper school student talent. Students may work on the staffs of the school newspaper, literary magazine or yearbook.

Varsity sports include league-winning volleyball and basketball teams, in addition to soccer, softball and tennis.

In their weekly "College Cluster," second semester juniors begin discussing the process of choosing and applying to colleges. This seminar continues through the middle of the senior year, when acceptances are received and final choices must be made.

Calhoun is a charter member of the Cum Laude Society and annually elects outstanding seniors for membership. Numerous awards are presented at Class Day, Athletic Awards Assembly and Commencement. There are named memorial awards in many subject areas as well as athletic awards. Commencement awards recognize character, integrity, maturity and service. Students can also graduate with distinction in a given discipline. Calhoun graduates go on to a variety of colleges, reflecting the diversity within the graduating class.

Popular College Choices   Brown University, Wesleyan University, University of Pennsylvania, New York University, Vassar College, Boston University, Cornell and Sarah Lawrence.

Traditions   Harvest Festival (annual school Thanksgiving celebration with activities organized around a common theme), fall and spring MS/US dramatic productions. Café Calhoun (upper school talent show), Book Fair and Gala Preview Party, Spring Carnival, Cluster Trip Days (special activities for grades 2–12), Wednesday

141

evening volleyball for parents, alumni basketball (alternate Mondays), Career Day, artist-in-residence Program, annual trustees' fund-raising event, Curriculum Expo (which includes the Annual Arts Festival), Class Day, Athletic Awards Assembly, Commencement exercises

Community Service Requirement   60 hours

Publications   Newspaper: *The Issue*
Literary magazine: *Antithesis*
Newsletter/alumni publication: *Calhoun Chronicle*
Yearbook

Hangouts   Riverside Park, student lounge, the plaza on 81st Street outside Calhoun, neighborhood coffee and pizza shops, Barnes & Noble Bookstore

The Cathedral School

1047 Amsterdam Avenue
New York, NY 10025–1702
(212) 316-7500, FAX (212) 316-7558
e-mail: ethurber@cathedralnyc.pvt.k12.ny.us

Coed
Kindergarten–8th grade
Not accessible

Phillip G. Foote, Headmaster
Edith Thurber, Director of Admission

Uniform   Flexible dress code: white blouses/shirts, navy or khaki skirts, pants, shorts (in warm weather)

Birthday Cutoff   Children entering kindergarten must be 5 by September 30

Enrollment   Total enrollment: 227
Kindergarten places: 24–28
Graduating class 1998: 20

Grades   The lower school (kindergarten–grade 4) is on a semester system
The upper school (grades 5–8) is on a trimester system
Letter grades begin in 5th grade
Full departmentalization begins in 5th grade

Tuition Range   1998–1999 $14,250 to $15,200, kindergarten–eighth grade
Fees are included in the tuition

Financial Aid/Scholarship   40% of the student body receive some form of aid based on financial need

Endowment $2,425,000

After-School Program   The school has an extended day enrichment program for Cathedral School lower school students. In addition, the Cathedral of St. John the Divine's A.C.T. program,

143

open to all students, offers after-school and holiday programs. A.C.T. is open to students from other schools but Cathedral students have priority when registering; an additional payment is required

Summer Program   A.C.T. uses the 13-acre Cathedral close for the summer program; a variety of creative and athletic activities are offered for an additional payment

———

The Cathedral School was founded in 1901 to provide choristers for the Cathedral of St. John the Divine. Now a fully coeducational independent school, the tradition of providing the choristers for the Cathedral is still one of the School's unique features. When the strains of evensong float out of the gothic cathedral over the 13-acre close of flowering shrubs and herb gardens, shade trees and strolling peacocks, Cathedral School seems like a place out of time, yet this school is very much in sync with modern life and the latest educational practices. One of the best kept secrets on the Upper West side, Cathedral School is a vibrant community. Its growing popularity is due to not only its extraordinary location but also a strong academic program, an enthusiastic new head of school, and a diverse and talented pool of students.

Phillip G. Foote, former headmaster of the Horace Mann School in New York and the Greenhill School in Dallas (which became the top school in Dallas during Mr. Foote's tenure), was appointed headmaster in 1995. It appears to be a good fit.

Getting in: Parents can attend information-gathering open houses in the fall. They have ample opportunity to observe classes, and special events and ask questions of school administrators and parents. The School retains an affiliation with the Episcopal Church but admits students of all faiths. The ERB is required for admission. Parents come for a tour and applicants are interviewed individually at the school. Cathedral School has always valued diversity and a full 40% of students receive financial aid. The school roster reads like a mellifluous mix of nationalities. Entering kindergarten and first grade students visit the school in late May. All new students attend a one-day orientation at school before opening day.

Parents: The parent body at Cathedral School represents a hip cross-section of city life and includes some prominent writer/editors, well-known actors, academics from Columbia University, professionals, musicians, and artists. Parents value the inclusiveness of the community and everyone is made to feel welcome. Though most parents work, the Parents Association is very active and sponsors fundraisers, book fairs, class dinners, workshops, picnics and produces an impressively literate monthly newsletter.

Program: Classes throughout the school are small. The atmosphere is academic but nurturing and the curriculum is multicultural and experience-based. The lower school is composed of grades kindergarten through four, and the upper school is composed of grades five through eight. Each division has its own academic director, faculty, schedule and special facilities. Lower school students, working in a self-contained classroom setting, master basic skills in the three R's and science. French or Spanish is introduced in kindergarten. Whenever possible, teachers in different departments join together to write and teach an interdisciplinary curriculum so that students see connections between subject areas. For example, when lower school students study the history and culture of Native Americans in social studies, they visit Manitoga in Garrison, New York, a living archeological site replicating an Indian village. They read Native American myths and folk tales and create their own, make Indian artifacts in art, write and perform original plays in music class and study indigenous animals in science.

Cathedral School is currently implementing a $500,000 technology initiative creating a technological structure that is curriculum driven and promotes active learning and critical thinking. The school has a T1 line and a new school-wide computer network. All classrooms have at least one computer and printer. The computer lab has 16 networked Power PC's; the library has five networked computers. The upper school science lab is equipped with four networked PowerBook computers and one desktop computer. Recent projects include: a multimedia research project on ancient Rome, The International Children's Literature Project, the Glove Science Environment Project, and the Mighty Math M&M Internet Project.

Art is integrated into the curriculum wherever possible and student artwork is prominently displayed throughout the school. Students work in traditional media as well as untraditional art forms like mosaic, architecture, and book-making. For good reason, the Medieval Studies curriculum at Cathedral School is the best in the city. Students tour every inch of the Cathedral and seventh graders celebrate the period's art, music, English and Latin in a Medieval Evensong, held in the Great Choir of the Cathedral of St. John the

Divine. They carry personal coat-of-arms banners and cardboard gargoyles, wear period costumes, recite original sonnets of courtly love, and sing and perform a regal dance that they choreograph themselves.

The interdisciplinary music curriculum emphasizes fun and appreciation. Children learn musical concepts, songs, instruments, movement, and the music of different cultures. The Suzuki method of violin instruction begins in first grade. Approximately 25 fifth through eighth grade boys and girls are choristers. All fourth graders are auditioned for the choir, a very selective process; however, joining the choir is optional. Choristers receive superior musical training, a stipend towards tuition and a wealth of performing experience. Student choristers recently performed at Shea Stadium for the opening game, at Harvard University, and at the memorial services for Jim Henson, creator of the Muppets, and jazz-great Louis Armstrong.

The physical education department uses Cathedral School's two gymnasiums and two outdoor playgrounds, as well as the adjacent playing fields in Morningside Park. Major playground and library renovations are underway. Intramural and varsity sports, both single-sex and coed, include basketball, soccer, softball and volleyball.

Hot lunch (a salad bar and sandwiches are also available) is served family style with mixed age groupings at tables; grace is led by student volunteers, including kindergarteners, and sung by all. Older students take turns as waiters and servers, helping the younger students. On specific days throughout the year lunch features traditional ethnic cuisines like African-American, Caribbean, Chinese, Greek and Jewish.

Every Friday morning lower school assembly is held in the Common Room. One parent said assembly reminds him of why he chose Cathedral School in the first place: "The spirit, the mix of interests, the obvious involvement of the teachers." The assembly room overflows with parents who act as both audience and participants, we were told.

The upper school at Cathedral (grades 5–8) is departmentalized. Each student carries a full program in English, social studies, math, science, French or Spanish and Latin. Latin is required in the seventh and eighth grades in addition to French or Spanish. For the last few years, Cathedral School's top Latin students have won first place in a New York City public and private school competition. In the Cathedral School Newsletter Latin teacher Dr. John Vitale wrote a compelling treatise about the relevance of studying classical Latin today (and not just as a vocabulary booster for the SAT's).

Students visit the cathedral twice each week for services led by the chaplain. While the services concentrate on stories, feasts and values derived from the Judaeo-Christian tradition in the West, students are also exposed to the world's great religious traditions. For example, first graders and their parents built a succah for the Jewish holiday of Succoth and celebrated a multiethnic Passover seder. Students at the school represent a variety of religious traditions, including Buddhist and Muslim, or atheist. "The goal is to affirm the religious tradition of every child." Parents praise the spirituality which infuses learning at Cathedral School. Each fifth grade student works with the Chaplain in an experiential course called "Introduction to Spirituality" which is intentionally non-denominational.

Students say they wish the school had a high school so they could stay on another four years.

High School placement counseling emphasizes self-awareness and a search for a school that would be appropriate for each individual's talents and interests.

Popular Secondary School Choices Friends Seminary, Trinity School, Riverdale Country Day School, Horace Mann School, Stuyvesant High School, LaGuardia High School of Music and Art and the Performing Arts, Fieldston School

Community Service Requirement Students develop projects to support Cathedral outreach and environmental programs care for Cathedral Close or raise funds for outside organizations; Inspired by the twentieth anniversary of Earth Day in 1990, sixth grade students formed an environmental group called L.I.S.T.E.N. (Loving Interest to Save the Environment) which emphasizes recycling

Traditions New parent dinners, all-school picnic on the grounds, class dinners, an annual fundraising auction, theater parties, Arts Festival, Earth Day, Alumni Day, Grandparents Day, Class Reps, Spring Fair, Field Day, Upper School Camp Trip, Chorister Tours, Peace Tree Ceremony, Passover Seder, Kwaanza Assembly, Eighth Grade Musical, Eighth Grade Pinning Ceremony, Eighth Grade Class Day, Chorister Divestiture and graduation

The Chapin School

100 East End Avenue
New York, NY 10028
(212) 744-2335

All girls
Kindergarten–12th grade
Limited accessibility (elevators and stairs)

Ms. Sandra Theunick, Head of School
Miss Martha Hirschman, Director of Admissions

Uniform   Lower school: light green or dark green jumper, white blouse
Middle school: dark green pleated skirt with white shirt, corduroy pants
Upper school: dress Gordon or dark green kilt or skirt, white shirt or blouse, corduroy or khaki pants
Uniforms can be purchased from the Corey Uniform Exchange

Birthday Cutoff   Children entering kindergarten must be 5 by October 1

Enrollment   Total enrollment: 630
Kindergarten places: 48
Graduating class 1998: 35

Grades   Semester system in the lower and middle school
Trimester system in the upper school
Kindergarten–3rd grade: detailed progress reports
Classes 4–12: letter grades and comments
Departmentalization begins in 4th grade
First final exam in 7th grade

Tuition Range   1998-1999 $14,800 to $16,250, kindergarten–12th grade
Additional fees: for books, lunch and school bus, approximately $600 to $1,800 (less for older students who no longer take the school bus)
School bus available for K–6; cost depends on type of service

148

Financial Aid/Scholarship $1,330,000 in tuition aid for 17% of the student body in school year 1997–1998

Endowment $33 million

Diversity   The school welcomes applications from Early Steps, A Better Chance Students and the Albert G. Oliver Program 21 Prep for Prep students enrolled as of Fall 1998

Homework   Class 2: 20–30 minutes
Class 3: 30–40 minutes
Class 4: 20 minutes per subject (average 3 subjects)
Classes 5–8: approximately 2–3 hours spent on an average of 4 subjects, depending on grade level
Classes 9–12: 3 hours

After-School Program   The school oversees the organization of various activities in fine arts, computer science and physical education for middle and upper school students
Middle school intramural program
Green and Gold team competition (girls in classes 4–12 at Chapin are either Green or Gold)
AAIS League interscholastic competition
Elective offerings in both the middle and upper schools

Summer Program   June Jamboree, 2 week summer camp

———

The Chapin School was founded by Maria Bowen Chapin in 1901 as an elementary school called "Miss Chapin's School for Girls." After the death of Miss Chapin, in 1934, it became The Chapin School, Ltd. Throughout the years Chapin has had strong leadership: Miss Ethel Grey Stringfellow, headmistress for twenty-four years, was succeeded in 1959 by Mildred J. Berendsen, who, after leading Chapin into the nineties, retired after thirty-four years in 1993. Ms. Sandra Theunick was named head in July 1993.

In the 1920s and 30s Miss Chapin's School groomed New York's young women to take their place in society. At that time, there were no afternoon classes. Some girls had great academic potential, and some less; classes were designated "general" or "college," depending on the aspirations of the individual.

Chapin in the nineties has an excellent academic reputation and sends its graduates on to the very top colleges throughout the country, but the tone of the school remains decidedly traditional. A parent told us "We wanted a place where our daughter would feel valued and loved. They care about keeping our girls sweet." And she added, "They highlight what she does well."

The departure of Mrs. Berendsen in 1993 was like the retirement of a CEO who has led a company for thirty-four years. Mrs. Berendsen was a gifted fund-raiser and a major building program was completed in 1990. Improvements to the school included an additional gym, new science labs, more classroom space and new dance, art and computer facilities. Additional construction completed in 1998 includes: A two-floor library/multimedia center, a new gymnasium, a drama classroom/black box theatre and a foreign language lab. The greenhouse and outdoor play yard were also renovated and a third kindergarten space was added.

Mrs. Berendsen's successor, Sandra Theunick, hails from a parochial school background and was formerly head of school at the Stuart Country Day School in Princeton, N.J. Parents find Ms. Theunick a mix of the traditional and popular: committed to women's studies, forward thinking, but very academic, not trendy. Parents say, "we are all trusting that she will preserve the character of the school while taking it forward." When asked about the importance of single sex education Mrs. Theunick responded: "It's not yet an even playing field for women . . . We give them [girls] experience and strength; nobody can tell you 'You can't do it' if you've done it before."

Spring 1998 marked the official opening of the new library called The Annenberg Center for Learning and Research. An outdoor play-roof was converted to create this "titanic" space which features port-hole windows and a grand staircase. The library has a multi-media center with capabilities for video-conferencing, private study rooms and in one section—plush purple armchairs! On previous tours The Chapin School felt like a renovated mansion; the effect of the current renovation is like taking down the heavy drapery and letting in the light.

Modernization is underway in other areas of the school as well: In 1998 the upper school at Chapin voted to add Gap khaki pants to the school uniform (from November to February), supplanting the Gordon Plaid kilt. The traditional Friday Morning Prayers have been updated to include recognition of other cultures, while retaining the name "Prayers." The girls now have a part in designing the program

150

on Fridays that might include a reading from the Koran or a song about spring. The Christmas program has been renamed the "Holiday" Program and includes Chanukah songs.

One result of a wide scale strategic planning initiative to re-evaluate Chapin's mission for its graduates was a mandate to create a comprehensive Life Skills program. In addition to a rigorous academic focus, students in Kindergarten through twelfth grade now address such issues as effective communication and leadership, self-awareness, respect for differences, and personal wellness.

Extensive research that included a review of existing data as well as input from students, alumnae, faculty and parents, launched the Life Skills Committee which has begun a successful process of reshaping life at the school. Two outgrowths of this committee are 1) Appointment of a full time coordinator of counseling services and life skills education who oversees the social and emotional growth and health of the school. 2) The introduction of a Peer Leadership program which prepares a select group of twelfth graders to counsel ninth graders.

Getting In: Parents don't have to apply in order to tour Chapin. Once an application is filed, parents make their appointments. Prospective kindergarten parents meet with the lower school head in the Reception Room for a short talk. Each family is given the tour individually by a parent tour guide and interviewed by the director of admissions Martha Hirschman, whom we found to be the warmest and most welcoming part of our Chapin experience. Parents return with their child for a group interview during which Mrs. Theunick and an upper school student answer questions. Every applicant receives a plant from Chapin's greenhouse. After admissions decisions have been made, a wait list is maintained. The wait-list letter informs parents how to notify the admissions office of their continued interest in The Chapin School.

Parent body: The Chapin parent body is very involved and supportive of the school. For example, Chapin does not have an after-school program as such in the lower school, but if a number of girls are taking ballet or ice skating or gymnastics after school, mothers will take turns escorting the girls to these activities sponsored by the Parents' Association. The school, in turn, is supportive of parents: "There is total emphasis on the whole child; kindness and warmth pervade the lower school. They are sensitive to individual needs and are concerned when there is a divorce or sickness in a family," parents say. "They are interested in making life easier for parents." For example, one parent said, "If your child forgets her lunch on the school trip they don't bother you at work or at home, they will provide her with one."

Chapin is also social in the traditional sense. "You would never dress informally for a school event," we were told although we noted that khakis and hair clips have replaced suits and headbands at drop-off and pick-up. Beginning in the '96–'97 school year, annual class cocktail parties were no longer held in parents' homes. The school now hosts a reception for parents in each division with faculty attending. The mixing of parents within each division has been positive and removing any social implications from these parties makes everyone more comfortable.

Parents with a particular skill or interest are invited to share it with the class. In one kindergarten class, for instance, parents were invited to celebrate the Japanese holiday "Girls Day" with rice cookies and tea. Parent involvement is welcomed, as always, with discretion; one parent who wanted to do a classroom photography project using some of the children was told, "No pictures."

Program: The lower school consists of kindergarten through class 3. Separation is handled gradually. By the second week the whole kindergarten group is staying until 2 P.M. Monday through Thursday and until 12:45 on Friday. Parents had praise for the kindergarten teachers' warmth and skill. The days have a predictable structure, which gives the girls a sense of security: They know what to expect. Attention is paid to students' different learning styles. Although traditional in tone, there is a lot of creativity in the classroom. Art projects are used to enhance units of study. For example, a kindergarten group built its own solar system with tinfoil stars and plaster of Paris planets. As one parent said, "These are sophisticated projects; there's no macaroni and glue here." Another commented, "It's very well rounded. Activities are transformed; the doll corner or blocks might be changed into a restaurant or doctor's office for dramatic play." The Scribner Laidlaw Beginning Program (with workbooks) focuses on both expressive and receptive language as well as reading and writing readiness. Each letter sound is reinforced in other activities: art, cooking, literature. Independent decision making is fostered.

Manipulative materials and everyday experiences are used to teach math concepts. Girls go out of their homerooms for music, dance, science and library, as well as physical education including gymnastics.

Classes 1 through 3 stay until 3:00 P.M. each day except Friday when dismissal is at 12:50. The curriculum is a continuum, each year building upon previous experiences. In Class 1 reading, writing, spelling and oral expression are emphasized using both phonetic and sight word instruction. Creative writing begins with the girls keeping journals in which they record their poems and stories. Class 2 and 3 students begin expository writing and research. Work is published, bound and illustrated. Class 3 girls participate in a strong writing program emphasizing creativity and clarity of expression as well as reading with an emphasis on critical inferential thinking and critical analysis.

Where possible social studies is integrated with language and performing arts. Social studies in Class 1 includes a unit on Women in History in which role models who have faced challenges and been successful are studied. One unit presented Betsy Ross. The girls read the story of her life, compared her original flag with today's, and learned a variety of patriotic songs in music class. Second graders studying India visited a Hindu temple, made curry and had lunch at an Indian restaurant. A Rajistani puppet troupe performed at an assembly. Another unit in Class 2 focuses on China, integrating many disciplines. The girls read Chinese folk tales and try their hand at writing in a similar style. They watch Chen dancers in Chinatown with follow-up workshops at school. A visit to The China Institute corresponded with Chinese New Year. A Chinese watercolorist and calligrapher taught her skills to the class. Symmetry was studied in mathematics using Chinese paper cut-outs. Both the Maya culture and the Victorian times are studied in Class 3. The girls construct a Mayan town and sew cross-stitch pillows, write diaries, and visit the Tenement Museum and a Victorian brownstone.

Throughout classes in the lower school, mathematics continues to be taught using an array of manipulatives and concrete objects, and focusing on basic operations and problem solving. The students practice many life skills such as measurement, time-telling and understanding money. Homework begins in class 2. Multiplication, division and fractions are studied in Class 3. Use of the computer lab is an integral component of the curriculum with lessons in a new computer lab as well as the availability of computers in each classroom. The students learn to type, to create a database, to word-process, to program, and to illustrate/animate.

Quaint traditions that persist in the lower school are Teddy Bear Day, Hat Day and Sock Day: You bring your own from home or make one.

Middle school at Chapin includes class 4 through class 7. Again, the English and history/geography curricula are coordinated where possible, and studio art is integrated with other subject areas. Clear and expressive writing is stressed, and writing skills are reinforced. Classes 4 through 7 meet weekly to put out one annual edition of the middle school literary magazine, which is called *The Cog*. Class 7 is introduced to Shakespeare with *A Midsummer Night's Dream*. The study of foreign language begins in class 5 with French or Spanish. Latin is introduced in class 7. Social studies units in middle school cover U.S. geography and Native Americans, a study of ancient and medieval civilizations and American history. In class 7 there is an immigration project in which each student does individual research on a specific country.

Science highlights: Several classes at Chapin work in the greenhouse and class 4 does trimester course work in botany and horticulture. Formal health education begins in class 1 with a unit on nutrition. Class 6 offers an introduction to biology that covers all the systems of the body, including reproductive, and the effects of drugs, alcohol and tobacco on the human body. At the end of class 6 students go on "an intensive three-day field trip, an experience that focuses on environmental science."

Beginning in class 5 girls go to nearby Asphalt Green for outdoor sports once a week. Field hockey, soccer, softball, track and swimming are offered. Afternoon electives in physical education are available for classes 5–7 including fencing and gymnastics. Chapin girls are separated into the Green and Gold teams for intramural competition culminating in an entire day of competition at Bear Mountain in May known as Field Day. Interscholastic competition begins in class 5 with gymnastics, in class 6 with soccer, track and swimming, and broadens in class 7 to include basketball, fencing and volleyball. The number of different sports offered and access to outdoor playing fields increases in the upper school, and Chapin has several strong interscholastic teams.

Extracurricular activities in the middle school include chess club, computer club, intramural and interscholastic sports teams, model rocketry, the literary magazine, readers' club, puppetry, baby care, art, drama, dance, music, debating and science. In addition, self-government begins in the middle school.

The upper school at Chapin consists of classes 8–12. Chapin's upper school remains "a caring, close-knit community" with "a shift in ninth and tenth grades as some girls leave for boarding schools or coed schools." Sixteen academic credits are required for graduation but, according to the brochure, most students complete more than twenty-two. There are sixteen AP's offered, including art history, French literature, calculus I and II and physics. For upper school students the Individual Study option, Interschool courses and the Chapin/Brearley academic exchange and residential term away (abroad, Vermont, or Maine) add breadth as well as depth to Chapin's curriculum.

Multicultural perspectives are explored in the class 8 Asian and African History which covers the cultures of Japan, China, India and Africa and the Americas. For example, English students contrast and compare a Japanese novel to Shakespeare's *Romeo and Juliet*. And during Humanities Week, class 8 explores another culture in depth. In 1998 it was Spain, the Spanish explorers and the Spanish colonies in the Americas. A parent said, "The Spanish influence in South America was studied and girls learned about Renaissance music, Mayan math and architecture, literature, religion, art and dance of Spain. A dance workshop introduced the girls to authentic Spanish flamenco dancing." The week's activities culminated in a fiesta.

Tenth graders are required to take an English course called "Self Discovery: a Thematic Approach to Literature and Writing" in which students read literature from many different cultures. Juniors and seniors can choose from a variety of English electives including "Southern Voices" (Toni Morrison, Josephine Humphreys, *et al.*), "The Urban Scene" and "The Lost Eden." History electives include "Women in China," "What We Believe," a comparitive religion course, and "European History."

The upper school curriculum includes a class 9 unit entitled "Urban Study." Class 10 attends an Interschool conference on environmental issues. Class 11 travels to Washington, D.C., where they visit the Holocaust Museum in addition to the usual sites, and class 12 explores the New York City art world.

Physics, chemistry and biology are offered in the upper school, with AP courses available for juniors and seniors. Students in the upper school take algebra, geometry and trigonometry with calculus A and B offered to juniors and seniors.

In the upper school, Chapin students continue active participation in studio art, dance, drama and music with opportunity for advanced work along with a wide variety of electives. For serious artists there is a portfolio course in preparation for the AP Studio Art Program, and there are courses in photography as well. For drama students there is an Acting and Directing Lab for classes 10–12, and a course called "Visions and Revisions," a theatre studies course that compares texts such as Sophocles' *Antigone* and Anouilh's *Antigone*. The Drama Club involves all areas of theatre production. There is a Forensics Club for students interested in developing their public speaking and debating skills. A Choral Club performs at holiday time as well as throughout the year. Dance Club members choregraph and perform their works in an annual performance. Club Night is a unique tradition in the upper school. The Halloween Club gives a party for the lower school girls; Dance and Drama Clubs put on student performances at night; and Holiday Club in December provides an evening for students, faculty and parents to join in singing together.

Upper school girls can participate in the student Self-Government (established in 1909), Science Club, S.A.V.E., an environmental organization, Amnesty International, Volunteer Community Activities, the Cultural Awareness Project, Model U.N. AIDS awareness, French, Latin, Spanish/Latin American Club, Literary Magazine, and Yearbook.

One parent says, "The curriculum is geared for the above-average girl." A former teacher says that "honor, achievement and academic rigor are valued at Chapin and that adds up to competition." But nobody describes Chapin as a "pressure cooker." "Chapin never gives up on a child," one former teacher said. "People seem to hop out of the woodwork to help each other, there's lots of cooperation and teamwork." Individual attention and concern for the development of the individual are hallmarks of a Chapin education. One parent described Chapin as "the most well-rounded girls' school." Another parent said that although "nastiness is discouraged, cliques form early." One parent described a common scenario (seen in one form or another at all schools): "Cliques form between third and seventh grades. Seventh-and eighth-grade cliques form around physical development and looks and competition for clubs and boys." The *Limelight* (school newspaper) has a regular feature on fashion, spring and fall. The parent of an alumna said that the girls "individualize their uniforms and can frequently be heard chatting away about the latest party." The net result of all this sociability is a boon for the school. Chapin's alumnae remain connected to the school long after they have left. The alumnae bulletin is bulging with notes and snapshots as if this were the largest extended family on the East Coast, and perhaps it is. It's no wonder that Chapin has had great success in fund-raising.

Chapin is working had to overcome the White Glove image. (The school used to emphasize "good form" in everything from dress to term papers an alumna recalls.) Today, the rigor of the curriculum and the variety of cultural perspectives cater to the interests of a more diverse student body. One parent said, "People don't know what a jewel Chapin is except for the Chapin parent."

Ann Klotz now works along with Ms. Louise Henderson who has been the college advisor at Chapin for over twenty-four years. During this time Ms. Henderson has cultivated excellent relationships with the Ivy League schools, which translates into a high proportion of acceptance to the top Ivys for qualified Chapin girls.

The day before commencement for the middle and upper schools there is a final assembly at which awards are given for achievement in athletics, fine arts and academics. Chapin commencement is held at the school. The girls graduate as a class with no special recognition for any individual student.

Popular College Choices Barnard, Brown, Dartmouth, Duke, Harvard-Radcliffe, Middlebury, Princeton, Stanford, University of Pennsylvania, Yale

Traditions Fall Book Fair, Club Nights, Grandparents' Day, lower school Halloween party, Holiday Program, Field Day, Chapin (Movie) Palace (Saturday movies with popcorn, cookies and juice during the winter months only), Chapin Spring Benefit (Family Night at Tavern on the Green or The Puck Building, etc.)

Publications Upper school literary magazine: *The Wheel* (since 1917)
Middle school literary magazine: *The Cog*
Newspaper: *Limelight*
Computer news publication: *The Chapin Chip*
Yearbook
Alumnae Bulletin

Community Service Requirement Community service is encouraged but there is no specific requirement

Hangouts The purple chairs in The Annenberg Center for Learning and Research, student lounge, Agnes B. clothing store, The Mansion (coffee shop on 84th Street and Second Avenue)

The Children's Storefront

P.O. Box 1313
70 East 129th Street
New York, NY 10035
(212) 427-7900

Coed
Nursery 2's–8th grade
Accessible only at 70 East 129th Street

Birthday Cutoff   None

Enrollment   Total enrollment: approximately 153
Preschool places: approximately 5
Graduating class size: approximately 15

Tuition Range   Tuition free

Financial Aid   100% of the student body

Endowment $2.7 million

After-School Program   After-school programs in conjunction with the Manhattan School of Music; 3:00 P.M. to 5:00 P.M.; free of charge

Summer Program   July preschool drop-off from 8:00 A.M. until noon
Six-week (beginning of July til mid-August) summer camp in Lyme, Connecticut

———

Ned O'Gorman came to Harlem in 1966 and opened a "grass-roots school" in a storefront on Madison Avenue. The school subsequently moved into four converted brownstones. The Children's Storefront is one of a few private schools that are tuition free. The Storefront receives the bulk of its funding from foundations, corporations and individuals. The Children's Storefront's annual fundraiser attracts many of New York's "A-list" partygoers. The school is accredited by The New York State Association of Independent Schools. O'Gorman describes The Children's Storefront as "a school to heal and educate and liberate the children who come to us." There is a broad range of ability within the student body. O'Gorman says, "We have children with learning disabilities, gifted children and average children, like me." As of June 1999, O'Gorman retired and a search is underway to replace him. O'Gorman will serve as a consultant to the school. Until a new Head of School is hired, Children's Storefront will be administered by a three-member committee of staff. Average class size is fifteen, providing students with the attention they need to succeed. There is a waiting list of approximately five hundred students.

City & Country School

146 West 13th Street
New York, NY 10011
(212) 242-7802, FAX (212) 242-7996
website: projects.ilt.columbia.edu/schools/C&C/

Coed
Nursery–8th grade (ages 2–13)
Not accessible

Ms. Kathleen Holz, Principal
Ms. Lisa Horner, Director of Admissions

Birthday Cutoff   November 1

Enrollment   Total enrollment: 258
Nursery 2's places: 19
Nursery 3's places: 12
Nursery 4's places: 6
Kindergarten (5's) places: 8–10
Graduating class 1997: 12

Grades   No grades; detailed narrative reports, and effort checklists starting in second grade

Tuition Range   1998–1999 $7,750 to $13,950, nursery–8th grade
Additional fees: $200 enrollment fee. II's and III's pay $250 building fee; IV's to XIII's have a $500 building fee.

Financial Aid/Scholarship   20% of the student body receive partial financial aid

Endowment   None

After-School Program   Open only to City & Country students; a variety of creative and recreational activities and sports programs from 3:00 P.M. until 5:45 P.M.
Extra charge for 3–7 year olds; no extra charge for 8–13 year olds
Specialty classes for all groups, including: chess, dance, music, art, cooking; additional fee required

Summer Program   June group: two-week camp for 7–13 year olds;

160

week-long courses in video, journalism, bookmaking and dance; museum trips

Summer day camp at The City & Country School: for ages 2–7; from mid-June until the end of July

These programs require an additional payment

———

City & Country School, founded in 1914, is one of the oldest progressive elementary schools in the United States. Located on a historic block in Greenwich Village, the school occupies three adjoining brownstones. Parents may tour the school and attend the open house before submitting an application. The ERB is not required for admissions but a screening is done of each applicant for kindergarten and of older applicants. Younger children come for a group visit (about an hour) and are observed at work and play in a classroom by teachers and the director of admissions. In addition, applicants are often observed in their nursery schools. Older applicants spend a day with a group of their peers and are observed by the group teacher and special teachers. A general skills assessment is administered during the visit.

The parent body runs the gamut from "corporate lawyers, bankers and doctors to writers and illustrators." What they have in common is that they want their children in "a quintessential progressive school."

Visionary educator and founder Caroline Pratt believed children learn best through practical and meaningful experiences. The process of education and the tools of learning are important here. The kindergarten usually consists of two groups of sixteen to twenty students each. From the earliest years, students work with open-ended materials: blocks, water, paint, clay, woodworking. V's through VII's plan their work as groups, which they sustain for a week or longer, creating cities with building blocks, wooden people, handmade signs, fabric and plasticine items and even electricity and running water. Frequent trips to observe the community at work are an important part of the program. In the outdoor yards, students create their own play environment each day with large boxes, blocks, boards, ladders and sawhorses. Older groups use the yard for running and ball games and team sports. Students bring their own lunch, and milk is provided as is midmorning juice and snack.

Reading and writing begin with frequent exposure to literature, experience charts, language arts games and activities, and early story-writing. Spanish is taught to all students beginning with the three-year-olds. Beginning with VII's all students have half an hour of independent reading in the library every day.

As a practical application of their academic skills and to develop self-esteem and responsibility, older children participate in the Jobs Program—running the school post office or store, operating printing presses, working with younger children writing and publishing the school newspaper. Group and individual research using primary and secondary sources, literature, and trips rather than textbooks to study a civilization, time period, or major issue forms the core of the middle and upper school curriculum. This curriculum is integrated with the Special Subjects and Jobs Program for the eights through thirteens; for instance, a study of "living documents" of the Revolutionary period in American history is coordinated with the older children's job of running the school newspaper. The annual IX's week-long country trip to Connecticut is a highlight. After completing a unit on the Oregon Trail, the students reenact everything they have learned. For example, they maneuver a covered wagon through the countryside, construct trailside rock-heated "ovens" and cook and eat real buffalo meat. Parents say the trip "really bonds the group; they come back changed."

All students participate in Rhythms (the music and movement program), and older children use the fully equipped woodshop, the art room, the science lab and the technology center. The music program includes a singing and instruction in recorder and stringed instruments. Chorus and orchestra are required in the upper grades.

Parents whose children have been in the school for several years note several changes which indicate that City & Country is not the bastion of progressive education it once was: "Traditionally each class has a job in the school (takes part in running the school mail system, prints the school calendar, and so on) but because the school has nearly doubled in size in the last 8 years there is less opportunity for children to actually take part in running the school."

Popular Secondary School Choices Stuyvesant High School, Fiorello LaGuardia High School of Music and Art, United Nations International School, The Trevor Day School, Brooklyn Friends, The Fieldston School, Friends Seminary, Packer Collegiate

Collegiate School

370 West End Avenue
New York, NY 10024
Tel (212) 721-2300 Admissions x552
FAX **(212) 877-8928**

All boys
K–12th grade
Accessible

Mr. Jacob A. Dresden, Headmaster
Mrs. Joanne P. Heyman, Director of Admissions and Financial Aid

Uniform   Lower school: no dress code for Kindergarten–grade 2, just "clean and neat"; by grade 3, long pants and a shirt with a collar
Middle school: grades 5–12, jacket (blazer) and tie, turtleneck allowed, shoes or sneakers, hair can be worn short or long

Birthday Cutoff   It is recommended that boys be 5 by the start of Kindergarten

Enrollment   Total enrollment: 590
Kindergarten places: approximately 40
7th grade places: approximately 8–12
9th grade places: approximately 6–10
Graduating class size: approximately 50

Grades   Trimester system
Grades Kindergarten–4: detailed anecdotal reports and conferences
Letter grades begin in 6th grade
Departmentalization begins in 5th grade
First final exam is given in 7th grade

Tuition Range 1998–1999 $16,570 to $17,900, Kindergarten–12th grade
Tuition at Collegiate includes lunch, books, fees and most additional costs, but no overnight trips, athletic equipment or special functions
There is an alternative payment plan through Academic Management Services

Financial Aid/Scholarship   Approximately 20% of the student body receive financial assistance

Endowment   Approximately $36 million

Diversity   Approximately 20% children of color
28 Prep for Prep students enrolled as of fall 1998
Collegiate was awarded a DeWitt Wallace-Reader's Digest Fund Independent School Opportunity Program Grant in 1989 and 1993
Collegiate has a Diversity Office with two faculty members
JAMAA: an organization for student families and alumni and faculty of color founded in the 1960s
Collegiate Teaching Institute for prospective teachers of color

Homework   Classes I and II: $1/2$ hour reading every night
Classes III and IV: 45 minutes plus reading, but not on weekends
Classes V and VI: approximately 2 hours
Classes VII and VIII: approximately $2^{1}/_2$ hours
Classes IX–XII: 2–3 hours

After-School Program   In-house after-school activities program available for Kindergarten–4. Collegiate boys participate in various sports clubs, chess, hockey and tennis programs; Athletic teams practice after school

Summer Program   Two-week June basketball clinic for lower and middle school boys
For older boys there are summer exchange programs in Europe and Latin America

---

Collegiate is the oldest independent school in the United States. It marked its 370th year in 1998. The school maintains a continuing relationship with the Dutch Reformed Church. Collegiate's strength is an emphasis on classical education combined with modern innovations. Collegiate is a well-rounded, academically rigorous school with a superior college placement record.

Headmaster Jacob A. Dresden came to Collegiate in 1991 from the William Penn Charter School in Philadelphia, the third oldest independent school in America. An alumnus told us that he is well-

164

liked by students and faculty: "Dresden is a good advisor, personable and knows the students' names." A parent told us that Dresden is a cheerful and determined person who tries to alleviate school and academic pressures.

Collegiate has had a long-standing relationship with the West End Collegiate Church. In 1940 the church and school separated but they still share some facilities. The Minister of the Church serves on the faculty of the school. The "Moving Up" ceremonies for the lower and middle school are held at the West End Collegiate Church, as is graduation. There is a school chaplain who is also an upper school advisor. The Holiday program, held in the church, includes various religious traditions. Seventh grade students study world religions. In the upper school, students must choose two three-credit religion courses.

All Collegiate students benefit from a recently completed series of renovation and building projects. In 1990, the school added a fabulous new gym and weight room, two new art rooms and a music room. In September 1997, Collegiate opened a kindergarten in the West End Plaza building of the school. Two spacious classrooms with an adjoining playroom provide room for academic centers, computers, creative movement, music, blocks and art projects. In the same year, the new science laboratories were installed for lower and middle school students. In 1998, a roof-top play area for kindergarten and lower school boys opened on top of the school's new six-story structure. The school's dining facilities were expanded, a two-story middle school center was completed and state-of-the-art biology, chemistry and physics laboratories were built for upper school students.

Getting In: The application fee is $40. Parents are encouraged to tour when their sons are eligible for kindergarten. Once parents have applied, they bring their son to the school. Kindergarten applicants visit in small groups with members of the faculty. Middle and upper school applicants have interviews and student guided tours of the school. Parents of applicants are interviewed on an individual family basis. There is a policy favoring siblings and legacies but admission is not automatic. Is there a typical Collegiate Boy? An alumni said, "He is self-confident, slightly preppie, a social, smart kid."

Parents: The parent body at Collegiate runs the gamut: Academics, artists, writers, professionals, musicians, and some Wall Street types mingle comfortably in what most say is an intellectual atmosphere. About half come from the East side and half from the West side. "It is a fun loving group, easy to connect with," said one parent.

Another told us, "The parent body at Collegiate is tremendously diverse and not stuffy; cocktail parties might be held in an apartment in the Village with people eating cross-legged on a futon or in a Park or Fifth Avenue apartment." Jewish parents have long been comfortable at Collegiate. There are many Jewish legacies attending Collegiate and school is closed on the major Jewish holidays. Parents Association meetings are scheduled on the school calendar and all parents are invited to attend.

Program: Academically, the early years at Collegiate are "challenging, yet comfortable." Learning is developmental and low-key. A former lower school teacher said the style of the school "is not extreme, not too traditional or informal, but they've borrowed what's best and held onto the things that have worked." Throughout the kindergarten and lower school there is the understanding that boys develop at different rates. Table groupings in classrooms are informal; no rows. The heterogeneous classrooms (approximately 20 boys in each with one teacher and a full-time assistant) often break into small groups for activities. There is an eclectic approach to reading instruction: some boys come in reading and some don't, it's not an admissions requirement. There is recognition of different learning styles.

There is no uniform in grades kindergarten through third "in recognition that little boys really need to move", said our tour guide. There is gym every day and recess either on the rooftop playground or in nearby Riverside Park.

First grade homework is approached with the attitude that parents are partners and a monthly sheet is sent home by the librarian for parents to fill in the books that they've read together with their sons. Parents are encouraged to come in to the classroom to share their skills and talents, or to simply read to the boys during library time.

Lower school boys leave their homerooms to go to specialists in art, music, physical education and science. Kindergarten boys have science in their classroom while all lower school students go to a specially designed new lower school science lab. In second grade there is a teacher and a shared assistant for each class. The boys are divided into skill level groups for math. Each boy has his own "Math Toolbox," containing ruler, eraser, and so on, for a hands-on approach to math. All kindergarten, first and second graders have access to computers in the classrooms. By third grade, the boys go to the new lower school technology lab. The full-time lower school technology coordinator works closely with teachers to support computer-related activities. In the lower school, boys learn keyboarding, basic computer skills and begin to use computers as tools to create documents and multimedia presentations.

In the early grades reading and math are "geared to the individual." The Fisher Landau Program (an in-house remedial program) is used to assess the boys and give support and enrichment.

In memory of the founders, third graders celebrate Dutch Day. They make spice bags and paint Delft tiles. In social studies, third graders learn about the Dutch settlers of New Amsterdam and Native Americans. Students are encouraged to bring in articles from *The New York Times* and discuss them. One year, third graders doing a unit on Japan studied haiku, learned calligraphy and made kimonos in art, read Japanese fables, and went to a tea ceremony. They clipped articles about modern Japan and read them aloud to the class.

The music program at Collegiate is very strong; renowned pianist Emanuel Ax is a former trustee and parent. Lower school boys have music twice a week. In fourth grade recorder is introduced; in fifth and sixth grades students study a stringed instrument; in seventh grade guitar is required. Each year students are given an instrument for use at school or practice at home. On our tour we saw eight boys playing their violins in a practice room. Private and semi-private instruction is available and music theory is taught. Third and fourth graders have a string ensemble and chorus. One year, the fifth and sixth grade chorus sang at Carnegie Hall as part of the Canterbury Choral Society's Fortieth Anniversary Celebration. Eighth graders are introduced to music technology and composition. The boys explore music and creativity through the use of computers and synthesizers.

In fourth grade the work load is stepped up and letter grades begin in the second half of sixth grade. Parents stressed, however, that "Nobody is pressured at Collegiate, the boys are encouraged to do their best."

The middle school at Collegiate consists of grades five through eight. According to parents, middle school demands a greater amount of independence. In fifth grade, departmentalization has begun. Fifth graders get lockers; desks are still organized in groups, not rows. There are regular forty-five minute periods. The middle school technology lab is easily accessible and often used. Technology skills are put to use as boys write papers, examine data and learn to use digital information sources for research. Students use computer-generated graphic materials in oral presentations in many of their classes. Fifth graders select either French or Spanish which they take until eighth grade when they can also begin Latin. An additional three years of foreign language is required for graduation (seven years in all).

Beginning in fifth grade, students are given long term assignments. Students learn to plan their weeks and organize their time. At Collegiate, students really know how to think. "My fifth grader was asked to write a paper about one of Robert Louis Stevenson's books from the point of view of a minor character," a parent told us. Another fifth grade assignment was to write a piece of historical fiction. One student wrote a piece on a Vietnamese teenager and the assignment was graded by both the history and English teachers.

Fifth and sixth graders take regular tests during the school year. At the end of seventh and eighth grades there is a formal exam period.

The social studies curriculum begins in the lower school with the study of families and communities, and expands in the upper grades to include the wider world. Fifth graders study ancient civilizations and read Greek myths and English folktales. Seventh graders study the Middle Ages, the exploration of the New World and the Cultures of the Americas. Eighth graders study World History (Asia, Africa, Islam and Europe) and write research papers.

There is a non-academic elective and activities program for middle schoolers "to broaden and enrich the boys' experience." Course offerings include: community service projects, computer, photography, drama, architecture, student government, middle school newspaper, literary magazine, and excursions away from school to take advantage of the urban setting.

Experience in public speaking is gained through weekly assemblies, morning meetings and many opportunities to perform in dramatic and musical productions. Recently, fifth graders put on a version of *Les Miserables*. One trimester of drama is required in seventh and eighth grades. Arts for grades seven and eight includes the opportunity for the boys to play in a chamber music group, study photography and produce two dramatic pieces during the year.

Middle school boys can participate in coed afternoon activities with Brearley girls. Seventh and eighth graders can take woodworking, sports, and a variety of other classes which are conducted at Collegiate or Brearley on a regular basis.

Summer reading is required for grades five through ten. Most boys purchase their books at the Paperback Book Fair held in the Spring. They also gather books at the Annual Book Festival organized by the Parents Association in the fall. Guest authors often include Collegiate parents. Sixth graders produce their own anthology of original literature. Each middle school grade takes a three-day trip to locations of interest. Past destinations have included a trip to Mystic, Connecticut with a stay overnight on a boat. Sixth graders visit a nearby city (Philadelphia, Boston), and seventh graders begin the school year with a three day trip to Frost Valley. The eighth graders end their year with a trip to the Princeton-Blairstown Center.

Prep for Prep students enter in either seventh or ninth grades. There are several programs for prospective students of color in the fall to introduce them to Collegiate and to encourage them to apply.

Interscholastic sports begin in seventh grade; participation is stressed over competition. After spring break, eighth graders can sign out for lunch and join their older peers at "Big Nick's Pizza." After school the courtyard handball court is the social gathering spot.

Upper school at Collegiate consists of grades nine through twelve. The upper school curriculum, according to a trustee and former P.A. president, is both "traditional and innovative." The school is not rigid in its approach to education, though the backbone of the curriculum is classical. There is an academic core program with electives offered in eleventh and twelfth grades. Some readings focus on the classics: Shakespeare, Dante's *Inferno*, *The Iliad* and *The Odyssey*, and the *Death of Socrates*. Other perspectives are explored in courses such as: Japanese Literature, African and Caribbean Writers, and Women in Literature. In history, American Urban Political History, Twentieth Century China, Russian Civilization, History of Psychological Thought, and History of South Africa are offered in addition to the normal selection of required courses. In math and science, AB and BC Calculus, Statistical Modeling, Geology and Astronomy are among the courses offered.

Parents say there is an emphasis in all grades on good writing and research skills. A former P.A. President told us that Verbal SAT scores are consistently high because of the emphasis on language arts and the academic core program. There is no summer reading list for grades nine through twelve. Summer reading is encouraged for pleasure at all grade levels.

The Technology Department offers an expanding program in computer and technology education and there are numerous opportunities for students to use computers in conjunction with course work in all disciplines. An academic local area network connects computers in the computer labs, the library, the science department and in selected classrooms. Access to the network allows students to "plug-in" to the many resources available through the system, including the Internet, the library catalog and reference materials on CD-ROM.

In addition to the yearly course offerings, Collegiate students can design an Independent Study course in an area of interest, taken in addition to the minimum course load of twenty classes per week. A senior project in an area of the student's choice (usually some form of internship) can be undertaken in the last trimester of the senior year if all other requirements are completed.

"The faculty at Collegiate is extraordinary," says an alumnus. A parent said, "They are a very senior faculty. Teachers average ten to twelve years of experience and three-quarters have advanced degrees." There is an assistant teaching program in the lower school in which less experienced teachers work with a mentor, eventually becoming head teachers. A big incentive to keep faculty is housing provided in a building connected to the school. A former P.A. President said, "Collegiate has one of the lowest tuitions yet offers the highest remuneration for independent school teachers which is why it keeps and attract good teachers." The faculty is part of the larger Collegiate community: there is a parent/faculty chorus which performs yearly at a "Celebration of Music" event.

Student government at Collegiate consists of three representatives from each grade. The middle school student government meets regularly and plans student programs and special events. Upper school student government has tackled furnishing the student center, finding summer jobs for students and relaxing the dress code.

Theater continues to be a strength in the upper school at Collegiate. Upper school students put on two to three plays per trimester, both in the school's two hundred and sixty-seven seat theater auditorium and in the recently enlarged "black box" theater.

Clubs at Collegiate are popular. The Model U.N. Club and JAMAA, an organization for students, families, alumni and faculty of color are among the more active ones.

There is a community service requirement at Collegiate of one hundred credit hours, twenty of which must be done outside of school. Programs include: tutoring at IS 44 at 77th Street, working at the St. Bart's or West End Avenue Collegiate Church soup kitchens, or at the West End Intergenerational Residence and Soup Kitchen. Many Collegiate boys give academic as well as peer support to the homeless children at the West End Avenue Intergenerational Residence. There are numerous food drives throughout the year and the proceeds are donated to the Residence. In-house tutoring performed at Collegiate is one way to fulfill the other half of the requirement. In 1998, the students also sponsored a blood drive.

As far as contact between grades, one alumnus said, "There's sports and chorus. It's too small a school for hazing." "Of course, you can only get a Collegiate varsity jacket if you play on a varsity team," an alum mentioned. The Dutchmen's colors are orange and blue, the same as the the Knicks and the Mets. Collegiate's biggest rivals are Trinity, Poly Prep, Riverdale and Fieldston. The Traditional Friday night basketball games are popular. Collegiate also has a championship cross-country team that runs in Riverside Park as well as championship teams in soccer, basketball, track and wrestling.

A recent alumnus told us that more important than the traditions themselves is the sense of success you get at Collegiate: "When you've been there a long time, you begin to think 'I can do anything.' If anything, Collegiate boys spread themselves too thin." Another alumnus said, "Athletes are also actors or musicians too, depending on the trimester."

The school stresses values, particularly integrity. "They are sticklers for honor and principle; competition is stressed in a healthy way. But it's tough and demanding," according to an alumnus. Collegiate is structured but students may choose from a growing number of electives from ninth grade on.

Collegiate enjoys great success at college placement due in large part to Mr. Bruce Breimer, Class of 1963, Director of College Guidance, who also teaches tenth and eleventh grade history and is known in independent school circles as one of the most powerful figures in college admissions. Since the graduating class usually numbers about fifty, it not difficult for him to know each boy. Parents and alumni say Briemer is a strength of the school, as he has over twenty years experience. "It's a highly personalized process. He helps each senior take control of his own college search in an independent fashion and he encourages each boy to go beyond the obvious in the quest for the most felicitous match." A 1991 graduate told us, "He makes or breaks your career; he's the guy you want on your side."

There are no academic prizes at Collegiate. Juniors and seniors with outstanding grades are inducted into the Cum Laude Society (the secondary school equivalent of Phi Beta Kappa). The Collegiate faculty and graduating class vote for the Head Boy each year, a senior who shows a combination of leadership, sportsmanship and citizenship.

There is a genuine school spirit at Collegiate demonstrated at

171

class dinners, the holiday assembly and at Moving Up Day. One parent said, "They all sing the school song and you cry no matter how many times you've seen it." A traditional graduation ceremony is held in the West End Collegiate Church. Cap and gown are worn and the alma mater is sung.

Popular College Choices   Yale, Harvard, Brown, Dartmouth, Princeton, University of Pennsylvania, Columbia, Wesleyan, Williams

Traditions   Lower School Book Day, Halloween parade, Parents Association Book Festival, Paperback Book Fair, 2nd grade trip to Manhattan Country School Farm, 3rd grade trip to Frost Valley, 6th grade trip to Philadelphia or Boston, 7th grade trip to Frost Valley, 10th grade Interschool trip to Frost Valley, Lower and Middle School Field Day, Middle School Fair, 5th and 6th grade music evenings, Grandparents Day, Moving Up Days for lower and middle schools, Athletic Banquet, graduation at Collegiate Church, alumni dinner

Publications   Newspaper: *The Collegiate Journal* (monthly)
Yearbook: *The Dutchman*
French publication: *Charabia*
Spanish publication: *La Herencia*
Literary magazine: *Prufrock*
Science and Technology publication: *Technically Speaking*
Opinion publication: *Issues*
Lower school: *Journal*
Middle school literary magazine: *Jabberwock*
Collegiate publication: *News From Collegiate, The Collegiate Review*
Alumni publication: *The Red Door*
Parents Association: *Newsletter*

Community Service Requirement   Grades 9–12: 100 credits by graduation (40 minutes–1 hour = 1 credit)

Hangouts   Collegiate cafeteria (the menu is in French, Spanish and English), the courtyard, library and technology labs

Columbia Grammar and Preparatory School

5 West 93rd Street
New York, NY 10025
(212) 749-6200

Coed
Pre-kindergarten–12th grade
Grades 7–12 accessible

Dr. Richard J. Soghoian, Headmaster
Ms. Simone Hristidis, Director of Grammar School Admissions
(Pre-K–12)

Uniform   No torn jeans, sweatpants, T-shirts with inappropriate messages, tank tops, cutoffs, boxers, gym shorts or bicycle pants

Birthday Cutoff   September 1

Enrollment   Total enrollment: 687
Pre-kindergarten places: 20
Kindergarten places: 60
7th grade places: 20
9th grade places: approximately 20–30
Graduating class size: approximately 60

Grades   Semester system
Letter grades begin in 7th grade
Departmentalization begins in 5th grade
First final exam is given at the end of 7th grade

Tuition Range 1998–1999 $15,000 to $18,850, pre-kindergarten–12th grade
There are no additional fees
A revolving loan policy requires that each family make an interest-free loan ($1,500 for grades K–9, $1,000 for grades 10–12) to the school for each child enrolled
A Tuition Refund Plan and a Student Accident Reimbursement Plan are available

Financial Aid/Scholarship   In 1997–1998, 18.2% of the students received aid totaling $970,690

173

Endowment $1,000,000

Diversity   14.3% students of color K–6,
17.3% students of color grades 7–12
55 families of color out of 120 received $665,975 (69%) of the year's total aid in '97–'98
MECA, Multi-Ethnic Cultural Awareness Club
12 Prep for Prep students enrolled as of Fall 1998
Focus, Families of Color United in Support

Homework   Kindergarten: none
1st: 20 minutes
2nd: 30–45 minutes
3rd, 4th: approximately 1 hour
5th–8th: $1\frac{1}{2}$–$2\frac{1}{2}$ hours
9th–12th: approximately 3 hours

After-School Program   CGPS After School Program for grades K–4 offers a variety of creative and recreational activities until 4:30 P.M., Monday–Friday
Sunrise Club 7:45 A.M.–8:30 A.M.
Math Club for grades 1–4
Chess Club for grades K–6
Rollerblading for grades 2–6
Intramural and Interscholastic sports grades 5–12

Summer Program   CGS Summer Camp: for Pre-kindergarten–6 from the end of school until the end of July, staffed by CGS teachers, an additional payment is required

———

Columbia Grammar School was founded in 1764 and functioned as a feeder school for King's College (later, Columbia University). Now CGPS graduates go on to a much wider range of universities and colleges. CGPS became a nonprofit school in 1941 and merged with a nearby girls' school. Since 1981 CGPS has been guided by Richard J. Soghoian, who holds a Ph.D. in philosophy from Columbia University and is also an International Fellow at the School for International Affairs. His expertise is manifested in the innovative social studies, history and geography programs throughout CGPS. Dr. Soghoian recently guided the school through two major construction projects: a

$6.5-million high school building completed in 1986 and a new $8.5 million building for grades 7–9 completed in 1996 which has five art studios, three science labs, a theatre and a new cafeteria. Columbia Grammar offers a well-rounded but structured program for able students. Columbia Grammar & Prep was restructured beginning in the 1996–97 school year to take advantage of the new space. The Grammar School is now composed of Pre-kindergarten through sixth grade (the first Pre-kindergarten class of eighteen children was admitted in 1996–97.) The Prep School consists of seventh through twelfth grades.

The director of the lower school, Stanley Seidman, was formerly head of Dalton's lower school. Parents say Seidman is well liked, knows all the children's names and is very accessible. Parents say they feel free to call the teachers at any time, and their calls will be taken even during classroom hours using the school's new voice mail system.

Getting in: The application is very straightforward. There are one or two essay questions. The ERB/ISEE is required. Please note that all applications for kindergarten and first grade must be filed by December 1. CGPS holds Friday afternoon teas for prospective applicants to pre-kindergarten and kindergarten. After a short slide presentation, Dr. Soghoian as well as other representatives from the school are available to answer questions, followed by a brief tour of the lower school (the grammar school). Parents may return for an optional tour of the new building and the upper school. These events are not part of the admissions process but a service to parents who want information about the school before making application for their child. Once an application has been filed, parents are taken on a more extensive tour of the school while their child is being interviewed (a small group interview of four children at a time, which lasts about one hour during which the child is observed by the lower school head as well as admissions personnel). After the tour, parents meet with Mr. Seidman over coffee. Parents say that the admissions process at CGPS is low-key and comfortable. "They are really interested in the child, not scrutinizing the parents," we heard. CGPS has an active wait list. What are they looking for? Hristidis told us "a bright child who can handle an enriched curriculum, eager to learn; nice, well adjusted children; we're not looking for a type, a range of children would do well here but they must be academically inclined."

Prospective applicants to the Preparatory School attend one of several evening meetings in which the program is described followed by a tour. Applications are considered on a rolling basis and there is no deadline though interested families are encouraged to begin the process as early as possible.

The typical CGPS student? "This is not a jock school," said one parent. "The typical student usually has some artistic bent." "The *atypical* student," one parent said, "is pushy, snotty or overly competitive."

Parents: The parent body at CGPS consists of many professionals. There is an equal division between West Siders and East Siders. Social competition is negligible. According to one mother, the parent body is "unpretentious, no limos or jewels, and if they have it, they leave it at home." "CGPS has a lot of generally liberal parents who might otherwise have sent their children to public school," said another. There are a number of Parents' Association events such as the Skating Party, Theatre Party and Spring Benefit (held at Denim & Diamonds in 1996). They are fun, low-key events. At the annual holiday concert "First Noel" as well as "O Chanukah" are sung. "What you see is what you get," says one parent with two children at CGPS. "There are absolutely no surprises."

Program: The pre-kindergarten and kindergarten year begins with a fall picnic in Central Park, held before the beginning of school. The school provides a very informative handbook for each division (lower and upper). Parents say CGPS is supportive about separation when school actually begins.

All students have a well-rounded schedule, which includes a strong swimming program (required for grades kindergarten through fourth grade and optional for fifth grade.) Kindergarteners swim twice a week for forty minutes, once a week in the middle grades) plus art, music and academics. CGPS swimming parties are a popular, inexpensive birthday party option; ice-skating and rollerblading parties are also in.

Presently, the grammar school (composed of pre-kindergarten through sixth grades) is housed in five interconnected brownstones on West 94rd Street connected to the original school building on West 93rd Street (now housing grades five and six). Children and adults develop strong legs because of the many stairways in the school. The classroom space is long, with windows at either end, but well laid out and bright. There is a courtyard play area for recess. Parents say that the kindergarten teachers are warm, and make learning fun, although by third grade they get more serious. "The children respect the teachers," a parent commented.

Throughout the grammar school learning is viewed as a progression, especially in math and reading. The brochure says: "Each grade's work builds on the work of previous years." Individual rates of learning in math and reading are accommodated. Wherever possible, art is coordinated with work in other subjects in the grammar school. Pre-kindergarten and Kindergarten have two teachers and one assistant. For first through third grades there are two teachers for approximately twenty to twenty-two children. Although it is considered a "structured school," the teaching at CGPS is flexible, "using a variety of approaches and techniques." Parents praise the well-paced reading program. In kindergarten reading readiness is the focus; in first grade "a phonics sequence is the basic method used for the teaching of reading." Whole Language literature based books are used. Math instruction in kinder-garten stresses experiential learning through the use of manipulatives and games. There are at least three computers in all of the classrooms and LOGO and word processing are taught in the grammar school. Fourth graders go out to the computer lab.

The extensive music program begins with the Kodaly and Orff methods, which are used for ear training. Second graders learn to play the recorder. Instrumental instruction begins in fourth grade and stu-dents are given an instrument to take home. Opportunities to perform include the third- and fourth-grade choir, a recorder ensemble for second and third graders, a string ensemble and a chamber music ensemble for more advanced students. In fifth grade students pick one instrument for further study.

The social studies curriculum for pre-kindergarten through fourth begins with families and community and broadens to include a study of ethnicity and immigration in second grade (including a trip to Ellis Island with students dressed as their immigrant forebears). Native Americans are the subject in third grade, explorers and Colonial America in fourth.

Fifth graders study the Revolutionary War and slavery. They use primary sources and read Early American folklore. Sixth graders study ancient civilizations and the Middle Ages and write a research paper. The Writing Workshop is a standard part of the curriculum in which students practice the steps of good writing (see Glossary, p. 50, *supra*). Fifth and sixth graders also take public speaking, engage in debates and practice speech writing.

A highlight of the grammar school is the Earth Fest in which mixed-age groups engage in a five-day study of an ecological or envi-ronmental topic. The unit concludes with a special assembly in the upper school gym at which each group presents a project.

The approach to science in the grammar school "is firmly experimental and based on the scientific method." Environmental awareness begins as early as first grade with a discussion about how waste leaves Manhattan island. First graders study endangered animals; second graders learn about water pollution and testing; third graders study air pollution; fourth graders examine wind and solar energy and travel to Nature's Classroom, an environmental study center in Connecticut. Sixth graders take a unit on environmental issues.

Parents say that by third grade the academic pace picks up and the work gets much more serious. Extra help is readily available. One mother said her daughter received extra help with reading during recess time.

Foreign language study begins in second grade with exposure to the Spanish language and culture, and is integrated with the social studies curriculum. (This is a pilot program that currently extends through fourth grade.) In seventh grade, students have a two month sequence in each of four languages, and choose one of the four for in-depth study in the eighth grade. The four languages currently available are French, Spanish, Latin, and Japanese.

In mathematics, the focus is on problem-solving skills. There are enrichment topics in each grade. In fifth grade these are palindromic numbers, tangrams and hieroglyphics. Other enrichment projects include curve stitching and M.C. Escher's tessellations.

Reports and grades come home twice a year. The anecdotal reports in the lower school are extensive and detailed. In addition, there is a checklist in each subject area showing that the student is either "progressing well," "developing" or "needs strengthening."

If a child has a learning deficiency, CGPS will "provide some degree of professional skills remediation on a temporary basis." CGPS also has a highly specific and intensive in-school treatment of learning disabilities called the Learning Resource Center, staffed by ten highly trained professionals. The program is limited to forty students, grades kindergarten through twelfth, who are otherwise fully mainstreamed students. There is an *additional* cost of approximately $15,000 per year, and use of the Learning Resource Center is contingent upon admission to the regular program. Applications are currently being accepted only when an opening is expected to occur.

For physical exercise students play in the courtyard, on the roof turf playground or go to Central Park, which is located only a block from the school, weather permitting. Physical education is required in all grades. Intramural and interschool sports begin in fifth grade. After-school sports are available. A Field Day with games is held at the end of the year for each division.

The Prep School (grades seven through twelve) is on a semester system. Grades are issued quarterly, there are two parent conferences and two narrative report cards. The school day begins with a ten minute homeroom period and is divided into forty minute periods, ending at 2:55 PM.

The new building housing grades seven through nine serves the "middle schoolers" exceptionally well; bright, and spacious, with special space for the arts: photo lab, filmmaking, jewelry-making and so on. The "underground" theatre holds 300. Stagecraft models (made by students) on display in the lobby are wonderful.

In seventh and eighth grades students are required to take English, science, social studies and math as well as art, music, computer and P.E. Foreign language study begins with a two month sequence in each of four languages: French, Spanish, Latin and Japanese. In eighth grade students choose one of these languages for continued study.

Seventh graders are ready to think critically and express themselves clearly and sensitively on issues of social relevance. In history the horizons have broadened to include examination of the effect of historical policies such as apartheid and colonialism on emerging nations and current events. Seventh grade English is coordinated with the seventh grade history curriculum and covers the themes of prejudice, tolerance and freedom. Readings include *The Crucible* and *To Kill a Mockingbird*.

In grades nine through twelve students are required to complete four years of English, math and social studies, as well as three years of science. Foreign language must be studied through the end of eleventh grade. Other requirements include a course in computer literacy (there are two computer labs, one with Macs and the other with PC's) two of three offerings in the history of art, theater or music, and a community service requirement of one hundred hours to be completed by the end of the senior year. Electives are available in all the major subject areas. Six courses are the normal course load, except during the senior year when five are required. Students can arrange independent study projects in their final semester.

Ninth and tenth grades are assigned to full year English classes. In ninth grade, the class addresses the fundamental human theme of coming of age and exposes the students to a wide range of literature. In tenth grade the course focuses on the fundamentals of good writing, as well as a selection of British and American literature. Eleventh and twelfth graders choose from a variety of electives but they must take at least one course in each of the following: British literature, American literature, and pre-twentieth century literature.

When asked about a multicultural curriculum at CGPS, Dr. Soghoian responded that "CGPS has always emphasized Africa, China, Japan and South America on nearly an equal footing with the study of Europe in the preparatory school program." CGPS also uses its extensive assembly program to emphasize multicultural performers and themes. Latin America and African history, culture and geography are the focus of the history curriculum in eighth grade and students make African masks, symbolic flags and maps and graphs. The study of geography at CGPS is considered "essential to the appreciation of today's international interdependency." A unit on "the origins of the U.N. and the vital role it plays in the international environment" is included in the eighth grade year.

The history sequence reads like a description of an advanced college history program. Students in ninth and tenth grades study Western Civilization, including European history from Greek and Roman times to the French Revolution and continuing through the Reactionary Era, Imperialism, World Wars I and II, and the Cold War. Eleventh graders study U.S. History, and juniors and seniors can choose from electives such as economics, philosophy, the Holocaust, and a course taught in conjunction with Tufts University as well as AP courses in comparative government, modern European history, and U.S. government.

Calculus BC and AB (college calculus and preparation for the AP exams) are offered by the math department, and graphing calculators are used in the calculus classes. At the annual Math/Science Fair, student teams present the results of their research on a variety of topics such as the mathematics of sound or an analysis of hurricane paths. The science department offers AP biology, chemistry and physics as well as electives in astronomy, consumer chemistry, human evolution, and a three year research course.

There is a great range of choice in the arts at CGPS. Photography, drama and filmmaking are popular. The ceramics room is full of inspired and beautiful work ready to be fired in the kiln. Wood shop and jewelry-making areas are busy places too.

The Prep School has its own Winter and Spring Concerts, (choral and instrumental) and a three day Arts Festival. There are several major theatre productions each year and at least one musical.

The student government, with elected representatives from each grade, helps coordinate activities such as the annual Field Day and fundraising for various causes. Clubs include MECA (the multicultural awareness group), Model U.N., Model SADD Congress, (Students Against Destructive Decisions) and Environmental Awareness.

At the Annual Social Issues Day a topic of importance is examined in depth through seminars and small group discussions. One year Gay Men's Health Crisis was invited to participate in small group question-and-answer sessions.

About 60 percent of high school students participate in a varsity sport. The new spectator gym is large and cheerful with wooden bleachers. At the end-of-the-year Sports Award Banquet the year's outstanding teams and coaches are recognized and individual achievement is honored. CP has strong teams in soccer, cross-country and varsity basketball. There is a trophy case in the school lobby.

Moving Up Day at CGPS reinforces the feeling of a warm community. It is a special day when all the students from pre-kindergarten through twelfth grade, faculty and staff gather together in the gym to share awards for academic excellence, citizenship and character, success in sports and so on. Songs are sung and class banners are handed down from one class to another to signify graduation.

Alumni speak about fond memories of CGPS: "Reunions hold good memories," "CGPS was a little more laid-back and less pretentious than some of the other schools but we all did well there."

Popular College Choices   University of Wisconsin, Boston University, Brown, University of Michigan, Tufts, Cornell, Columbia, Vassar

Traditions   Grammar School Science Fair, Earth Fest, Field Day, Prep School Math/Science Fair class dinners, kindergarten Grandparents' Day, Holiday Concert, Skating Party, theatre benefit, Winter Concert, Spring Concert, Instrumental Concert, 4th-grade trip to Nature's Classroom, Gymnastics Week, Spirit Week, Spring Benefit, The Reading Club, Operation Santa Claus, Social Issues Day, Sports Award Banquet, Moving Up Ceremony, Young Alumni Reunion

Publications   Alumni magazine: *Columbiana Today*
Literary magazine: *Chimera*
Yearbook
Newspaper

Community Service Requirement   Grades 9–12: one hundred
hours, cumulative

Hangouts   Central Park, deli around the corner

Convent Of The Sacred Heart

1 East 91st Street
New York, NY 10128
(212) 722-4745

All girls
Pre-kindergarten–12th grade
Not accessible

Nancy Salisbury, R.S.C.J., Headmistress
Mrs. Barbara S. Root, Director of Admissions

Uniform   Pre-kindergarten: gray smock jumper or navy overalls; regulation sneakers and shoes must be purchased at East Side Kids (15% discount on sneakers when buying SH shoes *and* sneakers)
Grades K–4: gray jumper, white blouse with McMullen collar, white anklets (warm weather), red long-sleeved mock turtleneck shirt and medium gray knee highs (cool weather); red-and-white-check pinafore worn every day, navy stretch shorts worn every day under gray jumper
Grades 5–7: gray kilt, medium gray knee socks or white anklet socks, white long-sleeved blouse, oxford-collar or white polo shirt with collar or white turtleneck; tights must be white, black or beige and can be worn under knee socks; seventh-grade privilege: crew neck or cardigan sweater with detail or pattern may be worn except for formal occasions
Grades 8–12: blue pinstripe cotton kilt; solid blue or white blouse with collar or turtleneck (spring and fall); solid color tights, no long underwear or leggings; Coburn plaid kilt; white, red, yellow, or navy blouse or turtleneck; no oversized clothing; white, yellow, red, green, navy or black socks or tights; no sweat pants, long underwear or leggings

Birthday Cutoff   Pre-kindergarten 3's applicants must be 3 by May/June before entering
Pre-kindergarten 4's applicants must be 4 by May/June before entering
Children entering kindergarten must be 5 by September 1

Enrollment   Total enrollment: 590

183

Pre-kindergarten 3's and 4's places: 28
Kindergarten places: approximately 35
Graduating class size 1999: 45

Grades   Trimester system
Letter grades begin in 5th grade
Departmentalization begins in 5th grade
First final exam is given in 8th grade

Tuition Range 1998–1999 $9,000 to $16,600, pre-kindergarten
3's –12th grade
There are some additional fees (*i.e.*, lunch, technology)

Financial Aid/Scholarship $1,392,957 (14.5% of the operating
budget)
24% of the student body receive some form of financial assistance

Endowment $4 million

Diversity   26% students of color
Women of Proud Heritage (founded 1991)
Women's History Assembly
4 Prep for Prep students enrolled as of 1998

Homework   1st: 15–20 minutes
2nd: 30 minutes
3rd and 4th: 45 minutes
5th–7th: 1–2 hours
8th–12th: 2–4 hours

After-School Program   All lower school (K–4) after-school programs require an additional payment; ballet, ceramics, cooking,
dramatics, gymnastics, photography, violin, arts and crafts,
recorder, dance, tennis, sewing, puppets, computer, music, team
sports, stichery, math for fun, swimming, ice-skating, typing.
Private instruction in piano is available for students in Kindergarten and up
Middle school: required middle school electives are offered from
3:40–5:00 P.M. (the elective fee is included in the tuition); choices
include a variety of recreational and creative activities, gallery and
museum visits; sports activities and teams include: soccer, swim-

ming, volleyball, basketball, softball, track, running club, tennis and gymnastics according to the season
Upper school: Junior Varsity and Varsity interscholastic athletic competition in the Athletic Association of Independent Schools of New York City and the Ivy League

Summer Program   Summer Playgroup: a six-week program from late June through July; creative and recreational activities including swimming are offered for 3–5 year olds; additional payment required; open to children from the community
Creative Arts Summer Program: a multi-arts summer program for boys and girls ages 6–15 (junior program for ages 6 and 7) offering instruction in art, drama, film, computer, science and athletics; all-day arts festival at conclusion of the program; an additional payment is required (limited financial aid is available)

––––––––

Chartered by the International Society of the Sacred Heart in 1881, Convent of the Sacred Heart is the oldest independent girls' school in Manhattan. Sacred Heart is housed in two magnificent land-marked buildings—the former Otto Kahn and James Burden mansions. The winding marble staircase leads from the vaulted lobby to bright and spacious classrooms as well as banquet hall and ballroom in the manner of Versailles complete with tapestry and marble. The ballroom was a wedding gift to Adele Burden née Sloane (great-granddaughter of Commodore Cornelius Vanderbilt) and the scene of many splendid parties and dances in the 1890s. Today the ballroom is used for Sacred Heart commencement, dance classes and assemblies, and is rented out on the weekends for corporate and charitable events and weddings, providing the school with additional income.

Sacred Heart, although a Catholic girls' school, is neither cloistered nor parochial in its outlook. Sacred Heart is governed by a lay board of trustees; the nuns are elegantly dressed (habits are not worn) and approximately one-third of the students have a mixed religious background. As one parent said, "It's a Christian school because Sacred Heart stresses how you lead your life—there is an emphasis on ethics."

The idea of social service is built into a Sacred Heart education. The catalog states: "A primary aim of a Sacred Heart education is the development in each individual of a personal faith that impels to action." All schools claim to care about every student as an individual;

at Sacred Heart, parents say, "They really mean it." Service begins with age appropriate projects in the lowest grades and continues through the upper school where Sacred Heart has led other city students in the Conference on Homelessness and intensive summer service programs.

Sacred Heart has enjoyed a decade of enrollment growth. Additional sections have been added in most lower school grades, facilities have been upgraded, technology has been integrated into the curriculum, amenities have been added (including a lunch program and cafeteria, weight-training room and exercise studio, automated library accessible via Internet, new science labs, upgraded libraries and renovated classrooms.)

Off campus, Sacred Heart is experiencing a historic expansion of its recreational and athletic facilities. The school has joined the Black Rock Forest Consortium providing access to a forest and an environmental sciences center shared with several other independent schools. Sacred Heart has also endowed lanes at the Asphalt Green Aqua Center; and it is one of the seven schools pioneering the renovation of sports fields on Randalls Island. Sacred Heart has committed to an extensive athletics rentals program to supplement its capabilities and 80% of the students participate in one or more JV or Varsity teams, often bringing home the championship trophies.

Getting in: Parents can request a tour of the school or attend one of the open houses before applying for their daughter. Largest points of entry are Pre-K, Kindergarten and ninth grade. The application fee is $50, and the application asks for baptism, communion and confirmation dates, as well as parents' education and employment. After applying, parents come for their tour and interview on the same day. Brick Church, Park Avenue Christian, Episcopal, West Side Montessori, International Pre-school, and St. Thomas More Nursery Schools are all considered "feeders" to Sacred Heart. The admissions office is sensitive to the needs of parents: "They are very courteous," one parent said, "and particularly accommodating to families from abroad." A parent from abroad told us, "It's like going to a Hilton, you know what to expect." Sacred Heart provides an instant community for New York City parents: "When you're accepted at Sacred Heart you're accepted as part of a large international family," said a parent. Another parent said she found Sacred Heart's geographical and ethnic diversity "with a lot of families from Europe and Latin America," refreshing after her daughter's homogeneous nursery school.

Parents: Sacred Heart parents say that social competition is negligible. They don't need to dress up to pick up their daughters at school. Parents are considered partners in their daughters' education. Newsletters are sent home three times a year. Communication from teachers, the PA, and administration is frequent. There is a new parents' cocktail party and family dinner held in May for incoming families, as well as a welcoming party in September. The Parents Association consists of officers, school representatives and class representatives and hosts an annual spring meeting and cocktail party and the annual auction or benefit fund-raiser and family events. There are two or three dinner dances held each year including the bi-annual Spring Ball (held at the American Crafts Museum one year) and the Hatter's Ball featuring custom or homemade hats, "ostrich plumes à la *My Fair Lady*," which benefits the Creative Arts Summer Program Scholarship Fund. Other Parents' Association functions include Christmas caroling, tree lighting and sale (neighbors are welcome) at which you can buy your tree as well as the ornaments and have a picture taken with Santa Claus by the Otto Kahn fireplace outside the former dining room where Enrico Caruso once sang.

Program: Nancy Salisbury, R.S.C.J., previously headmistress at Sacred Heart in Greenwich, Connecticut has been headmistress at the New York City Sacred Heart since 1980. At a recent upper school open house, Sister Salisbury described five elements of a Sacred Heart education: 1) faith: You will learn "what you are going to be and give in this world"; 2) academic challenge: Sacred Heart's rigorous academic program will impart a love of learning and enable each girl to become an independent thinker and grow in her own particular gifts; 3) social awareness: Everyone does service at Sacred Heart, and "we do not count hours"; 4) growth as a community: There is a strong relationship between faculty and students, and a diverse student community; 5) personal growth: To recognize your strengths, gifts and limitations, "you come as you are and are loved into being the very best that you can be." A lower school parent said that what she likes best about Sacred Heart is that the headmistress and the heads of the divisions "have a real concern for each and every family—people are what matters."

Religion and social service go hand in hand at Sacred Heart. According to the brochure, the "basic intent of the lower school religious program is to build in each student a positive sense of herself in relation to God and to her community." Ethics and spirituality are stressed—the basic premise is "you have a friend in God." There is mass once a week in the beautifully appointed chapel and parents are always welcome. In middle school "the link between faith and action is forged by social action activities that reach out to communities beyond the school." Middle school service projects include working in a day care center and participation in walkathons, God's Love We Deliver (meals delivered to AIDS patients) and Amnesty International. In the upper school community service is coordinated through the campus ministry and the Student Activities and Service Program. Students are expected to volunteer on a regular basis in a social service agency outside of school, keep a journal and share their experiences in a weekly meeting. Students in class ten must complete a final project in which they examine a social issue in depth through academic research and field experience.

The lower school at Sacred Heart is composed of grades pre-kindergarten through grade four. In lower school, the girls wear the signature Sacred Heart uniform: a gray jumper with a red-checked pinafore (both machine washable). Each lower school girl has an "Angel" or "Big Sister" to guide her. The fourth graders are partners with seniors in the upper school and middle school girls read weekly to lower school children. There are three kindergarten classes of approximately seventeen children each and two teachers in each classroom (plus a rabbit). Beginning in kindergarten the following subjects are taught: language arts, math, science, social studies and, in third grade onward, French. Students meet weekly for religion, art, music, library, gym and drama/movement. There are formal as well as informal assembly presentations. Exercise is taken on the two play terraces, which have views of the reservoir, or in Central Park across the street.

Parents say academics in the lower school consists of "good old-fashioned teaching combined with some of the newer methods" and "there's a lot of structure." Conferences are held twice a year but parents say you can schedule one any time if necessary. A tone of "warmth and acceptance" prevails along with academic rigor. Director of Admissions Barbara Root describes Sacred Heart as "not overly pressured, but everyone is expected to do serious work." The mother of a third grader concurs: "Sacred Heart is competitive but each girl is encouraged to do her best." Collaborative learning is emphasized in the early years, and there are no individual desks until third grade.

The reading program begins in kindergarten and becomes more formal in class one. Phonics is taught as an essential reading skill along with creative writing, Writers' Workshop, "whatever works." If a student is not progressing well she will begin working with a reading specialist. There is individual as well as small group instruction and basal texts are used. Girls are taught to experience mathematics "as an integral part of everyday life" through cooking, manipulatives and math games. For example, to learn the value of a million, one class is collecting and counting tea bag tags. The project is on display in the classroom.

Lower school science emphasizes the skills of observation and investigation. There is a two-day field trip to an environmental center in fourth grade. The social studies curriculum begins with a study of the students' own families, then extends to a study of the community. Students in class three research topics such as the rain forest or deserts. Class four studies Early Explorers and American History.

Art is integrated into the science and social studies curriculum in many ways. Students in class two pick an animal to study and model it in clay, then the entire class works together to create a Calderesque circus from wood, wire, foam and fabric. Students in class three made "incredible" papier-mâché vegetables in art and studied the growth of plants from seed through maturation in science. Fifth graders studying antiquity create a museum of ancient cultures.

Drama and movement activities are "designed to enhance the students' understanding of dance as a means of communication and expression." By class four the girls create and perform their own original dance/drama pieces.

George Orio, Convent's Director of Technology, is credited with seamlessly integrating technology into the classrooms and curriculum. Formal computer instruction begins in first grade. The classes are team taught by a computer specialist and the classroom teacher and use multimedia CD-ROMs and related software. Fifth graders work with LEGO LOGO, a robotics application, and by sixth grade students and teachers use *Hyperstudio* to create multimedia research projects.

Study of the French language begins in class three through songs and games to teach vocabulary and pronunciation.

A team of lower school psychologists and learning specialists give additional help where necessary. Project Charlie, an anti-drug program that focuses on self-esteem, is taught in the lower school. A comprehensive health program which focuses on nutrition begins in grade two.

Birthdays in lower school are special because the birthday girl can wear a party dress, bring in cupcakes or another sweet and can donate a book to the library in her name. Another fun event in lower school is the Halloween costume party. The lower school Christmas Pageant "can make you weep" it is so beautifully produced, parents say.

Middle school at Sacred Heart consists of classes five through seven. All six middle school homerooms are located on the fourth floor. Each new middle school student has an "angel" for the first weeks of school. New students and their angels are invited to school for a luncheon and orientation day the week before school begins. Flexible ability grouping in mathematics begins in class six. French ability groups begin in class seven. The first half of French I or Spanish I is offered to all seventh graders. The second half of this course is given in eighth grade. In middle school, a study skills and research course and Latin (class seven) and Spanish (class seven) are added to the core curriculum of English, math, science, social studies, and religion. Students say there is an increased workload in class six and the development of good study skills is emphasized.

By class five, computer work is integrated into the English, math, social studies and science curricula. Fifth grade students explore the physical concepts of simple machines through LEGO LOGO. A unit in class six on computer database filing uses *ClarisWorks*. Seventh grade students create multimedia presentations on the American Colonies using the *Hyperstudio* application.

Art continues to be integrated with the curriculum at many levels. Students in class six studying Medieval and Renaissance Europe create family crests and banners, work on tapestry projects and make stained-glass windows. The study of South America in class seven is supplemented by the creation of relief sculptures and the study of pre-Columbian art.

The middle school elective program is a required weekly enrichment elective. Among the choices are sports, drama, literary magazine, photography, ice skating, swimming and ceramics.

There is a middle school musical production in the fall as well as smaller productions in the winter and spring. Other highlights include the class seven father/daughter volleyball game, the pancake breakfast and the mother/daughter liturgy.

The middle school has its own student government, a Committee of Games, that oversees the sports competition between the Green and Buff teams. There is also a Big Sister Program. Each class takes an overnight trip, which is coordinated with the curriculum. Class five travels to Mystic, Connecticut, sixth graders to a Pennsylvania Renaissance Faire and seventh graders to Plymouth, Massachusetts.

Beginning in middle school and continuing through upper school, academic achievement awards are given to students who maintain an A average for the year in four or more academic subjects. At the end of the year there is a Sports Banquet to honor athletic achievement.

The upper school at Sacred Heart consists of classes eight through twelve. Class eight is a transition year at Sacred Heart. In class nine there is an influx of new students from parochial and independent schools in the New York City area. While some of the students who have been at Sacred Heart since pre-kindergarten or kindergarten opt to leave for a coed or boarding school in ninth grade. Incoming ninth graders have an overnight immersion program and each new student in the upper school has an "angel" for the first weeks. Upper school students at Sacred Heart say they feel they have more opportunity to take risks and to be more articulate in an all-girls school. (But we are told that Sister Salisbury continues to be strict about skirt length.)

Students say that the academic expectations are high—Sacred Heart was recognized by the U.S. Department of Education as a National School of Excellence. "The teachers work you hard, and honors courses are pushed," they say. The sense of community continues in the upper school: "It's not so competitive because we're all friends and we help each other." There has been an enormous change in the emphasis on the sciences in the past four years—now 90 percent of the students take an advanced science course during their senior year. Students take six or seven academic subjects in classes eight through ten and add electives in classes eleven and twelve. A former Parents Association president told us, "The upper school is rigorous but there is a lot of support." The study of religion includes textual study, literary exegesis, historical background, comparative religions, ethics and philosophy. In the eleventh grade the interdisciplinary approach culminates in a thirty-page baccalaureate level thesis and oral presentation of a topic combining Christology and the Arts. Recent topics have included examinations of the films of Fellini, the music of J.S. Bach, and Beguin lace makers.

Mrs. Price has been head of the upper school for over seven years. Because the upper school is small, the teachers know each girl very well. Teachers are approachable and there are peer tutors.

There is an intensive five-year writing program in the upper school and students become familiar with all literary genres. Students are expected to write well in all disciplines. In class nine there is an interdisciplinary social studies and English project that produces

Medieval Magazine and culminates in a banquet. Juniors and seniors can choose from courses in Asian and African-American literature. The "Memoirs" course examines feminist thinking through the stories of women in a variety of cultures. For "New York City in Literature," students read the work of an author (such as Edith Wharton, who lived in New York City) and visit his or her home and/or sites in the novel.

Students who excel in mathematics can take calculus AB and BC. Members of the Mathematics Club compete with other Catholic high schoolers in the tristate area.

The school has a standing research internship program at Rockefeller University where several girls study each year. Students have also interned at the Museum of Natural History, the New York Academy of Sciences, the Cooper Union Engineering School, and the Columbia Science Honors Program. A lab science research internship is available to students in eleventh and twelfth grades. Interns spend six hours a week in a laboratory and write a research paper.

The art department has been expanded in recent years.

In May there is a three-week Festival of the Arts when students celebrate their accomplishments in many areas. Artwork is on display throughout the school, and there are dance recitals, as well as performances by the handbell choir and the Speech and Drama Clubs.

Many of the extracurricular activities in the upper school are coed. There are upper school dances in September and at Christmas each year, and Sacred Heart students can audition for roles in the Collegiate, Regis and Browning Schools' plays and musicals. At Sacred Heart the drama department produces one-act plays or Shakespeare in the fall and a musical in the spring in which boys play some parts. There are also Service Days together with neighboring boys' schools.

There is no Sacred Heart orchestra but students can join the Interschool Orchestra or the Sacred Heart Handbell Choir.

Other extracurricular opportunities include student government, Peer Support, Archeology Club, Drama Club, Environmental Club, yearbook, literary magazine, newspaper and Women of Proud Heritage. Sports are popular and plentiful: There are eighth grade teams, intramural clubs and eight varsity sports. Two of Sacred Heart's chief competitors are Trinity School and Brearley.

Sacred Heart students in classes nine through twelve can participate in the exchange program at other Sacred Heart Schools either here or abroad. Students have studied in France, Belgium, Spain, California and Louisiana.

College guidance begins in class nine, and there are assemblies with alumnae. Students say that because the teachers know and remember them so well it is easy to get recommendations. A young woman, a senior, who came to Sacred Heart from a public school, says she "holds school dear, it has molded me into what I am."

Popular College Choices Columbia, Georgetown, Harvard, Kenyon, Middlebury, Princeton, University of Pennsylvania, Vassar, Yale, Boston University

Traditions Big Sister/Little Sister Cookout, used uniform sale, class coffees, Middle School Mother/Daughter Liturgy, Upper School Mother/Daughter Tea, Senior Mother/Daughter Breakfast and induction into the Alumnae Association, tree sale and caroling party, Christmas Pageant, Sacred Heart Antiques Show, Father/Daughter Dinner Dance, Dad/Daughter boat cruise, Black History Month (February), Women's History Month (March), Ring Day, Sacred Heart Feast Days, First Communion Confirmation, May Festival of the Arts, Spring Book Fair, Grandparents' Day, archeology trip, class nine Blairstown trip, class eleven retreat, upper school service trip in March, Sports Banquets, Hatter's Ball, Senior Dinner Dance, alumnae mothers lunch, conge, Senior cut day, Spring Street Fair, Prize Day, Homecoming

Publications Newspaper: *Spirit*
Upper School Literary magazine: *Zenith*
Yearbook: *Cornerstone*
Women's issues: *Women of Proud Heritage*
French Literary Magazine: *Sous Presse*
Middle School Literary Magazine: *Millenium*
Annual report
Parent/Alumnae Newsletter
Alumae Magazine: *Les Amies*

Community Service Requirement Each student is expected to give of herself to the school community and to the community at large—hours are not counted

Hangouts Jackson Hole (hamburger restaurant), Million Dollar Deli (candy store on Madison), Timothy's, Pintaile's Pizza

Corlears School

324 West 15th Street
New York, NY 10011
(212) 741-2800

Coed
Nursery–4th grade
Not accessible

Ms. Marion Greenwood, Head of School
Ms. Rorry Romeo, Director of Admissions

Birthday Cutoff   Children entering kindergarten should be 5 by September 1

Enrollment   Total enrollment: 150
Largest point of entry is 2/3's
Kindergarten places: varies from year to year
Graduating class 1998: 12
1999: 19

Grades   Anecdotal reports and checklists

Tuition Range 1998–1999 $9,765 to $14,290, 2/3's–4th grade
Additional fees: $500 building fee; reduced to $300 for a second child in the school

Financial Aid/Scholarship   30% of the student body receive some form of aid

Endowment   None
Each family makes a non-interest-bearing loan of $1,000 per child
There is a 3-year staggered payment system for this loan

After-School Program   Child care available after school Monday–Friday until 5:45 P.M.
Corlears After-School Specialty Program: open to Corlears students only; weekdays from 3:15 P.M. to 4:15 P.M.; an additional fee required; activities include music, drama, sports, chess, gymnastics, chorus, Spanish, art and cooking

Summer Program   Corlears Summer Program: six weeks from mid-June to the end of July for children ages nursery through 7; recreational and creative activities, swimming and trips; an additional payment is required

———

Corlears was founded in 1968 on the Lower East Side and moved to West 15th Street in 1971. Corlears has well-equipped classrooms, an art room, wood shop, library, two gyms and a lovely play yard. Children bring their own lunches. Admission is based on a personal interview and available school records. Corlears is small and nurturing and parents describe it as a neighborhood school. Corlears goes to fourth grade, specializing in education of children in the early years. There are interage classroom groupings throughout. There is a supervised early-morning drop-off for children age four and older. Spanish is taught beginning with the 4/5's. Classroom computers are available for children six to nine years of age. Use of the computers is integrated into classwork. An extensive counseling placement program assists fourth grade graduates with entrance to middle schools.

The Dalton School

108 East 89th Street
New York, NY 10128
Tel (212) 722-5160, FAX (212) 423-5259
e-mail info@dalton.org
website: www.nltl.columbia.edu

Coed
Kindergarten–12th grade
Accessible

Dr. Richard Blumenthal, Headmaster
Dr. Elisabeth Krents, Director of First Program Admissions
Ms. Eva Rado, Director of Middle School/High School Admissions

Uniform   None

Birthday Cutoff   None (but prefer applicants to be 5 by September 1)

Enrollment   Total enrollment: 1,290
Kindergarten places: approximately 85–90
Graduating class size: approximately 100–115

Grades   Semester system
Letter grades begin in 8th grade
Full departmentalization by 6th grade
First midterm and final in 9th grade

Tuition Range 1998–1999 $17,270 to $19,130 kindergarten–12th grade
No additional fees other than minimal PTA fee

Financial Aid/Scholarship   Approximately 20% of families receive some form of financial aid
$2.9 million available

Endowment   Approximately $9 million

Diversity   Approximately 16% children of color
29 Prep for Prep students enrolled as of fall 1998

196

Affiliated with Early Steps Program, A Better Chance, Albert G. Oliver Scholarship Program for children of color, Faculty Diversity Committee, PTA Diversity Committee; Full Time Diversity Coordinator

Homework   Kindergarten: none
1st: once a week, 15 minutes
2nd: ½ hour nightly (15 minutes of work, 15 minutes of reading, except for weekends or vacations) building to ½ hour of homework and minimum of 15 minutes of reading
3rd: 45 minutes plus reading (not on weekends)
4th–6th: 1–1½ hours
7th–9th: 2–3 hours
10th–12th: approximately 3 to 4 hours a night

After-School Program   The Dalton Serendipity Program: a variety of creative and recreational activities including computer, The Dalton Chess Academy, cooking, cartooning, sports and games; an additional payment is required; Kids Club: afterschool care daily on premises until 5:45 P.M.; an additional payment is required Interscholastic athletic competition, clubs and committees for middle and high school students

Summer Program   Summer camp for lower school students, open to children from other schools; an additional payment is required

———

Since its founding in 1919 by visionary educator Helen Parkhurst, The Dalton School's mission has been the improvement of education. Dalton is often described as having "one foot in traditional education and one foot firmly planted in the progressive movement." Known for inculcating independence of thought combined with intellectual rigor and for having a plethora of innovative programs with an emphasis on the use of technology to enhance education, The Dalton School serves as a model for other schools around the world and Dalton clones can be found in England, the Netherlands, Australia, Korea and Japan. Dalton is a famous school well known for its philosophy and historically rich in people and programs.

The foundation of a Dalton education is still the Dalton Plan which is not as complicated in actuality as it appears in writing. It consists of *House* (the home base for each student); *The Assignment* (the

197

work: a type of contract between student and teacher); the *Laboratory* (one-to-one or small group sessions between student and teacher that augment traditional classroom work). Dalton is unique in that Lab time is built into each teacher's schedule and students say that teachers are very accommodating and Labs often take place on the same day they are requested. Throughout the First Program and the early years of middle school, the House Advisor is also the classroom teacher. House groups change each year and are comprised of students of the same age until high school. Then there are mixed grade levels in each group and these students remain with the same House Advisor for four years. The role of the House Advisor is to act as an advocate for each child and as the key contact person for parents with the school. The Assignment is a document created by the individual teachers that covers a period of time and details the academic expectations in a unit of study. It is introduced at the First Program (lower school) and increases through middle and high school.

Getting in: Dr. Elisabeth Krents, a Dalton alumna with a doctorate in Education, was recently appointed Director of Admissions of the First Program. Parents describe her as "knowledgeable, enthusiastic and warm." She brings a welcome professionalism to the process. Parents interested in learning more about the school can attend spring tours conducted by Elisabeth Krents or attend open houses at both the First Program and middle and high school in the fall before applying. Dalton now takes a close look at parents to make sure they have a clear understanding of the school's philosophy and to see if they have solid values. For First Program applicants, Dalton requires both a parent tour and a meeting with Elisabeth Krents or another senior admissions staff member. Children are either interviewed at Dalton in small groups or observed in their nursery schools. Letters of recommendation from Dalton parents who really know the applicant's family are helpful. Don't waste time with letters from every celebrity or politician you ever met unless they really know your child.

Dalton doesn't merely pay lip service to diversity. The school follows through with respect and support, providing an afterschool program for children whose parents work, anti-bias retreats for faculty, parent and student support groups and a superb mentoring program that pairs high school students of color with successful professionals of color. These high school students, in turn, mentor younger students coming up through the middle school and in First Program. Beginning in 1996, high school students join with the PTA diversity committee to organize the First Program Cultural Festival featuring, art, food, music and storytelling.

What are they looking for? Elisabeth Krents told us "We are trying to get away from the myth that there is a 'Dalton type' of child. We look for *all* kinds of children. Helen Parkhurst's goal was to have a community of different individuals and to educate every type of child, preparing each for the real world. We want to admit students (and families) who reflect the diversity of the real world and that means geographic, socioeconomic, racial and religious diversity." Parents say that eccentricity and ethnicity are valued. The 1998 kindergarten class was composed of 21% children of color and children from all over the city. One does not have to be a genius to be accepted to Dalton; a former admissions director told us they look for "the child who is not just a sponge, but who will contribute." Dalton has a policy of preferring, but not automatically admitting, siblings and children of alumni. Dalton will accept an "at risk" child and does mainstream children with moderate physical disabilities provided they can keep up academically.

Parents: The School views parents as partners in the education of their children and they are invited to be involved in many different ways: There are committees that focus on ethics, gender, community service, the Book Fair, safety, and children's entertainment. Ongoing parent dialogues are conducted at the First Program. Kindergarten to grade twelve parents are invited to "Rap sessions", meetings for parents and administrators to discuss developmental and social issues.

Dalton is working hard to eradicate its glamorous, materialistic image of the 1980's. In the past, students have been labeled "spoiled." A student described the problem as particularly acute in middle school "where students are not as considerate of one another as they could be." The newly formed PTA Ethics Committee hopes to rectify all that. Values education is at the top of the school's agenda and an Ethics Task Force is at work to find ways to integrate ethics into the curriculum in a meaningful way.

Dalton families have changed over the years although Jewish families have long been comfortable at Dalton. The Downtowners Committee meets regularly since Dalton has an ever increasing number of children who live below 23rd Street. A three division PTA Diversity Committee exists to support families of color. If there's any question as to how Dalton families align themselves politically, just peek into the lower school library where, instead of the chiseled faces of Dalton's former headmasters, you'll see portraits of John and Robert Kennedy and Martin Luther King. In the 1960's, during Donald Barr's tenure as headmaster, Dalton gained a reputation for enrolling many "children of culture" from "show-biz" families; a sweet sixteen party at Studio 54 or a bar-mitzvah attended by Barbra Streisand was not unheard of. Dalton no longer has the monopoly on glitz which is spread more uniformly among the private schools today including those which were traditionally more staid such as Trinity and Spence. And according to a parent who is also a trustee: "In the nineties there's no fuss over famous families; it's old news." Still, with so many prominent families in the school, networking opportunities abound. For instance, a Dalton high schooler working on a journalism project was advised by a senior writer at *The New York Times* who has a child at the school. An alumna told us she landed her first fashion internship with Diana Vreeland at the Metropolitan Museum Costume Institute thanks to a Dalton connection.

Dalton parents are generous in their financial support of the school. A recently completed capital campaign funded major improvements in the school's facilities. A new 32,000 square foot Physical Education Center was constructed at 200 East 87th Street with a spectator gym (the basketball team is a strong draw) and other amenities. A new floor was added to the top of the 89th Street building that houses a visual arts center with seven skylit studios. A new state-of-the-art 8,000 square foot science center was recently built increasing the space allocated to the science program by 25%.

Program: First Program (affectionately known as Little Dalton) consists of kindergarten through third grade. It is housed in three interconnected townhouses on East 91st Street. Recent renovations added 2,000 square feet of instructional space to the school which includes a new science center plus a spacious commons area used by all the grades. The children still find Little Dalton "cozy" and move about the building freely.

Ellen Stein, a Dalton alumna, and former vice principal at Friends Seminary, is the Director of the First Program. The lower division went through a series of directors during the early 1990's and Ms. Stein's arrival in 1994 brings a much needed stability to the school. Parents speak highly of her commitment to ethics and the establishment of a strong sense of community in the school. "While Dalton is noted for its individualization, we also want to develop children's senses of their responsibility as members of the school and to the community at large." Since Ms. Stein's arrival, parents note that the First Program has tightened the kindergarten through third grade curriculum to create a more even balance between rigorous skills and "process learning."

Academics are approached in a structured but relaxed setting. In kindergarten the school becomes acquainted with a child's learning style. Instruction is individualized, some parents say "to a fault." While the day is highly organized, children are encouraged to proceed at their own pace within the context of curricular goals for the year that are consistent across the grade levels. "The children learn how to think, how to take risks and how to make mistakes," according to a parent. Children are not expected to read by the end of kindergarten but if they do individualized work is planned for them. Careful attention is paid to the placement of each student with the right teacher and right class.

From the very beginning of the learning process at Dalton, young students are actively and creatively involved in what they study. Dalton is historically known for its strength in the arts which are integrated into the curriculum. Dalton's First Program is based upon a social studies "core" where language arts, math, science, music and art are directly related to the core study. Second graders focus on New York City. The children create a model city which reflects what they have learned about city needs and urban design. They write and revise written reports about landmark buildings on the computer. In music classes the children put their own city poems into song and in art they paint murals of city scenes. In science class they study the ecosystems of Central Park. Divided into groups they are assigned parcels of land to "plant." They research plants and trees to determine which would best thrive in that specific environment and ultimately present their plans to New York City Park personnel. Two years ago, the Parks Department was so impressed with the children's plans that they were given permission to actually make their plantings. In addition, second graders created their own multi-media magazine on the theme of "diversity in the city." One class photographed neighborhoods, buildings and faces, another class focused on jobs and workers, interviewing parents in their workplaces and analyzing the data they collected, creating graphs (and posting data on the Internet). Another class concentrated on schools, foods and neighborhoods.

Art teacher Sheila Lamb, a Dalton institution, has guided the creative work of First Program students for thirty-one years. "I treat every child like an artist," she says. Her approach "is to be with the children with their imaginations . . . nurturers of their visual language." First Program art integrates all forms of arts and crafts. Creativity carries over to the sciences as well. One of our favorites is a third grade unit in which students study the unusual properties of planet "Oobleckia" (the name is based on a Dr. Seuss book, the planet is made of cornstarch, water and food coloring). Students must come up with solutions to problems such as "How would you land a spaceship on Oobleckia? They work in groups and make a final report at a mock conference.

Dalton is at the forefront of independent schools for its commitment (both financial and philosophical) to technology and education. The school has maintained a high-speed connection to the Internet since 1994. Under the Dalton Technology Plan, faculty have designed projects and curricula that utilize advanced multimedia technology. According to a former headmaster, technology does not replace traditional educational methods: "It allows us to deliver the Dalton plan more powerfully than ever and is consistent with Dalton's individualized approach, sense of community and mission to prepare students for life after Dalton. Technology shifts education from adults giving answers to students seeking answers to their own meaningful questions."

Walking through the halls one can see kindergarten children making their own interactive counting slide shows, sixth grade students being introduced to history and scientific principles through simulated excavations of Assyria and Greece, high school students participating in advanced astronomy simulation, and English students exploring the ideas of Shakespeare's *Macbeth* through online resources, including digitized versions of scenes from the play by three different repertory companies.

Specialists enrich the Dalton experience. It's the only school we know of with an archeologist in residence who spends six weeks with each third grade class excavating a dig set up in the backyard. Sixth graders participate in the Archaeotype program, "a computer-based, integrated curriculum unit" developed by Dalton faculty in which they examine artifacts from ancient Greece and Assyria, conduct their own research and discuss their findings. It is also the only school in the city to have a special lecturer who teaches Dalton classes at the American Museum of Natural History. Chess is taught to kindergarteners and first graders by a Yugoslavian chess master and the school has a composer-in-residence who writes musicals related to what the children are studying which the children perform. A story teller works with kindergarten children using a multicultural and gender sensitive approach to teaching fairy tales.

Don't worry if your child is fidgety—there's plenty of opportunity for the children to stretch their limbs as well as their minds here. In addition to daily play on the two play roofs and at gym several times a week, beginning in second grade students use Dalton's newly constructed Physical Education Center.

At the end of third grade the children at Little Dalton pass through the arch during the traditional Arch Day Ceremony in June and move on to Big Dalton. Before they do, each makes his or her own colorful ceramic tile that is permanently mounted in a hallway of Little Dalton. The transition to Big Dalton seems to be an easy one since the children have frequently visited "buddy Houses" and attended a variety of events at the ivy covered 89th Street building.

In middle school, fourth and fifth graders are taught in self-contained classrooms in which the House Advisor teaches most subjects. Departmentalization begins in sixth grade and all students in sixth through eighth grades are taught math, social studies and English by a core group of three teachers who work together. The core groups make Big Dalton seem small and provide a comfortable transition to the more demanding high school. Each core teacher is an advisor and each student has a sense of belonging to a particular core. Students are placed in different core and House groups every year. Individual differences in levels or skills are recognized by grouping within the classroom, by the individualized assignments and by the enrichment and support provided in the classes and in Labs. The annual Greek Festival is a highlight of the middle school.

Student life at Dalton's high school is informal. There are no bells and the dress code is relaxed. "There's a small grunge element," said a student, "But most people look good." Starting in late spring ninth grade students can sign out and leave school during a Lab period. Students who serve as peer leaders or peer tutors are involved with faculty in programs for incoming freshmen. A parent told us, "They do a superb job to ensure that the transition is smooth."

There is no Dalton "type" per se; there are jocks and artists and techies, and cliques form around interests. There is a strong drama group, a newspaper group, and athletic teams. Dalton students have embraced the new technology and communicate through Forum, an active e-mail message system. Amusing top ten lists are popular, we were told. Students also discuss community and current events online. Contrary to what's been written about Dalton students most do not carry cell phones although the beeper has become something of a fashion accessory. With the new ethics task force in place, students are paying more attention to how they treat one another, including keeping the cafeteria clean.

Community Service is one avenue for teaching ethics and values and it is integrated into the curriculum at every grade level. A recent project brought senior citizens from a local center to Dalton for computer lessons. Paired together with individual Dalton children, seniors learned how to operate a mouse and access the Internet. The students, in turn, learned about life in the city before the advent of television. Other community service projects occur throughout the year: making bread for a homeless shelter to distribute, or First Program parents and children getting together to decorate bags for God's Love We Deliver Program for homebound patients with AIDS.

Dalton students are politically savvy. During the war in Iraq, they held town meetings, and during the presidential election, students had an electoral college discussion and expressed their views through political videos, radio ads and cartoons. Dalton students have created their own video news program modeled on CNN and do not shy away from open and difficult discussions concerning race and gender. There are diversity groups such as: DAALAS (Dalton Alliance of African-American and Latino Students) and the more inclusive group Another Perspective. A discussion might be sponsored by Another Perspective, or Gender Issues or Human Rights or by the Exploration Committee and speakers such as Ralph Nader and Katie Roiphe are invited to address the students in groups both large and small. Environmental issues are important to the community and the student government instituted a recycling program and convinced the cafeteria to stop using styrofoam products.

In general, teachers are addressed formally (Mr. Smith, Mrs. Brown) but it depends on the teacher. Students describe the staff as "relaxed, intense, knowledgeable." And because of Lab time, students have the opportunity to develop close relationships with their teachers. Dalton nurtures its faculty providing some of the highest salary and fringe benefit programs offered by the independent schools. Dr. Judith Sheridan, High School Director since 1990, takes special pride in a talented caring and charismatic faculty.

Faculty are encouraged to take advantage of sabbaticals, travel grants, workshops and funded summer curriculum grants. During the summer of 1996 teams of Dalton apostles were abroad in Taiwan, Turkey and Australia to spread the word about the Dalton Plan and the use of technology in education.

Beginning in July 1999, Dr. Richard Blumenthal will assume the role of Headmaster. He brings to the position a familiarity with New York City as he grew up in Manhattan and graduated from Trinity in

1963. In addition, he is fluent in six languages and has a doctorate in comparative literature from Harvard. Before coming to Dalton, Dr. Blumenthal was head of the Harley School in Rochester with which Dalton shares an educational philosophy.

Dalton's requirements and course offerings in the high school seem quite traditional in scope. Freshmen, sophmores and juniors have to take at least five major courses. Core courses are English, history, languages, math and science. Students take elective courses as juniors and seniors. A junior can choose among five different courses in American literature, each with a different focus and reading list. A senior can choose among such humanities courses as "Asian Literature: East Meets West" and "Postmodern America," or "All the News That's Fit: The Press and the Public Interest." AP level courses are offered in many subjects. Seniors can create a senior project and Dalton high school students can take any undergraduate course for credit at New York University and Barnard/Columbia Colleges. For the motivated and able student, the sky's the limit.

Personal exploration is also provided in lab time throughout the students' years and particularly in the high school as students become increasingly independent learners. "It's not an easy school to go to," said a junior, "because you can't squander your free time—You do have to go to lab." The Assignment might be a month long project; for instance, students studying the pre-Civil War years might write a newspaper typical of the period.

At Dalton, there is tremendous support and encouragement for students seeking their own personal vision in the arts. Whether developing an energetically choreographed piece set to hip hop, studying the complexities of a Schubert Mass, designing an original set for Stephen Sondheim's *Company* or studying life drawing for three consecutive years, a Dalton student is guided by professional artists who are committed to teaching. One student described his experience this way, "If you're interested in a certain area, you are given a great deal of support and encouragement to pursue it in depth." According to a senior art teacher, "The new skylit art center has become a place where everyone uses every inch of space for the creation and consideration of art."

Dalton students display an array of musical gifts. There are two orchestras for the middle and upper school, a wind ensemble, a percussion ensemble, and a jazz-rock ensemble; a high school chorus and madrigal group. And all groups perform at the Annual Spring Concert.

In keeping with the emphasis on creative expression, Senior

Prank is a school tradition at Dalton. One of the most memorable was Chevy Chase's (1961) "cow in the library" and "trip wire in front of the elevators." Recent pranks have been more tame: purple footprints painted up the wall and over all nine floors, the dean of students' office filled with popcorn or balloons, or more imaginative: the creation of a surreal "twilight zone" on three floors of the high school.

Dalton's logo shows a child confidently leaving a mother's embrace. After thirteen years of self-discovery and academic adventure, Dalton's graduating seniors sing the words of the school motto: "Here we have learned to go forth unafraid."

After you read this entry you can visit The Dalton School Home Page on the World Wide Web. And don't forget to sign the Dalton-Web Guestbook.

Popular College Choices   Brown, Harvard, Cornell, Yale, University of Pennsylvania, Wesleyan, Amherst, Williams

Traditions   Greek Festival, Candlelighting, Arch Day, Dance Theater Workshop Concert, Spring Concert, parent discussion days, annual trips beginning in Little Dalton and throughout middle school, school street fair on 91st Street, Senior Prank, high school prom

Publications   Monthly student newspaper: *The Daltonian*
Literary Magazine: *The Blue Flag*
Middle School Literary Magazine: *Whispers*
Art, photography: *Fine Arts Magazine*
Public Affairs Journal: *Macrocosm*
Science publication: *Quantum Leaps*
Yearbook

Community Service Requirement   90 hours over four years

Hangouts   Starbucks, Stargate, The Bagelry, the new gym

The Dwight and the Anglo-American International Schools

291 Central Park West
New York, NY 10024
(212) 724-2146 ext. 1
website: http://www.ingress.com/~dwight/
e-mail: admissions@server.dwight.edu

Coed
K–12th Grade
Not Accessible

Mr. Stephen H. Spahn, Chancellor
Dr. Joyce Robinson, Head of School
Mrs. Kristina McCoobery, Dean of Admissions
Mrs. Elizabeth Callaway, Director of Admissions
Ms. Pema Shakabpa, Director of Admissions

Uniform   K–8 boys: khaki or gray slacks, blue blazer or sweater with Dwight crest, collared shirts or turtlenecks
K–8 girls: jumpers, gray or dark blue skirts, white collared shirts and blazers or sweaters
9–12 boys: collared shirt with tie, no denim or turtlenecks
9–12 girls: skirt or slacks (not denim), collared shirt, or turtleneck

Birthday Cutoff   Children entering Kindergarten must be 5 by December 31

Enrollment   Total enrollment: 400
K places: 13
1st grade places: 15
Graduating class 1995–1996: 70

Grades   Trimester system
Letter grades begin in 5th grade
Departmentalization begins in 5th grade and is completed by 7th grade
First final exam is offered in 5th grade

Tuition Range 1998–1999 $16,000 to $18,000, K–12th grade
Additional fees for registration, graduation and support activities

range from $900 to $1500

A tuition payment plan is available for families

Financial Aid/Scholarship $800,000 in financial aid is available
30% of students receive some form of financial assistance

Endowment $4 million

Diversity   15% students of color
35% of the students were born in a foreign country
The International Baccalaureate (IB) is offered
English as a Second Language (ESL) instruction is available
Dwight has an expanded language program offering French, Spanish, Italian for native speakers, Japanese, Hebrew and Chinese
2 Prep for Prep students enrolled as of Fall 1998

Homework   K: 15–20 minutes
1st and 2nd: $\frac{1}{2}$ hour
3rd and 4th: 45 minutes
5th and 6th: 1–2 hours
7th and 8th: 2–3 hours
9th–12th: 3–4 hours

After-School Program   Dwight's After-School Program is not open to students from other schools
Grades K–4: creative and recreational activities for an additional fee
Grades 5–12: there are approximately 37 clubs and activities offered before and after school, including an after-school study program; Minivarsity, junior varsity and varsity sports beginning in 5th grade

Summer Program   The Dwight Intensive Review Program is an academic summer program for students who need extra support or wish to accelerate; the program runs from mid-June through the end of July; an additional payment is required
An intensive ESL summer program is offered to current and incoming students; there is an additional charge for this program

The Dwight School was founded in 1880 as an academy of classical studies, became coed in 1967 and added a London campus in 1972. Dwight merged with the Anglo-American International School in 1993 and is now a comprehensive school which also offers the option of study for the International Baccalaureate (IB) Diploma. This consortium works out very well because the Spahn family has had a long association with both schools. Stephen Spahn, the chancellor of The Dwight School, attended Anglo-American and his father headed that school for more than thirty years. The Dwight School retains its identity as "a small traditional school" while adding the international elements of the Anglo-American School. The Dwight School follows the International Baccalaureate Curriculum from Kindergarten through twelfth grade. The Dwight School also offers a fully mainstreamed program for children with mild learning difficulties (the Quest program).

The school occupies three buildings—a five story building on 89th Street, a brownstone on 88th Street and a new space on Central Park West. In addition to classrooms these buildings contain a photography darkroom, two computer centers, a theater space, and two gymnasiums.

With students and faculty from over thirty nations, the school has a unique social as well as academic environment. Multiculturalism has been a natural part of the curriculum for many years. Students learn that there are many ways to celebrate and observe holidays. One of the highlights of the primary school is the annual holiday show. Each grade selects a country (often the country of origin of a classmate) and celebrates the country's most important holiday. Middle and upper school students attend and some are involved in production and musical elements.

The Dwight School is one of the few New York area schools to offer the International Baccalaureate diploma. As described in the brochure, "11th grade students may enroll in this challenging curriculum in six subjects requiring solid academic skills and the ability to think clearly and communicate effectively. The IB curriculum is a deliberate compromise between the specialization required in some national systems and the breadth preferred in others." Foreign students planning to return to their countries of origin are often required to have passed the "bac." The IB program is acknowledged as an excellent preparation for the more competitive U.S. colleges and can often represent a year's college credit.

The school believes that everyone has the capacity to excel at some endeavor. The curriculum that Dwight has used in the lower and middle schools for over twenty years, relates to Dr. Howard Gardner's theories of "Multiple Intelligence." (See Glossary) The Dwight School also appreciates the differences in students' learning styles and utilizes a "multi-sensory" approach.

In addition, the low student/teacher ratio (12:1) allows for small classes and individual attention. The faculty create many of the imaginative programs that prepare students to think critically while demonstrating common sense, the ability to work with others and manage time, people and information.

"Any child can succeed here," says Mr. Spahn. "We can take an average youngster and motivate him, provide positive reinforcement and transform him into a learner." There is nearly constant communication between the school and the families. "We welcome comments," Mr. Spahn says. "We have an open door policy." Parents say the warm, dedicated faculty come in early and leave late—help is there when help is needed. Student progress is monitored through standardized tests including the SATs. Grades are given on most work in the upper houses (grades). Parents meet with teachers three times a year.

Some students who are really struggling in the fast-paced, highly competitive independent middle and high schools transfer to Dwight, resulting not only in better grades, but improved self-esteem as well. A student who transferred into Dwight from Dalton said, "At Dwight teachers and peers give you lots of attention; everybody knows your name. Dwight has a traditional curriculum. They don't offer as many courses, but there is more structure." One mother said her daughter went from "just keeping up" at her old school to "doing very well at Dwight." The amount of homework was the same, about two to three hours, but she made honor roll. "She got so much out of it," says her mother, "real values and friendships." One parent whose child had a vision problem said it was handled so that her child never felt bad about herself.

Getting in: Upon request, parents can tour The Dwight School before filing an application. Once an application is filed the child's current transcripts are requested. The school will call the parents to arrange dates for their child's interview and a parent tour. Parents say the setting is relaxed. All applicants have a one-on-one interview. Applicants spend part of the day visiting classes.

Program: Dwight is described as "a family school" with many siblings in attendance. The lower school is small; all of the primary schoolchildren know each other and the teachers. However, some European formality prevails, as the teachers are addressed as "Mr. Jones" or "Miss Smith." In the after-school clubs a first grader can get to know a fourth grader. Because reading and math are taught on an individual basis, a child can advance at his or her own pace.

Perhaps the most distinctive feature of The Dwight School, in the words of a student, is that "there is no norm here." The student body is composed of children from diverse cultural, religious and geographic backgrounds. There is also a broad spectrum of academic ability at Dwight: a talented and superior group of international students who take advantage of a well-arranged ESL program and the opportunity to take the rigorous International Baccalaureate; average students taking the regular college preparatory curriculum and students with mild learning difficulties who are taking regular college prep with the support of the Quest program. There is a positive emphasis on differences. But all see themselves as part of the school.

The Quest program was started at Anglo-American in 1976 to provide additional support for children with minor learning problems (not behavior problems) so that they could participate in a full college preparatory curriculum without having to go to a tutor every day after school. All Dwight students are expected to develop a solid foundation of basic skills but the teachers at Dwight understand that children learn differently. Quest teachers provide extra support outside and within the classroom allowing students to be part of the group. Approximately 15 percent of the school is involved in the Quest program and parents must pay an additional fee for Quest program specialists. A parent said, "The teacher-student relationships are very personal and caring. The individuality of the students is stressed." Parents say that the program instills confidence: "My child thinks that he's a good learner now," said one parent. Parents with children enrolled in the Quest program say that reports are informative and elaborate with over thirty categories. Parents also learn the results of special testing in speech, reading and hearing.

The Quest program can serve students with mixed abilities; for instance, one student who is in the Quest program for science takes the International Baccalaureate course in history. Quest teachers also provide enrichment in English during the schoolday. Foreign students taking English as a second language often need assistance in certain subject areas.

The Timothy House students (grades K–4) play in Central Park or the gym every day. Reading is taught using an individualized eclectic

211

approach. A combination of literature, phonetics and basal readers is used through third grade. First graders use invented spelling but the work we saw on display was corrected. There are spelling tests every Friday in first grade. Lower school students have computers in their classrooms. Writing is incorporated into all areas of the curriculum: In addition to science and social studies reports, daily diaries are kept. Second through fourth graders use Writers Workshop, in which they learn the steps for effective essay writing: brainstorming, first draft, editing, final draft. Timothy House students study French.

Lower school students go to the art and music rooms twice a week. There is a darkroom, a music room and a painting annex.

Dwight's middle and upper schools are divided into three houses. Each house has its own Dean. The first class period is a House Community meeting. Advisors are selected by matching students and teachers.

"Bentley House" is composed of grades five through eight. Average class size is fourteen to fifteen students. Study skills are taught in fourth and fifth grades. Students learn how to prepare for tests and quizzes. In addition to the usual academic offerings, all students take art and music. Fifth graders study ancient Egypt and Greece. They read such classic children's literature as *Charlotte's Web* and *Treasure Island*. They are introduced to LOGO and word processing on the computer. (Spahn says that when handwriting is a problem, the student can write on a word processor and the ideas flow.) Spanish and French conversation and culture are introduced.

Sixth graders study the history of Europe from ancient Rome until the early eighteenth century. Latin is introduced in this year. Hebrew is offered after school. Seventh graders read *Of Mice and Men* and *Animal Farm*. In mathematics they study pre-algebra and algebra I. Native Americans and American history as well as geography are part of the curriculum. Life science and the environment are part of the science curriculum along with a health course.

There is an honor roll. There are intramural and mini-junior varsity teams. Extracurricular activities include Photography, Riding, Drama, Chorus, Newspaper, Yearbook, and the Dwight Environmental Action Committee.

"Franklin House" is composed of grades nine and ten. Students learn computer programming—Hypercard and Pascal. A course is offered in world cultures, "a thematic study of global diversity: Latin America, Africa and Asia." Tenth graders write a weekly essay in English class and complete a research paper. There is an honors humanities course in which students do readings in historical and political classics. The study of foreign language in Franklin House expands to include Spanish, French, Italian for native speakers, Latin, Japanese and Hebrew.

The ninth grade human relations course covers the issues of substance abuse and AIDS awareness. Counselors will not break a confidence if a student wishes to discuss a personal issue.

"Anglo House" is composed of grades eleven and twelve. Students are prepared for the SAT and achievement tests in English, mathematics, history and language. In response to student interest Dwight has added courses in constitutional law, military history, psychology, sports medicine and physiology and filmmaking. There are AP and/or IB courses in computer science, chemistry, physics, biology, art, English, Drama, music and foreign languages.

For students interested in science and the study of medicine, Dwight offers internships and courses at Memorial Sloan-Kettering Hospital and Rockefeller University. In 1993 a group of students worked in a cancer research laboratory. One student participated in the creation of the shark exhibit at the American Museum of Natural History.

The Adventure-Based Curriculum for grades five through twelve offers various outdoor experiences including orienteering, whitewater rafting, backpacking and caving. The Adventure-Based Curriculum has a three-part goal: 1. To develop the student's maturity and ability to interact with groups; 2. To impart key academic concepts in new and innovative ways; 3. To familiarize and acclimatize a primarily urban group of young people to the natural world.

The school considers building character an important part of its mission through community service, extracurricular activities, and sports. The Dwight Sports Institute works with students who have the talent and determination to become potential world class athletes and provides them with a flexible academic program combined with superior coaching. Self-esteem is bolstered through participation in athletics, and Dwight's trophy case is full. Dwight has a championship boys basketball team and championship soccer and softball teams as well as strong girls volleyball and basketball teams. The track and baseball programs are being expanded. Scholar-athletes at Dwight have included six ranked tennis players and a women's U.S. Sailing champion. Students can play on mini-junior varsity, junior varsity or varsity teams.

Students are encouraged to participate in extracurricular activities including the Model U.N., Newspaper, yearbook, Inward and Outward Bound, the literary magazine and social service.

Popular College Choices Brown, Columbia, Dartmouth, Bowdoin, Boston University, Ithaca College, Cornell, Georgetown, Miami University, MIT, Northwestern, NYU, Syracuse University

Traditions Science Fair, History Research Paper Competition, Art Exhibition, Camerer Essay Writing Contest, Shakespeare Competition, Doris Post Oratory Competition, annual Benefit Gala, Bronx Zoo trips, assemblies with guest speakers, International Food Fair, International Street Fair, Inward and Outward Bound, Model U.N., Spring Arts Festival, holiday show

Publications *Camerer Essays* (winning essays from the Camerer Essay Writing Contest)
Yearbook
Literary magazine
Dwight School newspaper: *Dwightonian*

Community Service Requirement All students are required to do community service; in addition to the Community Service Club, Dwight students volunteer in soup kitchens, Dwight Environmental Action Committee, Make-A-Wish Foundation, tutoring, SAVE THE CHILDREN

Hangouts Micro Grill, Columbus Star, McDonald's

The East Manhattan School for Bright and Gifted Children

208-210 East 18th Street
New York, NY 10003
(212) 475-8671, FAX (212) 477-9151

Coed
Toddlers (9 mos)–6th grade
Not accessible

Mrs. Irina Pigott, Director and
Director of Admissions

Birthday Cutoff   Toddlers must be 9 months old by September of the year they enroll
Children entering Nursery School must be 2.6 years by September
Kindergarten: No firm cutoff; it depends on the child's readiness

Enrollment   Total enrollment: 135
Nursery and Kindergarten total enrollment: 59
Kindergarten places: approximately 10-15
Graduating class size: approximately 5 to 10

Tuition Range 1998–1999 $3,600 (pre-Nursery three days a week) through $11,900 (full day) $7,000 (half day); includes hot lunch but there are additional fees

Financial Aid/Scholarship   Limited. Agency for Child Development (ADC) vouchers are available for some families in need

Endowment   None

After-School Program   Early morning program from 8:00 A.M.- 9:00 A.M., afternoon program until 6:00 P.M. A variety of recreational and creative activities including weekly singing class, Tumbling Time, computer, homework help; open to children from other schools; an additional payment is required. Holiday Program

Summer Program   Summer in The City Program: Two four-week sessions in July and August. Half-day program also available. A

215

variety of recreational and creative activities including field trips and swimming

———

The East Manhattan School was founded in 1968 by the current director, Irina Pigott, a worldly woman who speaks with a hint of a Russian accent, to nourish the creative potential of bright young children. The school is situated in the historic Gramercy-Stuyvesant District in two four-story converted brownstone houses. Helen Hayes, the late actress, and Anthony Haden-Guest are listed as sponsoring members of the Board. The slightly disheveled classrooms still reverberate with an arty sixties ethos.

In addition to ten classrooms the school has a gym, kitchen (hot lunch is eaten in the classrooms), library and art room and a backyard with structures (a castle, stagecoach and space shuttle) for imaginative play. The NYNEX multimedia center contains four IBM computers and CD-ROMs.

Getting in: Open Houses are held at various times of the year. Young children are admitted based on "their potential with much consideration given to their personality and interests as well as to the parents' acceptance and understanding of the school's philosophy and willingness to support it in its practices."

The school's brochure states: "We believe in the innate giftedness of almost all children" and "Almost all children can have a superior mind, irrespective of their origin, socio-economic background or gender." Still the school's admissions process selects students based on superior I.Q. scores.

Children four years of age or older are required to submit the results of an I.Q. test; 130 is the cutoff score but the school says it gives special consideration to demonstrated abilities or talents in a particular area. "Younger children are admitted with the belief that the school, with the cooperation of understanding parents, can discover, nurture and develop giftedness in a child."

The East Manhattan School has long incorporated poetry, drama and music into the curriculum. The first thing you notice when you enter, aside from the classical music playing in the background, is the "portrait gallery" wall of the schoolchildren in full dress personifying mythical and historical figures. There is almost a Diane Arbus-like quality in the children's remarkable, though dwarfed, resemblance to their character. Shakespeare, Mother Theresa, Eleanor Roosevelt, Marian Anderson and Margaret Thatcher are among the many figures depicted. Ms. Pigott explained that the school was once situated next to a costume factory and the school took all of their discards, eventually accumulating over 2,000 costumes in its collection. The costumes are used as part of the school's annual Winter Shows. Every year the students dramatize a different theme: "Democracy and its Birth and Development," "Women in History," "Composers," and "Revolutions Around the World" are some themes from past years. Another big event at The East Manhattan School is the annual Spring International Luncheon: a feast of foreign foods and art. Parents are asked to contribute a dish representative of their culture and also to share their talents (dancing, singing, performing).

Of course the traditional subject areas are covered at the school. There is an awareness of current events: the fourth through sixth grades took part in a computer simulation project on the topic of Arab-Israeli Conflict.

Some of the curriculum seemed rushed to us, even if most of the children are "gifted." For example, students in the first grade were already memorizing their times tables while still mastering addition and subtraction. Reading is taught with the understanding that developmental readiness varies even amongst bright children. Parents with children in the school must have faith that Ms. Pigott, who has a Masters in Early Childhood Education from NYU, and many years of experience, knows what she's doing.

In order to chart their progress, the school requires students to take the Metropolitan Achievement Tests each year. There are no grades in the school but written narratives go home once a year and there are two parent/teacher conferences.

About half of the graduates attend various public school programs, the rest go on to independent schools including Saint Ann's and Dalton.

The Ethical Culture Fieldston School

The Ethical Culture Fieldston School encompass three schools: Ethical Culture School, Fieldston Lower School and the Fieldston School. Each school has its own principal and there is a central Administrative Committee, consisting of three principals and the heads of centralized administrative offices.

Ethical Culture School

33 Central Park West
(at 63rd Street)
New York, NY 10023
(212) 712-6220 (main number)
(212) 712-8451 (admissions)
FAX **(212) 712-8441**

Fieldston Lower School

Fieldston Road
Bronx, NY 10471
(718) 329-7300 (main number)
(718) 329-7313 (admissions)

The Fieldston School

Fieldston Road
Bronx, NY 10471
(718) 329-7300 (main number)
(718) 329-7306 (admissions)

Coed
Pre-kindergarten–12th Grade
Elevator at ECS
Fieldston Lower and Fieldston partially accessible

Dr. Joseph Healey, Director ECFS
Ms. Francine Berk, Director of Admissions and Financial Aid ECFS

Ms. Joyce Baron, Principal ECS
Ms. Carole Chaim-Owitz, Admissions ECS
Ms. Beth Beckmann, Interim Principal Fieldston Lower
Ms. Rita McRedmond, Admissions Fieldston Lower
Mr. David Shapiro, Principal Fieldston School
Ms. Taisha Thompson, Admissions Fieldston School

Uniform No uniform is required at any of the Ethical Culture Fieldston campuses

Birthday Cutoff Children entering pre-kindergarten must be 4 before the day school starts
Children entering kindergarten must be 5 before the day school starts

Enrollment Combined enrollment: 1,560
Total enrollment Midtown: 510
Total enrollment Fieldston Lower: 305
Total enrollment Fieldston: 745
Kindergarten places: approximately 36 at Midtown and 18 at Fieldston Lower
Size of graduating class: approximately 125–130

Grades Semester system
Scheduled parent-teacher conferences pre-kindergarten through 12th grade
Kindergarten–6: detailed anecdotal reports and checklists of skills. Letter grades begin in Form I (7th grade)
Grades 7–12: letter grades with teacher's comments; first final exam given in Form IV (10th grade)
Students taking accelerated science have a final exam in Form III (9th grade)

Tuition Range 1998–1999 $15,475 to $18,175, pre-kindergarten–12th grade
Additional Fees: books, supplies and other course-related expenses are approximately $250 for grades 7–12 only; lunch and yearbook are included in the tuition

Financial Aid/Scholarship The Ethical Culture Fieldston School has one of the largest financial assistance programs of any independent day school in the country. Almost $4 million was granted in 1998

23% of the students schoolwide receive some form of financial aid; there are outright grants for eligible families, pre-kindergarten through grade 12

Monthly payment plan with no interest charges available to all enrolled families.

Low-interest loans are also available

Endowment $43 million

Diversity   22% students of color throughout ECFS

30 Prep for Prep students enrolled at Fieldston School as of fall 1998

Fieldston enrolls students in the Early Steps, Albert Oliver and Summerbridge programs.

Multicultural Concerns Committees at Midtown, Fieldston Lower and Fieldston; Minority Students Association; the S.U.M.E. club (Students United for Multicultural Efforts) and *Kaleidoscope*, a multicultural club and newspaper at Fieldston

Homework   Kindergarten and 1st: no homework

2nd: $1/2$ hour and an occasional worksheet

3rd and 4th: varies from 10 minutes–45 minutes plus additional $1/2$ hour of reading each night

5th, 6th: 1–2 hours

7th and 8th: no more than 3 hours

10th–12th: $3^1/_2$-$4^1/_2$ hours a night

After-School Program   At ECS and Fieldston Lower: after-school program for kindergarten–6 with some mixed-age groups; selections include sports, cooking, drama, arts and chess (for fun) for an additional payment; classes meet from 3:30–5 P.M., Monday through Thursday; Friday after-school programs begin and end earlier. Drop off and extended hours options at ECS and Fieldston Lower. Helping Hands, and Cookies and Dreams, for grades 3–6 at ECS introduce children to community service; activities include helping at a church day-care center or Head Start Center or befriending children confined to hospitals via computer

7th and 8th: intramural sports (8th grade), extracurricular clubs, middle school newspaper and play

9th–12th: interscholastic sports, extracurricular clubs, newspapers (3), literary magazines and yearbook, two theatrical productions and several student-written and produced plays

Summer Program Winter vacation and June Weeks: a variety of creative and recreational activities are offered for an additional payment
Intensive sports camp: Fieldston campus, ages 5–13; last two weeks in June; an additional payment is required
Fieldston Outdoors Day Camp: for ages 5–12, at Riverdale campus, full activities including swim instruction; focus on nature, environment and Hudson River region; trips. Head counselors are experienced teachers, supported by college and high school assistants; an additional payment is required
Fieldston Summer Science Academy: for 10–15 year olds, fieldwork (visits to Metropolitan area sites), photo lab, computers and ecology; an additional payment is required
Fieldston Summer Service Institute: academic enrichment for public high school students
Young Dancemakers Company

———

The Ethical Culture Fieldston School was started in 1878 by Felix Adler, the founder of the Ethical Culture Society, to develop the "potentialities" in children. The school was tuition free until 1890. The school has remained true to Adler's original vision of learning by doing, and has always been diverse ethnically, racially, financially. Writes Jeanne Amster, former director of The Ethical Culture Fieldston School, "The school is faithful to its mission of providing educational excellence in a community characterized by service, tolerance and innovation." In 1994–1995 an agreement was reached separating the schools from the Society.

Today many schools boast about "educating the whole child"; it is in vogue to have a child-centered curriculum. The Ethical Culture Fieldston school has been doing this from their inception, and is way out front in developing an integrated curriculum and emphasizing experiential learning. Children are active participants in their education here. ECF offers broad-based nonsectarian moral instruction with the emphasis on ethics in action. ECF backs up its values with financial support and personal commitment. The school gives out more financial aid than most other independent day schools in the country.

Getting in: Don't be intimidated by the imposing turn-of-the-century stone edifice on Central Park West, the Ethical Culture School is a warm and friendly place. One parent described the admissions process at ECS as "humane." Parents bring their child for a group interview. The interviewer asks, "Who's ready to come and play?" "Whose name begins with A?" and so on. After some leg hanging, all the children go off to play while the parents tour the school and ask questions of the admissions personnel and/or parent guides. In 1994 Joyce Baron, former assistant principal and head of the middle school at Fieldston, became principal of ECS (midtown).

What are they looking for in a candidate? A child who feels good about himself, who is enthusiastic, who enjoys being part of a group (there's an emphasis on collaborative learning). The child should enjoy his visit. If your child was unusually cranky at the interview and you go home that night and he's got a full-blown ear infection, let them know. "Admissions looks at the nursery school report to see that it corresponds to behavior in the interview, and the ERB should reaffirm both. If a piece doesn't make sense then we have to look further," says director of admissions Fran Berk. After admissions decisions have been made, the wait list is active. There is no typical student, but one parent said the children are "bright, laid-back and outgoing."

Parents: The parents are "a low-key mix" with "some sixties throwbacks." West and East Side professionals, artists and media people predominate, "but without the pretentiousness you find at other schools," parents say. Perhaps there is a larger percentage of working mothers. Is the Ethical Culture Fieldston School just for liberals? Of course not. The child is the applicant, not the parent. But it must be acknowledged that there is a strong association between Ethical Culture and the liberal tradition and progressive thinking. For example, Killooleet, a Vermont summer camp run by the family of Pete Seeger, held its annual "Sing" at the Ethical Culture Society. The director of the camp, John Seeger, is a former principal of Fieldston Lower.

Manhattan parents should note that while Fieldson Lower School, a second ECF elementary school located in Riverdale that primarily serves families from Upper Manhattan, all sections of the Bronx, Northern New Jersey, Riverdale and Westchester, almost 15% of the students travel from Manhattan. Parents should request a copy of the Wheel Book from Fieldston Lower School which offers a true "core" curriculum, if they are interested in this unique program.

There are many opportunities to socialize, and interesting lectures are offered for parents on child-related, nonacademic topics such as discipline and allowance. There is often a Fathers' Forum. Class dinners are potluck, usually at a family's apartment. (In the high school, parent support groups are held at a parent's home with the dean for the child's grade.) Social competition is minimized and celebrity parents (there are a few) enjoy their anonymity. Parents get involved in the school in the early years and stay involved. Parent volunteers come in and take dictation for kindergarten and first graders' stories. Here, you can have lunch with your child whenever you want. Parents can help with the Fieldston Directory, used book sale or the newsletter for parents. School events include theatre parties, concerts and auctions. Birthday parties run the gamut. Three-fourths of the parents are in town over vacations or weekends, one mother said.

Program: An awareness of ethics is implicit from the moment children begin their Ethical Culture Fieldston education. Formal ethics instruction begins in second grade with environmental ethics, and continues with community responsibility and decision making. The emphasis is on ethics in action. The million-penny drive began as a math exercise at Fieldston Lower, then quickly expanded to include all three schools. The goal was to collect a million pennies, or ten thousand dollars, to give to the homeless. Children in both lower schools helped collect, sort and count. Once they'd reached their goal they had to find a bank that would take a million pennies, which they did. A committee of fourth, fifth and sixth grade students, with teacher supervision, researched the many homeless organizations and chose to give the money to three that they believed would most directly serve the people in need. Community service is part of the ECF experience, from ethics in action in the lower schools to the ninth graders who stay after school to write letters for Amnesty International.

Students serve within the school as well. Children in fourth, fifth and sixth grades work with children in the lower grades on a regular basis. Interage writing collaborations allow fourth and fifth grade editors to assist first and second grade authors to publish.

One parent described her daughter's move from nursery school to Ethical as a "warm to warm transition." Pre-kindergarten and kindergarten separation is handled gradually; parents can stay for the first week if necessary. There is a staggered schedule. It is a hands-on, experiential kindergarten. Under the guidance of two full-time teachers, children often work on group projects. For instance, one kindergarten class designed and constructed a miniature playground from cardboard, paper clips and paper.

In pre-kindergarten, children begin going out to specialists in half groups but are not fully departmentalized until sixth grade. Most "specials" (library, movement, music, computer, social studies workshop and so on) are taught by the specialist in half classes. The other half of the class either attends another special class or remains in the classroom, allowing the core teacher to work with small groups in math and writing.

Since the advent of Ms. Baron at Midtown parents say there's a new emphasis on building a collaborative approach between child/faculty and parents, a greater openness. The most noticeable change is improved articulation of the curriculum through the grades. The emphasis is still on full mastery and competence with awareness that children work at different paces. A parent told us that her son, who has exceptional ability in math, now has an enriched course. Students with exceptional talents receive an additional level of challenge and those who need extra help receive it. (Remediation and enrichment are always provided within the classroom.) Baron says, "The focus is still on what's developmentally appropriate."

During the elementary years, students learn how to gather, organize, analyze, evaluate and communicate information. The work load increases appropriately as children are guided toward internalizing the learning process and becoming independent learners.

Ethical Culture has resisted pressure from high-powered parents to "hurry" the curriculum. Departmentalization doesn't begin until sixth grade, and no final exam is given until tenth grade. (Most schools start these in seventh grade.) Parents say, "Children at Ethical Culture develop a positive attitude about learning, which prepares them for the academically demanding high school." Proof that children with different learning styles can find success here is that more than 95 percent go on to the Fieldston School, which is considered a "very selective" high school. It is one of the three "hill" schools (along with Riverdale Country School and Horace Mann School) located in Riverdale, New York, just north of the city proper—a twenty minute drive that might take forty-five minutes at some hours. The catalog describing the curriculum in the early years states, "Our first aim is to provide an anxiety-free environment"; the development of self-esteem is as important to the later learning process as the acquisition of skills. Every activity in the lower school is coed. No basal textbooks are used in the first years. Homework is given in appropriate amounts, not as busywork or evidence of academic rigor. Some parents, who grew up in schools that stressed rote memorization and drill, are a little perplexed by these methods and a commonly voiced concern is, "Is my child learning enough?" They can be reassured that standardized diagnostic and achievement tests are given and regular assessments are made, so the school knows exactly where ECF students stand in relation to their peers at other schools. Second graders do have spelling tests, and begin to learn how to write a research paper.

While there is a definite curriculum for each grade, Ethical's developmental approach to learning anticipates that not everyone will get to the same place at the same time. Children learn at their own pace. The catalog says, "Emphasis is placed on conceptual development along with sequential and spiraling skills work in reading, writing and math." Because the program is responsive to children's needs and interests, it varies from year to year. Most of the children will learn to read in the first grade. From pre-kindergarten on, you see words all over the classroom. Kindergartners and first graders keep a daily response journal; they can fold in half what is private. The teacher responds to what the child has written. There is mixed-ability grouping throughout the school and at various times throughout the week students break into half groups. Ethical Culture and Fieldston Lower both have have math consultants, and have recently adapted a new problem solving based math program, Investigations in Number and Data and Space. There is math lab. On one blackboard was written: "fifteen reasons to learn math" (practical applications suggested by the children).

The Ethical Culture School has three science centers: one is a fully equipped laboratory with sinks, microscopes and computers. Wherever possible, science is hands-on and the scientific process is stressed: collect data, analyze it, construct a hypothesis, test it, reach a conclusion. In one classroom the students were studying the use of earthworms for indoor composting. On visiting day parents can crawl through a tunnel into the Star Lab, an inflatable planetarium brought into the classroom that illustrates the constellations. Fifth and sixth grade students chart the constellations on the computer. The school is in the midst of a five year plan to enhance the level of technology in the classrooms, establishing common areas for the use of technology, and creating "libraries without walls," i.e., information network accessibility to and from classrooms, homes, major universities, as well as Library of Congress. The computer curriculum focus on computers as tools to expand thinking and problem solving skills. The computer coordinator works with the classroom teachers. The curriculum for the fourth through sixth grade focuses on the ethics of computer use, use of spreadsheets, databases, word processing, drawing, painting and animation and on-line communications. Internet use is taught and access is provided under supervision. LOGO programming is introduced in fourth grade and continued in increasingly sophisticated ways through sixth. CD-ROMs are integrated into classroom, library and computer room instruction.

Ethical says it educates the "whole child," bringing out his or her natural creativity and encouraging its expression. The creative arts are considered intellectual disciplines; it follows that the arts at Ethical are strong. Four full-time workshop teachers are available; there is an art studio with a pottery center equipped with a kiln. Art is integrated into the curriculum at many points. Social studies workshop, a hands-on program relating to the social studies core, includes woodworking, sewing and cooking.

A hallmark of education at the ECS is an integrated curriculum, with subject areas overlapping in many different ways. Creativity and writing ability are also fostered. These elements combine in dramatic play. As part of the kindergarten curriculum, children learn that people live in communities, including the home, classroom, school, as well as the larger world. One classroom creates a bakery. They bake breads, and run a classroom café. Another class sets up a school-wide post office.

Critical thinking skills are emphasized from early on. A fifth grade class studying Greek myths switched the gender roles—Hercules became a she—and there was much discussion about the implications. There are many ways in which students are asked to examine the underlying assumptions about our culture. A parent told us that when a student brought in a Barbie doll for a model science fiction project the class got into a discussion about cultural artifacts: If Barbie were found by an advanced civilization, what conclusions would be drawn about our civilization? Students brought in other objects. A fifth grade class studying ancient Egypt and Rome had a discussion about heroes. "Malcolm X, Superman and Audrey Hepburn" were some of the names written on the board. At Fieldston Lower, fifth grades have a Medieval Fair; one class built a model cathedral and played roles in the social hierarchy of the time.

Ethical has two full-size gyms: the sixth-floor gym, which is large enough to be subdivided, and a spectator gym with an overhead track, on the lower level. The gym program stresses individual skills development, games and sportsmanship. Ethical makes use of its location next to Central Park in many ways. The park is used as a laboratory and of course, the children get to play in the snow and mark the changing of the seasons. Fieldston Lower first graders become experts in North American bird life. Third graders in both lower schools enact the lives of the Northern Woodland Indians who once inhabited the school's site.

The Fieldston School is "a big school that seems small." In good weather, the grassy quad surrounded by fieldstone buildings is full of students. But the "Graduation Grass" is not to be trod upon from mid-April until graduation. Freshmen can leave school premises during their free periods and lunch. The Tate Library is a beautiful facility (students say it's the best of the three "hill" school libraries) with almost 50,000 volumes, and Proquest and Dialogue search systems. It also houses a multimedia center. Unique to Fieldston are an observatory with a mirror telescope and a state-of-the-art print shop where everything from invitations to personal notepads are printed. In the spirit of founder Felix Adler, who believed in learning by doing, Fieldston is the only school that produces its own school publications from composition to final product. There are no bells, dress is casual and students seem relaxed. But by first form (seventh grade), college preparation has begun in earnest.

Fieldston's course guide is clear, descriptive and informative. The curriculum is broad, with electives that reflect a diversity of interests in the student body. Requirements are similar to those of the other independent high schools: a minimum of five academic courses per semester, with more elective choices as the students progress. Students do make choices about their academic careers; ninth graders have electives in language, arts and science. By senior year students can choose electives in English, math, history, language, science, art, music or computer. Six year sequences are offered in French, Spanish, and Latin, beginning in seventh grade. Conversational Spanish is part of the Fieldston Lower experience. Courses are offered in Modern and Ancient Greek as well. An ethics course is required each year in forms I through IV (grades 7–10). AP courses are offered in all areas.

Although independence is fostered in the high school, support is always available. A tenth grader said that she could talk to her advisor about anything and that students feel "the administration is on your side." Respect for individual learning styles continues at Fieldston, and the Learning Center helps students with individual learning differences. Generous grants established a Writing Center and History Writing Center where English and history teachers and peer instructors are always available. Students can also meet with teachers during free periods. Outside tutors are recommended if necessary but in the words of one student, "Most people don't hire a tutor unless it's a desperate situation." Students say that although a lot is expected of them and they work hard, homework is not oppressive. One student said she has friends who are "drowning in work" at other schools.

Elective choices in English include "Social and Political Issues," "African-American Literature," "Southern Literature" "Russian Literature" "Women and Literature" "Dramatic Literature" and "Theatre in the Modern World." Course offerings change annually.

All seventh graders are required to take "Patterns in Human History," an anthropologically based course. Survey courses in eighth through tenth grades provide a solid footing for later electives, which may include: "The Middle East," "African Studies," "African-American History," "China" and "Russian Civilization."

For students who are proficient in math there is a six-year unified mathematics sequence as well as "Calculus AB," "Calculus BC" and many offerings in computer science.

At Fieldston there is a continued commitment to the artistic development of the students. As at Ethical, the arts at Fieldston are considered an essential part of the curriculum and the offerings are extensive. Seventh graders begin with a visual arts sampler. In tenth, eleventh and twelfth grades an art major is available. Elective offerings include "Pottery Studio," "Life Drawing" (with live models), "Architectural Drawing" and "3D Art."

Also available to high school students is ALP (Alternative Learning Period), a Tuesday program of academic and nonacademic activities outside the traditional classroom setting.

Dance at Fieldston is considered a key part of the performing arts program. In addition to modern, jazz and ballet, electives include "Movement for Actors," and "Performing Arts Intensive." Fieldston football players take dance to improve their balance and coordination. There are numerous opportunities to perform: The dance company tours and there is an annual dance concert with student choreography.

Students who like drama can take advantage of a well-developed theatre program. There is a theatre concentration for juniors and seniors. There are four student-directed shows every year, plus one major drama (*The Crucible* one year) and a musical (*Into the Woods* one year). Students can take a course in stagecraft and practice their skills in the Alex Cohen Memorial Theatre. The drama and dance groups tour elementary schools. All seventh graders must study a musical instrument or sing in an ensemble. Upper school students can elect an arts, music or jazz major. Small group and ensemble instruction is available.

In addition to arts there is a full athletic program. Fieldston has a three season interscholastic sports program for eighth graders. Ninth through twelfth graders have a full interscholastic sports schedule, including strong teams in girls' field hockey, boys' cross-country and boys' basketball. Fieldston has two large gyms, four tennis courts, a weight room and a renovated pool. There is a healthy competitive spirit. One student said, "At Fieldston team sports are for fun; at Riverdale and Horace Mann they're out for blood." That doesn't mean Fieldston doesn't play to win. The Collegiate-Fieldston basketball game draws a good crowd, and the baseball team won the Ivy Prep League Championship in 1997–1998. During football season the school mascot, the Eagle, walks around campus. Homecoming is a major event at Fieldston. First there is a pep rally the day before big games, which besides football include soccer, tennis and field hockey. A cabaret talent show is held the night before, with a big party afterward. One year at the annual Halloween costume parade, Fieldston Principal David Shapiro dressed as an injured Horace Mann football player.

Student government is the PAC or Principal's Advisory Committee, a longstanding organization that meets regularly to discuss academic and social affairs. Many students will never forget the AIDS awareness assembly when Alison Gertz spoke to Fieldston students. One year students initiated a program to get teachers to bring a mug from home instead of using Styrofoam cups. The money saved was donated to a charity to benefit the environment. PAC also deals with social aspects of life at Fieldston and the bolstering of school spirit. PAC recently organized a fall barbecue and Big Brother, Big Sister program to foster relationships between the grades. In addition to SAC there is STS, a student-to-student counseling program. In the high school there are electives in ethics including an advanced course in peer leadership.

Tolerance and respect for difference are at the heart of Fieldston, and by and large relations between different groups are harmonious. One student said, "Fieldston is a lot more politically correct than other schools: I've become a lot more aware here." There is a multicultural club and magazine and a new Gay and Straight Alliance Club. Concerns about the voluntary separation of ethnic groups have led to a variety of responses: multicultural dinners, cultural awareness assemblies. At an awareness assembly on race relations actor Giancarlo

Esposito spoke to a rapt audience about the importance of getting along. Hugo Mahabir, Director of Multicultural Programs says, "The Office of Multicultural Programs supports and enhances the school's commitment to building a diverse community and develops in students a respect for others and knowledge of cultural diversity as students prepare to inherit a pluralistic and complex world." The Director serves as an advisor to students and as a resource for the faculty in working with students and parents from many different backgrounds.

There are over thirty clubs at Fieldston that vary from year to year, depending on the interests of the student body. An activity period is built into the school day so that students can participate in a club and perform in a school play or compete in interscholastic sports. Some recent clubs are the ever-popular Model U.N., Students for Change (Democratic politics) and S.H.O.P. (Students Helping Other People— community service). There is even a Lawn Sports Society Club.

Politically aware, Fieldston students flew yellow flags during the Gulf War; in the 1996 schoolwide election, Clinton won by a landslide.

David Shapiro, principal at Fieldston, said, "There is an overall emphasis on the process of learning at Fieldston: thinking, doing reflecting. What they learn here they take out of the classroom and into the world."

Popular College Choices   Brown, Columbia, Connecticut College, University of Wisconsin, Wesleyan, Cornell, Oberlin, University of Pennsylvania, Tufts, Vassar, Harvard, Haverford, Skidmore, Radcliffe, Yale

Traditions   Theatre party, Parents' and Grandparents' Visiting Day, auction, Toy Fair, potluck dinner, Swimathon, Ballathon, carnivals, Founder's Day, cabaret talent show, spring musical, Halloween costume parade through the Quad, 7th graders being called "Firsties," "Graduation Grass" on the Quad, homecoming football game, homecoming party and pep rally, Awareness Days, school song sung in Latin

Publications   Yearbook
Newspaper: *The Fieldston News* (since 1929)
Newspaper: *The Fieldston Chronicle* (about the impact of events outside school on Fieldston)
Multicultural paper: *Kaleidoscope*
Literary magazine: *Semprini*

Alternative literary magazine: *The Ice Weasel*
Alumni paper: *The ECF Reporter*
Art magazines
All Ethical Culture Fieldston publications, including the year-book, are printed at Fieldston's own printing press

Community Service Requirement 60 school hours or 120 summer hours beginning in 9th grade; Super Saturday, a day of community services activities; S.H.O.P. (Students Helping Other People)

Hangouts The Quad, student-faculty center, Jasper's Pizza, the little Irish café with music, Riverdale Diner (if you have a car), The Sandwich Shack, the cafeteria for breakfast

The Family School

323 East 47th Street
New York, NY 10017
(212) 688-5950, FAX (212) 980-2475

The Family School West

308 West 46th Street
New York, NY 10036
(212) 582-1240

Coed
Nursery (18 mos) through 6th grade
Not accessible

Mrs. Lesley Nan Haberman, Headmistress
Mrs. Ann Baker Reed, Director of Admissions

Birthday Cutoff   Children entering nursery school must be 18 mos by September 1st
Children entering kindergarten must be 5 by September 1st

Enrollment   Total enrollment: 140
Nursery places: 24 (18 mos-3 years)
Kindergarten places: 20
Graduating class size: 8–10

Tuition Range 1998–1999
FAMILY SCHOOL EAST
Toddler Program (18 mos-3 yrs): 2 Half Days—$4,500; 5 Full Days (8:30 A.M.–3:00 P.M.)—$10,000
Pre-Primary Program (3, 4, 5 yrs):
2 Half Days—$4,700; 5 Full Days (8:30 A.M.–3:00 P.M.)—$10,200
Elementary Program (6–12 yrs)—$10,500
Enriched Extended Day (3:00–6:00 P.M.)—$3,000
FAMILY SCHOOL WEST (2½–7 yrs): 2 Half Days—$4,100; 5 Full Days (8:30 A.M.–3:00 P.M.)—$9,200
Enriched Extended Day (3:00–6:00 P.M.)—$3,000

Additional payment is required for children with special needs who require additional support

Financial Aid/Scholarship   None

Endowment   None

After-School Program   Monday through Friday, 3:00–6:00 P.M., supervised homework time and a variety of recreational and creative activities for an additional payment; vacation programs are also available

Summer Program   Weekly camp program from mid-June through the end of August, 8:45 A.M.–5:45 P.M.; a variety of recreational and creative activities and academic maintenance, weekly field trips, older campers swim three times a week; if families enroll for the entire summer they receive one week free

---

Founded in 1975 by the current Headmistress Lesley Nan Haberman, The Family School East is a member of the American Montessori Society. "We call ourselves eclectic Montessori," explained the admissions director; a comfort to those who think of pure Montessori as too rigid. All of the teachers are certified Montessori teachers and traditional Montessori materials are used in the classrooms. Children are placed in heterogeneous mixed age groupings, also characteristic of the Montessori approach.

Getting in: Nursery candidates are interviewed. Applicants to kindergarten and above are required to take the ERB.

The Family School was founded as a nursery school, added a toddler and elementary school program, and now serves children through twelve years of age. The Family School is housed in a bright, up-to-date (and meticulously clean) building adjacent to the Holy Family Church. Although the school rents space from the church there is no religious affiliation. The school has a large gym downstairs but children also play outdoors in McArthur Park next to the United Nations building. Children bring their own bag lunch and a snack is provided by the school. The Family School West serves twenty children (ages 2½ through 7) in a one room school house, the former gym of a Lutheran Church.

As its name suggests, The Family School is an inclusive, warm community. The students come from all parts of the city. Some parents commute to work in the neighborhood. Thirty-five percent of the student body is composed of children of color. The school also has a limited program for children with special needs, some of whom receive additional support services.

In a pre-primary classroom (ages three to six) each day begins with the morning circle. Children then choose materials and work either independently or in a small group. Areas of study include geography, math and practical life. Children experiment in all art media, and the school has a kiln and potters wheel. Music and foreign language classes enrich the curriculum, and creativity is encouraged. Examples of the children's work adorn the walls of the school. In the primary school children continue learning in a practical context (for example using math manipulatives) and begin to move toward the understanding of abstract concepts. Reading is taught using several methods including the use of "Mack and Tab" readers.

Parents receive written narratives twice a year and the ERB is offered each spring. The school-parent partnership is an essential component of the Montessori experience and parent-teacher conferences are held three times a year. Parent classroom observations are mandatory.

School traditions include Grandparent's Day, holiday programs and Family Field Day in Central Park's Sheep Meadow.

On-going school choices include independent schools such as Riverdale, Dalton, and Browning; and various public school programs.

Friends Seminary

222 East 16th Street
New York, NY 10003
(212) 979-5030, FAX 979-5034
website: www.fsnyc.k12.ny.us

Coed
Kindergarten–12th grade
Partially accessible

Richard Eldridge, Principal
Harriet Burnett, Director of Admissions

Uniform   None

Birthday Cutoff   Children entering kindergarten must be 5 by September 1
Children entering first grade must be 6 by September 1

Enrollment   Total enrollment: 600
Kindergarten places: 38
6th grade places: 18
9th grade places: 20–25
Graduating class size: approximately 54

Grades   Semester system
Lower, middle and upper schools: conferences and written reports
Letter grades begin in 9th grade
Departmentalization begins in 5th grade and is completed by 7th grade
Final exams begin in 7th grade

Tuition Range 1998–1999 $15,150 to $16,175, kindergarten–12th grade
Additional fees: Building Improvement Fund, PTA dues, accident insurance, beverage plan, $860. Books and supplies are additional after 8th grade
There is an optional lunch program

Financial Aid/Scholarship   26% of students receive some form of financial aid

Endowment $3.5 million

Diversity   20% students of color
14 Prep for Prep students enrolled as of Fall 1998
Friends participates actively in the Early Steps, Prep for Prep
Albert G. Oliver, and ABC (A Better Chance) programs
Friends Seminary was the recipient of a DeWitt Wallace–
Reader's Digest Fund ISOP Grant. This grant was used to establish additional tuition aid funds for needy students of color, to
actively recruit new teachers of color, and to establish programs
related to cultural diversity
CARE (Cultural Awareness Reaching Everyone) is a student-run
organization that "takes an active role in discussing and educating
the community about cultural diversity"
Director of Multi-Cultural Affairs: liaison for both students and
parents; Multicultural Parents Committee and the Multicultural
Faculty Committee provide a forum for issues of concern
Student-led "Day of Concern" (most recent topic: Race in America)
Student committee on gender issues

Homework   Begins gently in 1st grade
2nd and 3rd: 20–30 minutes per night
4th: $1/2$–1 hour per night
5th and 6th: up to 1–$1^1/2$ hours per night
7th and 8th: up to 2–$2^1/2$ hours per night
9th–12th: up to 4 hours per night

After-School Program   Early Bird Program: 8:00 A.M. to 8:45 A.M.
Friends After Three Program: 5 days a week for ages 4–9; creative
and athletic activities from 3:00 P.M.–4:30 P.M., Monday–Friday
Extended coverage available until 5:30 P.M. each day
Vacation program during school breaks
All of the above programs require an additional payment
Athletics: middle school intramural sports, upper school junior
varsity and varsity team sports

Summer Program   Summer Friends: A three-week program in
June, open to lower and middle school-age children from all over
the city, offering a variety of recreational and creative activities

Friends Seminary is the oldest continuing coeducational day school in New York City, yet it is hardly the most traditional. Friends is distinguished by its Quaker heritage. Founded in 1786, Friends is owned by the New York Quarterly Meeting of the Religious Society of Friends. The brochure says: "Administering the school is viewed as a team effort." There is a principal rather than a headmaster. Friends provides a value-based program that is centered on the tenets of Quaker philosophy: The belief in each person's unique strengths and possibilities; the value of community and the individual's role within the community; decision-making by consensus; and the peaceful resolution of conflict.

Richard Eldridge, a Quaker, has been the Principal of Friends for over nine years. Mr. Eldridge is described as "gregarious, charming, intensely focused and spiritual." One parent said: "His office is a welcoming place; he's always quoting something wise and thoughtful and knows all of the kids' names." Another parent said that at Friends "there are no walls up around anyone; my children feel free to go to the lower school head if they are having a problem."

Academically, Friends begins gently and becomes increasingly rigorous as students progress. A former Parents' Association president told us: "Friends is not a socially competitive school but Friends does create competitive students."

Getting in: Parents are invited to tour Friends before making application to the school. For kindergarten and first grade, a group of six students meet with two teachers for one hour during which time each family has a twenty-minute interview. Friends is a very popular choice not only for downtown parents but also for families throughout the city, and admissions are competitive. Preference is given to members of the New York Quarterly Meeting of the Religious Society of Friends. There is a sibling and legacy policy for qualified candidates but admission is not automatic; one parent told us her daughter was deferred a year even though she had an older sibling at Friends. There is a wait list.

Parents: Parents talk about the family feeling at Friends. One mother described the school as "a community of shared values. Everyone is on a first-name basis." There is a buddy system to help parents get involved in the school. Parents say there are more working mothers than not. Fathers are very involved in the school; in fact, several fathers serve as class representatives and pick up their children at day's end. In response to the changing needs of two-career families, Friends provides programs before and after school and during vacations.

Socially the parents are very low-key; there is a form of reverse snobbery: "Downtowners don't flaunt," we were told. A prominent parent in the media business makes a point to park his limo down the block and walk his child into the school. "Nobody really knows who's wealthy," says one parent.

The Friends Fair is an annual spring event made possible through the efforts of hundreds of parents and students. In addition to the Friends Fair, there is an auction every other year and annual class potluck suppers. Many Friends parents remain involved long after their children have graduated; the book sale is still run by a parent who no longer has any children in the school. Because it is a Quaker school, raffles and games of chance are prohibited. A capital campaign is in place to raise money for improved technology, faculty salaries, financial aid, and a new upper school science, math and technology facility which opened in September 1998.

Friends parents really feel they have a voice. Throughout the year the PTA sponsors dialogue meetings for each division of the school. Examples of topics discussed include seventh graders and their need for independence, the role of the advisor, substance abuse and conflict resolution. Recently the PTA has inaugurated a PTA-community service partnership in which parents and students work together in support of a specific community service project.

Program: "Quaker philosophy permeates the school and after you've been there a while you recognize it," said one parent. Service to the community is important at Friends. It begins in kindergarten and extends through grade twelve. Walking through the hallways you might see eighth graders working with first graders; fifth graders serving family-style meals to lower schoolers, and parents working with students of all ages in workshops to decorate bags for God's Love We Deliver. At night, a common room at Friends is used to shelter and feed the homeless. A few years ago, when some parents expressed fears about tuberculosis, alterations were made to the building to provide adequate ventilation rather than do away with the program.

Quaker Meeting is the heart and soul of the school. Meeting is a time for students and teachers to come together in silence, and if moved to do so, to share thoughts and feelings with their community. In lower school, Meeting takes place in the classroom during the first five minutes of circle time. In the middle and upper schools, Meeting is held in the landmarked Meeting House. Middle school Meeting always begins with ten minutes of silence, followed by announcements, assemblies and so on. Upper schoolers have silent Meeting twice a week for twenty-five minutes. Most of these Meetings focus on relevant issues and school business. The mother of a fifth grader says, "Everybody thinks that because it's a Quaker school there are hours of silence, but that's not so; Meeting is a quiet time to come together and discuss the day, to hear announcements." A former PTA president said that "even the shy child will speak out and feel comfortable at Meeting." Parents are invited to attend Meeting whenever they can.

In the lower school, Friends is concerned with academics as well as with the child's emotional and psychological needs. Friends recognizes that children learn at their own pace and that the development of good self-esteem early on will lead to later success. Mixed-age grouping supports this thinking and is an important aspect of the lower school program. Although you will find an age span of almost a year within a grade at most traditional schools, at Friends chronological age does not determine placement. The aim of mixed-age grouping (which covers a two-year age span) is to help "students master skills at the appropriate level in their development." In the early years some students benefit from being the oldest in a class, others learn well from older peers. Placement is considered carefully at Friends. Teachers know their students well and consider a variety of factors before making placement decisions. A father told us that his children's reports were "wonderful, detailed, with a huge space for comments."

Parents say the emphasis at Friends is on learning how to learn. "Students don't just memorize the date of a battle but rather what really happened at the battle," said one. "Learning is an ongoing process," said another. "My daughter's teacher said, 'Just because you turn it in doesn't mean it's over.' " Some parents whose own educations stressed rote memorization have asked, "Are they getting enough facts?" But while the students may not realize that when they are measuring and baking they are using mathematics, this integrated approach to education in the lower school is becoming the norm in even the most traditional schools.

The lower school classroom is a "combination of teacher-directed instruction and self-directed exploration and learning." Children spend much of their time working in groups toward a common goal (collaborative learning), and learning is hands-on whenever possible. No one approach to the teaching of reading is used because teachers consider the approach that is best for each child. Students use math manipulatives as well as workbooks, and they learn LOGO on the computer. Conversational Spanish begins in kindergarten. In social studies students begin by looking at themselves and their families, widening their perspective to include the city, the country, and the world of other cultures. Lower school children at Friends leave their classrooms for art, music, library, gym and multi-media workshop.

Middle school consists of grades five through eight. Middle schoolers hang out in the courtyard, cafeteria or library; not in the hallways. The head of the middle school, Pam Wood, is well-liked and students feel they can talk to her about almost anything. Students and parents say that the workload increases in fifth and again in seventh and ninth grades. In fifth grade departmentalization begins. Concrete work (including plenty of homework) is given "and the kids crave it," one mother said. A parent said, "The kids are more comfortable and really show progress quickly and early in the year." Math for fifth and sixth graders is grouped by homerooms with subgroups based on ability. One mother said her daughter started to slack off and wasn't keeping up with her math work. The teacher discussed the problem with the student before it became a pattern, and she got back on track without her parents having to exert pressure. Students who need enrichment can get it. One mother said her son needed more work, so creative homework, not just busywork, was given.

Beginning in fifth grade students have increasing opportunity to make choices for themselves in the areas of foreign language and performing arts. French or Spanish begins in fifth grade. In seventh grade students are required to add two years of Latin.

Literature, grammar, and good writing are emphasized in English. Eighth graders have weekly writing assignments using creative and analytical skills. Topics in social studies begin with the study of ancient civilizations in fifth grade and progress through Medieval and Renaissance history in sixth grade, including the history of civilization in Africa or the Americas. Seventh graders study the American Constitution and government, African-American history and "The Immigrant Experience." Eighth graders examine topics in anthropology including gender roles and ethnocentrism.

The middle school science program is comprehensive, beginning with a hands-on general curriculum for grades five and six and extending to earth science and ecology in seventh grade and an introduction to physical science in eighth grade. Middle schoolers also take a human relations course that examines the physical changes and social issues of adolescence.

The visual arts program at Friends includes both two- and three-dimensional offerings as well as many performing arts electives. In addition to two art studios there is the newly renovated Seegers Arts

240

Center that houses a photography lab and art gallery. Seventh and eighth graders can take art electives. Under the direction of Jennifer Fell Hayes, an award-winning playwright, the Friends Seminary drama program features three major theatrical productions annually. Recent productions include: *Three Penny Opera, The Crucible* and *A Midsummer Night's Dream* and *Oliver*. In addition, drama electives are available to students in seventh through twelfth grades. Theatre is performed in both the meetinghouse and in the new "black box" theatre.

In middle school each day begins with Meeting, and Quaker values continue to play a central role in school life, particularly regarding discipline. Each student from seventh through twelfth grade has an advisor who offers curricular guidance and is an advocate in matters of discipline. At Friends, one incident does not make for a bad reputation. A mother told us that when her son was in lower school, a middle school boy picked on him. The middle school boy was suspended for four days, then required to work in the lower school student's classroom. "He turned out to be a good kid," said the lower school parent.

The middle and upper school music program at Friends is focused in two areas: classical and jazz. Students can also choose from a range of electives including chamber music, instrumental music and vocal jazz ensemble, wind ensemble and instrumental instruction. Students can learn an instrument in 5th grade; jazz instruction begins in 7th grade. Bob Rosen, Friends' jazz impresario, exemplifies the private school teacher who not only teaches but *does*. Mr. Rosen is a clarinetist, saxophonist, composer and conductor. He arranges for Friends students to jam with noted jazz musicians: A recent fundraiser brought Chuck Mangione to the school for a session. Students perform at a year end concert. Some graduates pursue jazz as a vocation.

Athletics at Friends is competitive. There are varsity and junior varsity teams in soccer, basketball, softball, baseball, volleyball and tennis as well as coed teams in squash, track/cross-country and swimming. (One seventh grade boy said he longed for football.) Friends has championship varsity boys and girls basketball teams as well as boys soccer.

President Theodore Roosevelt, an alumnus, would be pleased to note the schoolwide emphasis on experiential education. The wilderness and outdoor adventure programs at Friends begin in kindergarten with apple picking and become more sophisticated in the middle and upper schools. First and second graders make their own maps of their routes from home to school and go to a nature study workshop. Third and fourth graders go to Nature's Classroom in Connecticut for an outdoor education program. Middle schoolers also travel to Nature's Classroom and learn mountain climbing and rappelling. Upper school students take backpacking trips, go sea-kayaking and master rock-climbing skills.

A large number of new students enter Friends at sixth grade. "Friends is an easy school to start," says the mother of two. "There are many new kids and there's an enormous effort to be welcoming." Current upper school students mentor ninth graders. Ninth graders and above can leave school for lunch or relaxation in adjacent Rutherford Place (but have to sign out first).

The upper school consists of grades nine through twelve. It is considered rigorous, with up to four hours of homework a night. Minimum requirements for graduation include four years of English, three years of history and math, two years of foreign language, two years of laboratory science, and twenty hours of community service per year. Students must demonstrate proficiency in the use of the computer. Advanced Placement courses are given in all major disciplines. If a student is interested in pursuing an AP course and if there are not enough students to form a full class, a teacher will mentor that student so he or she can sit for the AP exam. Friends has a relationship with New York University, enabling juniors and seniors to take courses for high school credit.

One upper school parent commented that the upper school course offerings looked like a mini-college catalog. For example, English electives include "Regional American Writers," "African-American Literature," "World Literature," "Fiction and Ethnography" and "Fiction and Film." Choices in history include "History of Ideas: East and West," "International Relations" and "Multi-Ethnic New York."

Friends has made a serious commitment to technology. There are two newly renovated computer labs in addition to computers in most classrooms. Network systems are in place, and the new upper school facility houses multi-media classrooms. Students interested in media can take advantage of the outstanding Chapman Media Center which houses a screening room with editing capability.

Upper school students can participate in School Year Abroad, a semester at St. Stephen's School in Rome, and The Network of Complimentary Schools, to name a few.

The Social Action Committee "informs the upper school on issues and activities of community and global concern." Friends students volunteer to help the less privileged or donate time to Amnesty International, "Children of War" or to an environmental group. Friends students are not afraid to speak up and speak out. They are socially aware and committed to service. A father of two children at Friends told us, "The philosophy of the school prepares children to deal with the outside world. They become independent and self-assured."

The centerpiece of the Friends graduation is Quaker Meeting. One parent said that out of the silence of the Meeting "the students speak with remarkable self-possession; some of their speeches are political and some are nostalgic." There are no caps and gowns.

Popular College Choices   Brown, Cornell, Oberlin, Georgetown, Wesleyan and University of Chicago

Traditions   Quaker Meeting, nature and wilderness trips, Friends Spring Fair, Book Fair, Potluck Suppers, concerts, God's Love We Deliver bag decoration workshops, Lower and Middle School Field Days, Halloween Party, drama and musical theater

Publications   Literary magazine
Yearbook
Middle school newspaper
Upper school newspaper: *The Penn*
Photography journal

Community Service Requirement   Kindergarten–Grade 6: performed within the school
Grades 7–8: minimum of 15 hours, within the school
Grades 9–12: minimum of 20 hours, within or outside of school
Eleventh graders take a required service seminar

Hangouts   Mariella's Pizza, Joe Jr.'s Coffee Shop, Gramercy Coffee Shop, Rutherford Square Park

The Geneva School of Manhattan

250 East 61st Street
New York, N.Y. 10021
(212) 755-5269, FAX (212) 755-5971
E mail: Genevanyc@aol.com

Coed
Pre-K 3's–6th Grade
Not accessible

Ms. Rim An, Director

Uniform   Girls wear a plaid jumper or navy skirt, a white blouse, and a navy sweater with the school logo. Boys wear navy or khaki pants, white shirt, and a navy sweater with the school logo. The sweater, and girls' jumpers, must be purchased through the school

Birthday Cutoff   Children entering pre-kindergarten must be 4 by November 1
Children entering kindergarten must be 5 by November 1

Enrollment   Total enrollment: 53 in 1998, increasing each year as the school grows
Pre-K places: 12
Kindergarten places: 4
First grade places: 4
Second grade places: 4
Third grade places: 4
Sixth grade places: 4

Grades   Parent conferences six times a year. Report cards are issued three times per year. The Stamford Achievement Test is given each year in the spring

Tuition Range 1998–1999 $1,800–5,500 for pre-kindergarten (half-day program)
$2,800–$9,500 for kindergarten–2nd grade
Additional fees are approximately $200

Financial Aid/Scholarship   Tuition is based on a sliding scale so as

244

to make it affordable for families of all income levels. Tuition is further reduced for families with more than one child

Diversity   Approximately 20% students of color

After-School Program   None

Summer Program   None

———

The Geneva School of Manhattan was founded by a small group of Christian parents and educators who wanted to provide a classical education based on Christian tenets. Funded by private individuals and foundations, the school opened in 1996–97 with pre-kindergarten through first grades. Each subsequent year the school hopes to add one additional grade, continuing through grade six. The school is located in the Trinity Baptist Church building on East 61st Street, but is not affiliated with any church. A Christian-based independent school, the first in Manhattan, is likely to appeal to many parents who now home-school their children and to others who want a correlation between their faith and their children's schooling.

The founders were inspired by Dorothy Sayer's essay "The Lost Tools of Learning." The school name refers to Geneva, Switzerland, a center of the Protestant Reformation in the 1500's. "Geneva was a training ground for missionaries who went out all over Europe to spread the word," says the school's Director, Ms. An.

Getting in: A personal interview and a screening test, administered by the school, are required. The school has a non-discriminatory policy but parents must sign a statement of faith and a statement of cooperation. (The school will discipline children but corporal punishment is not permitted.) The registration form asks parents to describe their children and also to "Please give a short explanation of who you understand Jesus Christ to be and what His death and resurrection means to you," as well as to "Describe briefly your relationship with Jesus Christ."

Parents: All parents are required to volunteer three hours per week at the school. Parents are also involved in planning field trips and other extracurricular activities.

Program: The Director of the School, Ms. Rim An, taught mathematics at UNIS for six years and at various public schools before that.

She explained that the school will be "teaching the truth from the Bible," including creationism, but adds "Our school doctrine is not specifically in support of the fundamentalist movement." According to the school's literature, the educational program is founded on the principles and values set forth in Scripture. The Geneva School will revive the educational style that uses the classical "trivium," a three phase model that corresponds to the different phases in child development. The Geneva School's distinctive characteristics include: 1) curriculum based upon the Bible as God's Word; 2) classics taught as enduring works of excellence; 3) rigorous academics and small classes; 4) emphasis upon languages with foreign language instruction beginning in pre-kindergarten; 5) disciplined and nurturing Christian faculty; 6) involved parents who volunteer time and talents; 7) affordable tuition based on financial need. Latin instruction begins in third grade, and all students are required to go on weekly field trips.

Grace Church School

86 Fourth Avenue
New York, NY 10003
(212) 475-5609, FAX (212) 475-5015
e-mail: zwarner@gcschool.org

Coed
Junior Kindergarten–8th grade
Accessible

Mr. George Davison, Head
Ms. Zelda Warner, Director of Admissions

Birthday Cutoff   Children entering junior kindergarten should be 4 by October 1
Children entering kindergarten should be 5 by October 1

Enrollment   Total enrollment: 380
Junior kindergarten places: 30
Kindergarten places: 15
Graduating class size: approximately 33

Grades   Semester system
Letter grades begin in 5th grade
Departmentalization begins in 5th grade

Tuition Range 1998–1999 $13,973 to $16,823, junior kindergarten–8th grade
Additional fees: lower school approximately $60; upper school approximately $300
Families with more than one child enrolled receive a discount on the additional tuition

Financial Aid/Scholarship   25% of the student body receive some form of aid

Endowment $3.6 million

After-School Program   The GCS After-School Program is for Grace Church School students only; Monday–Friday until 5:30 P.M., for an additional fee; however, each child is entitled to take one class free each semester, but may sign up and pay for as many as space allows

Play groups meet every day and there is an hourly charge that is billed monthly (reductions are given to families who receive financial aid); advance registration for play group is not required

Vacation play groups are available

Summer Program   June School from the close of school until the end of June; a variety of creative and recreational activities for an additional payment

———

Grace Church was founded in 1894 as the first Choir Boarding School for Boys in New York City and celebrated its centennial year in 1994. Coeducation at Grace Church began in 1947. The school occupies nine renovated adjoining buildings. ERBs are required for admissions as well as an interview. (Kindergarteners are interviewed in groups of three.) The school is traditional and follows a structured curriculum. There is a dress code and teachers are addressed formally ("Mr. Smith," "Miss Jones"). A renovation in 1993 created a new dining room (hot lunch is included in the tuition) and a greatly enlarged library with state-of-the-art computer catalog and research facilities. The computer lab was updated and relocated next to the library. The computer center, all classrooms, and the library are connected via a local network with internet access. The Technology Access Project will make modem-equipped computers available to all upper school students for home use. E-mail links the community. There is a separate playroof for the junior kindergarten and kindergarten children in addition to a gymnasium, outdoor play yard and dance studio. Park facilities, Chelsea Piers, Basketball City, and a neighborhood indoor swimming pool are used to augment the physical education program.

Grace Church School has three divisions: junior kindergarten and kindergarten; lower school: grades one through four; upper school: grades five through eight. A choice of French or Spanish is offered in fifth grade. Latin is offered in seventh and eighth grades. The arts play a vital part in the curriculum. GCS has two art studios, each with its own kiln and children gain experience in a variety of media. Students in grades seven and eight may elect a major arts course in place of a second language. Instrumental music is offered beginning in third grade. Children may sing in the school chorus or audition for the church choir, which now includes girls. Three major drama productions are staged each year. In a recent year students performed in *Through the Looking Glass*, *Oliver* was the spring musical and *Through a Glass Darkly* completed the season. Younger children perform at music and dance assemblies and in class plays.

There is weekly chapel and students study the Bible: The Old Testament for grades three and four, and The New Testament for grade five, and ethics (grades six and eight). Seventh graders complete an overview of world religions. Grace Church School families observe a wide variety of faiths. Community service is required in the upper school. Grace Church School was the recipient of a DeWitt Wallace-Reader's Digest Fund ISOP Grant for increasing its representation of teachers and students of color and expanding the Grace Opportunity Program, an academic enrichment program for students in public and parochial schools. Grace Church School has a support group for parents of color. In 1998, Grace Church enrolled three students from Prep for Prep.

Graduates attend independent day schools, boarding schools and the specialized New York City high schools.

The Hewitt School

45 East 75th Street
New York, NY 10021
(212) 288-1919

All girls
Kindergarten–12th grade
Not accessible

Dr. Mary Jane Yurchak, Head of School
Ms. Anita S. Edwards, Director of Admissions

Uniform   Lower school: a Blackwatch plaid jumper; a white blouse tights or socks and sensible, non-skid shoes
Middle school: a Blackwatch plaid kilt, a white blouse, tights or socks and closed low-heeled shoes with non-skid soles. Casual options for both Lower and Middle school include uniform slacks, skirt, and a variety of uniform shirts, blouses, and sweaters. Sneakers can be worn
Upper school: a dress code requires comfortable and school-appropriate clothing. No sweatpants, jeans, shorts, T-shirts, no excessive makeup, jewelry, clogs, high-heeled platform shoes or sandals

Birthday Cutoff   Children entering kindergarten must be 5 by mid- to late October but readiness is the most important factor

Enrollment   Total enrollment: 355
Kindergarten places: 36
Average graduating class: 20-24

Grades   Semester system
Letter grades begin in 6th grade
Semester exams begin in 7th grade

Tuition Range 1998–1999 $14,338 to $16,091, kindergarten–12th grade
Additional fees: for activities, publications, trips, $252–$709. For

books, \$221–\$578. Food service, \$861, for grades 8-12 laptop purchase or lease required

Financial Aid/Scholarship   \$450,000 available

Endowment   Approximately \$2 million

Diversity   4 Early Steps, 5 Prep for Prep students enrolled as of September 1998
Cultural Awareness Club

Homework   Kindergarten: none
Grade I: 15 minutes
Grade II: 30 minutes
Grade III: 45 minutes
Grade IV: 1 hour and 15 minutes
Grade V: 1$1/_2$ hours
Grades VI, VII, VIII: 30–45 minutes per subject (4 or 5 subjects a night)
Grades IX, X, XI, XII: 45 minutes–1 hour per subject (4 or 5 subjects a night)

After-School Program   Hewitt Afternoon: (primarily a service for lower school girls) 3:15 to 4:45 P.M. Monday–Friday; study, sports, music, crafts, field trips; open to girls from other schools; an additional payment is required
Clubs that meet after school include gymnastics club, crafts club, computer club, French club, and chess club
After-school study hall: a supervised study period Monday–Thursday 3:15–4:00 P.M., for grades V–XII

Summer Program   None

Hewitt consists of two connecting five-story townhouses on East 75th Street. The library, quiet and cozy with a fireplace and piano, also has several computers with networking and CD-ROM capabilities and a periodical room. The marble winding staircase and floral wallpaper lined with class pictures of girls in white dresses holding bouquets harks back to the 1920s, when the school was known as "Miss Hewitt's

Classes" and educated the daughters of the city's socially prominent families. In the seventy-plus years since then, Hewitt has evolved to meet the needs of modern young women. In July 1990, Dr. Mary Jane Yurchak became head of school, and "her commitment to enhancing the science and technology programs and to making the school more intellectually challenging is having a positive effect," according to parents. "We all want to keep the friendly and supportive atmosphere. At the same time we all want to make the program more rigorous." Additional AP courses, a Ford Foundation grant for the computer sciences and a new curriculum have been the results. Goals according to Dr. Yurchak are: "a more integrated curriculum, more computer- and technology-based components, while continuing to use the city as an educational, ethical and ecological resource."

Getting in: The application fee is $50. Parents visit Hewitt with their daughter for a tour and interview. They are interviewed by the director of admissions in her office. Kindergarten and grade one candidates take a brief screening test before visiting classes. The director of admissions and the early childhood specialist also observe every kindergarten candidate at her own nursery school. One parent told us "Hewitt spent one and a half hours with the family and demonstrated a real appreciation of who my daughter was. Not only did they remember us but they were able to describe her whole personality." She felt the other girls' schools were much more aloof. Parents of girls who will be entering Hewitt in the fall are invited to a breakfast to meet the head of school and lower school head. In recent years Hewitt has set record levels in kindergarten enrollment.

Another parent said, "Hewitt lacks some of the social crustiness of the other girls' schools"; Hewitt is "definitely nurturing and traditional, with a less aggressive atmosphere than some other places." There are achievement assemblies for the lower, middle and upper schools that recognize accomplishment in academics, athletics, art and community service. A parent said: "They play down competition but there are prizes and awards." One mother said her "tomboy/nonconformist child fits in just fine at Hewitt." The brochure says that Hewitt provides "an environment of understanding, trust and affection." Many parents describe Hewitt as "a very comfortable environment."

Parents: Hewitt is a multicultural community. Although most mothers and fathers work outside the home, parental involvement is encouraged. One parent describes the Hewitt atmosphere as "small, cozy and inviting; you never feel out of place. You can be there as much as you want." In addition to open Parents Association meetings, there are many social and fund-raising events throughout the year. Some highlights are the annual Book Fair and Art Show, the Spring Benefit Dinner Dance, the Father/Daughter Dinner Social for grades eight through twelve and the Hewitt Barn Dance for lower school families. Parents may accompany their daughters to breakfast at Hewitt, from 7:45 A.M. until 8:15 A.M.; working and nonworking mothers say it's a nice way to spend some quiet time together each day. Siblings are invited and there is no additional charge.

Program: Each morning Hewitt students shake hands with the head of school. During the first week of school, lower school students are met downstairs and the teacher escorts them to the classroom. One mother whose daughter had trouble separating said the lower school head "saw me struggling and together we designed a strategy that worked."

The lower school at Hewitt consists of kindergarten through fourth grade. The kindergarten is a full-day program. Girls stay until 3:00 P.M. Monday through Friday. A parent said that Hewitt girls are very busy after school; she has to book play dates at least three weeks in advance because girls are enrolled in ballet, swimming or religious classes.

Hewitt has a "spiral curriculum." Academic subjects are introduced in kindergarten and are built upon in developmentally appropriate ways in the succeeding years. Kindergartners are introduced to reading, literature, writing, math, science, social studies, music, dance, physical education and library. French is introduced in kindergarten "without pressure" twice a week through songs and oral and verbal games such as "letter of the week." There are computers in the kindergarten classrooms and computer instruction in the computer lab. In 1990 Dr. Yurchak oversaw renovation of the computer labs with help from a $50,000 Edward Ford Foundation Grant.

Individualized attention is a hallmark of instruction at Hewitt. The teacher-student ratio at Hewitt is high. About three-quarters of the faculty hold advanced degrees. Students learn at their own pace and teachers pay careful attention to different learning styles. There is individual as well as small-group instruction in writing and reading. Kindergartners begin journal writing. One mother said her kindergartner came in reading and received one-on-one reading enrichment.

Math is taught with manipulatives like unifix cubes and games like chip trading. There's no one way to do something. "There are a lot of creative children here," the director of admissions told us. One mother told us her daughter, who has musical ability, takes private lessons at school and was encouraged to write a song that she'll sing at Grandparents' Day with her class.

In addition to physical education and dance classes, kindergarten girls go to the playroof, which is equipped with tricycles, wagons and jump ropes. After-school options include ice skating, swimming, art clubs and chorus.

In the first grade classrooms are furnished with tables in clusters. By second grade there are weekly spelling tests. Parents receive anecdotal reports twice a year; letter grades begin in sixth grade. Friday assemblies begin with the pledge of allegiance followed by a presentation: The author of a children's book might speak, or a dance or musical group might perform. One assembly featured the Yale Whiffenpoofs. A highlight of the lower school year is the annual Hewitt Barn Dance, a traditional square dance held in the gym.

Parents say at Hewitt, which is committed to single-sex education, "there is an implicit validation of female values." One mother praised the emphasis on women in society: "Hewitt parents enthusiastically participated in the 'Take Your Daughters to Work Day.'" In each division students gain experience with leadership in the Student Council.

Middle school at Hewitt is composed of grades five through seven and occupies the 75th Street building. The girls have a homeroom teacher for each grade in middle school. Departmentalization begins in sixth grade. Girls continue to study a full schedule of subjects including English, history, math, science, computer, French or Spanish (with the addition of Latin in grade eight), studio art, drama, music and gym. There is a new emphasis on math and science in the middle and upper schools. Eighth grade students take algebra I or II and conduct experiments and write lab reports in eighth grade earth science. For a history assignment, a seventh grader told us students had to pick a country or state and write a research paper about a cultural aspect of it; topics chosen included African dancing and photography in China.

The middle school has its own student council and its own literary magazine, *Enterprise*.

Overnight trips begin in middle school. Sixth graders travel to New Jersey for a forest conservation trip; seventh and eighth graders travel to Blairstown, New Jersey. One student who didn't want to go was given the option of writing a paper on the environment instead. There is an eighth grade trip with boys from Browning to Washington, D.C., and ninth graders travel to Frost Valley, New York.

The high school at Hewitt is composed of grades eight through twelve. Students have faculty advisors. A minimum of four academic

254

subjects per year is required but most girls take five major subjects and one or two minors in the arts. Three lab sciences are required in the upper school. Four years of English and three years of math, history and foreign language are required in the high school. There are six AP classes offered, significant since Hewitt is so small. In addition, the school offers "Anytime, Anywhere Learning" through an upper school laptop computer program that gives students universal access to the Internet and other digital resources such as CD-ROMs and integrated software.

Since 1972, Hewitt has coordinated certain classes with its "brother school" Browning (a twelve-year all-boys school on the Upper East Side). Electives with Browning include: psychology, religion, economics, twentieth-century political geography, Latin/African/Asian Studies and physics. In addition, there are coed French, Greek and Finance Clubs. There are two dramatic productions a year, one of which is performed in conjunction with boys from The Browning School. Everyone participates in the production, either as cast or crew. A recent musical was *Pippin*.

There is a Field Day for lower, middle and upper schools. After interscholastic sports games, Hewitt girls are expected to give a cheer and a handshake to their opponents.

Clubs at Hewitt include: Art Club, Drama Club, Glee Club, Model U.N., Cultural Awareness Club and Environmental Club. There are also junior and varsity sports teams. Students can work on the school newspaper, *The Hewitt Times*, or the art and literary magazine, *The Venturer*. Students also produce a yearbook, *Argosy*.

Senior privileges include using the front staircase the "Senior Stairs," instead of the back stairs and a three-week year end independent project with an individual faculty advisor. Eleventh and twelfth graders can leave school with parental permission.

Community service is required at Hewitt. Beginning in lower school, there are many opportunities for students to volunteer. One lower school class held a bake sale to benefit the Jewish Guild for the Blind. There is a Birthday Book Club—girls may donate a book to the Hewitt Library on their birthday. Middle schoolers often work in the school in the library, cafeteria or art room. Outside of school students visit the Marymount Nursing Home, participate in "You Gotta Have Park," walk for The March of Dimes and volunteer in the St. James Church soup kitchen. Faculty advisors and student council leaders publicize and coordinate many of these activities.

Highlights of the upper school include the spring musical, the

December chorus and handbell concert and the Sports Banquet. On Founder's Day flowers are laid at the foot of Shakespeare's statue (Miss Hewitt's favorite) in Central Park. Hewitt has teams in volleyball, basketball and softball as well as a very strong gymnastics program.

Commencement exercises at Hewitt are traditional. The seniors gather onstage and the kindergarten class walks in wearing white dresses and white gloves. Each kindergarten student presents a senior with a small bouquet and then walks, hand in hand with her, down the aisle.

Popular College Choices   Brown, Duke, Skidmore, Vassar

Traditions   Parents' Association Annual Holiday Fair, Arts Festival and Book Fair; new parents' breakfast, Parents' Association luncheon, Father/Daughter Dinner Social, Parents' Visiting Day, Grandparents' Day, Thanksgiving Concert, Holiday Concert, Lower School Square Dance, Science Fair, Hewitt Birthday Book Club, Hewitt Corner (school store), major givers' cocktail party at Dr. Yurchak's apartment, class trips to Blairstown, New Jersey, Frost Valley, New York, Model U.N. trip to Washington, D.C., fifth grade musical, upper school play, upper school musical with Browning, Lower, Middle and Upper School Field Days, Founder's Day, Lower School Final Assembly and Concert, Sports Banquet and Upper School Achievement Assembly, senior projects, commencement, young alumnae play

Publications   Upper school newspaper: *The Hewitt Times*
Middle school literary magazine: *Enterprise*
Lower school literary magazine: *Safari*
Art and literary magazine: *The Venturer*
Yearbooks: *Argosy*
School magazine: *The Hewitt Anchor*
School newsletters: *Hewitt Happenings*

Hangouts   La Viande Coffee Shop, 3 Guys Coffee Shop (on Madison Avenue)

Horace Mann School

Horace Mann Nursery Division
55 East 90th Street
New York, NY 10128
(212) 369-4600

Horace Mann Lower Division
4440 Tibbett Avenue
Riverdale, NY 10471
(718) 432-3300

Horace Mann Upper Division
231 West 246th Street
Riverdale, NY 10471
(718) 432-4000
e-mail: admissions@horacemann.org
web-site: www.horacemann.pvt.k12.ny.us

Coed
Nursery–12th grade
Accessible for Nursery Division and Upper Division
Not accessible for Lower division

Dr. Eileen Mullady, Head of School
Dr. Lawrence Weiss, Head of Upper Division
Ms. Marian Linden, Head of Middle School
Dr. Steven Tobolsky, Head of Lower Division
Ms. Lisa Oliveira, Director of Admissions
Ms. Wendy Steinthal, Director of Admissions, Lower School
Mrs. Patricia Yvan Zuroski, Director, Nursery Division
Mrs. Lydia Hechter, Director of Admissions, Nursery Division

Uniform   None; casual, comfortable, no baseball hats in class

Birthday Cutoff   Children entering nursery 3's must be 3 by September 1
Children entering kindergarten must be 5 by September 1

Enrollment   Total enrollment nursery–12: 1,605
Total enrollment nursery division: 160
Kindergarten places: 35

Total enrollment lower division, grades kindergarten–6: 530
Total enrollment upper division, grades 7–12: 915
Graduating class size: varies, from 150–170
The largest point of entry is at nursery level (approximately 40 places) and you must call for an application to the nursery school the first week after Labor Day
Horace Mann also has a kindergarten with one class of up to 21 children located in Riverdale, serving families from Riverdale, Westchester, the Bronx and New Jersey
The sixth grade admits 30 new students

Grades   Trimester system
Kindergarten–3: detailed anecdotal reports, conferences and checklists; check, check-plus or minus grades; weekly quizzes
Letter grades begin in 4th grade, and anecdotal reports continue
Departmentalization begins in 4th grade, is completed by 5th grade
First final exam is given in 7th grade

Tuition Range 1998–1999: $11,710 to $17,690, nursery–12th grade
Additional fees for books, transportation, lunch and trips approximately $1,300 to $2,000 in middle and upper divisions

Financial Aid/Scholarship   Over 3 million is awarded annually for financial aid
There are 12 named scholarship funds in the upper division

Endowment   Approximately $28 million

Diversity   52 Prep for Prep students as of Fall 1998
The Union is an organization of students of color at Horace Mann
There is a parent support group

Homework   1st grade: Worksheets, always due on Fridays
2nd: 4 times a week, 10–15 minutes in the beginning of the year going up to 20 minutes, 2 worksheets per night
3rd and 4th: 30–45 minutes a night
5th: 1 and $1/2$ hours a night
9th: 2–$2^{1}/_{2}$ hours per night
10th–12th: 50 minutes per subject per night, approximately 3 to 4

hours; more time is required for studying for exams and long-term projects

After-School Program For grades K–6: a variety of recreational and creative activities; an additional payment is required
Upper division: 40–70 clubs, which vary from year to year depending on the interests of the student body
Competitive sports in the Ivy Prep League

Summer Program Six weeks of courses for credit or review for Horace Mann students and new students; many summer camp programs available.

"Harvard man" is what many parents are wishing for when they enroll their four year olds at this very selective school. If you have a vision of your youngster in crimson uniform cavorting on a grassy field with the best and the brightest, then this might be the right place. (HM's colors are crimson and white.) And as at an Ivy League campus, most of the old stone buildings at Horace Mann High School are named after former headmasters and founders: Tillinghast Hall, Van Alstyne Auditorium, Pforzheimer Hall, the Loeb Library, The Pretty-man Gymnasium.

The school opened two new buildings in 1999: a new middle school building for grades 6 through 8 and an Arts and Dining Center serving grades 6 through 12. A complete renovation of most of the other buildings is planned for the year 2000–2001. The new buildings and renovation will highlight the middle division programs, increase student and public spaces, focus on art and music offerings, and make the existing T1 Internet and WAN accessible from every classroom.

It is somewhat ironic that this prestigious private school is named after a man known as the father of public schools. Horace Mann actually had nothing to do with this namesake. According to HM's history *The First Hundred Years*, it was founder Nicholas Murray Butler who chose the name because "at the time it was the only household name in American education." Blessed with strong leadership through the years, HM has served as a model for both public and private schools, combining the traditional and the innovative, and has always encouraged physical hardiness as well as academic rigor. Originally coed, except for a forty-year hiatus when the campuses were separate (under Inslee "Ink" Clark), Horace Mann readmitted women in 1974.

259

Along with Clark, Dr. Mitchell Gratwick, HM's head for seventeen years, left an indelible stamp on HM: "High standards, conservative values and innovative methods." Gratwick was a founder of the AP program and acquired the John Dorr Nature Laboratory, two strong components of the HM experience.

HM uses the building-block approach to learning: "Each step leads to the next." This philosophy is carried all the way through HM, ultimately leading to preparation for advanced college study. HM's bottom line: With superior preparation, a good measure of ability and the willingness to work like an ox, a student can achieve excellence here.

Horace Mann Nursery Division was originally established as a service for the children of alumni "who wanted to start their offspring in a Horace Mann system." It is located in a tight but tidy converted coach house on 90th Street between Madison and Park. There is no indoor gym but children use a rooftop playground or a yard for at least an hour a day and go to Asphalt Green once a week. Classrooms are colorful and well ordered—if crowded—reflecting a structured but stimulating "hands-on" curriculum. The staff psychologist is available to parents for consultation. All the head teachers have a Master's in Education.

Getting in: You must apply to the Nursery Division (HMND) when your child is two and a half years old. Getting in at the nursery level is far easier on the parents because the WPPSI-R (administered by the ERB) is not required for admission at that time. However, there is a caveat here. At the age of three there is really no way of knowing if your child will be able (or willing) to keep up with the high expectations and the work required later on. Also, potential learning differences that might be picked up by the WPPSI-R are not apparent. We know too many parents who boasted about their children getting into HM Nursery only to have to tutor them after school or (like one parent we know) over the summer. Parents may have to consider a change of school by third grade because a child is falling behind. It is not that HM weeds out children. The school is prepared to give as much support as is needed but there is a process of self-selection.

Applicants to lower, middle and upper divisions come to campus for a student and parent interview. Tours are led by student "ambassadors." Applications should be filed by December 15th and must be completed by January 15th. Families who request an application are invited to Fall Open Houses. The ratio of applicants to places is about ten to one. It's easier to get into HM at sixth or ninth grade.

The relocation of the sixth grade to the middle school campus has led to a significant change in middle school division admissions. By September of the year 2001, HM expects to enroll approximately 40 new sixth graders and 15 or fewer seventh graders; this change will be phased in during the interim years. Lisa Oliveira, Director of Admissions, says she expects the transition to result in three applications for every place in sixth grade and more than five applications for every seventh grade opening.

The upper division enrolls approximately 30 new students each year in ninth grade with six applications for every place and receives 30–40 applications for 5 to 10 tenth grade places. Few openings are available at eighth and eleventh grades.

Kindergarten applicants may be observed at their nursery schools if there are many children applying from those schools, but most children are observed in a group interview at HM in the afternoon (1:30 or 3:30). "By kindergarten," one interviewer said, "it doesn't bode well if a child doesn't separate well in the interview." It is very helpful if an HM parent who really knows your child writes a letter of recommendation.

Some entering students don't know how to write their names while some come in reading. But by the end of kindergarten most kids have "cracked the code." Formal instruction begins in first grade, and reading is expected to be well under way by second grade. "The curriculum in the early years is geared to the readiness of the children," says the brochure. There is a strong emphasis on basic skills balanced with new techniques and tools. Experiential learning is stressed, and computer, chess and other learning games are introduced. There is a resource room with six computers for kindergarten. One parent praised the fact that here children "capture the enthusiasm for learning young." During the second half of the year kindergartners travel up to Riverdale to get acquainted with the elementary school campus. (We suggest that parents applying to the nursery division take a tour of the elementary division, because before you know it your child will be up in Riverdale.)

Parents: The nursery division is homogeneous. Parents describe it as predominantly Jewish and financially mixed. One said, "I thought the parents would be a lot hipper." There is a very active Parents Association. One mother recalls attending her first parents' meeting thoroughly underdressed. Where do many families go on weekends and vacations? "You know," said one parent, "it's the triangle: the Hamptons, Boca, Vail." But parents report that once they reach

Riverdale the school community is more mixed. Communication with the parents is frequent, and there is a Parents Association newsletter. Nursery division parents can be class representatives and they may also serve as elected members on the Horace Mann Board of Trustees.

Since the elementary division, located in Riverdale, is "no one's neighborhood school," communication between home and school is very important. Teachers often call and chat with parents. There are many student-teacher conferences.

Program: Horace Mann is very honest in acknowledging that this school is not for everyone. Director of Lower School Admissions Wendy Steinthal says, "There is a quick pace with lots of enrichment." Most children thrive on the stimulation—the classrooms are buzzing with activity and the students are clearly engaged. The P.A. president said that the school "breeds independence." At the beginning of third grade a letter is sent to parents urging them not to help their children with their homework, and parents must sign it. Parents may only suggest, "Try this or that." Wendy Steinthal stresses that Horace Mann is supportive and committed to each child. "Yes, there is a lot to do but the children meet the challenge," she says. "This is a school for children who really like to learn." There is a real emphasis on teaching study skills and on learning how to be a student. One parent summed up the issue of competitiveness at HM astutely: "It's not that the school or the kids are necessarily so competitive; it's the high-powered parents behind them." The same can be said for all the top tier schools in New York City.

The elementary division has large open areas, although there are no "open classrooms." Some of these large areas are shared by four classes, with cubbies in the center. Some classes have two sections, one for reading lab or language arts, one for math. Formal reading instruction begins in first grade with an eclectic approach. There are three reading specialists and a communication skills specialist. Emphasis is placed on the writing process. HM children are tested for reading each year and there is a full reading lab.

HM is known for having strong math students. The elementary school hired an additional math teacher for sixth grade pre-algebra. There are many classroom projects: The computer program begins in kindergarten. Elementary students have computer lab (Macintosh) at least once a week for forty-five minutes. Beginning in fourth grade, they learn word processing and keyboarding; in fifth grade, graphics and programming. By fifth grade nearly 90 percent of the students use a computer at home.

The new middle division facility prompted a re-evaluation of the middle school curriculum. There is increased emphasis on interdisciplinary works and team teaching at the sixth, seventh, and eight grade levels. Students have more choices to make and more accountability, including the introduction of "free periods." Lower school PA president Pam Stuchin says: "It's wonderful for the sixth graders to experience the independence and increased responsibility that comes with the middle school environment. Until my older daughter started seventh grade I didn't realize how much they crave that sense of freedom."

There is an Artist-of-the-Month Program and three art teachers on staff. The Art Enrichment Program is an enhancement to the lower school curriculum. Using a variety of media (painting, collage, papier-mâché, ceramics, metal tooling and felt appliqué) students create two and three dimensional forms to go with a topic being studied in English, reading, social studies or science. Students from first grade through fifth work to create individual as well as large group projects. The completed work is often used as a learning tool or teaching aid in the classroom.

Foreign language study begins in first grade. First through third graders take *both* French and Spanish. In fourth grade students choose French or Spanish for the remainder of the lower school. In seventh grade students can elect Latin, German, Spanish, French, or Japanese.

Parents of active children will be glad to know that there is time for physical exercise: In first through fourth grades gym meets five times a week in a huge gymnasium. Fifth graders have gym four times a week. Students use a playground and the AstroTurf field year-round, and can use the tennis courts and pool at the upper division.

Special trips: Fifth graders take a three-day trip to Washington, D.C.; all second, third, fourth and fifth graders spend time at the John Dorr Nature Lab.

Mr. Norman Fountain (Trinity 1945) who first encouraged New York City parents to send their children to school in the Bronx, retired in spring of 1994. Dr. Steven Tobolsky is now head of the lower division. Another recent change at Horace Mann was the retirement, after thirty-one years, of beloved teacher Tek Lin. Mr. Lin was a "grammar guru, a weaver and the planter of most of the trees and flowers around Horace Mann Elementary." An embodiment of community spirit, he provided an oasis of Taoist calm in a demanding environment. Both men left their marks on Horace Mann and will be missed.

263

Programs are held at the John Dorr Nature Lab for incoming sixth and incoming seventh, eighth, ninth, and tenth graders for orientation and exploration, which includes the Searchers program, an adapted Outward Bound program.

The upper division: Now the group is larger and more diverse (26 percent are children of color), "large enough to be happy as they grow and change." In general "students respect the school" and enjoy the freedom of an open campus. There are no bells, and teachers are addressed formally. In 1992 Phillip Foote, former headmaster of the Greenhill School in Dallas, where he was very successful in recruiting talented students of color, became head of Horace Mann. Foote met with department chairmen to insure a sequential curriculum and unity among the three schools. Mr. Foote stepped down in the 1994–1995 school year. Dr. Eileen Mullady became the first woman to head the school. Her background is in higher education (Columbia and Princeton.) Parents say she has already begun to "clean house" and has launched a capital campaign. One of Dr. Mullady's goals is to "build an exemplary middle school." She notes that while HMHS is known to be hard and rigorous it is also "a school that celebrates intellectualism; a joyful, adventurous place."

In preparation for the challenge of the upper grades, students who need review attend the six-week summer session. Seventh and eighth graders also take mandatory study skills courses. The foundations course in seventh grade is a unique program combining English, history and anthropology described as "an explanation of the human experience." Readings include *Inherit the Wind*, *Things Fall Apart* and *Ishi: Last of His Tribe*. Students gain experience in creative and critical writing. Eighth graders celebrate "Pi Day" (on 3/14 of course) and build solar houses which are tested for temperature and heat retention on the football field on a cold day.

Historically HM has been strong in English and history, and now HM's science labs are state of the art. Four out of ten faculty members hold Ph.D.'s and the chemistry department has three research-quality lab instruments. The science library and resource room has six microcomputers and is often open for independent study. Science teachers are very accessible to students with an interest in advanced study.

The course catalog says that most of the eighth grade courses are equivalent to ninth grade courses at many high schools. And even the introductory courses move along at quite a clip. One alumnus said, "It was like going to college before college." In keeping with Dr.

Gratwick's legacy, HM was a pilot school for the AP program, and HMHS offers more AP courses than any other school, including "AP Psychology," "AP Latin: Epic Poetry" and "AP Economics." The math department offers calculus AP, AB and BC, including calculus with computers. English courses stress the classics but there are interesting electives in South African literature, Women's literature and an interdisciplinary course: "Explorations in English and Biology." Other opportunities for interdisciplinary study are available to students through IIRS (Independent Interdisciplinary Research Seminar). Internships and tutorials can also be arranged.

One Horace Mann (class of 1990) and Cornell (class of 1994) alumna says, "Academically there's lots of freedom and choices but there are no gut courses at HM, no course can be blown off." The average grade is a B⁻, which, one student boasts, "would be a B⁺ anywhere else." One HMHS student says, "Some people work hard for grades, and some people work harder for excellent grades." "It's as hard to get an F as it is to get an A" is also heard. Testing is so frequent (quizzes every week, exams every other), "you always know how you're doing." What is not listed in the catalog is the advanced level of maturity and independence required of students at HMHS, qualities already ingrained in students who came up through the HM system. The pressure is real, but one student said, "It's mainly self-inflicted." Yet another student told us that "teachers go to extremes to make the homework challenging." All homework requires a lot of time and thought, and one student said that he might blow off homework in one subject to study for an exam in another but if he missed two nights of homework assignments, he would fall behind.

Some students thrive under pressure and rise to the challenge of the competitive atmosphere, like the young woman (a HM "lifer" who has been at HM for twelve years) who takes three AP courses, does four hours of homework a night and still manages to watch *Dawson's Creek*. The minimum amount of homework is three to four hours each night, more on weekends. "This school makes you hungry," a student told us. "You get used to working hard and getting what you want, and you take that with you." One private school advisor tells families who are considering a most demanding school like Horace Mann to consider their family lifestyles. Some students will be able to accompany the family on weekend ski trips and still get their work done (one student trains for competitive ski racing). Others will be hitting the books in the chalet.

Contrary to popular belief, students at HM do support one

another. There is a peer leadership training program and a student tutorial program, and most evenings HM students spend lots of time on the phone discussing homework or exams.

Does this leave time for extracurricular activities? One student put it this way, "If you want to be in a play or a sport and you don't mind sacrificing that time, then you do your work when you get home." Still, extracurricular activities are encouraged even for kids who aren't excelling academically. Lisa Oliveira says, "Because the academics are so challenging, it's even more important for students to pursue their other interests. We want every student to experience successes, to explore abilities in and out of the classroom."

The community service requirement also contributes to personal growth. One alumna told us that HM helped her find a job as a counselor at a summer camp for homeless children and she then returned for four consecutive summers and found it an invaluable experience.

HM students are far from one-dimensional math nerds, as evidenced by the variety and number of their extracurricular activities. Every year there is a huge musical, and three smaller plays are put on annually. HM produces more than a dozen publications. Students can choose from up to seventy clubs in any given year. Popular ones include The Union (formerly the Joint Minority Coalition), which is open to everyone, political clubs (there is a Young Republicans of HM Club), the East Wind, West Wind Asian Club, Glee Club, Model U.N., Junior Statesman Club (debating) and a Shakespeare Club. The Glee Club and Chamber Chorus are very popular; they have made their own CD and traveled to Europe and the Middle East.

Students do have a voice in setting policy affecting student life at HM through the governing council, comprised of twenty-four students and fifteen faculty members who are elected annually. There is an annual tenth grade health survey (anonymous), and students are required to take health courses. In 1997 the Governing Council passed the "Teacher and Course Evaluation Bill." The Council spent three meetings debating the document, which called for written evaluations by the students twice a year. The bill compelled the school faculty and administration to pass a similar resolution, making teacher and course evaluations a reality.

One day a year HM students get a chance to break out. On Senior Absurdity Day they can be anyone they want. Recent choices include: the androgynous Pat (from *Saturday Night Live*), a can of Spam, Scarface and Brearley girls.

They say that Harvard is tough to get into, but easy to stay in; HM is tough to get into and tougher to remain in, but there is no question that the child who stays the course at HM will receive a superior, accelerated education. One alumna told us, "Horace Mann's great strength is it instills good work habits and is superior in college placement: HM goes above and beyond to get you into one of the colleges of your choice." It's prep for success. If your child makes it through, maybe you'll get to the Harvard-Yale tailgate picnic after all.

Popular College Choices   University of Pennsylvania, Cornell, Yale/Columbia, Brown/University of Wisconsin, Harvard

Traditions   Gilbert and Sullivan production in the lower school once a year, the Buzzell basketball game (vs. Riverdale), Senior Absurdity Day, Holocaust Remembrance Assembly and Martin Luther King Assembly, Native American Day, East Wind–West Wind Dinner (Asia Night), Lower School Family Picnic

Publications   Yearbook: *The Mannikin*
Newspapers: *The Lower School View*, *The Record* and *The Journal*
Literary magazine: *Manuscript*
Prose literature: *Legal Fiction*
Science magazine: *Spectrum*
Math magazine: *Mantissa*
Business journal: *Businessman*
Journal of opinion: *Outlook*
Multicultural paper: *The Drum*
Photography: *Insight*
Music: *The Riff*
Alumni publication: *Alumni Bulletin*
Student Opinion Journal: *The Horace Mann Review*

Community Service Requirement   80 hours in grades 9–12; special activities in grades 7–8
Student Voluntary Service Organization

Hangouts   Riverdale diner, the library or cafeteria, The BBQ or the field outside on nice days

La Scuola D'Italia G. Marconi

12 East 96th Street
New York, NY 10128
(212) 369-3290, FAX (212) 369-1164

Coed
Pre-kindergarten–12th grade
Not accessible

Ms. Bianca Maria Padolecchia, Headmistress
Ms. Pia Pedicini, Vice Principal
Ms. Olympia Federico. Middle School Coordinator
Ms. Marisa Laroca Piccioli, High School Coordinator

Birthday Cutoff   Children entering at the nursery level must be 3 and toilet-trained by December 31
Children entering kindergarten must be 5 by December 31

Enrollment   Total enrollment: 170
Pre-Kindergarten 3/4's places: 24
Kindergarten places: 20
Graduating class 1998: 8–10

Tuition Range 1998–1999 $8,100 to $10,500, pre-kindergarten–12th grade
Additional fees: for application, registration and activities supplemental fees are approximately $850 for grades 1–12.

After-School Program   For children in grades Pre-K through 5, from September 5 through June; Monday–Thursday; 3:15 P.M. until 5:30 P.M.; for an additional charge activities include: English and Italian homework, Italian Language, Arts & Crafts, Singing, Acting, Piano, Creative Movement, Computer, Ballet
Evening Italian language and culture classes for adults

Summer Program   Summer camp is available if enough students are interested (additional charge)

La Scuola D'Italia G. Marconi, of New York was founded in 1977 by the Italian Ministry of Foreign Affairs and is dedicated to Guglielmo Marconi, the inventor of the wireless. Due to the increasing interest of Italian and American families, the school has grown into a unique bilingual educational institution that reflects the best features of both Italian and American instruction. The bilingual curriculum is rooted in the European classical tradition. La Scuola is now housed in a historic building, once a private mansion, on East 96th Street. Students must bring their own lunches. Students must become fluent in at least two languages: Bilingual instruction in English and Italian begins in pre-kindergarten. There is a four-year requirement in Latin for the ninth through twelfth grades and in French for the seventh through ninth grades. Students graduate with the Maturita, the equivalent of the International Baccalaureate.

La Scuola is legally recognized by the Italian Ministry of Education and chartered by the Regents of the University of the State of New York as a private, independent American school.

Graduates attend European universities and major American colleges.

Little Red School House and Elisabeth Irwin High School

Lower and Middle Divisions
196 Bleecker Street
New York, NY 10012
FAX (212) 677-9159

Upper Division
40 Charlton Street
New York, NY 10014
(212) 477-5316 (main number), FAX (212) 675-3595

Coed
Pre-kindergarten–12th grade
Not accessible

Mr. Andrew McLaren, Director
Ms. Sally Tannen, Director of Admissions
Miss Ridie Lazar, Assistant Director of Admissions,
Middle and Upper divisions

Birthday Cutoff   Children entering pre-kindergarten must be 4 by
October 31
Children entering kindergarten must be 5 by October 31

Enrollment   Total enrollment: 435
Pre-kindergarten places: 24
Kindergarten places: 30
Graduating class size: approximately 15–20

Grades   Semester system
Letter grades begin in 5th grade
Departmentalization begins in 5th grade

Tuition Range 1998–1999 $13,505 to $15,560, Pre-K–12th grade
Additional fees for lunch, trips, books, student activities, Parents
Association dues and graduation fee are approximately $1,500

Financial Aid/Scholarship   36% of the student body receive some
form of aid

Endowment $200,000

After-School Program   All programs are for LREI students only; all require an additional payment
Before-School Program: for 4–13 year olds, 7:30 A.M. to 8:40 A.M. The Early Childhood-Primary Program: for 4–6 year olds, 2:45 P.M. to 6:00 P.M.; a variety of creative and recreational activities The Intermediate Program: for 7–13 year olds, 2:45 P.M. to 6:00 P.M.; a variety of creative and recreational activities A 10-week Academic Enrichment Program: for 4–13 year olds, 2:45 P.M. to 6:00 P.M.
Vacation Program: for 4–9 year olds; a variety of creative and recreational activities; additional vacation programs are available for older children

Summer Program   Open to children from other schools; camps for 4–14 year olds from mid-June to mid-August (Day Camp for children ages 4–9; Specialty camps in French, Spanish, Chinese, Science and Technology; Sports Academy; Travel Camp). An additional payment is required.

––––––

Little Red School House and Elisabeth Irwin High School (LREI) was founded in 1921 by Elisabeth Irwin. Working closely with John Dewey and Eleanor Roosevelt, Ms. Irwin set up a "model school" within New York City's public school system with an emphasis on experiential (or active) learning. She eventually moved the program out of the public schools. Ms. Irwin selected students she thought reflected the diversity of New York City and aimed for a school with an exceptionally involved parent body. In the late 1930s Ms. Irwin was able to purchase the buildings where the high school is now located, and the lower and middle schools were moved to the Bleecker Street location.

The ERB is required for admission to grades four through twelve. The school is composed of three divisions. Lower school: four year olds through fourth grade; middle school: fifth through eighth grades; high school: ninth through twelfth. Hot lunch is available for an additional fee. Formal foreign language instruction begins in the fours with Spanish; in sixth grade students may choose between beginning French or continuing Spanish.

Little Red and Elisabeth Irwin recently celebrated its seventy-fifth anniversary and maintains a progressive approach which nurtures both intellectual rigor and a genuine joy of learning. The school retains its original emphasis on experiential and collaborative learning, and a commitment to diversity—both in the student population and curriculum. During the 1960s the "Red" in the school name supposedly implied sympathy for the leftist viewpoints. Today, Director McLaren says, "We are not a radical school, but we believe in critical thinking."

True to its mission as a model school, LREI provides an atmosphere in which innovative teaching thrives. The creative, young staff create exciting curricula which can then be replicated in other schools. We were particularly impressed by a fifth grade science/history project designed to introduce students to the problems of interpreting archeological artifacts. Three teams of students design clay artifacts that represent different aspects of ancient civilization and bury them in a dig box in the school's backyard. They dig up each other's artifacts, analyze them in the lab and write up an interpretation of each piece. The project culminates in the creation of a "physical museum" in the classroom as well as a computer museum where students can "click" on a fragment and see a picture of the whole artifact and text explaining its meaning. The project integrates art, science, history, English, computer and math; through their active participation, students are stimulated to think in new ways.

At LRE the classes are small and the student teacher ratio is seven to one. Classes are structured but informal; everyone is on a first name basis. "There are rigorous academic expectations while allowing for plenty of creative expression," says McLaren. Community service is a requirement beginning in the middle school. LREI enrolled five Prep for Prep students in 1998.

Parents say that LREI has always been in the forefront of innovative education. Essentially it provides a very comfortable learning environment with a solid academic foundation: "The day is tightly structured without being constraining; one subject flows into the next"; "The Gestalt at a school has to be right for learning and at Little Red, it is." A teacher at LREI told us "Their first priority is to really love and care about the kids . . . they feel it is their responsibility to find a way so that each child can grow and be challenged."

The Thanksgiving Assembly is a tradition that reflects the sense of community at LREI. The room is decorated with a beautiful display of autumn cornucopia and corn stalks. The children and teachers sit in chairs and on the floor and there is a big basket in the middle. Representatives from each class get up and read a poem and put something they've made—cornbread, for example—into the Thanksgiving basket (the gifts are donated to the needy.) One of the faculty talks about the origin of the thanksgiving tradition and they sing a Native American song. "It was not a spectacle for the parents, it had real meaning and was very moving," said a participant.

In 1996, the high school inaugurated a modular schedule; the academic year is divided into five modules or "mods" rather than semesters; during each mod, students focus on three major subjects rather than the traditional five or six. LREI is also the headquarters of the city wide Urban Citizen Project, which involves students in issues of urban life and governance.

High school students can take elective courses at the Colleges of Arts and Sciences at NYU through a special arrangement between the schools. Students have taken courses in anthropology, creative writing, religion and philosophy.

Traditions   Weekly Assembly Program, Buddy classes, Division trips, 7th grade Williamsburg trip, 8th grade trip to France or Spain, High School environmental studies trip, Book Fair, Halloween Fair, Spring Fair, Arts auction held in a Soho gallery featuring work by LREI parents and faculty, Fathers Who Cook Dinner, Father-Child camping trip, Literary Evening, Poetry Slam, Lower, Middle and Upper School Chorus

Publications   Several desktop publications related to the curriculum
Yearbook: *Expression*
Lower school yearbook: *Really Red*
LREI newsletter: *Monthly Mailings*

Community Service   Required in the Middle and Upper School

Hangouts   Student lounge, In the Black Coffee Shop

Loyola School

980 Park Avenue
New York, NY 10028
(212) 288-3522
website: http://www.loyola.nyc.org.

Coed
9th–12th grade
Not accessible

Rev. Joseph J. Papaj, S.J., President and Headmaster
Mrs. Audrey M. Grieco, Director of Admissions

Uniform   Dress code consists of blue blazer with Loyola patch for all students. Boys: collared shirt, tie, slacks. Girls: collared blouse, skirt or slacks. No jeans, T-shirts or sneakers

Birthday Cutoff   None

Enrollment   Total enrollment: approximately 200
Graduating class size: approximately 50

Grades   Semester system
Numerical grades for exams and report cards; letter grades for progress reports

Tuition   1998–1999 $12,200

Financial Aid/Scholarship   Approximately $400,000
Approximately 36% of the student body receives some form of financial assistance

Endowment $2.2 million

Diversity   As one student said: "Loyola has a very diverse group of students from different walks of life. When the student body comes together a very special atmosphere is created."

Homework   Approximately 2½–3 hours per night

274

After-School Program Extracurricular activities and clubs meet after school and during a mid-day period set aside for this purpose. Varsity and Junior varsity teams compete in the Independent School Athletic League, the Girls Independent School Athletic League, and the Independent Baseball Association

Summer Program None

Loyola School was founded in 1900 by Jesuits at the request of parents who wanted a Catholic alternative to non-sectarian prep schools. At that time the school was "up in the county" but featured the most up-to-date classrooms in the city. It became co-ed in 1973. The Loyola School is the only independent coed Jesuit high school in the New York tri-state area. Loyola combines Jesuit traditions with a strong college preparatory program. The school's motto, *Fide Fortis*, means "From Faith, Strength." The school is governed by a lay board of trustees and has been named a School of Excellence by the U.S. Department of Education.

The school is housed in an imposing stone building at Eighty-Third Street and Park Avenue. In September 1996, Loyola completed a half-million dollar renovation of the fourth floor. This expansion allowed the school to enlarge its science and computer labs. The school's technology coordinator is Mr. James Lyness.

In 1995, Father Joseph Papaj, S.J., (pronounced "PAPeye"), became President and Headmaster of the school. Father Papaj has served as Director of Campus Ministry at St. Joseph's University, had served on Loyola's board and was principal of two other Jesuit high schools.

Getting in: Applicants and their families are invited to an Open House in the fall. Applicants are evaluated on the basis of their academic and personal qualifications. Admissions requirements include: a transcript from the current school, a personal interview, two letters of recommendation, and Loyola's entrance exam, which is similar to the ISEE. In addition, the tour applicants are encouraged to spend a day visiting classes. Audrey Grieco, Director of Admissions, is warm and has a genuine love for the school.

Parents: A "New Parents" evening is held in the fall of the freshman year, an opportunity for parents to socialize and to familiarize themselves with their child's daily life. Parent-teacher conferences are held four times a year and either a written report or a report card is sent home every six weeks. There is an active Parents Association and the Headmaster distributes a newsletter to parents regularly.

Program: There is a warm and friendly family atmosphere at Loyola. As one student said: "At Loyola, they care about us as students and as teenagers getting through today's world." Every student has a faculty mentor who assists with student's academic, spiritual and extracurricular options. The Dean of Academic Affairs for over 17 years, Sister Nora Cronin, is role model and inspiration to the young women at Loyola, many of whom have gone onto successful careers in the sciences. One Loyola alumna is a recent graduate of West Point.

Loyola's goals are to promote religious, intellectual, cultural, social and physical growth in every student as well as a concern for social justice. "Jesuits are known for being very independent," we were told. While the majority of students are Roman Catholic, a wide variety of faiths are represented. According to the school, Loyola's philosophy is: "Strong faith must be founded on a solid understanding which extends to theology classes, where knowledge rather than belief is stressed." The curriculum in religious studies is complemented with a program of retreats, and each morning, before classes begin, optional Mass is available in the chapel.

The core curriculum consists of four years of theology, English and physical education; three years of history, math and foreign language; two years of science, one year of speech, composition skills, art history, computer, health and music history. Writing skills are stressed; freshmen are required to take seven periods a week in English and composition skills.

Students may take elective courses in art history, art studio, computer science, writing fiction, poetry, discrete mathematics, Latin, modern drama, modern American fiction, film study, chorus, ensemble, modern British and American poetry, philosophy in literature, global perspectives, political science and economics. French, Spanish, Italian and Latin are offered. Advanced placement courses are offered in American history, European history, biology, physics, calculus, computer science, English, French and Spanish. Advanced Italian is offered in conjunction with Fordham University as a college credit course.

Loyola students excel in speech and debating, and there is a trophy case filled with the forensic and debate clubs' winnings. Loyola usually places first in the small school division for State Championships. The school competes successfully in many local, regional and national competitions. In addition to Speech, Loyola also has a Model Congress.

There is a large art studio and students work in many media including drawing, pastels, prints, watercolors, and oil painting. Students' musical activities include solo, ensemble instrumental and choral performances. "The Loyola Players" produce two professional level drama productions each year, and a major musical every other year. Recent productions: *Marvin's Room* and *Picnic*.

The elected student government is an integral part of school life at Loyola. Representatives help plan school dances as well as address student's issues. The volunteer service program, whose motto reflects the Jesuit motto, "Men and Women for Others," provides opportunities for students to help others.

During Spring Break, fifteen to twenty seniors and some faculty spend two weeks traveling through Italy from Milan to Rome, with Easter at the Vatican. The school also sponsors three overnight ski trips a year. Loyola also offers a spring vacation trip to another country, open to all students. One year the trip was to France, another year it was to Austria and Germany.

The athletic teams at Loyola are competitive. For boys, sports teams include junior and varsity soccer, basketball and baseball. Girls teams include volleyball, basketball, softball and co-ed varsity track and cross country. In a recent year the girls won the GISAL volleyball championship. This year the boys' varsity and the boys' junior varsity basketball teams won the ISAL championships. A professional quality gym, paddle tennis courts, and a fully equipped fitness room are also available to students.

The school has a cafeteria that serves a hot lunch daily. Beginning in ninth grade with parents' permission, students may leave for lunch.

Popular College Choices Amherst, Brown, Boston College, Columbia, Georgetown, Holy Cross, New York University, Princeton, Williams

Traditions Freshman/Senior Night, Junior Talent Night, Arts Festival, Fall/Spring Drama Productions, Christmas Concert, Awards Convocation, Sports Night, Sophomore/Junior Semi-Formal, Senior Prom, Senior Trip to Italy

Publications   Newspaper: *Blazer*
Literary Magazine: *Knight*
Yearbook

Community Service Requirement   There is a four year Christian community service requirement. As part of the Jesuit philosophy students are encouraged to volunteer. Choices include: annual school-wide service projects at Thanksgiving, Christmas and during Lent, which provide food, clothing, toys and monetary donations. Students also volunteer to tutor underprivileged children, visit shut-ins, prepare and deliver meals to an SRO and to the homeless, work in metropolitan area hospitals, and help senior citizens. In addition to community service, students also volunteer in the weekend homeless shelter at St. Ignatius Loyola Church.

Hangouts   The Commons, Mimi's Pizzeria, the steps of the Metropolitan Museum of Art, Loyola Cafe and Senior Section (complete with pool table, lounge, TV and stereo, located on the bottom floor of the School)

Lycée Français de New York

The French Baccalaureate School

Pre–N through 5th grade
7–9 East 72nd Street and
12 East 73rd Street
New York, NY 10021

6th through 10th grades
Admissions and Administrative Offices
3 East 95th Street
New York, NY 10128

11th and 12th grades and Baccalaureate Prep.
60 East 93rd Street
New York, NY 10128

(212) 369-1400, Admissions x 3111, FAX (212) 423-1275
(for all three locations)

Coed
Nursery–12th grade
Not accessible

Mr. François Macheras, President
Mr. Gauthier Willm, Director of Studies
Nora Schaumburger, Admissions and Director, Early Childhood
Programs
Elise Maman, Admissions at all other levels

Uniform: Classical navy Lycée blazer, skirt for girls, trousers for
boys; white shirt

Birthday Cutoff Children entering at the pre-nursery level must be 3
by September, at the nursery level they must be 4 by September 30
Children entering kindergarten must be 5 by September 30

Enrollment Total enrollment: 925
Pre-nursery places: 26
Nursery places: 53

Kindergarten places: 70
Graduating class size: approximately 55–60

Tuition Range 1998–1999 $8,200 to $12,300, 3's–12th grade
Additional fees of under $1,000

After-School Program After-school program for nursery and kindergarten only; an additional payment is required

Summer Program Ecole Buissoniere ECP and Elementary

Founded in 1936 by a group of French and American individuals, the Lycée Français de New York offers a classical Franco-European education as well as an English/American Social Studies program. Fifty-four nationalities are represented in the student body. The tone of the school is formal and there is a uniform requirement. Applicants to nursery through fifth grade are admitted on the basis of interviews and school records. Applicants to the secondary school (sixth grade through *terminale*—thirteenth year) must take an entrance examination unless they are transferring from an accredited French School (in France or elsewhere). The school is accredited by the French Ministry of National Education and by NYSAIS. No knowledge of the French language is required for nursery through kindergarten. Applicants to grades two and above should have a working knowledge of the French language. Bilingual instruction is given in nursery and kindergarten. By first grade classes are taught only in French except for English, American literature and history and other foreign languages. Beginning in ninth grade, in addition to French and English, a third foreign language is required; choices include German, Spanish and Italian. An introduction to Latin and Greek is required in eighth grade, further instruction is elective. Because of an accelerated curriculum, a high school diploma may be awarded to students after *premiere*—twelfth grade. Most students continue to the end of *terminale* and take the French Baccalaureate.

Graduates attend a variety of American or European colleges and universities or take preparatory classes for the "Grandes Écoles" in France.

Manhattan Country School

7 East 96th Street
New York, NY 10128
(212) 348-0952, FAX (212) 348-1621
website: www.mcs.pvt.K12.ny.us
e-mail: mcs@mcs.pvt.K12.ny.us

Coed
Pre-Kindergarten–8th grade
Not accessible
Dr. Michèle Solá, Director
Ms. Mary Trowbridge, Director of Admissions

Uniform   None

Birthday Cutoff   Children entering the 4/5's must be 4 by October 31

Enrollment   Total enrollment: 180–190
4/5's places: 18
Graduating class 1998: 22

Grades   Detailed anecdotal reports
Three parent conferences required per year
No letter or number grades in the lower school (through 4th grade); Effort is graded in the upper school
Departmentalization begins in 5th grade and is completed by 8th grade

Tuition Range 1998–1999 $11,400 to $16,200, 4/5's–8th grade
All parents pay according to family income on a sliding scale. The maximum compares to full tuition at other schools
Fees are included in the tuition
Parents can pay tuition on a monthly basis
There is a 25% deposit required when contracts are signed

Financial Aid/Scholarship   Approximately 65% of the student body receive some financial aid

Diversity   50% students of color

281

Endowment $6.3 million

After-School Program   A variety of creative, academic, and recreational activities. MCS After-School Program meets Mondays–Thursdays from 3:00 P.M. until 5:30 P.M. for 4 year olds to 8th graders, an additional payment is required

Homework   Nursery and K—None
1st grade: Once a week, 30 minutes
2nd: 30 minutes, 3 x a week
3rd and 4th: 45 minutes, 4–5 x a week
5th and 6th: 1–1½ hrs per night
7th and 8th: 2–3 hrs per night

Summer Program   Three-week summer farm camp program in the Catskills; for 20 children age 9 and up; open to students from other schools; an additional payment is required

In 1966, Manhattan Country School was founded by Augustus and Martha Trowbridge, on Manhattan's Upper East Side, in an elegant private landmark building designed by Ogden Codman. Manhattan Country School's origins are deeply rooted in the social and ideological principles of the Civil Rights Movement. Its commitment to equality, social justice and cultural diversity are at the center of its curriculum. MCS has achieved what many independent schools with far greater endowments and financial aid claim is their goal: a truly diverse school. Fifty percent of the student body and faculty are people of color. There is a unique tuition/scholarship program at MCS. The school is a recipient of a five-year private family foundation grant to develop a gender-equity curriculum. In 1997, "Gus" Trowbridge, director and founder of MCS, retired. Michèle Solá, formerly Assistant Director, is the new Director.

Getting in: All parents applying to MCS should visit the school as a first step in the admissions process. From mid-September until mid-April, tours are held during the school day. Parents of children applying to Pre-K through first grade should attend a tour before January. In early November, an Open House is held at the school. Parents who have requested admissions materials prior to November will automatically receive an invitation.

For applicants from pre-kindergarten through first grade, MCS does not require the ERB test. However, if the test is administered MCS should receive a copy of the test results. Children are observed and asked to play games at the group interviews. For applicants for second grade and above, ERB test results are required, as well as the applicant's school report and an interview. "Most importantly, we're looking for a good match, families that are comfortable with a diverse community." says Michèle Solá, Director of MCS.

Parents: Parents at MCS, as well as parents of alumni, are active fund-raisers for the school. They help organize many events throughout the school year. The parents of each class are responsible for one event, a total of ten in any given year. These include: Farm Festival, Grandparents' Day, Kwanzaa Festival, Spring Benefit, Dr. Martin Luther King, Jr. Commemorative Walk, and Farm Outing Day. There are many opportunities for parents to come together with the faculty and administration, to discuss common issues relating to education and child development. Parents Association Meetings are well attended and committees meet regularly.

Parents are an integral part of the social studies curriculum. The 4/5's class take "home visits"; the 7/8's study a family in depth for one semester; the sixth grade invites parents and other relatives to share their histories as part of their project on the Civil Rights Movement. Teachers at MCS welcome the opportunity for parents to share stories and talents and accompany students on class trips. Parent-teacher conferences are held three times a year, and parents may meet more often if there's a need.

Program: The lower school at MCS is composed of six mixed-age groupings from 4/5's through 9/10's. The lower school groups span two overlapping age levels. These mixed-age groupings offer flexible academic and social placements for children and enable the school to meet the developmental needs of each child. Within this framework, a grade level for each student is designated by the school. The average class is eighteen, but many classes are taught in smaller groups of eight to ten students. Each of the four youngest classes has a head teacher and an assistant, as well as student teachers, in most classrooms throughout the school. One parent told us, "To me the most important characteristic of MCS is the deep respect shown to students and their individuality. In this school community, students learn to value themselves along with their peers. The artificial barriers that schools routinely set regarding the teaching experts and the learners are less visible in the MCS environment. Everyone is learning and everyone is teaching."

The core curriculum at MCS is its social studies program. It allows the school to apply its multicultural perspectives and fosters positive social values. In the lower school, social studies is integrated into all areas of the classroom through graphs, geography and mapping, creative writing, literature, drama and art. In the upper school, social studies and history follow a chronological organization. Students refine research skills, and learn how to write formal research papers, as well as point-of-view essays.

Formal reading instruction begins in the 5/6's class. In small groups, (approximately half the class), students are taught how to read and write. MCS takes into account that children learn to read in a variety of ways, and the teachers use many materials, including basal readers, structured phonics materials and literature. For students who need reinforcement, a reading specialist works in the classroom with small groups of students. If additional support is needed, a student will work with the specialist in another classroom. If a tutor is recommended, the school will work together with the student's tutor to help meet the student's needs.

The school considers Spanish to be an essential component to the multicultural experience at MCS. Beginning with the four-year-olds, Spanish is taught at every level in mixed-age groupings. Signs throughout the school are written in Spanish. The lower school Spanish program is culture-based and integrated into the classrooms. The upper school Spanish program is textbook based and prepares students for the New York State Proficiency Exam in Spanish.

The upper school at MCS is composed of grades five through eight. Departmentalization begins in fifth grade. Fifth and sixth graders study English, social studies and math with their group teacher. Specialists teach Spanish, science, art, music, shop and physical education. In seventh and eighth grades, students are divided into two mixed-age homerooms, and each student is assigned a faculty advisor. Classes for seventh and eighth grades are fully departmentalized.

The math program follows four fundamental themes: making sense of data, patterns and predications, numbers and number sense, and geometry and spatial sense. In the lower school, math is integrated into the children's daily activities and manipulative materials are used. Upper school students follow a common text.

MCS has taken a hands-on approach for the science curriculum. Teachers and science consultants make use of Central Park as a nature laboratory. Students learn to use the scientific techniques necessary for accurate observation, problem-solving and recording. Classrooms have work areas for experimentation, science displays, and science libraries. A goal of the science program is to instill a critical understanding of the ethical questions surrounding scientific issues.

Technology: In 1996 MCS was chosen as one of only two NYC private schools to work in collaboration with Teachers College's Institute of Learning Technology's Eiffel Project. As part of the project, MCS has been wired for Internet access via a T1 line and classrooms are networked. Seventh and eighth grades have computer and Internet access available in their classrooms. Fifth through eighth graders must complete a four-year computer literacy course and older children are offered electives in computer graphics and design. An after school computer class is offered to the fourth through seventh grades.

Computer use is directly related to the curriculum. For example, the seventh and eighth grades host their own website on Mammal Study; the eighth and ninth grades communicate via e-mail with the Zuni nation in New Mexico; shop students use AutoCAD to design woodworking projects, and the seventh and eighth graders produce a literary magazine, *Lit Mag.*, using desktop publishing.

Art, music and drama enhance the curriculum. Art is required of all students through sixth grade; seventh and eighth graders must meet a combination requirement in the arts, with additional electives available in each subject.

All students have weekly library classes. The library hosts presentations by visiting authors, such as Jamaica Kincaid, Milton Melzer, Brian Pinkey and Vera B. Williams. It is also where class plays and family story-telling gatherings are held.

Children in the 4/5's through 7/8's have daily outdoor activities at a nearby playground or in the meadow at Central Park. There are structured group activities with a physical education teacher once a week either in the school's music room or in the park. The 8/9's through eighth grade have outdoor time in Central Park three times a week and a structured physical education class twice a week at the Boys Harbor Gym, located on Fifth Avenue at 104th Street. There are elective classes in track, basketball and tennis for older students.

MCS owns a small working farm, located on 177 acres in the Catskill Mountains in Roxbury, New York. Students with their teachers, begin going to the farm in the spring of their 7/8's year. By fifth grade, they have three week-long trips a year. The farm acquaints students with a self-reliant way of life. "One of my favorite times was at the farm. My farm education gave me an appreciation for a completely different lifestyle, as well as teaching me various things like milking cows, tapping trees, creating textiles," says an alumna. The farm program leads to six graduation requirements: to milk a cow; to plan and cook an evening meal for the entire class and to bake bread or another yeast dough product without adult assistance; to identify birds, plants, animals and their tracks, to describe the life cycle of one animal; to produce an original textile from fleece to a finished garment, artifact or material; and to participate in a "town meeting" on an environmental issue. A recent graduate told us, "Looking back at my years at MCS, I realize that I loved everything about it. At the time I remember feeling that the school was so small and undeveloped. However, MCS had everything I needed. The diverse community and the close relationships with my teachers were experiences that I would not have gotten anywhere else."

Graduates: About half go on to the specialized public high schools; half go on to the independent schools including Riverdale, Fieldston, Friends, UNIS, Calhoun, Trevor Day

Marymount School of New York

1026 Fifth Avenue
New York, NY 10028
(212) 744-4486, FAX (212) 744-0163
website: www.marymount.K12.ny.us

All girls
(boys in nursery and pre-kindergarten)
Nursery–12th grade
Accessible

Sister Kathleen Fagan, Headmistress
Ms. Concepcion R. Alvar, Director of Admissions

Uniform Lower School—Fall/Spring: blue cord jumper, white short-sleeved blouse, navy blue blazer. Winter: navy blue jumper, white or red turtleneck, navy blue sweater or blazer
Middle School—Fall/Spring: blue cord skirt, white short-sleeved shirt, navy blue sweater, navy blue blazer. Winter: plaid or gray skirt, white turtleneck, navy blue or green sweater or blazer
Upper School—Fall/Spring: blue cord skirt, white short-sleeved, navy blue sweater, navy blue blazer. Winter: plaid or gray skirt, white turtleneck, navy blue green or yellow sweater or blazer

Birthday Cutoff Children entering at the nursery level should be 3 years old by August 31
Children entering kindergarten should be 5 by August 31st

Enrollment Total enrollment: 400
Nursery places: 15
Kindergarten places: 20–25
Graduating class sizes: approximately 40

Grades Semester system
Letter grades begin in class V. Grades are distributed each quarter, upper school grades given out at parent-teacher-student conferences 2x a year
Departmentalization begins in class IV

Tuition Range 1998–1999 $9,600 to $16,200, Nursery–12th grade
Additional fees for books and activities approximately $800

Financial Aid/Scholarship　Available to those who qualify
Approximately 27% of students receive some aid

Endowment　N/A

Diversity　Approximately 28% students of color
3 Prep for Prep students enrolled as of Fall 1998
Cultural Awareness Club, Multicultural Committee, Jazz Festival, Harambee Night, International Week, Senior Class trip to the U.S. Holocaust Memorial Museum, Native American Exchange Program

After-School Program　Marymount's after-school program for K–III requires an additional payment
After-School Activities Program: for grades kindergarten through 7th, Monday–Thursday until 6:00 P.M., Fridays until 5:00 P.M.; a variety of creative and recreational activities
The Instrumental Music Program offers private lessons
Supervised Study Program, Monday–Thursday until 6:00 P.M.

Summer Program　Marymount Summer Program: coed, ages 3–8, open to students from other schools; mid-June through July; a variety of creative and recreational activities; Drama Camp: a six-week coed program for ages 8–14; mid-June through July; acting, improvisation, and set design; the program culminates in the production of a full-scale musical or scenes; Science/Technology Camp: 2 weeks, coed, ages 8–14, exploration in laboratories, field trips; team sports and swimming are part of all of these programs

---

The Marymount School of New York was founded in 1926 as part of an international network of schools directed by the Religious of the Sacred Heart of Mary. The founder, Mother Butler, believed that women should be leaders in society and that, "the world never needed women's intelligence and sympathy more than it does today." The school became independently incorporated in 1969. Sister Kathleen Fagan, a graduate of the school, has been headmistress since 1976. She previously taught at Marymount schools in London and New York.

The Marymount School is housed in three adjoining Beaux Arts mansions on Fifth Avenue, part of the Metropolitan Museum of Art landmark district. The breathtaking ballroom on an upper floor must be seen to be believed. Sixty-five percent of the student body is Catholic and thirty-two different nationalities are represented. The director of admissions told us: "Religious education and chapel are the moral thread that binds the school." Chapel service, held once a week, may be conducted by students of any faith; social issues are discussed. Students attend Mass at least four times a year. Students can participate in an exchange program with any Marymount School in Los Angeles, London, Paris or Rome.

Getting in: Parents are invited to attend a fall Open House. After applying, parents meet with the director of admissions and tour the school. Children may accompany their parents on the tour. On a separate date, applicants are interviewed individually at the school. Beginning in kindergarten the ERB is required for admission. The school says it "thoroughly considers the unique qualities of each applicant including academic ability, special interests, and talents."

Parents: The parent body includes business people, artists, academicians, engineers, doctors, lawyers and government employees. Parents are an active and integral part of the school. They visit classes, set up exhibits, volunteer to read to children in the library and so on. Activities sponsored by the Parents Association, include parent meetings and conferences with teachers that strengthen school-family ties. Parents and alumnae give career seminars and offer their places of work for senior internships.

Program: The lower school is composed of nursery through third grade. Each morning students are greeted in the lobby by the division head. Each lower school classroom has a head teacher and an assistant. The program is structured and traditional but characterized by creativity and warmth. There are organized learning centers equipped with hands-on, interactive materials that encourage experimentation and collaboration. Students are grouped according to skill levels in reading and math. French begins in third grade. Science and technology education begins at the nursery level in the newly renovated science and technology laboratories. The children are taught by specialists in art, music, science, language, computers and physical education. There is a reading and learning specialist on staff.

Marymount has a unique relationship with the Metropolitan Museum of Art and was recently ranked number one among all city schools for use of the museum. Other city resources that the school uses include the United Nations, Ellis Island, the Stock Exchange, the Central Park Zoo, the Staten Island Observatory and various galleries and museums as experimental classrooms.

Each lower school student has a big sister in the middle or upper school. This bond is strengthened throughout the year by trips, events and shared projects.

The middle school is composed of grades four through seven. According to the brochure, in the middle school "Each student is encouraged to develop and pursue areas of interest, to think honestly and critically about the world around her and to acquire a sense of social responsibility in school, at home and in her community." The integrated core curriculum gradually increases in the degree of departmentalization at each grade level. Latin is introduced at grade five. Readings and written composition are incorporated into the study of French. Students begin the study of Shakespeare in sixth grade. They also begin a peer training program in seventh grade to prepare them to be peer counselors to the middle school students. Research and study skills with a focus on time management and organization are emphasized. Speech, debate and drama are incorporated into the program and students participate in weekly assemblies, chapel services and an annual drama production.

Marymount School has established a school-wide network of computers with Internet access. Computers are used across the curriculum and provide multiple tools for gathering data, sharing information and completing assignments. In addition, there is a state-of-the-art library network that offers access to the entire library catalog, a 14-slot CD-ROM tower, and an on-line periodical service on the Internet.

Beginning in nursery school, lower school students learn in the general science laboratory with its child-size tables and stools. Three spacious state-of-the-art science laboratories are equipped with Powerbooks and multimedia teaching stations to provide a variety of work space configurations. Upper school students take three years of laboratory science and 75% elect a fourth year of science. AP courses are offered in chemistry and biology as well as eight other subjects.

The upper school consists of grades eight through twelve. Students continue to study French or Latin or they may choose to study Spanish. Some students opt to study two languages. Graphing calculators, computers, and other technological tools are used frequently in math, science and computer courses. The ninth grade Integrated Humanities Program links interdisciplinary themes in English, history, art history, religious studies, and studio art. Students visit the Metropolitan Museum of Art at least once a week. In the second semester, seniors attend weekly seminars hosted by alumnae who discuss their careers and life experiences. In May, seniors begin a five-week internship program, sponsored by alumnae or parents, during which they are exposed to a wide range of careers. The student-interns return to school periodically to report on their experiences in a group setting. Seniors also participate in an ethics class and attend evening events with their parents, hosted by the Director of College Counseling, to prepare them for college.

All Marymount students are encouraged to participate in extracurricular activities and they can select from a wide range of sports and clubs. Ten team sports are offered, including swimming, tennis and fencing. The school's basketball team has won the AAIS League championships for the last four years and also won a recent NYSAISAA State Championship. In addition to varsity sports there are junior varsity and seventh and eighth grade intramural teams.

At weekly assemblies, students make presentations or outside speakers address the school community as part of the alumnae sponsored Lisanti Speaker Series. Marymount recently celebrated the "Year of the Word," and hosted well-known speakers such as Gloria Steinem and 1996 Inaugural Poet Miller Williams. Other speakers have included Nobel Prize winner Dr. Rosalyn Yalow, a Chinese dissident and a curator from the Museum of Natural History. Each year students from Classes nine through twelve spend time at retreats. Ninth grade students travel to Frost Valley to bond as a class, sophomores focus on community service, juniors on leadership and seniors on ethical values/transition into colleges and careers. All students participate in community and school service which is integrated into the curriculum. Students in tenth grade are required to contribute forty hours of volunteer service at hospitals or agencies in New York City as part of their Social Justice class. Lower and middle school students visit senior citizens and participate in holiday food drives. Students volunteer in the school as tour leaders and ambassadors, office helpers and peer tutors.

Federal Judge Katharine Sweeney Hayden, Class of 1959, described her experience at Marymount: "We were always encouraged to express ourselves! We read and read and learned to absorb, synthesize and digest large amounts of material. As a lawyer and judge, I draw upon the benefits of my Marymount training every day."

Popular College Choices   Columbia, Yale, Harvard, University of Virginia, New York University, Boston College, Duke, Tufts, University of Pennsylvania, Vassar, Georgetown

Traditions   Founder's Day, Father-Daughter Square Dance, Vespers, the Christmas Pageant, Lessons and Carols, Family Ice-Skating Party, Family/Friends Day, Grandparents Day, the Book Fair, New Parents Reception, Field Days, Upper School retreats, Parent Picnics, Science Fair, Athletic Awards Evening, Spring Benefit, Junior Ring Day, Alumnae Reunion, 100 Nights Dinner

Publications   Student Newspaper: *The Joritan*
Student Literary Magazine: *The Muse*
Yearbook: *The Marifia*

Community Service   Community Service is required of all students. Opportunities include participating in New York Cares Day and the Achilles Club; visiting the elderly at Katen Residence; and sponsoring food and toy drives for the families of New York's Incarcerated Mothers Program. Community service activities are coordinated through Campus Ministry, one of the largest student clubs at the school

Hangouts   Amity Coffee Shop, Metropolitan Museum of Art steps, Marymount teahouse

Metropolitan Montessori School

325 West 85th Street
New York, NY 10024
(212) 579-5525, FAX (212) 579-5526

Coed
Pre-kindergarten through 6th grade
Accessible

Ms. Ramani DeAlwis, Head of School
Ms. Mary Gaines, Head of Primary School
Ms. Margi Doherty, Admissions Director

Birthday Cutoff   Children entering Pre-kindergarten must be 2.9 years old by September 1st
Children entering Kindergarten must be 4.9 years old by September 1st

Enrollment   Total enrollment: 210
Pre-K and Kindergarten places: 30
Kindergarten places only: 2–3 per year, as available
Graduating class size: 16

Tuition Range 1998–1999 $8,250 (primary half-day) through $12,000 (upper elementary)
Additional $400 field trip fee for upper elementary only
For new students only, the school requires a one-time fee (or bond) of $750 paid upon enrollment, refundable without interest upon written request after the child leaves the school

Financial Aid/Scholarship   Limited aid available
33 students receive some form of aid
10% of the annual budget of $2.5 million goes to financial aid

Endowment $1 million reserve fund
A capital campaign was begun in 1996 to replenish this fund which had been used for the renovation of the new building

Homework   1st grade: 20 minutes
2nd: 30–45 minutes

3rd: 1 hour

4–6th: 1½–2 hours

After-School Program   Primary half day program for 3 and 4 year olds, 12 noon–3:00 P.M.: 9–12 or 1–4 program optional for those enrolled in morning half day

Elementary program for 1st–6th grade: hours 9–3

Clubhouse: hours 3–5

Creative Arts Program: a variety of creative, recreational and academic activities, Monday–Friday, 3:00–4:30 P.M.

Early morning drop off program (8:00–9:00 A.M.)

An additional payment is required for all programs

Summer Program   Metropolitan Montessori School Summer Camp is open to 2.9 to 6 year old children. There are two 3 week sessions available in the months of June and July

---

Metropolitan Montessori School, formerly St. Michael's Montessori, was founded in 1964 and took its name from its previous location in St. Michael's Church on West 95th Street. In August of 1996 this popular nursery and elementary school moved 14 blocks south into a stately red brick building in the heart of the gentrified West Side. The new building, an extensively renovated 1865 carriage house which once belonged to William Randolph Hearst, provided the growing school with an additional 5,000 square feet of space. Characteristic of this nurturing school, when digging the foundation for the new building they took great care to preserve two one hundred year old London plane trees at the building site.

Getting in: After submitting an application, parents are invited to tour the school. Tours are given twice a week in the mornings. There is a question and answer period after the tour. Children are invited back with their parents for a one-on-one visit with a primary teacher to "see if they are developmentally ready to start." ERB testing is required for applicants to first through third grades. Students of color constitute approximately 30% of the school.

Program: The brochure states that "While educational method and classroom materials are firmly rooted in the philosophy of Dr. Maria Montessori, the school addresses the unique issues and concerns of today's children." Parents are pleased with the way the school imparts the academic groundwork necessary for later learning.

Mixed-age groups of children remain with the same teacher for three years. Children in grades 1 through 6 keep journals for all subjects and continue working in them as they move up through the school producing a visible record of their academic progress. Grammar is taught through the use of symbols; it looks difficult but most children have achieved mastery by third grade. Attention is paid to individual development within a group setting and students are ability-grouped for every subject. For instance, a first grader might be reading at a fourth grade level, a sixth grader might be doing ninth grade level math.

Children leave their classrooms for music, art, French (or Spanish), library and physical education. The new lending library's computers are networked throughout the school. Quizzes and tests begin in fourth grade and students receive letter grades in all subjects. A checklist and narratives are sent home once a year and there are two parent/teacher conferences.

Community service is an important component of a Metropolitan Montessori education. Fourth through sixth graders are required to perform at least 5 hours of service per school year. An integrated program allows students to visit a local home for the elderly who are also invited for a holiday lunch prepared and hosted by the children. One year students prepared Easter baskets of toiletries which were delivered to AIDS patients at St. Luke's hospital.

Metropolitan Montessori has its own literary journal and yearbook. There are numerous special events at the school, including a yearly spelling bee for grades one through six. Fourth through sixth graders put on a theatrical production; one year it was *Wind in the Willows*, another year it was *Macbeth*. There is an annual Sports Day at John Jay College gymnasium, a day of family bowling at Leisure Lanes, the March auction fundraiser, and a welcome picnic each September for the entire school.

The majority of Metropolitan Montessori graduates attend various independent schools. At least fifteen graduates of the school currently attend Stuyvesant High School.

The Modern School

539–543 West 152nd Street
New York, NY 10031
(212) 926-4731

Coed
Nursery–6th grade
Not accessible

Mrs. Sandra Carter, Director/Director of Admissions

Birthday Cutoff   Children entering nursery school must be $2\frac{1}{2}$ by September 1st

Enrollment   Total enrollment: 105
  Nursery places: 10
  Pre-K places: 16
  Kindergarten places: 16
  Graduating class size: variable, approximately 11–23

Tuition Range 1998–1999 $3,480 to $3,885, Nursery to 6th grade
  Tuition can be paid in 10 monthly installments

Financial Aid/Scholarship   Limited amount available
  15% of the student body receives some form of aid

Endowment   None

After-School Program   Children can arrive as early as 8:00 A.M. Daily after-school program: homework and study skills supervision as well as creative and recreational activities from 3:00-5:45 P.M. for an additional payment of approximately $35 per week

Summer Program   Summer Day Camp and tutorial program for an additional payment

———

The Modern School might seem like an oxymoronic title for one of the oldest black independent schools in New York City and the nation, but the school's mission—to provide an alternative to dismal inner-city public schools—is just as relevant today as it was in 1934, the year the Modern School was founded. In the succeeding sixty years multicultural scholarship and diversity programs such as Early Steps and Prep for Prep have been instituted to help prepare and to place children of color in other independent schools. But the school is still essential and the choice of many families. In 1954 The Modern School moved to its present location on West 152nd Street, a former convent school purchased from the Sisters of Mercy. Some of the original ornate wood moldings and fireplaces were preserved. But the youthful optimism of these bright faces learning in the once grand but now somewhat seedy building should tug at the heart-strings of a potential benefactor. The charismatic founder, Mildred Johnson, is still actively involved in the school. The school's brochure states that Mrs. Johnson's composer-father J. Rosamond Johnson, and her author-diplomat uncle, James Weldon Johnson, were important architects of the movement known as the Harlem Renaissance. Mrs. Johnson's numerous awards for service, including a Martin Luther King Jr. Lifetime Achievement Award and a 1984 citation from Mayor Edward Koch for distinguished service to the children of the city, are displayed in the school's reception room.

Getting in: Applicants for nursery through first grade are tested in-house. Second through sixth graders must submit the results of the Metropolitan Achievement Test.

Program: Despite its progressive origins, The Modern School's methods are described by Mrs. Carter as "traditional and struc-tured." The students wear neat uniforms (white blouse or shirt, grey skirt, jumper or slacks; only sixth graders can wear the light blue top.) In the classroom desks are organized into rows. The teachers seem young and committed, the students are attentive and eager to learn. Portraits of black heroes (drawn by a former teacher) decorate one stairwell. Fifth and sixth grade projects on ancient Egypt and the Civil War were on display in the lobby. Columbia University donated computers to The Modern School's computer lab. In third grade and up there is a computer in each room. First through sixth graders bring their own lunch. Hot lunch is served to nursery school students.

Special events at the Modern School include: fifth and sixth grade plays in February, the annual Spring Festival and the Science Fair (both held in May).

Graduates attend many of the District 4 alternative programs as well as various independent schools.

The Nightingale-Bamford School

20 East 92nd Street
New York, NY 10128
(212) 289-5020 (main number), Admissions: x208 or x211
FAX (212) 876-1045
website: www.nightingale.org
e-mail: ceverett@nightingale.org
info@nightingale.org
All girls
Kindergarten–12th grade
Accessible

Ms. Dorothy A. Hutcheson, Head of School
Ms. Carole J. Everett, Director of Admissions

Uniform   Lower school: navy or houndstooth jumper with white collared shirt
Middle school and upper school: navy skirt, gray or light blue lightweight kilt, white blouse or turtleneck, navy knee socks or navy or white tights
Upper school: navy, light blue or gray skirt, solid-color collared shirt, solid-color ankle or knee socks or tights. Middle and upper school: navy corduroy pants, Thanksgiving to Spring Break. Seniors can be out of uniform on Fridays and after Spring Break
No boots, clogs, or sandals

Birthday Cutoff   "No strict birthday cutoff" but most girls are 5 by the start of school

Enrollment   Total enrollment: 540
Kindergarten places: 40–42
Graduating class 1998: 45

Grades   Semester system, K–IV detailed narrative reports and checklists. Comments continue through upper grades
Letter grades begin in 5th grade
Departmentalization begins in 5th grade
First final exam in 7th grade

Tuition Range 1998–1999 $15,645 to $17,380 kindergarten–12th grade

Additional fees: for trips, lunch, books, supplies, Parents Association dues and yearbook approximately $950

Financial Aid/Scholarship   20% of students receive some form of aid
$1,183,780 was budgeted for financial aid in 1997
Average grant per student is $12,180

Endowment $20 million
$37,037 per student

Diversity   22% students of color, 27 Prep for Prep students enrolled as of fall 1998, 5 ABC., C.A.F.E.: Cultural Awareness For Everyone (school multicultural club that meets biweekly) sponsors assemblies, dinners, evenings
Parents of C.A.F.E. (meets once a month) for potluck supper and discussion
Nightingale students participate in the Interschool Multicultural Coalition which meets monthly
The Nightingale-Bamford School received a second DeWitt Wallace–Reader's Digest Fund Independent School Opportunity Program Grant in 1993 for scholarships for upper school students of color, recruiting faculty of color and workshops and programs on diversity for the entire school community
S.E.E.D. (Seeking Educational Equity, Diversity) seminars for faculty and administrators

Homework   Lower school families are expected to read aloud with their children from kindergarten on, a half hour a night reading or being read to by the child.
Kindergarten: none
1st and 2nd: $1/2$ hour
3rd and 4th: 45 minutes
5th and 6th: $1^1/2$–2 hours with built-in study hall during the school day
7th and 8th: $2^1/2$ hours
9th–12th: approximately 45 minutes per subject a night (with one homework-free subject per night) Weekly assignments are given to encourage long-term planning

After-School Program   Hobbyhorse, co-ed, a variety of recreational and creative activities for kindergarten–Class 4 until 6 P.M.

Boys from Allen-Stevenson and St. Bernard's Schools also participate. 12–15 courses are offered including gymnastics, drama, dance, chess, swimming, cooking, magic, knitting, photography, computer; an additional payment is required.

Junior varsity and varsity sports for Middle and Upper School girls, NBS participates in interscholastic athletic competition and also the 12-team Athletic Association of Independent Schools. The NBS gymnasium is usually open every Saturday for "pick-up" games and practices and Nightingale girls can participate in Saturday sports at St. Bernard's School.

Some special interest clubs, Glee Club, drama and dance rehearsals, literary magazine and newspaper also meet after school. There is also music instruction available.

Summer Program Sunny Days Program: coed, a June program for children ages 5–12 from 8:30 A.M. to 3:00 P.M.; trips, arts and crafts, swimming, computer, cooking and so on; open to children from the community; an additional payment is required

---

The Nightingale-Bamford School began with classes held by Miss Nightingale in 1906. In 1919 Miss Nightingale was joined by Maya Stevens Bamford and together they founded The Nightingale-Bamford School in 1920. In 1989 the school began a $15 million renovation and expansion, completed in 1991. The school now has central air-conditioning, state-of-the-art science labs and a hi-tech theatre/auditorium, a photo lab, three computer labs and a new cafeteria. "Formal, but not rigid, for very bright girls who know where they stand; not overly competitive," is the way one mother describes the school.

Traditional in the early years, Nightingale offers more choices later on. There is a conscious attempt to avoid gender stereotyping, while still instilling the social graces. They've struck a nice balance— keeping the best of the old while incorporating the new. "Academic rigor with a soul," says one parent.

Only the sixth head in the history of the school, Dorothy Hutcheson was preceded by the formidable Mrs. Edward McMenamin, who reigned for twenty-one years. McMenamin's legacy is the new facility and a successful endowment drive. A parent calls the arrival of Ms. Hutcheson, a native Georgian and an educator her whole career, "a breath of fresh air; now women don't have to use their husbands' last names." "Ms. Hutcheson can be warm, accessible and fun and also strict and firm. She listens to and also takes action for the students," a senior said. Ms. Hutcheson knows each student by name and often greets them and shakes their hand as they enter the blue doors in the morning. A ninth grader told us, "Ms. Hutcheson cares and is very open to new ideas and suggestions. It's good to be able to tell her the way we feel." A full-time working mother, Ms. Hutcheson has already made her refreshing presence known in other ways too. She accepted the Student Government's proposal to add pants to the dress code (after allowing female faculty members to wear pants). She re-established the Senior Independent Study project which allows qualified seniors to drop some of their required courses and pursue in-depth a topic of their choosing. There is great emphasis on integrating technology into the classroom. One parent remarked after her tour, "At Nightingale there was a sign that said 'Have you checked your e-mail today?' " Nightingale's time to gather by division, a time to reflect, to make announcements, and to discuss issues of moral and ethical concern, was formerly known as "Prayers." By renaming it "Morning Meeting," which more accurately describes it, Ms. Hutcheson has shown that she is not afraid to break with tradition.

Getting in: One parent described NBS's application process as "warm and welcoming." Parents can arrange for a tour before applying. When the application is received, parents are given an appointment for a tour and an interview with a member of the admissions staff. On another date kindergarten applicants will have a group interview with lower school teachers while their parents meet with Ms. Hutcheson and Mrs. Blanche Mansfield, the head of the lower school. Middle and upper school girls take their tours with student tour guides. Individual interviews with the division heads are required. Girls do placement work during their visit. If admitted, girls and parents are invited to re-visit and spend time in the school. There are welcome parties for all new students and parents in the spring and early fall. A great deal of care is given to having families make a smooth transition to Nightingale. Preference is given to siblings and legacies, but they are not automatically accepted, and an active wait list is maintained after admissions decisions have been made. No letters of recommendation are required or desired as part of the process. Nightingale has made a major commitment to diversity and there are more girls from different racial, ethnic and socio-economic backgrounds than in the past.

A mother who eventually chose NBS said that she "couldn't sit up straight enough at some of the other schools," and while she noticed "a lot of scarves on the parents at other girls' schools," she was impressed by "the sensible shoes" she saw at NBS.

Is there a typical student? It depends on whom you ask. According to one parent, "She has blond straight hair, uses little or no makeup and carries an L. L. Bean bookbag." Yet another parent told us the typical student is "earnest, engaging, vibrant and aware," referring to an upper school student she felt exemplified NBS qualities. A tenth grader said "We are smart, involved in the life of the school and have learned to speak with confidence." Obviously!

A parent told us that NBS delivers "a ton of nurturing." She felt her daughter walked the line between "funny and fresh." Since it sometimes seems that outgoing girls receive the most attention, it was refreshing to see that Nightingale awards the Molly Hemmerdinger Scholarship Fund, in memory of Molly Hemmerdinger, "for support of a shy student with hidden potential." An NBS mother with two daughters at the school said she feels the school "is making little Eleanor Roosevelts out of the girls: self reliant, inner-directed and well versed." A father said, "They learn to be independent, to do for themselves." He also believes there is a hidden agenda, to teach the girls the social graces. He also said he thought "Nightingale makes feminists of the fathers."

Parents: The parent body is diverse and varies from class to class. "There are lots of mixed [religion] marriages," said one parent. Jewish and Christian holidays are observed. "When you give at Nightingale, you receive," said one parent. "It's good to be an involved parent and make yourself known." One father who admits he always shaves before attending a school event or dropping off his daughter, yet describes himself as "one of the youngest and loosest" parents there, said he enjoys serving on "Daddy Patrol" (safety patrol) and walking his daughter to school with other Nightingale fathers and daughters.

A mother remarked, "As a parent of color in the school, I wanted to be vigilant, vocal and visible. Nightingale has welcomed me and my daughter fully and made us feel comfortable and I've loved the C.A.F.E. dinners and volunteering for various committees."

The Parents Association plays an integral role in the life of the Nightingale community by providing communication among parents, staff, administration and faculty and by supporting the school. Many parents volunteer their time and talents for school activities and events such as Grandparents' Day, Father-Daughter breakfast, programs on parenting, Safety Patrol and the Book Fair. Other ways that parents are involved include speaking to classes and assemblies, asking friends with special areas of expertise to share them at school, inviting students to visit them on the job, singing at an all-School concert, performing in or helping with costumes and make-up for an all-School play, chaperoning class trips, volunteering in the library and cooking or baking for class get-togethers. In addition, the Parents Association sponsors the fair, a "Fathers Who Cook" dinner, and other major fundraising events to benefit the scholarship fund. There are other outings, including family picnics and skating parties. Courses are also offered for parents in the evening. One of the most beloved English teachers, Christine Schutt, who has just had her book of short stories, *Nightwork*, published by Knopf, has a parent reading/discussion group. Various faculty members will also teach classes in computers.

The Parents Association meets monthly to discuss issues of general interest; meetings are scheduled at convenient times for working parents, there is childcare provided and meetings are well attended. Mothers are listed by their first names with their husbands' names in parenthesis. Nightingale's Speaker Series is one of the best in the city. The series is sponsored by the Parents Association and seeks to address issues concerning girls' intellectual, social, and emotional development. Recent participants include Joan Jacobs Blumberg, author of *The Body Project*; JoAnne Deak, a specialist on "cliques" and girls' social development and author of *How Girls Thrive* (a NAIS publication, see *infra* p. 467); and Catherine Steiner Adair, author of *How to Counter the Culture: the Challenge of Raising Healthy Girls*. The public is invited to attend these lectures, an example of the N-B sense of community extending beyond the schoolhouse. Parents also publish a very helpful monthly newsletter, *The Nighthawk*, which includes calendars, updates on what is going on throughout the School, and thoughts from Dorothy Hutcheson, the Head.

"Socially the school is low-key," said a parent. The kindergarten new parents' dinner is usually potluck. The fundraising functions are "a lot of fun," said another. Class coffees to discuss parent concerns at each grade level are held at the school throughout the year. A parent who summers in the Hamptons told us that there is an annual August picnic there for about seventy-five NBS families hosted by a member of the NBS board.

Program: A great deal of care and intelligent planning went into the physical renovation and updated curriculum at Nightingale, taking into account the latest research into how girls learn. Carol Gilligan, author of *In a Different Voice*, which examines the differences in girls' and boys' approaches to life and learning, was invited to speak to the

Nightingale parents. Based upon some of this research, furniture in the math teaching rooms was changed. Even the rooftop playground is completely modernized with an emphasis on play that strengthens the upper body, an area where girls are traditionally weak. Math and science are taught by hands-on methods. Girls use math manipulatives and play math games such as chip trading. Extra math periods have been added at the lower school level to permit special attention to spatial relations, another area where girls tend to need reinforcement.

According to the brochure, in the lower school homeroom teachers in each grade teach reading, English, math, history, and geography, and all of them incorporate use of computers. Other lower school faculty, specialists in their fields, teach science, music, art, library and physical education. Collaborative learning, an interdisciplinary approach and other innovative educational techniques are used in the lower school. "Girls at Nightingale are not allowed to talk their way through understanding. When they study machines, they create an invention; they build castles in conjunction with the Class III study of the Middle Ages. This helps them with their spatial relationships and understanding of three dimensions." We saw a group of first grade girls on the floor doing a lesson with the Cuisenaire rods. Differences among teachers are also respected. Each classroom is set up differently, a few with desks in rows, most with desks in groups, depending on the teacher's preference.

Kindergarten at Nightingale is described as "nurturing," and we would add "busy." Each kindergarten girl is paired with a senior "big sister" who shows her to her room. There are four full-time teachers with master's degrees. Basic number concepts and reading readiness are stressed. The structured reading program emphasizes phonics, but is eclectic, employing a Whole Language approach as needed. Girls keep journals, and practice their D'Nealian handwriting. They study communities, cultures, traditions and occupations and endangered animals. Kindergartners use the computer in their classroom as well as in the computer lab. Art and music are integrated into the curriculum. Girls go out for library (cozy and carpeted) and cooking (a recipe each week for each letter of the alphabet). There are museum trips and visits to other local points of interest, as well as talks by parents. Independence is valued, cooperation not competition encouraged—all things to all parents!

The lower school curriculum is integrated where possible. Kindergartners studying communities make clay houses; second graders studying Native Americans make kachina dolls, clay animals and learn techniques of weaving. Third graders studying the Middle Ages make unicorns, swords, stained-glass windows and prepare a medieval feast; fourth graders studying colonial America examine early American crafts including quilting, and make traditional toys like dried apple-head dolls with currant eyes and cotton hair.

We noticed that the lower school science lab houses a live snake and rabbit. In a lovely example of how the lower school science curriculum is integrated, fourth graders studying skeletons in science also study the use of gesture in dance and art. Fifth graders construct papier-mâché whales in coordination with a unit on marine life in science.

Classes I through IV learn to read using an eclectic approach which stresses phonics but also employs elements of Whole Language and other programs. "Whatever will break the code," one teacher told us. Girls are expected to read every night. There is "daily practice in oral and written communication." A parent told us that her third grader has reading and writing homework every night. We saw work with corrected spelling hanging up on the walls; attention is paid to grammar and vocabulary too. By Class IV girls are writing book reports and short essays. Public speaking is reinforced through recitation in class, at assemblies and dramatic productions and on Class III's traditional Famous Women's Day. Older girls are required to take a public speaking course in Class XI.

History and geography in the lower school "draw upon materials from the Boston Children's Museum, which provides authentic artifacts and activities." The curriculum guide says, "An interdisciplinary approach incorporates trips, projects, novels and discussions of current events." For instance: in Class III girls create a persona and deliver a "famous woman monologue" while dressed in costume; Class IV girls create a Plasticine terrain model to learn about features of landscape. Projects are researched in the state-of-the-art computerized library and on the internet.

The school gathers together twice a week, once for Morning Meeting and once for assembly. Assembly is for discussion of current events or curriculum issues (environmental, cultural, political), with student participation.

In music, girls sing folk songs and songs from different cultures in various languages. They start with Orff instruments and the Kodaly system of sight-singing. They are introduced to opera and perform their own opera in Class IV. Girls learn to play the recorder in the lower school. Music appreciation classes are offered at many levels.

Each class presents musical performances integrated with other studies. Instrumental instruction after school is available.

There is always academic support available at NBS. In the lower school, tutoring in-house is a way of fulfilling the students' community service requirement, and a learning specialist is assigned to the lower school. After school, "labs" in math, languages and science are available four days a week with Nightingale faculty for girls who would like enrichment or extra help. In class, if there are two teachers, one will offer individual help. A third grader told us there is an "I did it" board in her classroom to mark achievements large and small. A parent said, "They feel it's really important for every child to have one special thing to be an expert at." Exams preceded by one week of review begin in seventh grade. "Some girls fall apart and some sail through," a parent said.

In the upper school there are built-in study halls during the school day and after school lab time when teachers are available for extra help. While many describe Nightingale as rigorous, no parent or student described it as a sweatshop either.

The lower school library was located on part of the upper school floor to facilitate interaction between divisions. "Younger girls see what is ahead of them and the upper school girls are reminded of where they came from," said an administrator. The girls consider it a real rite of passage to change from their lower school tunics to the skirts and blouses of middle and upper school. Few girls seem to object to the dress code, saying that it removes competition in clothing. Girls do accessorize with jewelry and hair items.

Middle School at NBS is composed of Classes V through VIII. The middle school homeroom teacher is the anchor. She says hello and goodbye each day and follows each girl's progress offering guidance along the way. The academic program includes English, history, math, science, Latin (beginning in Class VI), a choice of French or Spanish (beginning in Class V), visual arts, music, physical education and health. A parent said "They are building study skills all the way through."

An extensive offering of extracurricular activities begins in middle school. Choices include: Arioso, a select chorus for Class VIII; the middle school newspaper, *Bytes from the Bird*; the middle school literary magazine, *Out of Uniform*; dance club, recycling, student government and drama. There is an annual Gilbert and Sullivan production and a musical performed with boys from Allen-Stevenson.

Class VIII performs a Shakespeare play. Team sports begin and there is a no-cut policy.

Part of the middle school art program is the photography requirement for fifth through eighth graders. The photo lab has fourteen processing stations. The high quality of the photography program is evident from the results published in the *Philomel*, the upper school literary magazine, some of the best photography we've seen in terms of selection, subject matter and quality of the printing. For three out of the past four years, *Philomel* won the Gold Crown, the highest award given by the Columbia University Scholastic Press Association for excellence in writing and production. The ceramics studio is open to fifth through twelfth graders.

The upper school at NBS consists of Classes IX through XII. Tenth through twelfth graders have the privilege of being able to sign in and out of school during the day at the front desk, a privilege that can be revoked. The Nightingale school jacket cannot be purchased until tenth grade, and the entire class must raise enough money for every member of the class to purchase one.

Peer group counseling, in which a group of eight or nine freshmen meet with two seniors to talk about topical issues, such as dating or eating disorders, is a feature. Students pick their own faculty advisors in the upper school, and interaction among the grades is encouraged.

Most seventh through ninth graders carry six courses per semester. NBS's commitment to math and science is evident in the four-year upper school math requirement (algebra starts in eighth grade); two years of lab science are required. (Ninety percent of the girls take three or more lab science courses.) Eighteen credits are required for graduation, but most students complete more.

Grades are compared but not posted. The average grade is a C, one student said. Many teachers seem to go at the pace of the smartest students. Teachers notify students of forthcoming tests on a "test board" so that a balance can be maintained in students' workloads and schedules. Ninth grade is a big jump in difficulty from eighth grade, we were told. A new interdisciplinary unit in Class IX on Humanism continues the collaborative learning of earlier years. English, history, science, Latin, French, Spanish, art, music and drama teachers team-teach this unit.

"The Diversity and Richness of World Literature" is explored in tenth grade with a focus on the classics. There is a single semester requirement of public speaking. Eleventh and twelfth grade English electives include "Exiles: The Lost Generation in Paris" and "The New Woman in Shaw and Ibsen." After a solid grounding in modern history and non-Western history, eleventh and twelfth graders can take electives that include "Social Movements in the Twentieth Century," which examines reform movements, and "The Advent of Feminism, Black History and Civil Rights." Students can take advanced study in English, languages, history, math and science. A parent told us: "The girls are intelligent about current events; they have common sense. There are articles in the school newspaper about how much the students know about government, for example."

The science department offers a course in Applied Chemistry, "ChemCom" ("Chemistry in the Community") as well as Environmental Science and Marine Biology and Genetics. The new science labs (separate biology, physics and chemistry labs) are state of the art, complete with an air vent for working with hazardous fumes, emergency eyewash and shower, and a laser disc player. NBS has three computer labs with both IBMs and Macs. Josh Feder, Director of Technology at N-B, facilitates the seamless integration of technology into the curriculum. "At Nightingale our goal is to have every teacher in every subject be fully capable of using technology to augment the best methods of instruction." Feder, author of *Teaching With the Web*, designs and conducts workshops on multimedia, the internet, and Web site design for teachers at N-B as well as other independent schools. The school is fully networked and all students have e-mail addresses.

NBS students can enroll in Interschool courses, design an independent course of study, or take courses at Barnard, Columbia or other New York universities with school approval. There are some intriguing opportunities for travel and study abroad: The Japan trip and the Latin study trip to Italy are offered over spring vacation. For those who want to spend a semester or full year abroad Nightingale has sister schools in Australia, France, Switzerland and Spain. Two juniors and a faculty member visit St. Paul's Girls School in London. For those who love the outdoors there is The Mountain School option and a Maine coast semester.

Socially, one student noted, there was a definite "in" group, and because the school is so small, it can be quite obvious. But a ninth grader said she had made "friendships that will last for life" at NBS and the "family-like environment makes learning more bearable and enjoyable." On the subject of single-sex education, one ninth grader told us, "You won't get distracted by a guy you like, it's easier to focus on schoolwork. On the other hand, it can be very hard to feel comfortable around boys because you don't get to spend much time with them." There are ample opportunities, however, for coed experiences through Interschool activities. At a recent open house an eleventh grader commented: "I came to NBS from a downtown coed school in ninth grade and I thought I'd really miss boys. Instead, I feel liberated. I don't have to worry about distractions during classes and I've kept my old friends who are boys and made new ones through interschool activities."

AIDS is a prominent issue. Mary Fisher, who is HIV-positive and the mother of two young children (she was the AIDS speaker at the Republican convention), addressed the NBS community at an AIDS awareness assembly and people were moved to tears. The new health curriculum in the upper school uses *Changing Bodies, Changing Lives* as a text.

Community service is a requirement and in the upper school thirty hours in school and thirty hours outside of school are mandatory. The Nielsen Service Prize "endows an award to a student who makes a genuine commitment and important contribution in the area of social service." A student said, "Community service is stressed." NBS girls are very concerned about their community and participate in park cleanups, Special Olympics and AIDS walks and tutor at a nearby public school or volunteer at hospitals. In-house service includes library work, assisting the school nurse, stuffing envelopes, tutoring, helping in art studios or the school kitchen.

Popular clubs in the upper school include C.A.F.E. or Cultural Awareness for Everyone and the Gender Issues group. Other choices include the Drama, Dance and Glee Clubs, Interschool plays and musicals, student government, yearbook, newspaper, literary magazine, Model U.N, Photo and Film Clubs, Debate Club and Environmental Club. The Glee Club just returned from a tour of Italy where, among other events, they sang for the Pope. They also performed at a New York Knicks game. Students can work on stage crew or perform in the Interschool drama or musical. There is an Interschool drama production as well as an upper school musical in alternate years. A recent production was *Bye, Bye Birdie*, with Conrad played by a Collegiate student. Faculty, staff and parents join the students in producing the upper school musical. Those who have an interest in the visual arts can take a full year of studio art: design, painting, photography, video or ceramics.

The new gym has bolstered school spirit in the area of athletics. Teamwork is stressed. The Nightingale Nighthawks field strong teams in soccer, basketball, tennis, gymnastics, badminton and swimming.

During "Senior Weeks" girls take courses in everyday living including: "How to Manage Your Money," "How to Change a Tire," "Date Rape on Campus" and "Let's Experience New York's Cultural Life" with trips to the opera, ballet, Philharmonic or a play.

Seniors at NBS have the use of a senior lounge (all others hang out on the sunny back terrace), and can ride the school's elevators. There is an Honors and Awards Assembly the day before graduation: Achievements in academic areas are rewarded as well as effort and improvement.

Director of Admissions, Carole Everett, describes NBS girls as "wholesome" and well-prepared for life after NBS.

Nightingale alumnae feel a strong connection to the school. "During a recent visit last spring I was pleased by the friendliness, the familiarity of the uniforms, and the sense that Nightingale is still a superior learning environment and a safe haven in a frenetic city," said an alumna. According to a mother, "Nightingale is a traditional community where people really care about each other, the girls are well mannered and well behaved . . . there are high expectations and they measure up from day one."

Popular College Choices   Harvard, Brown, Cornell, Vassar, Wesleyan, Boston University, Dartmouth, University of Pennsylvania

Traditions   All-School Fair (proceeds support the Scholarship Fund), Big Sisters/Little Sisters, singing holiday songs before winter break; the Daisy Ceremony for Class IV; Honors Assembly; Athletic Awards dinner; Class VII Gilbert and Sullivan production; Class VIII Shakespeare play with Allen-Stevenson; Festival of the Written Word assembly; Famous Women's Day; Field Day; Cum Laude and other weekly assemblies with a mix of prominent speakers and student-led discussions; Winter Concert; Homecoming, an annual soccer and volleyball game against Brearley on a Saturday in the fall; C.A.F.E. (Cultural Awareness for Everyone) dinners for students and their parents each year; The Father/Daughter breakfast; Grandparents Day; Book Fair

Publications   Middle school newspaper: *Bytes From the Bird* Upper school newspaper: *Spectator*

Middle school literary magazine: *Out of Uniform*
Upper school literary magazine: *Philomel*
French Journal
Alumnae magazine
Yearbook
Monthly parents newsletter: *Nighthawk*

Community Service Requirement   30 hours in school, 30 hours of service in the community; a 9th grade social service project with Class IX at Collegiate

Hangouts   The upper school terrace, Jackson Hole Burger Restaurant, Ciao Bella, Timothy's, senior lounge, Student Center

The Packer Collegiate Institute

170 Joralemon Street
Brooklyn, New York, NY 11201
(718) 875-6644, fax (718) 875-1363
website:www.packer.edu

Coed
Nursery–12th grade
Not accessible

Mr. Geoffrey Pierson, Head of School
Ms. Valorie Iason, Director of Admissions, Preschool and Lower School
Mr. Matthew Nespole, Director of Admissions, Middle and Upper School

Uniform   None

Birthday Cutoff   Children entering at kindergarten must turn 5 in December
Children entering first grade must be 6 by August 31

Enrollment   Total enrollment: approximately 825
Kindergarten places: 25
First grade places: 20
Ninth grade places; 15–25
Graduating class size: approximately 55

Grades   Semester system:
K–4, detailed anecdotal reports and checklists
Letter grades begin in 5th grade; in addition, detailed anecdotal reports are sent twice a year

Tuition Range 1998–1999 $7,150 to $15,000, Nursery–12th grade
Additional fees: under $300 for books (5th–12th grades only)

Financial Aid   30% of students receive some form of tuition assistance

Endowment   10 million

Diversity   25% children of color

After-School Program   Open to Packer Collegiate students only; a variety of creative and recreational activities from 3:15 P.M. until 6:00 P.M.; for an additional charge
Extracurricular clubs and activities
Junior varsity and varsity athletic competition

Summer Program   Summer Camp: open to children from other schools; mid-June through the end of July; an additional payment is required

---

Founded in 1845 as the Brooklyn Female Academy, and endowed by Harriet Packer, The Packer Collegiate Institute is the oldest independent school in Brooklyn and was the first to offer higher education to young women. It became coed in the early seventies. Packer's architecturally unique landmark building boasts fully equipped science and computer labs, two theatres, music and art studios and two full-court gymnasiums in addition to an elegant chapel with a 1906 Austin organ and nine Tiffany stained-glass windows. Chapel attendance is required once a week at which social, political, environmental and ethical issues are discussed. The style of the school is informal and there is no dress code. Hot lunch is available for grades three through twelve only.

Packer's diverse student body represents the five boroughs of New York City and the outlying metropolitan areas. In 1998, Packer enrolled eleven students from Prep for Prep. Parents say a distinct feeling of community exists among children of all ages and backgrounds and the faculty.

Getting In: Open houses are offered throughout the Fall so prospective parents can tour the facilities and talk with students, faculty and administration. Applicants to kindergarten are tested at the school to assess their aptitude and learning style. Candidates for grades 1 through 4 are interviewed and tested individually at the school. Applicants for grades 2 through 4 have a classroom visit. Applicants to grades 5 through 12 have a personal interview and must submit previous school records, two teacher evaluations and results of the ISEE or the SSAT.

Program: The lower school at Packer emphasizes an interactive, individualized, developmentally appropriate approach. The junior first grade program is a transition program for children who will turn six in the fall of the year. The following year children move to first grade. Reading is taught using eclectic methods. "We use a wealth of materials to accommodate the variety of learning styles so characteristic of young children."

The middle school at Packer begins in fifth grade. Students have one extended core class in English and history and another in mathematics and science. Computer, music, dance, theatre, chorus, gym and health round out the curriculum. All fifth graders must take a course called Frameworks which reinforces good study habits and skills such as note-taking, test-taking, research and so on. In sixth grade, some students, upon recommendation by their teacher, continue in Frameworks II, with the expectation that they will begin foreign language in seventh grade. All other sixth graders begin study of a foreign language in French, Latin, or Spanish.

Each middle and upper school student has an advisor who is a teacher in the school. The Peer Support program involves juniors and seniors who are selected to attend a leadership training seminar preparing them to meet with freshmen in small groups throughout the year to discuss their transition to high school.

In the upper school, the freshman year is built around a collaborative program involving faculty from the English, History, and Arts departments as students study ancient civilizations through the Middle Ages. Freshmen also take a rigorous year of conceptual physics, foreign language and mathematics. The interdisciplinary approach continues in the sophomore year as students study "The American Experience" from historical, literary and artistic perspectives. Chemistry, foreign language and mathematics complete the academic program. Students in their junior and senior years have many electives from which to choose, including AP courses in 15 areas. A junior year English course, biology, and Modern European History are requirements. Graduation requirements include four years of English and physical education; three years each of foreign language, mathematics, history, and sciences; two years of electives; two years of arts; one year of Health; and 45 hours of school and community service. Older students can participate in independent study, Senior Emphasis Program, Maine Coast Semester, High Mountain Institute, or a Cultural Exchange Program.

Offerings in the arts are broad and include visual arts, photography, computer graphics, modern dance, orchestra, brass choir, woodwind ensemble, jazz band and women's ensemble.

Clubs and organizations available to students include AIDS Education Committee; Brothers and Sisters; CARE (environmental club); Chorus; Debate; Mock Trial; Model Congress; Multicultural Student Association; Drama Club, SAFE (feminist club); Social Action Committee; Student-Faculty Judiciary; Student Government; and various school publications. There are numerous athletic teams in middle and upper school, including a middle school coed soccer team, judo and fencing, girls' volleyball, gymnastics, basketball, and softball, and boys' soccer, basketball, baseball and volleyball.

Popular college choices   Brown, Wesleyan, University of Pennsylvania, Amherst, New York University

Publications Art and literary publication: *Packer Current Items*
Yearbook: *The Pelican*
Newspaper: *The Prism*

Community Service Requirement   15 hours per year in the Upper School (9th-12th), tenth grade service project at a day care center, senior center, or soup kitchen

Hangout   Upper School Student Center, McDonalds around the corner

Poly Prep Country Day School
Coed
Nursery—12th Grade
Not accessible

Poly Prep Lower School
50 Prospect Park West
Brooklyn, NY 11215
(718) 768-1103
(Nursery–4th Grade)
Maureen Walsh Heffernan, Head

Poly Prep Country Day School
9216 Seventh Avenue
Brooklyn, NY 11228
(718) 836-9800
website: www.Polyprep.Brooklyn.ny.us
(5th–12th Grade)
William M. Williams, Headmaster
Lori W. Redell, Director of Admissions

Birthday Cutoff Children entering nursery school must be 2.3 years old by September 1st;
Children entering kindergarten must be 5 years old by September 1st

Enrollment Total enrollment: 670
Nursery–4th grade: 140
Nursery places: 45
K–4th grade places: 10
5th grade places: 35–40
7th grade places: 30
9th grade places: 35–45
Graduating class 1998: Approximately 95
40 Prep for Prep students enrolled as of Fall 1996

Tuition Range 1998–1999 $5,000–$17,200, 1/2 day Nursery–12th grade
Additional fees: for lunch and graduation for grades 5th–12th approximately $750

No additional fees for grade N–4th
Transportation for students from Manhattan, Staten Island, Brooklyn and Queens is provided at no extra charge.

After-School Program   Arts Program Monday–Thursday for N–4th grades, an additional payment is required; for grades 5th–12th, extracurricular activities and clubs, Varsity and Junior Varsity athletic competition.

Summer Program   For grades N–4th, Day Camp and Drama Camp; For grades 5th–12th, Day Camp, Performing Arts Camp, Sports Camp and Computer Camp; from the end of June until the beginning of August; open to students from other schools; an additional payment is required

Founded in 1854, as part of the Country Day School Movement, Poly Prep has been located on a twenty-five acre campus in the Dyker Heights area of Brooklyn since 1917. The campus has playing fields, a theatre, swimming pool, tennis courts, squash courts and a new fitness center with a dance center for the Alvin Ailey program which is taught at Poly. ERB testing or the SSAT is required for admissions.

The school's motto, *Virtus Vitrix Fortunae*, or "Hard Work Conquers the Vagaries of Fortune" is as relevant now as it ever was. It's one of our favorite school mottos. Poly Prep is diverse—children of color represent approximately 27 percent of the student body. In 1998, Poly Prep enrolled thirty-four Prep for Prep students. In spring 1995, Poly Prep took over the Woodward Park School, in Park Slope, Brooklyn adding a lower division that will feed students into Poly Prep's middle school. The Poly Prep Lower School is located in an historic 12,000 square foot mansion overlooking Brooklyn's Prospect Park. The lower school emphasizes hands-on learning, and the use of manipulative materials across the curriculum. Transportation to the school from Staten Island, Brooklyn and parts of Manhattan and Queens is provided at no extra charge. Approximately 15 percent of students come from Manhattan and approximately 18 percent come from Staten Island. There is a dress code. Hot lunch is provided.

Popular college choices   Boston University, Carnegie Mellon, Columbia, Connecticut, Johns Hopkins, Lehigh, SUNY-Binghamton, Wesleyan, Yale

Professional Children's School

132 West 60th Street
New York, NY 10023
(212) 582-3116, x135 Admissions answer line,
x112 Admission Director
www.pos-nyc.org

Coed
4th–12th grade
Not accessible

Dr. James Dawson, Head of School
Sherrie Hinkle, Director of Admissions

Birthday Cutoff   None; applications are accepted at various times during the year

Enrollment   Total enrollment: 200
4th grade places: 10
Graduating class size: variable, from 35–60

Tuition Range 1998–1999 $13,650–$14,700, 4th grade—returning seniors; $16,500 for new seniors
Additional fees for books and supplies total approximately $500

After-School Program   Extracurricular activity groups are formed if there is enough interest in the student body

Summer Program   None

———

Professional Children's School was founded in 1914 as an academic program for children appearing in vaudeville or on the Broadway stage. Today, Professional Children's School is the only fully accredited independent school providing a college preparatory curriculum for children actively involved in the performing and visual arts as well as competitive sports. (It is to be distinguished from LaGuardia High School for the Performing Arts, one of the New York City specialized public high schools, depicted in the movie *Fame*.)
Applicants must have a serious interest in the arts/sports and aca-

demic ability—no auditions are required for acceptance. A transcript, personal interview and standardized testing complete the application process. About 32 percent of the student body receive partial financial aid.

Students follow a regular school day but the periods are slightly shorter so that students can schedule professional engagements during school hours.

A Guided Study Program is available for students whose professional commitments keep them away from the classroom for an extended period.

Approximately 70% of Professional Children's School graduates attend college on a full or part-time basis; another 15% go on to college after completing professional commitments. The rest pursue their careers and may enroll in college at a later time.

Rabbi Arthur Schneier Park East Day School

164 East 68th Street
New York, NY 10021
(212) 737-6900

Coed
2's–8th grade
Accessible

Rabbi Arthur Schneier, Dean
Mrs. Marilyn Meltzer, Principal
Mrs. Sarah Platovsky, Director of Jewish Studies
Mrs. Harriet Ingber, Early Childhood Director
Mrs. Toby Einsidler, Administrator

Birthday Cutoff   Children entering at the nursery level must be 2 by August 31
Children entering kindergarten must be 5 by December 31

Enrollment   Total enrollment: 300
2's places: 35
Kindergarten places: 10
Graduating class size: approximately 12

Tuition Range 1998–1999 $4,600 to $11,340, 2's (two half days)—8th grade
There is a discount for synagogue members
There is a discount for families with two or more children enrolled in kindergarten—8th grade

After-School Program   For Park East students only; a variety of creative and recreational activities Monday–Thursday from 3:30 P.M. to 4:30 P.M., 1:30 to 3:00 P.M. on Fridays; an additional payment is required

---

The Park East Day School was founded by Rabbi Arthur Schneier as a nursery school and merged with East Side Hebrew Institute in 1979, adding an elementary division. Park East Day School is affiliated with Congregation Zichron Ephraim and the adjoining Park East Synagogue (founded in 1890).

Park East's eight-story school building includes classrooms, a science laboratory, computer center, art studio, library, music room, auditorium, cafeteria, gym and outdoor playground. The program combines Jewish traditional religious values with a demanding secular curriculum.

Getting In: Students come from diverse Jewish backgrounds. ERB testing is required for admission to kindergarten and above. Admissions decisions are based on observation of the children, an interview with the parents and ERB test results.

Program: There are two teachers in each kindergarten classroom. The program is geared to the individual child's readiness and includes beginning reading and personal writing. A hot kosher lunch is served beginning in kindergarten. Kindergarten students eat lunch with their teachers in their classrooms. First through eighth grades eat together in the school cafeteria.

There is a dress code beginning in first grade. Class size from first grade through eighth grade averages 15 students. Beginning in first grade students take a dual curriculum, with half the day devoted to secular studies and half of the day devoted to Hebrew/Judaic studies. Formal Hebrew instruction begins in this year. Students are introduced to Hebrew grammar and vocabulary, Jewish culture, Torah, prayer and holidays. Both boys and girls participate equally in prayers. Thematic studies (Holocaust, immigration and the history of modern Israel) are integrated throughout. The curriculum is supplemented by trips to museums, Jewish theatre productions, and the study of Jewish authors. There is weekly instruction taught by specialists in science, computer, library, art, chess, gym and music.

Students who show proficiency in math receive enrichment several times a week. Park East students have the opportunity to participate in city, state and national math and chess competitions throughout the year. Students with a special interest or proficiency in English are enriched with in-depth assignments. Beginning in third grade students can attend a weekly book discussion club moderated by one of the teachers. There is a learning center staffed by a specialist for students who need strengthening in Hebrew, reading and mathematics.

The artist-in-residence program exposes students to various facets of the arts. Guests have included a classical pianist, songwriter, radio announcer, actor, stamp collector, opera singer, cellist and designer.

Literary Week, in November each year, is a school-wide celebration of books. Lecturers have included publishers, book designers, authors and illustrators.

A spirit of community is reinforced through various school assemblies such as the Biography Fair for grades 3 through 5, the first grade Siddur play, the second grade Chumash play and the Science, Math and Technology Fair presented by students in grades 1 through 8.

Extracurricular activities include: Chess, science, computer, painting, museum club, basketball, creative writing, cooking, costume design, team sports, softball and mathematics.

Graduates attend a variety of NYC private and specialized public high schools. Recent choices include Ramaz, Dalton, Columbia Grammar and Prep, UNIS, Solomon Schecter High School, Yeshiva of Flatbush, Elisabeth Irwin High School, Bronx Science, Stuyvesant, LaGuardia School for the Performing Arts, and Frisch High School.

Traditions Annual Purim Carnival, Chanukah party, Literary Week, Sukkoth dinner celebration, participation in the Salute to Israel Day Parade, Student Art Exhibit

Community Service Requirement Park East students are encouraged to participate in a wide-range of community service activities such as visiting nursing homes, helping to support synagogues on the Lower East Side, organizing coat drives, collecting Passover foods for Project Dorot, and entertaining the elderly during holidays

Ramaz

Lower School
125 East 85th Street
New York, NY 10028
(212) 427-1000

The Rabbi Joseph H. Lookstein Upper School
60 East 78th Street
New York, NY 10021
(212) 517-5955 (upper school and admissions)

Coed
Nursery–12th Grade
Accessible

Rabbi Haskel Lookstein, Principal
Mrs. Daniele Gorlin Lassner, Director of Admissions

Birthday Cutoff   Children entering at the nursery level must be 3 by August 31
Children entering kindergarten must be 5 by August 31

Enrollment   Total enrollment: 1004
3's places: 19
Kindergarten places: 25
9th grade places: 50
Graduating class size: approximately 100–110

Tuition Range 1998–1999 $10,850 to $14,700, nursery 3's–12th grade
Ramaz has a scholarship and special needs fund: nursery, $1,200; K–12, $2,200
Additional fees: for registration, lunch, student activities and overnight trips approximately $1,000

After-School Program   Lower school: a variety of creative and recreational activities until 5:00 P.M.; an additional payment is required
Upper school: a variety of creative and recreational activities until 6:00 P.M.; there is no additional charge

Summer Program   None

Ramaz is an Orthodox Jewish day school founded in 1937 by the late Rabbi Joseph H. Lookstein. The initials (in Hebrew) of the rabbi's name make up the acronym that is the school's name. Ramaz is committed to modern or centrist Orthodox Judaism. Applicant families may also be "conservative and committed" but all families keep kosher homes. Formal Hebrew language instruction begins in first grade. Half of the school day is devoted to Judaic studies and half the day is devoted to the general studies curriculum. Although all classes are coed, the sexes are separated during morning and afternoon prayers. Ramaz has a dress code and a kosher hot lunch is served.

Popular College Choices   Barnard College, Columbia University, Harvard University, New York University, University of Pennsylvania, Yale, and Yeshiva and Stern Colleges of Yeshiva University

Regis High School

55 East 84th Street
New York, NY 10028
(212) 288-1100, FAX (212) 794-1221
website: regis-nyc.org

All boys
9th–12th grade
Not accessible

Rev. Thomas H. Feely, S.J., Principal
Mr. Eric P. DiMichele, Director of Admissions

Birthday Cutoff   None

Enrollment   Total enrollment: 512
9th grade places: 135
Graduating class 1997: 120

Tuition   None: all students receive tuition-free scholarships and pay
only laboratory and activity fees

After-School Program   A variety of extracurricular activities until
5:30 P.M.
Varsity sports competition in the Catholic High School Athletic
Association

Summer Program   None

Regis High School was founded in 1914 by the Society of Jesus as
a tuition-free school for Catholic boys. Regis High School is sustained
through the original bequest of a generous parishioner of the Church
of St. Ignatius Loyola as well as contributions from alumni.

Regis High School is highly selective. Only baptized Catholic
eighth grade boys may apply. Regis does not accept transfers. The
admissions process is rigorous: Applicants must score in the ninetieth
percentile and above on standardized tests and have an outstanding
elementary school record. In addition, students must sit for the Regis
scholarship examination. Semifinalists are interviewed by faculty and

alumni, and approximately half of this group is selected for admission to Regis. Financial need is one factor in the admissions process.

Regis offers a traditional liberal arts curriculum. The pace is accelerated, and the work load and expectations are most demanding. The school also has a Director of Technology, Mrs. Michele M. DeCarlo. Four years of theology are required as well as participation in community service projects, liturgies and religious retreats. Catholic holidays are observed.

The average combined SAT score for the Class of 1997 was 1367.

Popular College Choices Columbia, Cornell, Fordham, Harvard, Georgetown, Yale, New York University, Johns Hopkins, Williams, Princeton, Holy Cross

The Riverdale Country School

Upper School or Hill Campus
5250 Fieldston Road
(at West 253rd Street)
Riverdale, NY 10471-2999
(718) 549-8810, FAX (718) 519-2795
e-mail:@riverdale.edu
website:www.riverdale.edu

Lower School or River Campus,
Spaulding Lane (between Independence and Palisades Avenues)
Riverdale, NY 10471
(718) 549-7780, FAX (718) 796-8241

Coed
Pre-kindergarten–12th grade
Not accessible

Dr. John R. Johnson, Headmaster
Mr. Kent Kildahl, Head of the Upper School
Mr. Sandy Shaller, Head of the Lower School
Ms. Ann Woodward, Director of Admissions
Mrs. Grace Ball, Director of Lower School Admissions

Uniform   Lower school: casual and neat, turtleneck, shirts with collars, no logos, no white T-shirts
Upper school: appropriate attire

Birthday Cutoff   Children entering pre-kindergarten must be 4 by September 1
Kindergarten: developmental placement

Enrollment   Total enrollment: 1035
Lower school: 412
Upper school: 620
Kindergarten places: 54
Graduating class 1998: 114

Grades   Semester system
Kindergarten–4th: detailed anecdotal reports and checklists

327

Letter grades begin in 4th grade

7th–12th: grades with comments twice a year; grades alone twice a year

Modified departmentalization in 4th–6th grade

Full departmentalization by 7th grade

First midterms and finals begin in 7th grade

Tuition Range 1988–1999 $16,400 to $18,900, pre-kindergarten–12th grade

Riverdale has a monthly payment option and a quarterly payment option running from June to March

Extended repayment plan (educational loan)

Tuition refund plan (insurance)

Busing from Manhattan is approximately $2,000 for lower school students, approximately $1,000 for upper school students

Financial Aid/Scholarship   20% of students receive some form of tuition assistance

$2.3 million available

Endowment   Approximately $16 million

Diversity   20% children of color

12 Prep for Prep students enrolled as of fall 1998

Lower school parents of color meeting held three times a year

Lower school multicultural literature program at all grade levels

The upper school has a diversity coordinator who works with the entire student body and faculty on issues of diversity and multiculturalism

Homework   1st: 15 minutes, Monday through Thursday

2nd and 3rd: 30–40 minutes, Monday through Thursday

4th: 45 minutes–1 hour, Monday through Thursday

5th and 6th: 1–2 hours a night

7th and 8th: 2–2½ hours a night

9th–12th: average of 3½ hours per night; more for those taking many APs

Assume 40 minutes per subject per night

In addition, parents of young children are encouraged to read to them for at least 20 minutes each night from the lower school recommended reading list

After-School Program   Riverclub: For grades Pre-k through 6th; 3:30–5:00pm; a variety of creative and recreational activities for an additional payment; transportation home is available
Grades 7–8: intramural and interscholastic sports
Grades 9–12: interscholastic sports, theatrical productions

Summer   Program   The   Summerbridge   Program: a   privately funded 6-week-long program (established in 1992) that prepares 90 talented middle school students from the inner city for competitive high schools; it is tuition-free and taught by Riverdale High School students as well as college students under the guidance of two directors and several other teachers.
Summer camp: 7 weeks, for ages 6–11; sports, nature and creative activities; for an additional payment

———

After coming upon an intoxicated schoolboy in the street in New York City, Riverdale Country School's founder, Frank Hackett, decided to found a school in the countryside, far from the degrading influences of city life and offering abundant opportunity to play in the open air. Hackett coined the term "independent school" to distinguish his school from the "hoity-toity private schools." From the outset, Hackett had a vision of a "world school" with an "international curriculum."[*]

Today RCS offers a strong community with a diverse population. The curriculum is grounded in liberal arts basics. Parents say academic expectations are high and many types of students can find success here, but they must be committed to doing the work that is expected of them. Moreover, gaining admission to RCS has become increasingly competitive. "It happened because we're making it better by maintaining our curriculum standards and staying committed to them. We have a really good academic program and a C.A.R.E. (Children Aware of Riverdale Ethics) package and we've worked hard on our physical plant and that attracts people. We're a school that never sleeps," says Sandy Shaller, Head of RCS's lower school.

The lower school consists of grades pre-kindergarten through sixth. RCS lower school Admissions Director, Mrs. Grace Ball, has been at Riverdale for over thirty years. She says, "There really is no typical student. We have a good metropolitan mix, and approximately

[*]*The Quickened Spirit*, by Allen Hackett (The Riverdale Country School, New York City, 1957), p. 51.

60 per cent of our students come from Manhattan. The others come from The Bronx, Westchester or Northern New Jersey." One parental concern is that a car is necessary if you send your child here. Not true. Parents can easily find a ride to Riverdale for Parents' Night, two conferences, one music program, three parenting evenings and one play (in each grade), the Academic Fair, Book Fair and the carnival.

Getting in: Respect and consideration for the individual is a hallmark of RCS, beginning with the admissions process. RCS is one of very few schools to grant each lower school applicant a one-on-one interview, either with Mrs. Ball or one of her assistants, Sarah Lafferty or Barbara Scott. Continued interest in the lower school by an ever-increasing number of qualified applicants has made it more difficult than ever to be accepted at RCS according to Mrs. Ball. Children who are shy in a group of strangers have nothing to fear here. "We don't have a mold that children must fit into," says Mrs. Ball. The mother of a girl who transferred from a single-sex school said, "My child has never been negatively typecast here."

Cake, cookies and hot coffee greet you on the morning of your tour. Leave the Chanel suit at home, and it will not count against you if your husband cannot make it to Riverdale for the tour. Please don't brag about *your* many accomplishments; RCS is not scrutinizing the parents. "We really look at the child. I never read a file until I meet the child," says Mrs. Ball.

Admission to the upper school is also very competitive. The RCS upper school admissions staff are personable and friendly and offer students and parents a one-on-one interview with either Ann Woodward, Director of Admissions, or one of her associates. "Careful attention is paid to making sure that RCS is the right personal and academic fit for each applicant," says Ms. Woodward. Once admissions decisions have been made, RCS maintains a small selective wait list.

Riverdale's pre-kindergarten program, at the River Campus, is helpful for parents of children with borderline birthdays and parents who know from the start that they want to send their children to Riverdale.

Parents: There isn't a typical student, nor is there a typical parent at RCS. All types can feel comfortable here. The class cocktail party might be held in an apartment on Park Avenue or on Riverside Drive. "There are as many Gucci loafers as there are Birkenstocks," one parent said after attending several school functions. Parent involvement is welcomed and parents can volunteer to go on class trips, work in the library or help teach computer. Communication between teachers and parents is just a phone call away, and one parent said her children's backpacks are always full of correspondence from Riverdale. One mother said, "A note came home the first day home-work wasn't done." The school's bus service says they will drop off homework at your door "every day if necessary" if your child misses school (lower school only).

Program: The upper, or Hill Campus, serves grades seven through twelve, and the lower school, or River Campus, serves pre-kindergarten through six. At the lower school learning is more experiential; the upper school is more traditional and structured.

Each morning as the younger children arrive at the River Campus, Sandy Shaller, head of the lower school, is there to greet them. He knows every child (and nearly every parent) by name, and is involved in almost every aspect of the lower school. Parents say, "Mr. Shaller *is* the lower school." Almost all prospective parents have a chance to ask Mr. Shaller questions about RCS, either when they tour or certainly after acceptance. Mr. Shaller and Ms. Terri Hassid (assistant head of the lower school) each teach a class a day. At the 1998 Spring Carnival, with booths operated by each class relating to the theme "Broadway Theatrical Productions," Mr. Shaller roamed the campus as The Phantom of the Opera, "complete with mask, black costume, hat and cape," said one parent.

An architecturally eclectic group of buildings make up the River Campus. The latest addition is a brand-new three-story, twelve-classroom building with a 6,000-square foot gymnasium (designed by an alumna whose sons and daughter attend RCS). The Perkins Building houses an auditorium, library, classrooms, administrative offices and science resource room. The Junior Building contains admissions, the cafeteria, a computer complex and music classrooms. The Senior Building (Arts Building) houses two art studios, special music classes and support services. In addition, there are four newly resurfaced tennis courts, a soccer/football field, an environmental education area, patios and a well-designed play area. The River Campus is large enough to accommodate all these facilities in one place, and intimate enough to feel like a community. Children have the freedom to jump rope, build a snowman, enjoy the playground or throw a football at recess, depending on the season. Students are not allowed to wander around the River Campus alone; they are always well supervised, particularly at busing time.

Like a traditional elementary school, RCS has recess (formal recess ends after third grade), and four gym periods per week. "It's an intense day and at recess there is an explosion of energy. This is a country campus and we use it," says Ms. Hassid. Each grade puts on a music and drama performance and there are weekly assemblies where folk songs are occasionally sung. Pre-kindergarten and kindergarten at Riverdale stress readiness and provide individualized attention. Classes in pre-kindergarten through first grade all have a head teacher and an assistant teacher. There is traditional circle time, along with job charts and journal writing with invented spelling. Since the school is in a country setting, much attention is paid to the study of nature and environmental issues. For example, every lower school student gets three seed pots and plants them in the wetlands area and will have a hands-on opportunity to work on the grounds. Pre-kindergarten and kindergarten children have garden plots where they plant flowers and vegetables as part of the Spring science program. Nearly every kindergarten and first grade class has a pet: guinea pigs, turtles or fish. Math instruction is hands-on in the early years. One kindergarten mother came in to make pizza for a math project that included grating the cheese and measuring the circumference of the pizza (she brought her own homemade sauce).

By first grade formal academics are introduced and the teachers have serious expectations. For those who need strengthening there is the Small Group Reading Program. By first grade there are daily homework assignments four times a week. The lower school recently began to administer the CTP III (a standardized test that measures academic skills and compares the test scores to other independent schools' test scores).

In second grade there is one teacher, and reading and math skills continue to develop and expand. Foreign language is introduced in third grade; those who need strengthening in language arts take "Fundamentals of Writing." Writing is stressed in all subject areas, and creative expression is encouraged. The lower school has its own publication called the *Rivulet*. In sixth grade, students pick topics and learn how to research and write term papers. The first final exam is given in sixth grade.

Many class trips are scheduled, including a train trip for kindergartners up the Hudson for a picnic lunch. Third graders tap maple trees and collect and process the syrup. The science resource room is a popular place filled with natural treasures such as materials, nests, leaves, bark and fish as well as all types of equipment for conducting hands-on experiments.

RCS students may breathe fresh air each day but the resources of Manhattan are not neglected. For example, sixth graders are introduced to independent research through "The Concrete Garden" project. They pick any building in New York City and write an in-depth report on it. Modified departmentalization begins in fourth grade but is not complete until seventh.

Computer study at Riverdale is strong. The school has recently installed a fiber optic cable that connects all of the buildings and allows the RCS community to gain access to the Internet in all of the classrooms. The usage of the Internet is curriculum driven and is primarily for educational purposes. An "Acceptable Use Policy for Technology and Computer Networks" is sent to all Riverdale families to inform parents of possible issues concerning the use of this technology. For parents who aren't as computer savvy as their children, RCS provides parents with on-line (internet) and off-line (books, videos, etc.) materials, a Parents Association course on computers and technology, and a list of books that offer guidance to new users. Almost all members of the administration, teachers and upper school students have e-mail addresses. Lower school students do not presently have e-mail accounts, but e-mail can be sent through their teachers. A publicly viewable list of e-mail names at RCS is in the works. General queries can be sent to webmaster@riverdale.edu, admin@riverlake.edu or postmaster@riverdale.edu.

There is a beautiful new computer lab and several mini-labs on both campuses. In addition, there are twenty laptops available for fourth through sixth grade students. RCS also has a Computer Coordinator (at the lower school), a Director of Technology (at the upper school), and a support staff of at least four trained professionals who run the computer science department and provide information on the use of computers. "Technology is a powerful tool. At Riverdale our curriculum drives technology, not the reverse," says Mr. Shaller in describing the lower school's integration of computers and academics. From kindergarten through second grade, parent volunteers (who are trained) work with students on games and problem solving. In third grade formal instruction starts, in fourth grade LOGO is introduced. Fifth grade students collected science data and set up a data base to coordinate, record and graph information. For students in grades seven through twelve RCS offers four computer science courses,

(Introduction to Technology is a required course for all seventh and tenth graders.) including two AP courses and Programming in C/C++. "The computer and the Internet are helpful tools, but they should be used sparingly. Children have a great deal of exploration to do away from the illuminated screen," says Mr. Shaller.

Although RCS is a coed school, there is concern about gender issues. In a recent year, the parents were invited to attend a Gender Issues Forum where the latest theories about gender and intellectual development were discussed. Mr. Shaller says RCS is sensitized to gender issues (and at least one kindergarten parent has seen him roll up his sleeves and invite girls into the block corner.)

When asked what values are stressed at RCS, many parents and students said "teamwork," both on and off the field. One student described Riverdale as "a healthy environment that promotes community feeling." In 1989 the RCS Lower School Student Council created C.A.R.E. (Children Aware of Riverdale Ethics), a program that emphasizes problem-solving strategies, respect for differences and consideration for the feelings of others. The official C.A.R.E. song was written by the lower school drama specialist, January Akselrad, and it evokes the spirit of the program in an entertaining way. This sense of consideration and caring extends to the larger community as well. Recently, lower school students held a walk-a-thon that benefited the Children's Blood Foundation. Another year, lower school students held a penny drive for the Pediatric AIDS Foundation.

There is positive interaction between the grades at Riverdale. Friendships between children in different grades begin on the bus ride to school, and also through various planned activities. Fifth graders prepare the Holiday Feast with pre-kindergarteners, second and fifth graders work together on a butterfly project, and second graders and kindergarteners work together sewing an alphabet with each pair of children working together on a letter square. Sixth graders interact with younger children during lunch or recess. This community of students extends all the way up to the alumni. One student said, "The alumni are not just donors, they are people you know because you've worked and connected with them." Every three years, former Riverdalians return to conduct workshops and talk to the students about their professions.

The upper school consists of grades seventh through twelfth; the two largest points of entry are seventh and ninth. The upper school is structured but not rigid. Bells mark the end of class periods. There are many required courses, but by eleventh and twelfth grades over sixty electives are available, including: "Masterpieces of Western Literature," "Philosophy," "World Religion in History and Literature," "African-American Literature," "Native American Literature," and "Race and Class in New York City." Math is "ability grouped" in the upper school: Students with aptitude in this area move at an accelerated pace and those who need more reinforcement get it. There are twenty four AP courses, and there are honors as well as regular sections. No class ranking is made. The curriculum is challenging and rigorous, however, students are supportive of each other and there is no cut-throat competition. "It doesn't matter what anybody else gets as long as you did your best" is the message. And one student talked about "growth in grades": As the work got harder, her grades improved.

In October 1997, Riverdale underwent a NYSAIS (New York State Association of Independent Schools) evaluation. RCS was reaccreditated, and in its official report the NYSAIS Visiting Committee stated that many aspects of the school impressed them. "The vitality of RCS's academic program; outstanding, dynamic, creative teaching; diversity; and the balance of academics, arts, activities, and athletics. Students are friendly and confident and display a strong sense of community. Riverdale students are outstanding examples of civility, which is a reflection of the care offered by the faculty and staff," states the NYSAIS report.

It's very difficult to fall through the cracks at RCS because there is a strong support network of people and programs. Advisors (for groups of ten or twelve) meet regularly. There is easy access to faculty, whose schedules are posted and who stay for the entire long day even if they finish early.

Seniors are required to take a year-long interdisciplinary course called I.L.S. or Integrated Liberal Studies. Introduced into the curriculum in 1980, I.L.S. surveys the cultural history of the West from the perspectives of four disciplines: literature, philosophy, the history of science and the history of music and art. The course culminates in a final oral examination.

Students help students in several ways. Eleventh and twelfth graders are selected, as an honor, and trained to act as peer counselors to seventh graders, dealing with academic and social issues under the Peer Advisory Leadership (PAL) program.

RCS welcomed Dr. John R. Johnson as the school's new Headmaster in 1997. Dr. Johnson previously served as the President of The Mary Institute and St. Louis Country Day School in St. Louis, Missouri where he is credited with orchestrating the merger of the two single sex schools. He also taught classes of European History, including AP European History during his entire twelve years at the school. Dr. Johnson was also the Director of Studies at the Harvard School in Los Angeles where he was responsible for the school's academic program. In addition, he has served as Director, UCLA Summer Sessions at UCLA (Los Angeles.) He is a warm and supportive leader and he attends almost every school event. Recently, he attended the Annual Fund committee's end-of-the-year bowling event held at Chelsea Piers where he fostered a feeling of support and appreciation among the attendees. When asked what Dr. Johnson's vision for Riverdale includes, he says "Riverdale has a balanced approach to education. It is a school that values first-rate training across the broad, in academics, the arts and athletics. We attend to the whole child. Our faculty really knows their students and their concern extends beyond the classroom."

RCS has recently acquired approximately seven acres and several buildings that were formerly part of the Manhattan College campus. The property is adjacent to the upper school campus and plans are well underway for its use. So far, plans include: the renovation of the existing gymnasium, swimming pool, locker room and physical fitness facilities, the complete renovation and slight expansion of the three hundred seat theater, an expansion of the center for the arts, ten to twelve classroom renovations, a new full-sized playing field, expansion of the existing practice field and four new tennis courts.

Mr. Satish Joshi, head of Visual Art, has been inspiring students for many years. Graduating seniors leave farewell messages to him painted on the walls of the art room: "Satish, you know me. That in itself is a great thing. I ♥ you." and "Thanks for the best homeroom ever." Riverdale's art and literary magazine *Impressions* recently won the 1997 award of the National Council of Teachers of English, the highest award for excellence in student literary magazines.

Seniors have their own lounge, complete with posters and comfortable couches, and can use the newly landscaped courtyard. Backpacks are dropped casually in the halls. Seniors can leave the campus for lunch and free periods. (These are privileges, not rights, and can be revoked for bad behavior.) Each year a Senior Leadership Conference is held at Frost Valley at which seniors explore their own leadership style; teachers conduct workshops on writing college essays and coping with senior-year stress. Class officers are elected at Frost Valley and seniors get a sense of solidarity as a class. The weekend launches them in their role as leaders of the upper school. The student government has three representatives from each grade.

The junior class is pushing for more privileges: RCS juniors can't leave campus until April of junior year. (At Horace Mann and Fieldston students can leave in ninth grade.) But one student maintained that having to stick around campus contributes to the feeling of community. Each year the senior class parents give a gift to the school.

Though sequestered from many of the ills of urban life, RCS students are concerned about the wider world. At the recent One World Day, students chose to focus on AIDS awareness. Upper school students spent the day in workshops and special events in the classrooms: They made an AIDS quilt, put on skits and dramatizations and listened to doctors who clarified medical aspects of AIDS and who advised students how to protect themselves.

Frank Hackett's "spirit of internationalism" is translated into respect for differences between people. Relationships between groups at RCS are good. A tenth grader told us: "It's not too cliquey; everyone knows what they like to do and no one gets in anyone else's way." In athletics, "Everyone works together on the field."

There are over thirty-eight clubs, and new ones are added each year. They include the successful Mock Trial Club, S.C.C. (Students of Color Committee), Film Club, Environmental Club, Amnesty International, Model Congress and Community Service. An activity period for clubs is scheduled during the school day, so that students can find time to engage in extracurricular interests.

School spirit at RCS is manifested through athletic competition in the Ivy Prep League. Riverdale has a newly renovated athletic center that was completed in the Fall of 1998. The athletic center houses an Olympic-size pool, where many trophies are on display. There are sixteen junior varsity and varsity sports teams including a swim team and a strong fencing team. Riverdale's football team achieved sports fame in the sixties when Frank Bertino coached Riverdale to seventeen undefeated seasons. Horace Mann alumni wince when they remember how future pro player Calvin Hill led RCS to a winning streak of fifty-one games. Today, the annual "Buzzell" basketball game in February against arch-rival Horace Mann draws a crowd of over one thousand people. The game was named for a Horace Mann student who died and the proceeds are donated to charity. In 1990, Riverdale made a politically correct decision to change the name of the school mascot and team name from The Indians to The Falcons.

A Riverdale junior who plans to be a litigator describes RCS as "a healthy, fun environment that promotes community feeling. If you work hard and apply yourself, you'll really succeed and help is always there if you need it."

Popular College Choices   Brown, University of Pennsylvania, University of Michigan, Harvard, Duke, Yale, Macalester, Wesleyan. Although RCS students apply and gain admission to the top Ivy League colleges, they select a variety of colleges, which is consistent with RCS's emphasis on perceiving students as individuals, rather than types

Traditions   Grandparents' Day, Spring Carnival, Winter and Spring Concerts, Book Fair, Academic Fair, Parents' Association Dinner/Dance and Auction, Buzzell games, Talent Show, Children Helping Children (charity outreach program), C.A.R.E. program (Children Aware of Riverdale Ethics), Homecoming Day, Career Day, One World Day, Shakespeare Recitation Contest, Policy Reading Competition, Friends of the Arts evening, Sixth and Twelfth Grade Graduation Ceremonies, Reunion and Winter Gathering for Alumni

Publications   Lower school publications: *The Rivulet*
The Flying Falcon
Upper school newspaper: *The Riverdale Review* (since 1916)
Literary magazine: *Impressions* (1997 National Council of Teachers of English Award)
Alumni magazine: *Quad*
Yearbook: *The Riverdalian*
Photography journal: *Exposures*

Community Service Requirement   14 hours on the River Campus for grade 6
20 hours for grades 7 and 8
72 hours for grades 9–12

Hangouts   Dino's Pizza, Riverdale Diner, Bagel Corner, RCS cafeteria (with a view of trees and fields) and library

Rodeph Sholom School

Nursery Division
7 West 83rd Street
New York, NY 10024
(212) 362-8800

Lower Elementary Division
Grades Pre-Kindergarten–1st
10 West 84th Street
New York, NY 10024
(212) 362-8769

Upper Elementary Division
Grades 2–6
168 West 79th Street
New York, NY 10024
(212) 362-0037

Coed
Nursery–6th grade
Accessible at 7 West 83rd Street and 168 West 79th Street
Not accessible at 10 West 84th Street

Mr. Irwin Shlachter, Headmaster
Mrs. Alice Barzilay, Director of Admissions and Placement

Birthday Cutoff   Children entering kindergarten must be 5 by September 4
Children entering at the nursery level must be 2.6 by September

Enrollment   Total enrollment: 500
Nursery enrollment: 130
Elementary enrollment: 370
Average graduating class size: 30–35

Tuition Range 1998–1999 $6,200 to $15,800, nursery 2 1/2's–6th grade
Temple membership is included
Additional fees: for registration, materials and insurance are under $600

Lunch fee grades 2–6 $800
There is a tuition reduction of $500 per sibling for each enrolled
child beyond the first

After-School Program for Nursery through 6th graders; weekdays
until 5:00 P.M.; a variety of creative, recreational and educational
activities for an additional charge

Summer Program Rodeph Sholom Summer Camp from late June
through mid-August; an additional payment is required

Founded in 1958 as a nursery school; the elementary level was
added in 1970. The Rodeph Sholom Day School is a Reform Jewish
day school affiliated with the Congregation Rodeph Sholom. It is
the only Reform Jewish day school in New York City. The nursery
division is housed in the temple building on West 83rd Street. Pre-
kindergarten through first grade are housed in a modern building
on West 84th Street, connected via a courtyard to the 83rd Street
building. Second through sixth grades (upper elementary divisions)
meet in a fully renovated facility on West 79th Street which houses
two gyms, three libraries (one is fully computerized and linked to the
internet), two computer labs, science labs and a cafeteria. The school
is renovating an adjacent building on 78th Street to meet its need for
expansion.

Getting In: Parents should call for an application and to reserve
a place in a group tour. ERB testing results, a school report, and a
playgroup interview with the child are required for admission to
kindergarten and above. "We choose not to be too elitist in admissions—our students have a wide spectrum of ability," the admissions
director told us. Students come from a variety of backgrounds; most
live on the Upper East and West Sides but some come from New
Jersey, Riverdale and Westchester. The school has no dress code.

Parents: A parent who has been at the school for several years
points out that as the school has expanded, the parent body has
evolved from a fuzzy West Side school to a school with more polish
and considerably more money: "Formerly the parents were psychologists, painters, a social worker—your basic West Side shleppers. Now
they're media executives, managing directors, executive editors;
people who golf."

An active PTA organizes several annual fund-raisers including the book fair (open to the neighborhood), and the Spring Auction held at an art gallery downtown. The PTA also sponsors dialogue meetings throughout the year; recent topics include: computers, Jewish studies, and neighborhood safety. The PTA frequently purchases blocks of tickets to sporting events and Broadway shows.

Program: The Rodeph Sholom School provides a combination of rigorous academics and a supportive environment. The school believes "the higher you place the bar, the higher the children will reach." Although there are three divisions (nursery, lower elementary, and upper elementary) there is interaction between older and younger students. For example, first graders read to nursery students and the entire school visits the Science Week exhibit created by the fifth grade.

The lower elementary division is comprised of pre-kindergarten through first grade. All classrooms have a computer and are filled with children's artwork and work in progress. Younger children play outdoors in the courtyard daily. Judaic studies is woven into the curriculum and each Shabbat (Friday) a different child's parent/guest is invited to participate with the class.

The school's approach to teaching is a balance of traditional/instructional and discovery-based methods. Social studies drives the integrated curriculum. In kindergarten the class is divided into small groups for individualized reading instruction which combines whole language and phonics techniques. Math, science, handwriting, writer's workshop and Jewish studies are taught in the classroom. Students leave their classrooms for special instruction in computer, library, art, music and physical education. Rodeph Sholom School uses the "Everyday Math" program developed at the University of Chicago (see "Chicago Math" in *glossary*).

Computers are used in all classrooms at RS. The technology curriculum includes: keyboarding, graphics, spreadsheets, database management, telecommunications, Internet, e-mail and desktop publishing. The science curriculum focuses on problem solving skills. Fifth graders study the weather. They run their own weather station, plot the readings, compare the metro forecast to the RS forecast and announce their weather watch results to the school.

Social studies is woven throughout the curriculum. Kindergartners focus on "me and my family." In first grade the social studies curriculum expands to "the neighborhood and the market." First graders learn how fruit is grown, transported and sold; they take field trips to various neighborhood and open-air markets in the city; they create their own market in the school lobby and sell produce to students and faculty; and they donate their profits to a charity of their choice. Second graders study New York City. Third graders study Native Americans; fourth graders examine Ancient Greece, Ancient Egypt and the Age of Exploration. The fifth grade focuses on Colonial America and the sixth grade studies 20th century World History.

The Jewish Studies program includes Hebrew language, Shabbat, the Torah portion, holidays and festivals, charitable deeds, and Jewish history, life and traditions. Beginning in first grade, Hebrew is taught using a combination of phonics and whole language techniques, including reading, writing, conversation and music. In addition to Congregation Rodeph Sholom's rabbis, Rabbi Matthew Gewirtz acts as friend, mentor and spiritual advisor to students.

The school has a partnership with Family Academy in Harlem to promote tolerance and awareness. Classes in kindergarten through fifth grade meet with classes from Family Academy throughout the year to work on projects together. Recently the first grade classes created a ten-foot mural that travels between the two schools.

Music is an integral part of the curriculum utilizing Orff instruments, Dalcroze Eurhythmy for movement and Kodaly Training for singing. Beginning in third grade, students study opera, including *The magic Flute*, *Carmen* and *The Marriage of Figaro*. Fourth through sixth graders have the opportunity to participate in band, string or flute ensembles and to give concerts/recitals. From Torah presentations to the Israel Day parade celebration, there are many opportunities for children to present and enjoy music.

In addition to after-school athletics, there are several active clubs including Girl's Math, Science, Pet Club, Orchestra, Band and Choir. The "Future Problem Solvers" team has been reigning State Champions for the past nine years.

Parents say that Rodeph Sholom provides a well-rounded education. One father told us, "They do a great job of combining Jewish identity with a solid academic grounding. It's a first rate education without any pretensions."

Popular on-going school choices   Riverdale, Horace Mann, Columbia Prep, Spence, Fieldston, Dalton, Hunter High School

Traditions   Jewish Holiday Celebrations (Purim Carnival, lunch in the Sukkah, etc.), Science Fair, Art Show, Book Fair, Frost Valley Environmental trip (fourth through sixth graders)

Publications: *The Rodeph Sholom Sun*
The Rodeph Sholom PTA Newsletter

The Rudolf Steiner School
A Waldorf School

Elementary Division
15 East 79th Street
New York, NY 10021
(212) 535-2130

Upper School
15 East 78th Street
New York, NY 10021
(212) 879-1101 (main number)
(212) 327-1457 (admissions), FAX (212) 861-1378

Coed
Nursery–12th grade
Not accessible

Ms. Carol Bartges, College Chair, School Head
Ms. Martha Masterson, Director of Admissions
Ms. Irene Mantel, School Administrator

Birthday Cutoff   Children entering at the nursery level must be 3 by September 1
Children entering kindergarten must be 5 by September 1
Children entering 1st grade must be 6 by September 1

Enrollment   Total enrollment: 270
3's places: 15
4's places: 3–6
Kindergarten places: 8–12
Kindergarten places: only if there has been attrition
1998 graduating class: 15

Grades   Semester system
Letter grades begin in 7th grade
Departmentalization begins in 9th grade

Tuition Range 1998–1999 $10,000 to $15,500, nursery 3's–12th grade
Additional fees under $200
Lunch is included through 2nd grade and is optional thereafter for a payment of $700 per year; Organic produce and milk used exclusively

Financial Aid/Scholarship   A fair portion of the student body receive some form of aid

Endowment $50,000

After-School Program   Grades 1–5, Monday–Friday
A variety of academic, creative and recreational activities for an additional payment

Summer Program   A 3-week June Day Camp is offered for children in preschool through grade 3 for an additional charge
A 3-week June Music Program is offered for children in grades 4 through 8 for an additional charge
Both summer programs are open to students from outside the Rudolf Steiner community

———

The Rudolf Steiner School of New York was founded in 1928 and is the oldest Waldorf School in North America. Rudolf Steiner (1861–1925), an Austrian scientist, artist, educator and founder of anthroposophy (wisdom of the essential human), began the original Waldorf school at the request of the owner of the Waldorf Astoria factory in Stuttgart in 1919. Integrating intellectual and artistic development, Steiner sought to sustain and deepen the child's capacity for life and creative thought. Despite being driven underground during WWII, Steiner's ideas survived and now inspire some seven hundred schools in over thirty countries. There are approximately 140 Waldorf Schools in North America. The curriculum, which was designed in 1920, is continuously updated within the original framework.

The lower school is housed in a Stanford White mansion just off Fifth Avenue; a sweeping marble staircase graces the foyer. Hot lunch is available. There are no uniforms; the dress code recommends appropriate clothing. Students address teachers formally. There is a spiritual ethos that permeates the school. The seasons and Christian holidays and festivals are observed creatively through drama and art. The preschool stresses imaginative learning and creative play. Children play with all natural materials such as birch logs, baskets of leaves and homemade dolls. Nature stories, myths and fairy tales are the core of the lower grades' language arts program.

Beginning in first grade, reading and math are taught with the aim of developing each child's pictorial imagination and children begin instruction in two foreign languages. Music, drama, and crafts are an important part of the Rudolf Steiner curriculum throughout. All students also take eurythmy: "the art of movement as developed by Rudolf Steiner," as well as visual speech and music.

In accordance with the Waldorf Method, class teachers move with the class through several grades. Narrative reports are provided and parent conferences are scheduled once a semester, but there is frequent informal parent/teacher communication.

Each morning includes a main lesson block in one subject area, which is studied for a period of approximately four weeks. All students write and illustrate main lesson books, which serve as their textbooks. Academic subjects such as English, math and foreign languages are scheduled regularly for several periods weekly. Afternoons are reserved for additional academic work, lab periods (there is a modern, fully equipped science lab) and drama/movement, art, music or crafts. German and Spanish are introduced in kindergarten and become part of the curriculum in first grade.

High School main lesson blocks are taught by specialists in each field; class advisors coordinate class activities and oversee students' academic and personal progress. High school foreign language is taught by levels beginning in the ninth grade. Students choose either German, French or Spanish.

All pedagogical decisions are made by the College of Teachers within The Rudolf Steiner School, composed of tenured teachers who have made a long-term commitment to the school. They serve as the central administrative body of the school and elect the faculty chair or school head.

All students, third through sixth grades, participate in the Farm Program at the school-owned Hawthorne Valley Farm in upstate New York. Seventh and eighth graders visit a Vermont environmental center. Tenth graders can participate in a foreign exchange program at any Waldorf School in Europe.

High school students participate in Community Service; twelfth graders take an internship at an organization in their area of interest. There is a strong athletics program which includes junior varsity and varsity competition with other independent schools in volleyball, soccer, basketball, softball, and track.

Popular College Choices   Boston University, Bowdoin, Columbia University, New York University, University of Chicago, The School of Visual Arts, Skidmore, Sarah Lawrence College, Princeton University, Wellesley, Swarthmore, Williams

Saint Ann's School

129 Pierrepont Street
Brooklyn Heights, NY 11201
(718) 522-1660
e-mail: admin@saintanns.K12.ny.us
website: www.saintanns.k12.ny.us

Coed
2's–12th grade
Not accessible

Mr. Stanley Bosworth, Headmaster
Ms. Linda Kaufman, Assistant Headmaster
Ms. Mary Russotti, Director of Admission

Uniform   None

Birthday Cutoff   None specified; readiness is stressed

Enrollment   Total enrollment: 1,040
Preschool total: 70
Kindergarten places: 30
9th grade places: 5–10
Graduating class 1997–1998: approximately 73

Grades   Semester system
No letter grades are given throughout the school; standardized tests are given each year, and the results in middle school and high school are reported to parents
Departmentalization begins in 4th grade

Tuition Range 1998–1999 $13,600 to $15,900, lower school (kindergarten–3rd grade) to 12th grade
No additional fees
A tuition refund plan is available
Private bus service (for an additional fee) is available from Manhattan; also accessible by subway or car

Financial Aid/Scholarship   15% of the student body receive some form of aid

Endowment $1 million

Diversity   17% children of color
23 Prep for Prep students enrolled as of fall 1998

Homework   1st and 2nd grades: none
3rd and 4th: 1 hour
5th and 6th: 1½ hours
7th and 8th: 2 hours
9th–12th: 3–4 hours
°The guideline is 20 minutes per class, but there is usually more

After-School Program   Open to current or new Saint Ann's students only
Kindergarten through 6th grade: 3:00 to 5:30 P.M. (6 P.M. if necessary)
Creative activities, computer, games, sports, study, art, theatre and so on; an additional payment is required

Summer Program   Open to current or new Saint Ann's students (preschool through 6th grade); Six-week program that begins at the end of classes and continues through the end of July, offering creative activities, sports and field trips
Three-week gymnastics program for grades 3–8

———

Saint Ann's School was founded with seventy children in 1965 under the aegis of St. Ann's Episcopal Church. The rector of the church envisioned a school for gifted children, "with uniforms and a healthy dose of religion." Founding Headmaster Stanley Bosworth (known to all simply as Stanley), a former French teacher at the progressive (now-defunct) Walden School, was only thirty-five years old when he came to Saint Ann's. He came with his own vision: "It was my vow all those years ago that this particular school would somehow provide 10 percent of our nation's poets." It was Stanley's vision that prevailed.

In 1981, Saint Ann's was chartered by the New York State Board of Regents; in 1982 Saint Ann's was formally disaffiliated from the church. The sixties are long gone but Stanley's idealism has not dimmed; he still says that "no student should approach us without stars in his or her eyes." Saint Ann's is a school where gym is called "Recreational Arts," where there are no grades, no class rankings and no rigid curriculum. Saint Ann's has produced award-winning playwrights as well as a Westinghouse Scholar. A parent said, "The unconventional tone of the school gives these kids a shared bond and a respect for the unconventional in life . . . these kids are not afraid to break the mold."

Saint Ann's is a progressive, arty school for very bright children. "It's what Dalton used to be," parents say. Located in Brooklyn Heights, now thoroughly gentrified, the school attracts many local families. Approximately one-third of the students come from Manhattan. Several years ago, the school renovated the basement of the main building and added a gym, a lecture room and an art gallery, plus five additional classrooms. More recently, the two-story dining room was redesigned to create two balcony rooms (which are used both as additional dining space and as classrooms). The entire area also doubles as a performing space.

Getting In: The brochure states: "We admit the talented." Saint Ann's students must be self-motivated and have the ability and maturity necessary to handle freedom and rigorous academic requirements. They use a "holistic approach" when it comes to admissions. Director of Admissions Mary Russotti says, "Our admissions process is an eclectic one that considers both achievement and glimmers of special talent." Candidate profiles are cross-checked with ERB scores where appropriate. In addition to testing and interviewing the applicant, the admissions director will observe a child in his or her nursery school on occasion. Parents of applicants to the lower grades are interviewed with special concern for receptivity to the values of humanism and the arts. The admissions director provides parents with an opportunity to offer insights and/or additional information about their child that might help in making a decision. The appropriate division head also interviews middle and upper school applicants. Parents say that there is little of the "admissions anxiety" found at the Manhattan schools because "kids at Saint Ann's don't get their sense of self-worth from outshining others; there is very little glitter or glitz." Another parent said, "The atmosphere was informal and friendly." Saint Ann's maintains a wait list but there is not much movement on it.

Saint Ann's is not a member of ISAAGNY (Independent Schools Admissions Association of Greater New York) but does adhere to the same admissions notification and parent-reply dates as the other independent schools. The school's midwinter break is scheduled in February, a week before that of the public schools. Spring break is scheduled to coincide with Easter and Passover.

The typical Saint Ann's student is "bright, arty, concerned for others and confident." Is there a self-consciousness about being gifted? A parent says, "It has the effect of creating among the children a sense of community and specialness that overrides all other differences including ethnic background, family income and gender."

Although admittedly it is more of an accomplishment to make an award-winning scholar out of a mediocre student, Saint Ann's is nonetheless remarkably good at encouraging bright children to fully realize their potential. A mother told us, "All of my children's special talents—repeat, *all* of them—were nurtured, developed and tested in the very loving laboratory of Saint Ann's." One parent told us that her son's first grade teacher recognized that he had a talent for art. "She was so enthusiastic and encouraging that it brought out more than his ability to draw and paint—it also developed his interest in art history and a strong sense of himself." He is now in college majoring in a different subject but he is on the staff of the humor magazine, and art will be his lifelong avocation.

Aside from the excitement of teaching exceptionally able students, teachers say Saint Ann's is a great place to work because of the freedom and flexibility: "Teachers get to teach exactly what they want to teach; there is no rigid curriculum." In the lower school most teachers have a special talent or interest; they are painters or writers, for example, "and the administration encourages these interests." A significant portion of the student body is made up of the children of faculty. In the middle and high school teachers are selected not because they have a master's in education but because they have expertise in a creative area: Stanley's original vision was to have actors, painters and musicians as teachers. There is a "master teacher" and the student is his "apprentice": The drama teachers are playwrights and actors, the English teachers are writers and so on. Many of the teachers are young and "There is an enormous energy, excitement and commitment." Twelve percent of the faculty are Saint Ann's alumni. Another of Stanley's tenets is that "art and literacy serve the scientist as well as the artist." However, a former teacher confided that Stanley's attempts to have poets teach science have not always been successful.

Parents: With respect to the parent body, one parent said she never felt that her bank account, background or lifestyle made a difference at Saint Ann's: "If I didn't fit in, I never noticed." Many fathers, such as those who work as full-time writers or illustrators or songwriters, are able to bring their children to and from school. One parent said, "Saint Ann's isn't interested in the parents; when you drop off your child, he becomes Saint Ann's child." Consequently, the Parents Association is not particularly strong. The same people have been running the Parents Association for several years. Parent events include Parents Night at school, cocktail parties, dance concerts, two middle school and high school productions each year, voice recitals and instrumental concerts. Saint Ann's students act as hosts. There is a welcoming party for new parents at the school. Because the alumni body is so young (the first alumna graduated from Saint Ann's in 1970), alumni fund-raising was started only recently. Saint Ann's alumni keep in touch: The *Saint Ann's Times* reports on news of over four hundred alumni.

Program: Lower school at Saint Ann's is composed of grades kindergarten through third. Separation is handled gently. Parents say: "They are unbelievably sensitive." A parent can stay in the classroom if necessary. Kindergartners come for a playtime in the spring and begin with half/class half/day for the first two days of school in the fall. The head of the lower school, Gabrielle Howard, is outstanding; she has been at Saint Ann's since 1973, initially as a teacher. Cathy Fuerst is the head of the preschool. She has served as a lower school master teacher for eleven years, as an assistant to the Director of Development, and as Coordinator of the lower school after-school program.

Classes are identified by teachers' names. In a kindergarten class of twenty children there is a master teacher and an assistant. Students in the lower school address teachers by their first names.

The brochure says, "Reading is central." Writing, math, science, art, music and dance round out the rest of the lower school schedule. Reading is taught with eclectic methods—"any way the child needs"—including phonics. By the end of first grade about 95 percent of the children are reading. A former lower school teacher told us that "many first graders are reading Beverly Cleary or Roald Dahl, but some are still on *Mack and Tap*. But by the end of the first year most are on a second grade reading level." A parent told us that one shortcoming at Saint Ann's is if a student needs remedial help his parents must pay extra for it. "Parents must be aware of any learning difficulties their child is having," she said. There is no learning specialist on staff at Saint Ann's; however, several trained specialists are permitted to use the school premises for private instruction.

Parents say, "You have to get the daily and weekly information from your child but the school will let you know if your child isn't working up to his potential." The anecdotal reports are extensive. And the ERB and standardized tests are given during the year as objective measurements of aptitude and achievement. According to the brochure, these tests are used to see if students are at the proper level or need to be moved along.

Although the student body is a narrowly selected group of very bright children, the academic atmosphere at Saint Ann's is not one of cutthroat competition. "It's very nurturing and informal; kids are allowed to be who they are." For instance, parents say, a first grader can take a sixth grade math class and not feel out of place. (In fact, a first grader once did take sixth grade math; a teacher accompanied him to the class and stayed with him.) And of course there is no competition for grades because there aren't any. (On longer research papers students might receive a "good" or a "check", in addition to extensive comments.)

In the preschool and lower school, students leave their classrooms for "specials" in art, music and recreational arts. Kindergartners also leave the classroom for dance. Beginning in second grade, students leave their homeroom class for math and computer, and in third grade for science. Third grade is the last year of the classroom-based program; there are still blocks in the classroom. Formal instruction in computer begins in third grade. Ten year olds learn LOGO and Pascal. One lower school group studying Greek mythology wrote an epic poem seventy pages long. Lower schoolers produce one play or musical each year.

Middle school at Saint Ann's is equivalent to grades four through eight. Bells ring between classes in the middle and high schools. It is up to the teacher whether or not students use their first or last names. Full departmentalization begins in the first year of middle school (fourth grade), which requires a lot of maturity. Says a former lower school teacher, "There's a lot of choice for a ten year old." Each fourth grader also has a locker with a lock.

The brochure says that "subject achievement and aptitude define placement, particularly in math and language groups. The makeup of English and history classes is largely determined by age." Sixth graders learn the structure of language. Formal language instruction begins in the seventh grade, and students can choose from Latin, Greek, French, Spanish, Chinese and Japanese. Science is part of the curriculum each year. Middle schoolers take five years of science, and health issues are part of the eighth grade biology course.

One parent said, "My fourth grader is learning what I learned in college. In our conversations she talks about Greek and Norse myths and Latin."

The arts are considered academic subjects at Saint Ann's. The middle school has its own literary magazine. Nancy Fales Garrett's playwriting course is so good that nearly every year a play by a Saint Ann's student is accepted for production by the Playwright's Horizons Festival's annual off-Broadway run in the fall.

Middle schoolers perform in mixed-age plays and musicals; recent productions include *Fahrenheit 451* and *Room Service*. A parent told us that when her son was in fifth grade, his drama teacher, an off-Broadway director (the kind that Saint Ann's delights in hiring), sparked his interest in performing and he eventually was selected as a member of a well-known theatre troupe.

Athletics are popular at Saint Ann's. There are varsity and junior varsity sports teams (including girls' softball, soccer, basketball, and volleyball) and coed baseball. In addition to A and B team gymnastics, yoga, running, weight training, exercise and fitness, fencing and karate are offered. There is plenty of school spirit exhibited at basketball games. Saint Ann's has several gymnasiums and uses nearby parks for playing fields.

Students cannot leave school for lunch until the second half of eighth grade. Milk and fruit are provided free of charge; lunch is available for an additional fee.

The high school at Saint Ann's is composed of grades nine through twelve. There is a tremendous amount of freedom and choice in the high school at Saint Ann's so students must be self-motivated.

The teachers in the high school—all "masters" in their disciplines—"love what they do and they communicate it to the students." The brochure describes the high school curriculum as "adventurous." Saint Ann's is progressive but the school is not embroiled in the multicultural debate rocking the public schools. Parents say the school stresses "Latin, writing, reading, theatre and playwriting." Stanley says the school has "a commitment to Western civilization" and respect for the Western canon. (In this way it's not so different from a "traditional" school like Trinity.)

We observed an English class discussing Nabokov's *Lolita*. Some of the students had their feet up on their desks, others were sprawled or supine yet the conversation was electric. In a classroom nearby, a young attractive Spanish teacher gave her student a high five for a correct answer. The history class down the hall was studying the recent elections in Russia. History classes often have seminars on current events. A parent had praise for many teachers and for one standout, Victor Marchioro, who teaches "The Bible as Literature", described as "an unbelievably rigorous and unforgettable class." Also singled out for praise were Ruth Chapman, an art history/English teacher, and Peter Leventhal, an art teacher. "It's worth insisting that your child take one of his classes just to read the evaluations he writes—you will not believe anyone could be so articulate about your child," said a parent.

Extracurricular activities keep Saint Ann's open seven days a week. Over the weekend the school may be used for play rehearsals, sports and yearbook meetings. There is a playwriting class for high school students and one for middle school students and a playwriting festival each spring. Students can work on photography or literary magazines.

Students with a scientific bent can participate in the science research program in addition to the broad range of science courses offered. And several each year are selected for the Science Honors Program at Columbia University, and junior and senior math teams compete in the New York Interscholastic Math League.

High school students travel to Washington, D.C., to get a first-hand look at government in action and participate in model congresses there (as well as in Boston). There are study abroad trips to France and Spain. The Saint Ann's Singers tour overseas.

A parent of two Saint Ann's students told us: "My son had four years that were so spectacular in every way that college was a bit of a letdown." Saint Ann's students are encouraged to strive for awards and honors (Saint Ann's produces numerous National Merit Scholarship Finalists and AP scholars), and these accomplishments are conspicuously listed in the *Saint Ann's Times* each year. In addition, Saint Ann's students outshine their peers at other independent schools in the Johns Hopkins Center for Academically Talented Youth Competition. (The CTY talent search is based on achievement on the PSAT and the SAT.)

Technology: In 1994 Saint Ann's had the foresight to create two administrative computer positions: 1) Director of Computers and Technology (she supplies an overview of the present and future role of computers at Saint Ann's, oversees purchases and maintenance of hardware, maintains the school-wide network and coordinates computing activities among various departments) 2) Coordinator of Educational Software (her responsibilities include training faculty, installing software, assisting with use of the Internet, and staff training). The Coordinator offers a wide-range of courses (from basic skills to HyperCard and web publishing) to *faculty* during school hours so that faculty have a chance to keep up with their students' technological expertise! "We've attempted to make computers available and useful to all of our students and staff, from the third grade to the twelfth, and from the Headmaster to the kitchen staff." Thus the Saint Ann's population is largely computer-literate.

The Main Library is fully computerized with Internet access. The school has a T1 high speed connection to the Internet in place and all students and staff have e-mail addresses and can create their own web pages if they wish. The school hopes to expand the Computer Center (now located across the street) and is seeking more space in the neighborhood to do so. The Computer Resource Center (located in the main building) is fully equipped and teachers can bring classes in to use programs such as A.D.A.M for science/anatomy, Civilization for history, and Geometers Sketchpad for mathematics. A part-time lab assistant staffs the Resource Center.

Two newly renovated science labs are wired for network access. In addition to networked computers, the Science labs have ten Power-Book computers and data acquisition instruments that enable students to conduct experiments and collect data in real time. The students then analyze the data on the spot as part of the lab.

The math department makes much use of computers as well. Students have published math papers on the school web site. The Middle School Problem Solving class visits the Resource Center on a regular basis to obtain new problems and share solutions on the MATH-COUNTS web site.

Ever aware of the arts, Saint Ann's is developing a music/computers lab in one of the music rooms, which will be expanded into a multimedia lab.

Saint Ann's students apply to and are accepted at a broad spectrum of colleges including the top Ivy League universities. Oberlin, a small liberal arts college in Ohio, is popular. A parent said, "Stanley and his team devote enormous energy to getting the students into the best schools—that means the best school for the child, not necessarily the parent."

Graduation is held in the Church of Saint Ann and the Holy Trinity. Caps and gowns are not worn but "Pomp and Circumstance" is played. According to tradition, the president of the board of trustees speaks as well as a member of the faculty. There are four student presentations that can be in any medium.

Popular College Choices   Yale, Wesleyan, Brown, Oberlin, Barnard, Amherst

Traditions   Fun Run, Parents' Night, Founders' Day, Fund-Raising Auction

Publications   Middle school literary magazine
High school literary magazine
Photography or art magazine
Publications on a variety of subjects including: art, humor, nonfiction
Development office publication: *Saint Ann's Times*

Community Service Requirement   None

Hangout   On the steps in front of school

St. Bernard's School

4 East 98th Street
New York, NY 10029
(212) 289-2878, FAX (212) 410-6628
website: www.stbdev.org

All boys
K–8th/9th grade
Not accessible

Mr. Stuart H. Johnson, III, Headmaster
Elizabeth B. Ketner, Co-Director of Admissions
Anne S. Nordeman, Co-Director of Admissions

Uniform   Kindergarten: St. Bernard's shirts, khaki pants, Grades I–III: Monday–Thursday: navy blazers must be worn to and from school, St. Bernard's shirt or turtleneck, khaki-colored trousers or shorts, belt must be worn if pants have belt loops;

Grades IV–IX: Monday–Thursday: navy blazers to and from school, polo or turtleneck or oxford shirts tucked in, khaki pants or shorts with belts; all clothing must fit; no jeans, no T-shirts with logos, no sneakers except at gym

Fridays: blazers, ties and oxford shirts required, all day

Enrollment   Total enrollment: 381
K places: approximately 40–43
Half of the 1998 graduates will attend city day schools, half will attend boarding schools

Grades   Kindergarten: checklist and written reports
Grades I–III: detailed anecdotal reports, no checklists or rankings, no grades given in sports or art
Grades IV–IX: letter grades accompanied by detailed written reports
Departmentalization begins in grade V
Grade VII: first final
Grade VIII: first midterm

Tuition Range 1998–1999   15,600 to $16,000 Kindergarten–9th grade

Additional fees: for lunch, books, supplies, physical education and trips total approximately $2,000
Tuition reimbursement and accident insurance plans are available

Financial Aid/Scholarship   16% of the student body received some form of aid in 1997

Endowment   N/A; reputed to be large

Diversity   Children of color represent 10% of the student body
8 Prep for Prep students enrolled as of fall 1998

Homework   Grade I: 10 pages of reading out loud to parent every two to three nights plus 1–2 pages of a workbook every other night, approximately 20 minutes
Grade II: spelling tests once a week; reading: 1 chapter every 2–3 days, approximately 20–30 minutes
Grade III: written compositions and journals, some math, approximately 30–40 minutes
Grades IV and V: compositions begun at home and math every night, approximately 1 hour; prep (study hall) begins 3:30–4:30 P.M.; most 4th and 5th graders use this time to complete some of their homework, but prep is not mandatory until Grade VI
Grade VI: $1\frac{1}{2}$–2 hours; prep is mandatory
Grade VII–IX: 2–3 hours

After-School Program   St. Bernard's boys can participate in the Nightingale-Bamford Hobbyhorse after-school program, Monday–Friday 3:15–5:00 P.M. or 6:00 P.M.; offered are crafts, sports, computer, ice skating, photography, chess, science; at moderate cost; financial aid is available
Grades III–IX participate in intramural games including soccer, basketball, baseball, softball, lacrosse
Varsity and junior varsity Red & White teams in all sports
St. Bernard's is a member of the Manhattan Private Middle School League
Lessons in ice hockey are offered for an additional fee
Saturday Sports Club in the St. Bernard's gym: open to children from other schools; Saturdays from 9:00 A.M. to 3:00 P.M.; $30 a day; supervised coed activities

Summer Program   Summer sports camp, June 15 through July 31st.

Although the school emblem shows a St. Bernard dog, St. Bernard's School was named after the rue St. Bernard, a street in Belgium. It is pronounced with the accent on the first syllable. Founded by an Englishman in 1904, St. Bernard's has always had an affinity for English traditions. It unself-consciously calls its alumni Old Boys, and many of the devoted faculty still hail from Great Britain. But St. Bernard's is a kinder and gentler place than its British counterparts. Parents say there is a family feeling here. As Mrs. Forster, former co-director of admissions, says: "There is a crispness of attitude, with fun." A parent said "There's enough leeway so that the boys can be boyish."

Stuart Johnson, a Yale man, was under thirty when he was appointed to his post as headmaster. He succeeded Englishman Amos Booth. Mr. Johnson is described as "unpretentious, caring, witty and a bright and stylish writer" and it is said that he "writes wonderful messages in bulletins and follows the traditions set forth by the other heads." "He goes out of his way to know everyone," said a parent. "He even came to a lacrosse game in Greenvale!" Manners are very important; Mr. Johnson shakes each boy's hand each morning. Mr. Johnson listens to all complaints and dispenses "punishments without tears." In addition to his administrative duties, Mr. Johnson teaches European history and directs the annual Shakespeare play. He knows all the boys by name and invites alumni to his apartment around Christmastime.

Getting in: Parents are advised to call for an application and brochure in September or October of the year before the child will enter Kindergarten. St. Bernard's does not require any application fee. There is no birthday cutoff because they try to judge each boy on his own merits. Readiness is what is important. Boys in this year's Kindergarten have birthdays spanning the entire year, including some younger boys with summer birthdays.

After the application is received by the school, they will call you to arrange a parent tour as well as a separate time for your child's interview. The tour is usually for two families at a time. Don't be afraid to ask questions, but you should be familiar with the catalog so that you can ask meaningful ones. "Really, we love parents to ask us *any* questions about the school and their child," say the co-directors of admissions. Leave plenty of time for the tour because it is very thorough. You are not rushed if you wish to linger in a classroom. After the tour, each set of parents meets privately with Mr. Johnson, for anywhere from ten to twenty minutes (longer if necessary). A parent at St. Bernard's recalls that she took her time on the tour: "I loved that we had the opportunity to tour the school and meet with the headmaster before we decided to apply."

The co-directors visit as many nursery schools as possible to see the boys in their current setting. All boys have a thirty minute interview at St. Bernard's. You are told not to prepare your son for the individual interview. It is a formal evaluation but the boys usually enjoy themselves (thirty minutes of undivided attention!) while their nervous parents sit and wait. Reading material is provided for those parents who are able to concentrate. There is a strong sibling and legacy policy. There is not a typical St. Bernard's boy although they look remarkably similar walking up Madison Avenue in their blue blazers.

Parents: A lot of Old Boys send their sons to St. Bernard's. Parents say the parent body is composed in part of "families with good values, 'Eleanor Roosevelt' types—women who work, even though they don't have to." One parent described the typical St. B parent as "an old New York family, with oil paintings of their ancestors on the walls and well-worn furniture." Certainly the tone of the parent body is "understated." Those who have means do not flaunt it.

Many parents who are prominent editors, writers or journalists send their sons to St. B's because of the school's emphasis on literacy. The beautifully written brochure says one of the basic premises at St. B's is "a regard for the beauty and power of English—in reading, writing, speaking, listening."

Class cocktail parties are held in the fall or winter and everyone gets a turn to host. The event can be casual or catered; the Parents Association reimburses parents for their expenses. The Parents Association sponsors events such as the Book Fair and Author's Night, a School Fair and a Raffle. On Parents' Night mothers and fathers gather in the gym and then go to the classrooms where they are joined by the teachers. There is a special visiting day for grandparents in the spring.

In the words of one alumnus, "In the old days St. Bernard's was a hatchery for the progeny of millionaires." The scions of some of New York's old families still attend. (St. Bernard's is rumored to have one of the largest endowments among city independent schools.)

Program: Traditions are an integral part of life at St. Bernard's, and parents say the boys—and Old Boys—look forward to many of them. Every morning St. Bernard's boys shake hands with the headmaster and then with their teachers. Every afternoon they say good-bye to their teachers with another handshake. Each day begins with an assembly in the gym. There are Tuesday-morning Bible stories followed by discussion with Rosemary Lea whose Bible stories were published in 1995. A school-wide assembly is held on Fridays. At assembly a hymn is sung, announcements are made and there is a program. After Christmas each grade I boy receives a hymn book with his name on it and the date that he received it, and he keeps it for the whole time he is at St. B's. Parents talk about the family feeling at assemblies, to which they are invited several times a year. Each boy gains experience in public speaking beginning in grade I. Each boy recites a poem or performs in a play at assembly. Topics at assembly range widely. There might be a group of Old Boys reminiscing about life at St. Bernard's in the fifties or a performance of music of the Middle Ages by the Interschool Orchestra. A particularly witty assembly used the theme Lingo Limbo to personify elements of bad writing. The Oxy Morons, the Euphemism Unit, Club Cliché and the Grammar Goons painlessly pointed out the pitfalls of poor writing.

There is a tradition at St. Bernard's involving a stuffed alligator given to the neatest class. At Friday assemblies the alligator is presented by one class to another with some original poetry or a song.

On your tour you will see desks arranged in traditional rows with the teacher at the front of the class speaking to the students. You might hear a student reciting a poem, or a nine year old reciting his multiplication tables, but don't be misled; although there is plenty of structure, there is flexibility and creativity within each classroom. Boys may stand upon their chairs, work on the floor in groups, sit in a circle and read aloud. "The combination of bright kids and unusual teachers makes St. Bernard's unique. The real beauty of St. Bernard's is its teachers," says Mr. Johnson. There is little turnover in staff at St. B, there are some eccentrics and there's a big age range. One parent described her sons' teachers as "warm, kind and intellectual." Another parent said, "Some teachers are rough and tough, but adored. Some teachers give the boys nicknames." Another parent said: "There are kids whose fathers had the same teachers, they are all well remembered, some revered, for generations." From fifth grade up all homeroom teachers are men. The "favorite rebel," Nik Milhouse, retired after twenty-two years as a teacher of science and photography. He founded the yearbook *The Keg*, and led groups of city boys and girls, teachers and parents on trips to various countries within Latin

America where they gained an appreciation of the entire region and its culture.

A major expansion of the building is complete. The renovations include: a state-of-the-art gymnasium, science wing with four new labs, a teaching theatre, two kindergarten classrooms with separate play-deck, and a carpentry room.

Junior school at St. B's is grades K–III. Parents told us that reading is expected to be under way by Christmas of first grade. Grade I boys are divided into two reading groups with much fluidity between them. Boys must read aloud to their parents ten pages every two to three nights. "From the first day of school boys get into the homework habit," says one parent. Homework is never unreasonable, but there is a certain amount expected every night.

There are two reading specialists and one math specialist on the staff of the special learning department. There is concern for the individual child. One mother told us her son needed a little extra help in math in first grade, and a St. B teacher who happened to be in the same summer community offered to work with him over the summer free of charge, so that he wouldn't have trouble with second grade math.

One mother spoke about the progress her son made in grade I: "It's a caring environment and they keep a close watch. My son is shy but they've helped him to socialize. Also, at first he couldn't write and now he writes pages; he also wasn't a team sports player and now he participates fully."

A typical grade I schedule: The day begins with an assembly in the gym and goes on to art, gym, library, science, sums, spelling, phonics, reading, math, recess, lunch, physical education, work-time/crafts and dismissal. The curriculum is well rounded, parents say, and there is time for physical activity every day, either on the outdoor play terrace or in the fields of Central Park just a block away. There is a computer in every classroom, in addition to a large new computer lab with PC's. The science room for grades I through V is very well equipped.

Third graders do a lot of written work. They study Greek mythology "and are very devoted to it," a parent said. Awards for best and most-improved handwriting are given in each class.

Music begins in first grade. We toured around Christmastime and strains of "O Come All Ye Faithful" were floating through the halls. Tryouts for the St. Bernard's singing group begin in fourth grade and most boys make it. Rehearsals are held twice a week before school. At performances, boys wear special ties and trousers. One recent year they sang at Carnegie Hall, and they have also appeared at Alice Tully Hall, the youngest musical group to perform.

Art is hands on, with an academic approach. One Christmas, boys made ornaments for the Florence Nightingale Nursing Home.

The middle school is grades IV through VI. Fourth graders have a meeting before the school year begins to discuss the transition to middle school.

Fifth graders always sponsor the Science Fair, a midwinter event in which experiments are demonstrated. There is a fifth and sixth grade environmental group that organizes an Earth Day program and raises money for environmental causes.

Every homeroom performs at an Assembly; one recent year a fifth grade class did the story of Prometheus. A parent described the play as "pure entertainment" with St. Bernard's characteristic wit and English humor." The boy who played Hercules was the skinniest boy in the class, but he came out swaggering, with his sleeves rolled up. "The boys really loved performing!"

From time immemorial every fifth grader has written a ten-page research report on an animal, and, says a parent, "Every alumnus remembers his animal." They also do a unit on Native Alaskans in the winter and Native Americans in the spring. Latin begins in sixth grade.

The Garrett McClung Prize is a special award given in grade V for achievement. Six prizes are given out at the end of grade VI.

The upper school consists of grades VII through IX. Special events during these years include the annual eighth grade Shakespeare production, directed by the headmaster. The play varies from year to year (in recent years it has been *The Tempest* and *The Taming of the Shrew*), and St. Bernard's boys play all roles. Another eighth grade tradition is a visit to Civil War battlefields in Virginia. There is an eighth grade debating society and an upper school public speaking contest.

In grade VII *To Kill a Mockingbird* is read and in grade IX, Solzhenitzyn's *One Day in the Life of Ivan Denisovich*. Parents say the boys are very well prepared for the ongoing schools because of St. B's emphasis on reading and writing.

The student council is composed of elected members from grades IV through IX. The council meets each trimester and each class elects its own president, vice president and secretary. The entire council meets with the headmaster. Recent issues have included the usual plaints: calls for better food, more recess, less homework, more holidays.

Clubs include the Computer Club, the Chess Club, the Photography Club and the St. Bernard's Singers. St. Bernard's boys can participate in Nightingale-Bamford's Hobbyhorse after-school program too. Ninth graders are permitted to go out for lunch.

The entire school benefits from the handsomely renovated Jenkins Library, in which an oil painting of the stern-faced founder overlooks the stacks. There are shelves of O.E.D.'s and study carrels for the older boys as well as CD-ROMs and other research tools. A separate section of the library is reserved for the younger boys so that they do not disturb the concentration of the older boys.

Intramural sports competition begins in grade III. Ninety percent of boys from grade V through grade IX play on at least one team each year. There are varsity and junior varsity Red and White teams in all sports. St. Bernard's teams excel in soccer and baseball. Ice hockey is offered in addition to the traditional sports.

Values are stressed throughout St. Bernard's and there is a code of conduct. In addition, one parent said, "High value is placed on both grades and awards." There are essay and composition prizes and a public speaking prize. At the final assembly numerous awards and prizes are given out; one of the highest awards is the Payne Whitney Honor Cup.

Consistent with the belief that "a good heart is finally more valuable than a well-stocked, well-trained head," community service at St. B's starts at the top with the headmaster, who is on the board of the Yorkville Common Pantry. Food drives are held at Thanksgiving, Christmas and Passover/Easter. Boys in grades I through II can work with the Clown Care Unit of the Big Apple Circus by writing poems or making gifts that the clowns take to children in area hospitals. In addition, each class does a project or community service work. Older boys visit the elderly at the Florence Nightingale Nursing Home or decorate the cafeteria or other common areas of the home for the holidays; the St. B's singing group performs or just visits informally. Other community service opportunities include the Environmental Club and recycling program, and bake sales for charities. There is usually a student-led response to a major disaster: For hurricane and earthquake victims, a well-decorated jar for contributions will be placed in the lobby and a check sent to a relief fund. There is a public school tutoring project in East Harlem at a school located at 115th Street and Second Avenue.

St. Bernard's imparts a palpable enthusiasm for learning, and the techniques for mastering any subject. An alumnus told us that the only times he wasn't at the top of his class were at St. Bernard's and The Harvard Business School. One parent said what surprised her the most about St. Bernard's was its warmth: St. Bernard's is not just for Anglophiles.

About half of the graduates go to boarding school and the rest transfer to independent day schools in the area, after either eighth or ninth grade.

Traditions   St. Bernard's book of school songs, Friday assemblies, eighth grade Shakespeare play, eighth grade trip (one week), fifth grade animal report, Alligator Award for neatness, Science Fair, Book Fair, Sports Day, Parents' Evening, Father's Dinner, Father/Son Soccer Game, The Caslon Spelling Bowl, Author's Night, Junior Old Boys' Lunch, Old Boys' Dinner, Grandparents' Visiting Day, Spring Concert, Middle School Music Festival

Publications   Yearbook: *The Keg*
Literary magazine: *The Budget*
Parents' Association Publication: *St. Bernard's Gazette*
Alumni Bulletin: *St. Bernard's School*

Community Service Requirement   No specific requirement but each boy must perform community service in a number of ways available through various programs within the school. There are also many opportunities to serve the local community: Yorkville Common Pantry, the Florence Nightingale Nursing Home, the Clown Care Unit at various hospitals

Hangouts   Richie's Deli on Madison, the Italian ices man outside school

Saint David's School

12 East 89th Street
New York, NY 10128
(212) 369-0058, FAX (212) 289-2796

All boys
Pre-Kindergarten–8th grade
Accessible (3 elevators)

Dr. Donald T. Maiocco, Headmaster
Ms. Janet Sughrue, Director of Admissions
Ms. Julie Sykes, Director of Admissions

Uniform Grades pre-kindergarten through pre-1st: collared or turtleneck shirts only, no jacket required, sneakers are allowed Grades 1–8: tie and jacket (jacket can be any color); Bermuda shorts allowed in September and May, no sneakers

Birthday Cutoff Children entering kindergarten must be 5 by December 31
Children entering 1st grade must be 6 by September

Enrollment Total enrollment: 365
Pre-kindergarten places: 16
Kindergarten places for incoming children: 20
Pre-1st places: 20
Graduating class size: approximately 35

Grades Trimester system
Pre-kindergarten through 3rd grade: detailed anecdotal reports and conferences
Letter grades begin in 4th grade
Departmentalization begins in 4th grade
First final exam is given in 7th grade

Tuition Range 1998–1999 $8,700 to $17,900, pre-kindergarten–8th grade
The cost for lunch, books, and athletics is included in the tuition
There is a new 8-month tuition payment plan available to parents
A 10 percent discount is given on the tuition of the second child

of parents with three or more children in the school; there is a discount of 25 percent for the third child and 50 percent for the fourth and additional children

Financial Aid/Scholarship   10% of the student body received some form of financial aid in 1997–1998

Endowment   N/A

Diversity   7% children of color
5 Prep for Prep students enrolled as of fall 1998

Homework   1st: 15–20 minutes
2nd: $1/2$ hour
3rd: 1 hour
4th and 5th: $1^1/2$ hours
6th: $1^1/2$–2 hours
7th and 8th: 2–$2^1/2$ hours

After-School Program   The Saint David's after-school program is open to Saint David's boys only; an additional payment is required Grades 1 through 8: Monday–Thursday, 4:30–5:30 P.M.; various activities including sports, art, cooking, computer, photography, woodworking, pottery, and rocketry and chess

Summer Program   The June Program for kindergarten and pre-1st boys during the last two weeks of June; an additional payment is required
June Summer Sports program (9:00 A.M.–3:30 P.M.) for grades 1–8, two weeks in June: a variety of sports, games, activities and field trips; an additional payment is required
March sports program for grades 1–8 either first or second week of spring vacation

Although Saint David's School, founded in 1951, is relatively young, it is interesting to note that the school has more traditions than most of the long-established East side boys' schools founded at the turn of the century. The school building, originally three private homes designed by Delano and Aldrich in 1919, retains much of the beauty, warmth and architectural detail of the period. Saint David's is a

Catholic school for boys but the Saint David's community is inclusive; almost half of the boys practice other religions, and the catalog states that St. David's "is a family school in every sense of the word." Parents say St. David's "offers a balance of academics, arts and athletics with a spiritual component." St. David's is known for an emphasis on literature, languages, history and art "bolstered by practical anatomy, mathematics and a growing computer science department."

Saint David's was founded by lay Catholics and, according to the mission statement, Saint David's remains grounded in the traditions of that faith. Saint David's students are taught "to respect and learn from all religious traditions, to prize diversity and to develop the spiritual and ethical values necessary for successful moral decision making." One parent described St. David's as a place where "the school and teachers work to develop boys who will be able to think critically about what life presents them with, and they do that by providing the boys with a foundation of ethical and moral instruction." One parent who is not Catholic and who recently relocated to New York City with her family from another country said she chose this school for her son because, considering the language and cultural differences, she felt Saint David's would provide "a challenging but nurturing academic environment with less pressure than at some other schools." Another parent said she chose Saint David's for "its heart, soul and mind."

Getting in: Applications must be filed by December 1. After the application is filed (there is a $40 fee), tour and interview dates are scheduled. Individual tours of the school are given by the directors of admission. Applicants for grades kindergarten through third have a one-on-one interview with a teacher. Applicants for grades four through eight spend a day in a classroom. The directors of admissions say that a diverse group of boys is chosen from a variety of nursery schools; approximately fifteen schools are represented in a class of thirty-six. Admissions at Saint David's is not stressful, and parents are made to feel comfortable about the process.

Parents: The parent body at Saint David's is described by a parent: "There is wealth and there are some limos but parents are far from ostentatious." Parents do dress well, and many wear suits to school events. An annual dinner dance is held in early March. A recent event consisted of a very successful dinner and auction. Parents mingle more informally at the frequent cocktail parties, teas, morning coffees, a theater benefit, and family skating at Wollman Rink.

Program: Saint David's has had remarkably few heads of school in its history; David Hume was headmaster for thirty-plus years. In

July 1992, Dr. Donald Maiocco became the school's fourth head-master. Parents describe Maiocco as "academically oriented and well travelled." (The original Normandy war maps we saw on the walls are courtesy of a former headmaster.) Dr. Maiocco greets the boys in front of the school almost daily, and parents say he is very accessible and returns calls promptly. When parents were concerned about their seventh graders hanging out at Jackson Hole (a hamburger restaurant), Dr. Maiocco established a setting in which parents could discuss these issues—like a fireside chat with coffee. Dr. Maiocco is the guiding force in the school's "rededication to the humanities." One of the first things he did was to change the names of the homerooms from A and B to Pi and Theta. The new school alma mater is sung to a Mozart melody. Dr. Maiocco teaches "Humanities VIII." According to the catalog, "Saint David's is deeply committed to exploration of the civilizations that most shaped our own: Democratic Greece and Republican Rome." Latin is required in the fifth grade and sixth grade and becomes an elective in seventh and eighth grades.

Dr. Maiocco has written that Saint David's mission is "to provide the finest education available within the best traditions of the church." Religious instruction at Saint David's is based on an inclusive, not exclusive, Catholicism. Requirements include: morning chapel, religion classes, mass (four times a year, third grade and up, held at the Church of St. Thomas More) and the celebration of Christian holidays. Preparation for First Communion is optional. Religion classes are ungraded, and holidays of other faiths are also examined during the course of the year. The catalog states that "students of all faiths are encouraged to draw from their religious traditions for class discussions and assignments."

The chapel is the former library and contains a fireplace and servant's bell in addition to pews. First and second graders attend chapel once a week for Bible stories. Third through eighth graders begin each day with chapel, at which hymns are sung and faculty members relate a personal story that reflects a particular moral or ethical lesson. These "chapel talks" can be humorous, serious, spiritual or merely enlightening, and range from an account of a close call with bears on a hiking trip to an explanation of the Book of Kells, an English teacher's description of the significance of the Jewish holidays to him or a well-loved member of the kitchen staff singing spirituals.

Saint David's calendar lists eight fêtes de l'écoles or celebration days. Each day is marked by a special program. There is a celebration for the founding of the city of Rome, and on every March 1, Saint

David's Day, members of the school community bite a leek to symbolize their becoming a son or daughter of Saint David's (in the year of his introduction Dr. Maiocco did his part).

Lower school is composed of pre-kindergarten through third grade. There is one pre-kindergarten class of approximately sixteen students, two kindergarten classes (of eighteen students each) and one pre-first classroom of no more than twenty students. The pre-first class serves a useful purpose for boys who may be reading, but are young or need more time before first grade. The brochure states, "In the early years the school seeks a balance between work and play." A parent told us about a wonderful celebration in the lower school for "Cinco de Mayo," a Mexican feast day: "They had a piñata, food and clothing from Mexico." One second grade project focused on how each boy could do his part to help save the earth. One year, the family of one of the second grade boys had lived in Japan and helped the class celebrate Children's Day with a Japanese Tea Ceremony.

In the lower school basic skills are emphasized. Homework is introduced in first grade. Formal reading instruction also begins in this year with special small group instruction. Manipulatives are used for math instruction. Math is tracked or grouped by ability starting in first grade. Fourth graders begin learning how to write a research paper. There is a computer in every classroom.

Drama, music and art are integrated into the academic curriculum. Lower school boys choose a famous painting to study. Parents look forward to the yearly first grade Christmas play. Students go outside their homerooms for instruction in pottery, woodworking, music, science and gym. Project Charlie, an anti-drug program, is taught in second and fourth grades. Sixth graders take a full health course called D.A.S.H. (drugs, alcohol, sex and health).

Lower school boys have a break midmorning for recess in the little gym, or they may go to the play yard. They change for sports in the afternoon. From kindergarten up, boys eat in the downstairs lower school dining room. Lunch is served family style, and, said one mother, the boys are expected to eat what is on their plates. Parents praise Lower School Head Jane Warwick: "She knows each boy as an individual—his strengths and his weaknesses."

Sports at Saint David's begins with intramural competition in third grade. From grade five on there is All-Star Team competition with other schools, but a hallmark of the sports program at Saint David's is that all fifth and sixth grade boys get a chance to play at the varsity level; there are no team cuts at this age. The school's athletic facilities have recently been expanded to include a new 16,000 square foot sports center located at 215 East 94th Street. The athletic director says, "a lot of attention is paid to skill development, and the coaching staff is strong," which enables the Saint David's boys to compete with the best of them. The Red Team has fielded championship basketball and soccer teams. On Friday afternoons some faculty and boys sometimes go to the park for informal sports, or play pickup basketball in the gym. There are seasonal parent/faculty games and an alumni soccer match. The Player of the Week program recognizes outstanding performance in a game, enthusiasm or sportsmanship.

Another incentive for boys in the lower school is the Saint David's armband, which is awarded at a monthly assembly to boys who did something special. The armband has been awarded for "recognition of academic excellence," for "neatness" or for "simply smiling." One parent said her son got it for mastering the "bird's nest" in gymnastics.

There is no middle school at Saint David's: Grades four through eight are considered part of the upper school. Letter grades begin in fourth grade. Boys begin lab science in fourth grade. Math continues to be grouped according to ability.

Latin, introduced in fifth grade, continues through eighth grade. In sixth grade boys can choose between French and Spanish. Fourth through sixth graders are taught the science of geography and they have a "map of the month" to study. April has been designated "Science Month" at Saint David's. Guest lecturers talk about the sonar systems in dolphins, the cardio-vascular system and advances in heart surgery and the impact of El Nino.

Drama continues to be incorporated into the curriculum. For example, Tom McLellan's fifth grade class stages a mock Revolutionary War battle, the Battle of Macgowan's Pass, in Central Park. Boys also take a field trip to Old Bethpage, Long Island. Class plays usually tie in with the history or English curriculum; past productions have included *Casey at the Bat*, *Philoctetes* and *The Pirates of Penzance*.

There are many opportunities for boys to practice public speaking: Sixth graders recite original poetry and eighth graders deliver research reports on art to students and teachers and sometimes give the chapel talks.

Opportunities for musical performance include handbell choir, recorder, Glee Club, Interschool orchestra, philharmonic and two ensemble performances with Brearley each year.

There is interaction between the grades in which students act as teachers. Eighth graders talked to third graders about Greek coins they had made; a fifth grade class addressed fourth graders about aspects of Native American cultures.

Visiting Day provides students an opportunity to interact with girls at the single-sex schools. They pick an activity such as library or music and go to a girls' school for the library or music hour in the fall. In the spring, they reciprocate and host the girls. Exchanges are matched by grade and age.

Boys in the upper school are assigned many long-term projects in order to develop their time-management skills. Seventh and eighth graders have trimester exams. In addition to Dr. Maiocco's humanities course there is an eighth grade course in comparative anatomy. The eighth grade "Foundations of Western Civilization" course, which is taught by the headmaster, is a "survey of architecture, music and literature of three distinct eras: ancient Greece, Europe during the Renaissance and the United States during WWII. The course includes fundamental Greek and culminates in a trip to Italy before the spring break. Eighth grade boys study Renaissance art and architecture in Rome, Siena and Florence.

Although there is a definite emphasis on the classics, Dr. Maiocco states that "Saint David's has increased its efforts to include in its curriculum the achievements of women and of members of a wide range of ethnic groups . . . what we strive for is contextual understanding." Observance of Martin Luther King Day at Saint David's is not just a holiday but an opportunity for discussion of Dr. King's contributions across many subject areas. For instance, a discussion of the poetry of Langston Hughes might serve as a springboard for discussion of "Dr. King's impact on the moral consciousness of the American people and the world." Similarly, a study of Gandhi's influence on Dr. King's "I Have a Dream" speech is part of an upper school study of the American civil rights movement.

Art is not an elective in the upper school. Seventh and eighth grade boys receive letter grades in art, with the emphasis on attitude and effort, not talent. Some boys objected, some boys thought it would encourage them to take the arts more seriously.

Saint David's is proud of its honors math program for grades seven and eight. Students participate in the annual Math Bowl.

Outdoor education takes place on the week long annual seventh grade Cape Cod trip in October, during which boys are led on explorations by instructors from the Cape Cod Museum of Natural History.

The sixth grade boys visit Frost Valley for two overnights and participate in an "Outward Bound" program.

Extracurricular activities in the upper school include working on the school literary magazine (*The Canticle*) or the yearbook and playing on sports teams. The student council president (grades five through eight) is elected and he then selects his cabinet.

The Saint David's Social Action Committee participates in many community service projects, such as contributions to charity boxes, the Annual Thanksgiving Drive, the May Flea Market and a sixth grade remote-control model car rally fund-raiser. Seventh graders make weekly visits to the Florence Nightingale Nursing Home. The soda machine profits go to a charity.

At the end of their eight-plus years at Saint David's, the school magazine asserts that the boys will have "painted grapes and dissected frogs, studied Greek and conversed with computers." Graduation takes place at the Church of St. Thomas More in a nonreligious ceremony (boys wear ties and jackets). Awards are given in athletics, music, art and academic areas. The ceremony is followed by a reception with hors d'oeuvres and cocktails on the terrace at Saint David's. Afterwards, many families get together for dinner. Saint David's graduates attend a variety of day and boarding schools.

Traditions   Morning chapel talks, class plays, Math Bowl, History Bowl, weekly poetry recitation in lower school, St. David's armbands, Player of the Week, fêtes de l'écoles, all-school Christmas concert, Gala Spring Art Show, clothing and book sales, seventh grade Greek play, Upper School Science Fair, Annual Dinner/Dance and Auction, faculty-father athletic contests, annual alumni soccer match, alumni Christmas party, Eighth grade Art History lectures with Nightingale-Bamford School

Publications   *Saint David's Magazine*
Literary magazine: *The Canticle*
Lower school literary magazine
Yearbook

Community Service Requirement   7th grade nursing home visits are required; class projects; upper school Social Action Committee coordinates community service activities

Hangout   Jackson Hole (hamburger restaurant)

St. Hilda's & St. Hugh's School

619 West 114th Street
New York, NY 10025
Tel (212) 932-1980
website: www.StHildas.org

Coed
Toddlers–8th grade
Accessible

Ms. Virginia Connor, Head of School
Ms. Roxandra Antoniadis, Director of Admissions

Birthday Cutoff   November 15 (N's–1st grade)

Enrollment   Total enrollment: 260
Toddler program places: 20
Nursery places: 20–40
Kindergarten places: 20–40
Graduating class 1998: approximately 15-20

Tuition Range 1998–1999: $3,200 to $14,600, 2's–8th grade
Additional fees: for materials and activities are approximately
$450
An optional hot lunch program is available for $650–$900

After-School Program   St. Hilda's & St. Hugh's After-School Program is open to children from other schools; a variety of creative and recreational activities; 3:00 P.M.–6:30 P.M.; an additional payment is required
Vacation camps in September, December, March, June for an additional charge

Summer Program   Summer camp is open to children from other schools; there is an additional charge; a variety of recreational and creative activities
First session: mid-June–July 4
Second session: July
Third session: end of August–second week of September

St. Hilda's & St. Hugh's is a coed Episcopal day school founded in 1950 by the Reverend Mother Ruth of the Community of the Holy Spirit, an Episcopal religious order for women. The Community of the Holy Spirit maintains its affiliation with the school through representation on the board of trustees. The curriculum at St. Hilda's & St. Hugh's is traditional and integrated. There is a uniform requirement in grades one through eight, and teachers are addressed formally as "Mr. Smith," "Miss Jones." Although chapel attendance and religious studies are required, the student body is diverse. French is offered from kindergarten on, Latin is offered in seventh and eighth grades. A new theater arts program has been added to the curriculum and also to the after-school and summer camp programs.

St. Hilda's & St. Hugh's Schools graduates attend a variety of secondary schools including the New York City specialized high schools (Stuyvesant and Bronx Science), independent day and boarding schools and Catholic high schools (Loyola and Fordham Prep).

St. Luke's School

487 Hudson Street
New York, NY 10014
(212) 924-5960
website: Admin@StLukeSchool.org

Coed
Junior kindergarten–8th grade
Not accessible

Ms. Ann Mellow, Head
Ms. Susan Parker, Director of Admissions

Birthday Cutoff   Children entering junior kindergarten must be 4 by October 1
Children entering kindergarten must be 5 by October 1

Enrollment   Total enrollment: 190
Junior kindergarten places: 18
Kindergarten places: between 5 and 10
Graduating class 1998: 20
5 Prep for Prep students enrolled as of Fall 1998

Grades   The lower school is on a semester system (grades junior kindergarten–4)
The upper school is on a trimester system (grades 5–8)
Letter grades begin in 5th grade
Departmentalization begins in 5th grade

Tuition Range 1998–1999 $13,590 to $14,260, junior kindergarten–8th grade
Additional fees: $460 (junior kindergarten), $645 (5th and 6th), $660 (7th and 8th)

Financial Aid/Scholarship   21% of the student body receive some form of aid

Endowment $275,000

After-School Program   St. Luke's After-School Program: Monday–

Friday, from dismissal time until 5:45 P.M.; a variety of creative and recreational activities; an additional fee is required

Summer Program St. Luke's Summer Programs: the last two weeks of June; Junior Camp for grades K–3rd, Sports Camp for grades 3rd–8th; a variety of age appropriate recreational and creative activities are offered for an additional payment

———

St. Luke's School was founded in 1945 and retains its affiliation with the Episcopal Church. The program is ecumenical but there is mandatory chapel from one to three times a week at the Church of St. Luke's in the Fields, a landmark building dating from 1822, rebuilt in 1985, and 15 percent of students take communion. ERBs are required for admission to junior kindergarten and kindergarten. Most classrooms in this West Village school face the tree-lined courtyard, affording good light and little street noise. The classrooms are spacious and bright. The school has a new library, media center, gymnasium, art studio, small theater, music, computer and foreign language rooms, a science lab, and a large dining room. There are three outdoor play areas, and students use the Carmine Street field for varsity sports. St. Luke's has no formal dress code—the only requirement is that students be clean and neat. Hot lunch is not provided; students bring their own.

The curriculum is highly structured but a variety of educational approaches are used. Interdisciplinary teaching is strong. St. Luke's is divided into two divisions: junior kindergarten through fourth grade; fifth through eighth grades. Students select either French or Spanish in sixth grade. There is a very active Parents Association. In 1998, St. Luke's admitted five students from Prep for Prep.

Popular High School Choices The Nightingale-Bamford School, Packer Collegiate Institute, Polytechnic Preparatory School, Riverdale Country School, Collegiate, Trinity School, the Brearley School, the Spence School, the Dalton School, and Friends Seminary.

The Solomon Schechter School of Manhattan

at Park Avenue Synagogue
50 East 87th Street
New York, N.Y. 10128
(212) 427-9500

Coed
Kindergarten–8th grade
Wheelchair accessible

Dr. Steven C. Lorch, Head of School
Sondra Weiss, Early Childhood Director, Admissions Contact

Uniform Boys: navy or gray slacks, blue shirt, navy sweater with crest
Girls: navy jumper or skirt or slacks, white blouse, navy sweater with crest

Birthday Cutoff No strict cutoff; developmental readiness is the main consideration

Enrollment (K–2): 65
Kindergarten places 36

Grades Detailed anecdotal reports

Tuition Range 1998–1999 Kindergarten–2nd grade: $500–$15,400 (Tuition is based upon a sliding scale depending on parents' ability to pay)

Endowment N/A

Diversity 9% students of color

After-School Program Available subject to interest

Summer Program None

The Solomon Schechter School of Manhattan opened its doors in 1996 with a kindergarten and will continue to grow, adding a new grade each year, through eighth grade. The school currently uses the religious school classrooms at the Park Avenue Synagogue at 87th and Madison. The Solomon Schechter School is one of a network of over 70 Solomon Schechter schools throughout the United States and Canada, the first of which was established in 1951.

The Solomon Schechter School of Manhattan was conceived in 1994 as an initiative of the United Synagogue of Conservative Judaism and the rabbis of the nine Conservative synagogues in Manhattan. During its formative period, a group of dedicated parents and community leaders came together to develop the school's mission and character. Elie Wiesel serves as Honorary Chairman of the Board of Trustees, Dr. Samuel Klagsbrun as Chairman of the Education Committee. The aim was to "establish a Jewish day school . . . where students will be given a rich understanding of their Jewish heritage, a fluent command of the Hebrew language, and a passion for Jewish learning. The goal is to nurture culturally aware, compassionate, and socially responsible individuals who will constitute the future leadership of the American Jewish Community."

Getting in: Parents are welcome to visit the school and meet with admissions staff members prior to applying. In addition, an open house is held in the fall at which time prospective parents can meet with the faculty and with parents of children already enrolled in the school. After an application has been filed, the child visits the school for an individual interview and testing: the Gesell developmental assessment is administered by the school. The results of ERB or any other standardized testing should also be forwarded to The Solomon Schechter School. Finally, the parents come in to meet with the Head of School, Dr. Lorch. To fulfill the family education requirement parents in the school must participate in a series of classes in Jewish life and texts but they are not required to know Hebrew.

Parents: One parent described the social mix as "An eclectic group who are down-to-earth and 'heimish,'" diverse geographically and religiously (although all the children are Jewish). Parents help out in the office, go on field trips and volunteer in the classroom. The PA sponsors brunches, and an annual kosher food tasting evening and Education Night. All parents are members of the PA and invited to attend meetings.

Program: Head of School Dr. Steven Lorch, who has degrees from Harvard and Columbia, has previously been the head of three other Jewish schools in North America, Australia and in Israel. According to Dr. Lorch, there are two language objectives for the Kindergarten year: 1) that every child will read and write in English by the end of the year; and 2) every child will become proficient in Hebrew. "To achieve these objectives the classroom has to truly be an enriched bilingual environment."

The classroom teachers are bilingual (English/Hebrew) and work with the Early Childhood Director to design the curriculum. The classroom emphasizes experiential or active learning. There are early childhood materials, including blocks, as well as computers in the classroom. The classes often break into smaller groups for math activities, block building, computers, and so on.

A main feature of the program in the early years is an interdisciplinary (or thematic) approach to learning. Topics of study are chosen on the basis of the interests of the children in the class and each topic is then investigated from a variety of perspectives: social studies, Jewish tradition, the arts, science, literature, mathematics, writing: all contribute to a rich and textured understanding of the topic at hand.

Reading is taught by combining elements of both Whole Language and phonics. Children use manipulative materials when learning math and sciences. Children are instructed by specialists in music and physical education twice a week. There is daily physical exercise, either on the outdoor playroof or in nearby Central Park.

Children are introduced to Jewish life through the Jewish Studies curriculum and Hebrew is taught using the natural method of language study. Religion plays a central role in the life of the school. Prayer, activities related to holidays, the observance of dietary laws and acts of kindness (charity) are stressed. Girls are offered full egalitarian privileges and participation.

Traditions: Monday and Thursday prayer in the Chapel (parents are welcome), Friday field trips, *Kabbalat Shabbat*, Family Holiday Programs for Sukkot, Chanukah, Purim, Pesach, and Yom Ha'atzmaut, First Grade Siddur ceremony on TuBish'vat, Grandparents and Special Friends Day "exhibitions," Class-wide celebrations at the end of a unit of study.

Publications: Weekly newsletter: *Daf Kesher*
Yearbook

The Spence School

22 East 91st Street
New York, NY 10128-0657
(212) 289-5940, FAX (212) 534-0118

All girls
Kindergarten–12th grade
Accessible

Ms. Arlene J. Gibson, Head of School
Mrs. Penual (Penny) Allan, Director of Admissions

Uniform   Grades kindergarten–5: plaid jumper and white shirt, solid-color stockings, tights, socks
Grades 6–8: navy blue skirt, blue cord skirt, navy blue pants in winter, and white shirt
Grades 9–12: gray skirt or gray slacks, any shirt with sleeves; no leg warmers, leggings or long underwear, low-heeled shoes only
Uniform is not required on Fridays
After fall trimester, seniors may petition to cease wearing their uniforms
Before the start of school uniform fittings are held at Spence
Gym outfits are given to the girls free of charge

Birthday Cutoff   Girls entering kindergarten must be 5 by October 15

Enrollment   Total enrollment: 590
Kindergarten places: approximately 40
9th grade places: 10–15
Graduating class 1997: 43

Grades   Semester system in lower school
Trimester system in middle/upper schools
Grades kindergarten–5: checklist (skill acquired, developing skill, needs support, marked improvement)
Grades 6–8: letter grades begin in 7th grade, detailed anecdotal reports plus a checklist
Grades 9–12: letter grades and detailed checklist

Departmentalization begins in 6th grade
First final exam in 6th grade

Tuition Range 1998–1999 $16,190 to $17,510, kindergarten–12th grade
Additional fees: for lunch, books, supplies, Parents Association dues and miscellaneous supplies approximately $1,100–$1,400

Financial Aid/Scholarship   Approximately 17% of the entire student body receive some form of tuition assistance, 32% in the upper school
Financial aid accounts for 9.5% of the operating budget

Endowment $31.6 million (as of June 1997)

Diversity   17% students of color; 26% in the upper school
18 Prep for Prep students enrolled as of fall 1998
Cultural Awareness Club
The Afro-Latino Alliance
Jewish Culture Club
Asia Society

Homework   Kindergarten: none
1st and 2nd: approximately 10–20 minutes
3rd and 4th: 30–45 minutes
5th: 1 hour–1$^{1}/_{2}$ hours, plus reading assignments
6th: 20–30 minutes per subject per night plus reading assignments
7th–8th: approximately 2$^{1}/_{2}$–3 hrs
9th–12th: approximately 3–4 hrs

After-School Program   Second Act After-School Program: coed, open to students from other schools; a variety of creative and recreational activities for an additional charge; Monday–Thursday from 3:00–6:00 P.M., Friday from 2:00 to 4:00 P.M.
Middle school: interscholastic sports program
Upper school: varsity teams
Some club meetings and choir, drama and dance rehearsals for grades 6–12 are held after school; choruses rehearse during school periods except for select choir and glee club

Summer Program   Second Act June Program: a two-week program
in June with a different theme each year; open to students from
other schools; there is an additional charge
Jumpstart: a two-week voluntary program for new students grades
9–12

The Spence School, founded in 1892 as Miss Spence's School for
Girls, is housed in an elegant red brick building on East 91st Street
and offers a well-rounded, rigorous academic program, strong in performing arts, the sciences, visual arts and foreign language studies.
Spence artfully combines the traditional and innovative; it was one of
the first independent schools to use the computer in the lower grades,
and multicultural perspectives add excitement and relevance to the
traditional core of studies.

"Relevance" is a key concept at Spence. Spence's mission, "to
inspire students to meet the ethical and intellectual challenges of life,"
is summed up in the school motto: "Non Scholae Sed Vitae Discimus:
Not For School But For Life We Learn." Spence is committed to a
diverse, academically talented student body. One parent said, "It's
very fast paced; you need to have a child who can handle that."

In 1998, Head of School Mrs. Edes Gilbert retired; she was the
last of a generation of Grand Dames who governed the prestigious
Manhattan girls' school over the past twenty years. Arlene Joy Gibson
was selected to lead Spence into the twenty-first century. Educated at
Bryn Mawr College, Ms. Gibson's area of study is Latin America; she
was a Fulbright Scholar in Political Science at the University of the
Republic, Montevideo, Uruguay. An advocate of single sex education,
Gibson was formerly headmistress of a girls' school in Summit, New
Jersey, and she was founding President of the National Coalition of
Girls' Schools. "What attracted me to Spence," Gibson told us, "was
the relationship between the students and the faculty. The atmosphere, which I observed in the classrooms, was positively electric.
Students were asking such intelligent and insightful questions that they
stretched the thinking of the entire class, while teachers challenged
students to probe ever deeper into the material. Everywhere, there
was the excitement that comes from learning. Even in the youngest
grades of the school, Spence truly forms a community of scholars."

Getting in: Spence is one of the few very selective schools where
parents can have an individual tour and interview before they even

apply. However, in recent years, because of over-enrollment in the lower school, transferring in after kindergarten has been very difficult. Admissions personnel told us, "No letters of recommendation and no photos please." What are they looking for? "We are offering a place to a girl who will take full advantage of everything a Spence education has to offer." One parent was very impressed by the upper school student who led her tour: "She was so open, obviously not scripted, and she answered all our questions, which indicated to me that Spence is proud of what it does, and the girls are not afraid to talk about it." Parents are given a card with the name of the young woman who led their tour so that they can contact her through the admissions office if they have any additional questions. Once the application is made, parents applying for kindergarten are given an appointment for their daughter's interview. In the lower school, this takes place with a small group of other girls at the school. In the upper and middle schools, the appointment is individual. Spence has a wait list.

One mother told us that there is no typical Spence girl: "What distinguishes Spence from the other girls' schools is that there is no norm here. The girls are individuals and all are enthusiastic about learning."

Parents: A parent described the parent body at Spence as dominated by two groups: "Those with well-worn, polished shoes (old money), and those with brand-new $450 Ferragamos (new money)." There is a growing contingent of media types. Another parent described the parent body as "some families who don't live on their salaries—attorneys, investment bankers, independent entrepreneurs." But the Upper School is more diverse. Many prominent Jewish families feel comfortable at Spence; we were told that "Ascension through the ranks of Spence's Parent Association requires a certain amount of social skill and savvy." The 1998 PA benefit was a casual evening of dinner, dancing, silent auction and raffle with a Western theme at the Puck Building. The class cocktail parties or suppers are now held at Spence. The Spring Event for new parents is a reception in the dining room at which fifth grade girls serve as hostesses.

Program: The lower school curriculum is integrated where possible; drama and art are often incorporated. The girls spend lots of time in the big block area in the kindergarten classroom, and each room has a pet rabbit or fish or guinea pig. Each kindergarten class has two teachers, and the class frequently breaks into small groups. Reading readiness begins in kindergarten. An eclectic method is used to teach reading, including Whole Language and phonics. There is a resource center for students who need support. A parent said, "They reinforce learning through writing, speaking, observation, drawing." Classes write and illustrate their own books.

Geography is taught as part of the multicultural curriculum in kindergarten and first grade. Students learn about boundaries and borders, and they explore their own and others' ethnic groups. Kindergartners do a units on various countries for which they make passports and cameras, and as the teacher reads from a book about a country, a student says "click" and later draws a picture of the mental image she had "taken." The girls bring in items from other countries and create their own museum in a corner of the room.

In kindergarten parents are invited to spend a morning with their daughters sometime during the year to share a special talent or interest with the class. They also come in for Parents' Visiting Day. In one kindergarten class a parent came to talk about his trip to China. If parents have any questions, teachers are always available.

Computer classes are part of the curriculum in all division of the school. Alumni from the late seventies remember an emphasis on computer even then. In grades kindergarten through fifth, LOGO, a computer graphics language, is taught. Keyboarding and word processing are taught in fourth. The lower school has its own computer lab with Macintosh computers. There is a fully equipped lower school science lab and two science teachers whose sole responsibility is to work with kindergartners through fifth graders. One computer science course is required in the upper school and several advanced courses are offered, including "AP Computer Science."

In addition to academic subjects, first graders take courses in art, music, computer and physical education. Art, dance and drama teachers are working professionals. In the spacious art room we saw highly individualized stick puppets and masks. Throughout the social studies curriculum, the brochure states, there is a "special emphasis on the role of women in history and focus on the rich diversity of cultures," and social studies is coordinated with language arts, music and art. For example, a parent told us about a unit on East Africa during which the girls "built African huts, lived in them, did homework in them." Second graders read biographies and write book reports about "someone who made a difference." Eleanor Roosevelt, Florence Nightingale and Ann Sullivan are particularly popular because the unit includes coming to school in period costumes.

Second graders are also introduced to chess with each devoting a semester to learning the intricacies of the game. The Spence Second Act Chess Team was the first all-girls chess team to compete in the NYC Scholastic Chess Championship.

One year, for an integrated second grade unit on baseball, a parent told us, "For English they read the biography of Jackie Robinson, for art they studied baseball murals and created their own, in history they examined integration and baseball and in gym, they learned the essence of the game—they played it!"

Third graders participate in an immigrant project; they study a person or family from another country. They also study the history of New York and take many field trips to places such as Philipsburg Manor, Ellis Island, The Museum of the City of New York and the Natural History Museum.

"Simulations" enrich the fourth and fifth grade social studies curriculum. Art is incorporated into these simulations as well as research and writing skills. At the end of the fourth grade geography unit (during which students study longitude, latitude and map reading), students break into teams for a transcontinental race—their assignment is to "navigate" across a mythical continent. They write creative, detailed diary entries along the way. As part of the fifth grade United States history unit, students imagine that they are colonists trying to survive in the New World. In the spring they take a "simulated" covered-wagon trip across the Western United States and construct detailed models of their wagon train.

Foreign language begins in third grade, with a choice between French and Spanish. One parent said games and songs are used to teach language in the early years. An optional second language can be elected in seventh grade. Japanese is offered in the middle and upper schools.

Health education starts early and covers a variety of topics from nutrition to body image and anatomy to peer and family relationships. A nonintimidating puppet show educates the girls about sexual abuse. One parent said it was very appropriately done. Spence also uses the anti-drug program Project Charlie. More important, parents say that self-confidence, self-esteem and leadership are constantly reinforced in the girls: "They are always supporting the girls in their choices and decisions," "The girls are self-confident from beginning to end."

Drama, dance and music are part of the curriculum in each grade. The head of the lower school told us, "Everyone should see herself as a dancer, researcher, geographer; there is always a place for each student to excel." Kindergarteners perform at the Holiday Pageant in December. Fourth graders perform a ballet. Lower school chorus begins in third grade. The sixth grade chorus, a middle school chorus and Glee Club are open to all. The Select Choir (which travels abroad) and three chamber ensembles in the upper school are open by audition. There is an instrumental music program for grades one through twelve, and private lessons at Spence are in great demand.

The dance program is extensive: folk, tap, ballet, in addition to physical education classes. One second grade mother said of her daughter's dance performance: "They were in unison doing these routines; we were all stunned." The middle and upper school dance company performs at Symphony Space each year.

All girls gain experience with public speaking. One parent said her daughter, who is normally reluctant to perform on stage, got up in front of the lower school to read her own poem: "She never would have had the confidence if she hadn't been at Spence." The other girls were supportive. "There was no competitiveness. All the girls' poems were great."

To mark the transition from lower school, middle schoolers (sixth through eighth grades) have their own floor at Spence, and their own uniform. The head of the middle school told us "there is a real esprit de corps in middle school; it has its own identity." Middle schoolers have their own student council. The sixth grade is fully departmentalized and in the seventh grade letter grades begin.

Art continues to be integrated into the curriculum. One sixth grade class did a unit on Egypt. The girls learned the names of the gods and kings and all their attributes and contributions and learned about Egyptian culture and religion. In math they studied the geometry of the pyramids. In art they made their own hieroglyphics. The Egyptian unit culminated in a visit to the Metropolitan Museum of Art.

Eighth graders read *Jane Eyre*, *Romeo and Juliet* and a selection of poetry and American short stories. In history both Western and non-Western cultures are explored, and students hone their research methods. Seventh graders study the Middle Ages and the history of Africa and Islam.

The middle school fields teams in basketball, softball, soccer, volleyball, track and field and swimming. These teams participate in interscholastic competition.

Middle schoolers participate in community service projects through the Community Service Club for grades six through twelve and volunteer in the lower school. Middle schoolers perform in the annual eighth grade play with boys from neighborhood schools. Annual dances for seventh and eighth graders provide other opportunities to socialize with the opposite sex.

Contact among grades is important to Spence girls. Middle and upper school students attend Wednesday morning assemblies together along with Tuesday full period assemblies. The middle school has its own assembly on Tuesday mornings, the upper school on Mondays. Mixing of grades occurs in the lunchroom: Upper school students eat all together according to their schedule, not by grade. The head of school and teachers eat with the girls. In middle school, during Secret Sisters Week, middle school girls from different grades are assigned to give small gifts to each other. Field Day offers students on mixed teams a chance to work together with girls from other grades.

If you go straight through Spence from kindergarten to twelfth you are known as a "survivor." Attrition occurs after eighth grade when some girls go to boarding schools or, occasionally, to a coed day school. According to a survivor, "The work builds up in eighth and ninth grades and then increases again in tenth and eleventh, but if you're good at budgeting your time you don't notice. However, if you get two D's or an F you're on academic probation."

The upper school at Spence consists of grades nine through twelve. The upper school is academically rigorous. Students who enter at ninth grade can ease their transition by attending the summer Jumpstart Program, an orientation program that is free of charge. Girls with a problem subject can attend special review sessions or go to the Resource Center. "If necessary," says a student, "teachers will even look over your notes with you." The school will also supply a tutor's name if needed. Classes are kept small, about twelve to fifteen students. The average course load is five to six full credit courses. In addition to the usual core subjects, computer science, performing arts, speech and health are upper school requirements, as are four years of foreign language or three of one language and two of another. Eight APs are offered, including foreign language, studio art, calculus, biology and physics. Students are required to take two years of lab science; most choose to take another advanced-level science course. In 1993–1994 the science labs were completely updated. Each of the science labs now has a computer with CD-ROM.

Students say that a friendly teacher-student relationship at Spence makes their school unique. One reason for this is that teachers in the middle and upper schools must teach a range of grades and as a result get to know the girls as they mature. Teachers also act as advisors to their students both as homeroom teachers and as faculty advisors to student-led clubs.

According to the brochure, in English a "special emphasis is placed on a cross-cultural study of literature so that students are exposed to a range of material outside the Western tradition that enriches their understanding of other cultures." An elective course in world literature is required. Senior Seminar and/or independent study are also available.

Clara Spence, visionary educator and founder of The Spence School, believed in a broad curriculum to meet the interests of the students. Today, many courses at Spence are developed based upon student interest or faculty initiative. For example, "Text and Image," a course that combines art and computer science for graphics and desktop publishing, was designed by two faculty members. Reflecting increased student interest in the Middle East, Asia and Africa, the history elective program in the upper school is largely non-Western. There is a course on the origin of the conflict in Southern Africa. In a thoughtful interdisciplinary course called "African-American Literature, students are introduced to the writings of the men and women who shaped contemporary black American culture: DuBois, Hurston, King, Baldwin, Malcolm X and others.

Students with proficiency in the arts can take advanced course work in studio art, photography and the performing arts.

Spence has wonderful opportunities for foreign language study abroad including "Adventures in Real Communication," open to tenth through twelfth graders, who can take a one- or two-month program in France, Spain or Latin America. There is the School Year Abroad option for eleventh and twelfth graders, the Swiss Semester in Zermatt for tenth graders, the San Patricio Exchange in Madrid for tenth or eleventh graders and for ninth graders, a one- or two-month spring program in Evreux, France. For those who prefer an experience closer to home, participation in the Maine Coast Semester in Chewonki, Maine, or study at the Mountain School in Vermont in association with Milton Academy is offered.

An eleventh grader told us that after school most girls either do homework, participate in school clubs or go out with their boyfriends, who pick them up at school. "Athletics are popular, chorus is fabulous and so is the choral master. Attendance at dance concerts and Glee Club events is good," she said.

Ninth graders have privileges; they can leave school if they have parental permission. Eleventh and twelfth graders can simply sign out. Ninth and tenth graders share "the Pit," a lounge area contiguous with the ninth and tenth grade lockers. Juniors and seniors each have their own lounge (visitors are not given a tour through it). Senior privileges include not wearing their uniform in spring of senior year, coming in late Thursdays and Fridays (if they don't have a class) and being allowed to use the elevators. "You'd think they'd never used an elevator before. They stop at every floor," says one parent.

There is an upper school student council. One student council event is Color or Theme Days: Themes are picked such as Western Day or Come As You Are Day and the faculty dress up too. Weightier issues recently tackled by the upper school student council include: 1) Issues relating to the challenges of living in a diverse community, both inside and outside of school, 2) environmental concerns (SEAC is an environmental concerns group at Spence) and 3) eating disorders, an issue common to all schools, coed and single sex. Spence takes a preventative approach to this problem. A senior says, "Spence has been phenomenal about helping girls with problems."

There are numerous opportunities for faculty-led and student-led extracurricular participation at Spence. Faculty-led activities include dramatic productions, dance company, athletic teams and chorus, while student-led activities include drama club, Amnesty International, French club and Spanish club. Because of the size and unique nature of its community, many students have the opportunity to assume a leadership position in a club or activity by the time they graduate.

Commencement is held at the Church of the Heavenly Rest. Awards are given out at the Athletic Awards Banquet for athletic achievement and sportsmanship. The White Blazer Award is given to a student who is well respected in the athletic community, demonstrating determination, sportsmanship, cooperation, dedication and leadership. At Final Assembly external academic awards, such as National Merit Scholarships, are announced, but graduates no longer have the traditional Spence prizes for special academic achievements bestowed upon them. It is thought this will discourage excessive competition, according to the school. And one junior told us, "They didn't acknowledge the good work that everybody did."

When asked what school event embodies the spirit of Spence, Head of School Edes Gilbert replied: "Opening Assembly and Alumnae Day. Each year at Opening Assembly the entire school welcomes the incoming kindergarten students and everyone cheers for them, and the seniors see how far they have come. At Alumnae Day in the spring, the seniors are inducted into the ranks of Spence alumnae . . . there is a great continuity of strong women here."

Popular College Choices   Harvard, Columbia, Georgetown, University of Pennsylvania, Princeton, Yale, Dartmouth, Cornell, Brown, Kenyon, Middlebury, Vassar, Wellesley

Traditions   Opening Assembly, Lower School Halloween party, Lower School New Parents' Dinner, Lower School Field Day, grade five sleepover and breakfast, spring drama, eighth grade play, eighth grade trip, skating party, Middle School Sing-Off Competition, middle school picnic, Saturday movies (winter), lower school holiday program, Father/Daughter Evening, Mother/Daughter Tea, third and fourth grade foreign language breakfasts, Grandparents' and Special Friends Day, Secret Sisters Week, Dance Concert at Symphony Space, Middle and Upper School Concert at Church of St. Thomas More, Book Fair, clothing sale, Choral group, Spence Boutique, student council 91st Street Fair, grade ten Interschool trip to Frost Valley.

Publications   Newspaper: *Spence Voice*
Literary arts magazine
Yearbook: *Threshold*
Newsletter on current political issues: *Spark*

Community Service Requirement   No specific number of hours: in grades 6–12 the board of the Community Service Club is made up of two elected representatives from each of the grades, along with an elected student head; weekly meetings are held to plan a variety of fund-raising and volunteer activities such as tutoring projects in local public schools, food and clothing drives, visits to the elderly or homebound, work in soup kitchens or daycare organizations. The service club plans an annual Community Service Day

Hangouts   Jackson Hole (hamburger restaurant around the corner on Madison), junior lounge, senior lounge

The Studio Elementary School
124A West 95th Street
New York, NY 10025
(212) 678-2416

Coed
Nursery (22 mos)–6th grade
Not accessible

Ms. Janet C. Rotter, Head of School, Director of Admissions

Birthday Cutoff   none

Enrollment   Total enrollment: approximately 90
   Nursery places (2's and nearly 2's): 10
   3's and nearly 3's places: approximately 10
   Early childhood: 16
   Kindergarten and up: 5 to 6 places in K, as available in upper grades

Tuition Range 1998–1999
   All day program, 5 days a week (8 A.M.–6 P.M.) 9/1–7/31: $14,025
   2's and nearly 2's: 2 mornings $3,160
   3's and nearly 3's: 3 mornings $5,240
   Early childhood: 5 mornings $7,650, 5 full days: $11,025
   K–6th grade: 5 days $11,025
   All fees are included

Financial Aid/Scholarship   10% of the student body receives some form of aid
   Approximately $75,000 budgeted annually
   A work exchange program is available for parents

Endowment   None

After-School Program   Extended day program until 6:00 P.M.; a variety of creative and recreational activities for an additional payment

Summer Program   Summer Camp from mid-June through the end of July; a variety of creative and recreational activities for an additional payment

The Studio Elementary School was founded in 1971 by Robert and Dolores Welber as a "one room schoolhouse" in Greenwich Village. Three years later Janet Rotter, a graduate of Bank Street, came to Studio as an assistant teacher. She is currently Head of the School, as she has been for the past fourteen years. The Welbers retain their affiliation as members of the board of trustees. In addition, Mr. Welber continues to teach Music and Movement classes.

In 1977 the school moved to a building on the Upper West Side which is leased from the adjoining synagogue. (The school has no religious affiliation.) In addition to several bright classrooms, the school has a well-equipped kitchen, a library, and a large common room which also serves as the cafeteria and a toddler gym. The Studio Elementary School has always emphasized a sound traditional curriculum combined with a developmental approach paying attention to each child's social and emotional growth. The school has a neighborhood feeling and parent involvement is welcome.

Getting in: Parents can attend an open house/tour before applying. Applicants meet with the head of the school and children over age 5 visit a classroom. ERB testing is requested for applicants age 8 and above.

Program: One of the founding principles of the Studio Elementary School is that children of all ages can learn from each other; the school still uses cross-age and cross-grade grouping. There is a teacher and an assistant in each classroom through first grade. Class groupings are reshuffled each year.

"The school's emphasis is on learning how to think and create and not just fulfill requirements," says Ms. Rotter. "Students learn that there is not just one way to get to the solution of a problem. Thinking, and the interaction between student and teacher, is the point." The school provides a lot of unstructured materials so children are free to experiment. Children can work independently within a group setting, focusing on the concepts and skills that will help them move on to the next level of development.

Attention is paid to the emotional life of the students. A parent told us, "The teacher is very aware of my child's attitude towards her work. They work with her on the development of self-discipline, organization and self-evaluation in addition to teaching the curriculum."

A unique aspect of the Studio school curriculum is the Kitchen Science class. Each day a hot lunch is prepared by a team of students (ages three and up) and served to the entire school. Cooking combines skill work in math (measuring), reading and writing (recipes and menus), science (mixing different things together) and social studies (a group studying colonial America will prepare a lunch representative of that period).

The block room is used by all groups through the six and seven-year-olds. After "walking and exploring" the neighborhood, younger children will recreate what they saw in blocks. For physical education, younger children go to the play yard every day, older children (five and up) go to Central Park.

Reading is taught using eclectic methods including Whole Language, sight words, basal readers, and phonics. Children are also read to every day. We noticed a cozy carpeted platform with cushions for independent reading in the hallway between nursery classrooms. In math students might have a group lesson then work independently on problem solving and skills.

Homework begins at age six (an assignment time is built into the school day) when they begin to introduce the requirements of the outside world. Parent/teacher conferences are held three times a year. Grading begins in the middle elementary classes.

Graduates attend various Independent schools including: Saint Ann's School, Ethical Culture/Fieldston, Friends, Trevor Day and Trinity, as well as various public school programs (including the Computer Schools and the Delta Honors Program at P.S. 54).

The Town School

540 East 76th Street
New York, NY 10021
(212) 288-4383
website: www.townschool.org

Coed
Nursery–8th grade
Accessible

Ms. Joyce Gregory Evans, Head of School
Ms. Natasha Sahadi, Director of Admissions

Uniform   None for nursery and kindergarten divisions
Lower and upper school girls: plaid kilt or navy jumper or navy and tan skirt; solid-colored collared or turtleneck shirt; girls may wear solid navy, gray or tan pants except on Fridays; sweaters, socks, leggings and tights may be worn in the colors of the plaid
Lower and upper school boys: solid navy, gray or tan pants; solid-colored, collared or turtleneck shirt in the colors of the plaid
Friday is dress-up day for assembly: Girls wear skirts, boys wear navy jacket, white or blue shirt and tie
The first Tuesday of each month is a nonuniform day: Denim and sweat clothes may be worn

Birthday Cutoff   Children entering nursery school must be 3 by September 1
Children entering kindergarten must be 5 by September 1

Enrollment   Total enrollment: 375
Nursery places: approximately 18
Kindergarten places: approximately 26
8th grade graduating class: approximately 36

Grades   Trimester system
Letter and effort grades are given in the upper school beginning with the second trimester of 5th grade
Departmentalization is begun in 5th grade

Tuition Range 1998–1999 $10,200 to $17,675, nursery–8th
Additional fees and Parents Association dues, approximately $1,100

A tuition refund plan, extended payment plan and accident plan are available

Financial Aid/Scholarship Approximately 14% of the student body receive some form of financial aid

Endowment $15 million (A portion of the funds from the sale of The Town School's air rights to the Glick Corporation went toward the endowment fund)

Diversity 8 Prep for Prep students enrolled as of Fall 1998
Multicultural Curriculum Guide developed by Town School faculty
Multicultural Families Committee: a school-sponsored committee comprising parents, teachers and administrators, for the purpose of sharing multicultural interests, concerns and suggestions; monthly meetings are posted on school calendar; the committee keeps the Parents' Association informed of all its activities

Homework Because of the long school day, homework in the early years is kept to a minimum:
Kindergarten–1st: occasionally
2nd: beginning in the second half of the year, about 15 minutes
3rd and 4th: 45 minutes–1 hour
4th, 5th and 6th: 1 hour–1½ hours
7th 8th: 2–3 hours

After-School Program The Town School After-School Programs are Postscript and Clubhouse
Junior Postscript Program: for pre-K and kindergarten students, Monday through Thursday, 2:45–4:00 P.M., Friday, 12:15–1:30 P.M., with extended day option until 6:00 P.M.: a variety of creative and recreational activities; an additional payment is required
Postscript Program: for grades 1–7, Monday through Thursday 3:45–5:00 P.M., Friday, 1:00–2:30 P.M., with extended day option until 6:00 P.M.; activities include: Rollerblading, computer, photography, swimming, woodworking, gymnastics, arts and crafts, CATS tennis, theatre; an additional payment is required
Clubhouse Program: a multi-aged option with rotating choices daily, beginning at 12:00

Intramural sports program
Interscholastic athletic competition for grades 5–8

Summer Program   Summersault program for ages 3–9, open to children from the community, an additional payment is required

---

The Town School is a coed elementary school that ends with eighth grade. It overlooks the East River on quiet East 76th Street, opposite John Jay Park. Although The Town School has had numerous heads over the years, parents say the school's essential identity and philosophy have remained consistent. The Town School emphasizes warmth and is sensitive to the developmental needs of young children. A traditional core of academic skills is taught using an innovative curriculum. The 1936 school brochure description of Town was accurate then and now: "Progressive but not radical . . . its object is to create an environment in which the child may develop the best that is in him and give him a thorough understanding of every subject he studies." Expectations are high but this is not a pressure-cooker environment. Because of the focus on the elementary grades, parents say there is an intimacy that provides an opportunity for leadership and the development of self-confidence. Students leave Town well prepared and well rounded.

Founded in 1913 by Miss Hazel Hyde and originally known as "Miss Hyde's School," The Town School acquired its present name in 1936 during the era of the town car and town house. The school motto roughly translates as "Be joyful in the pursuit of knowledge." Former head of school Fred Calder describes the committed faculty and administrators at Town School as "a group of people who [still] believe that the education of young children begins and ends with warmth, humor and good sense." Miss Hyde was known for attracting exceptional faculty who were very involved in running the school. To this day, the teachers at The Town School retain their influence through the "corporation" (once known as "the members"), who advise the head of school.

As of July 1993, Joyce Gregory Evans became the head of school. As head of an elementary school in California, Evans was successful in diversifying the school population, parent education, fund-raising, administration and curriculum development. Evans' view of the challenges in education for the twenty-first century indicate that The

Town School will be staying the course upon which it has already embarked: "Education used to be seen as filling students with a body of knowledge. Now we recognize that the process of learning is at the core. Critical thinking, problem solving, gaining access to information and learning cooperatively are all vital ingredients of a superior education." Parents agree that there has always been an emphasis on the process of learning at Town rather than the rote accumulation of facts. Parents say, "Children learn how to think, and they learn that it's OK to be wrong or to fail."

In 1985 The Town School sold air rights to Glick Development Affiliates for $7 million. Some of this windfall went toward a capital improvement and maintenance fund, some toward the school's sizeable endowment and a portion went into renovation and addition of facilities, including two new science labs for lower and upper school students, a new darkroom and a computer room. Town students have use of their own auditorium, as well as a full-size gym. The school is uncluttered, clean and carpeted (no echoing hallways here). It's easy to see why children are comfortable here.

Getting in: There are no essay questions on the application. Parents may tour the school before they apply for their child. Our tour guide was very knowledgeable and didn't mind answering numerous questions. At a later date, parents bring their kindergarten applicant in for a small group interview while the parents meet with the director of admissions.

Parents: The parent body at Town is relatively low-key. Says one parent, "These aren't all parents who went to private schools themselves." The Parents Association was founded in 1951. There is a monthly newsletter to inform parents about activities and meetings. Curriculum evenings and parent education seminars keep parents apprised of what's going on in the world of education and at Town (a recent panel discussed gender issues in elementary education). Head of School Evans realizes that "parents [today] particularly need to discuss the challenges they face with their children." Activities for Town families include the Welcome Back Picnic in the fall in Central Park, a parent-faculty musical, Science Night, the Book Fair and the Spring Benefit. One mother described the events she attended: "Everyone came, there were nice feelings, nothing was hyped up, just a wonderful, warm environment."

Programs: Kindergartners have a fairly long day, from 8:15 A.M. until 2:30 P.M. Monday through Thursday and until noon on Fridays.

First through eighth graders eat hot lunch at school; pre-kindergartners and kindergartners have to bring their own lunches. There are two kindergarten classrooms, each with two teachers. (All of the nursery and kindergarten division head teachers have a master's in Early Childhood.) In addition to the teachers, there are three language arts specialists and two school psychologists. The kindergarten rooms are situated at opposite ends of a short carpeted hallway where, during activity time, children from each class can play and socialize. Each kindergarten classroom has a block area, wood shop, listening corner, computer, a pet (we saw a hamster) and their own bathroom and kitchen. The children were busily working in small groups, some with clay or wood, some painting.

The Town School has traditionally celebrated the arts, and art is integrated into the curriculum at every level. Grades one through four visit the lower school art studio once a week. We saw bas-relief self-portraits and still lifes in the style of Matisse. There is a kiln for firing clay. Students frequently visit museums, and visiting artists come in to share their art, music, or drama expertise.

The music and dance curriculum begins in nursery when both are taught simultaneously. First and second graders learn the Orff method. Third graders learn to play the recorder. Private instrumental instruction is available both before and after school. Students who love to perform have the opportunity, and can work on costumes, scenery and stage managing as well. Children can perform at assemblies, and there are two full-scale musicals a year. The fourth grade musical typically has more than one lead: There were four Charlies for "Charlie and the Chocolate Factory" one year. There is an upper school chorus and band. A highlight of the year is the annual eight grade musical.

Unique to Town School is the River Community, used in kindergarten, and developed by Town School teachers. It is a curriculum revolving around a year-long study of the East River, The Town School neighborhood and transportation in the community. In science, children learn about water, and they experiment to determine what sinks and what floats. In social studies they discuss transportation on an island, and one kindergarten class built a model of the Triborough Bridge from Popsicle sticks. Field trips can include a walk across the Brooklyn Bridge or a ride on the Roosevelt Island tram. Students also learn to map their environment.

The language arts program is literature based and by first grade students are writing in response journals daily. Invented spelling is used, but spelling skills are taught in second grade. First graders move out of the classroom for science in the lower school science lab, library, gym, dance, music and art.

Students from kindergarten through second grade have computers in their classrooms. By third grade students use hallway stations with three or four MACs or the computer lab (which is equipped with IBM PC's and MACs) where they learn keyboarding skills and word processing. Students learn to use software related to the language arts, math and social studies. By fifth grade students take a trimester of math in the computer lab and use the LOGO Writer program, GEO sketchpad, and other programs.

Fourth graders study their own family unit, write letters to relatives, study their own country (countries) of origin and use this as a basis to learn about other immigrating groups. A book-publishing party is held in the spring. A multicultural curriculum is in place. We were impressed by a project in the first grade that examined the Cinderella myth from the perspective of different cultures, including Chinese and Egyptian. Assemblies often feature multicultural performers. Irish step dancers performed at one assembly and invited the students to come onstage and participate.

In math, using the University of Chicago Math Program, children learn to reason logically, see mathematical patterns and relationships, and understand the presence of math in everyday life. Manipulatives, math games and literature are woven into the curriculum to develop abstract mathematical thinking while reinforcing computational concepts. The lower school science lab features scaled-down versions of the familiar black tables and stools; the curriculum stresses the process of inquiry. For instance, second graders studying the Northeast woodlands create a nature mural; each child researches a forest animal to add to the mural. Fifth graders studying oceanography use *The Voyage of the Mimi*, a computer companion program. There are numerous trips to reinforce laboratory learning: Third and fourth grade students travel to a working farm; fifth graders go to Mystic, Connecticut, and live on a schooner; sixth graders go to Nature's Workshop, an environmental center in northwestern Connecticut. Seventh graders go to Blairstown, New Jersey, for an Outward Bound-type program.

Parents say that The Town School really "honors individual learning styles." Educators recognize that some children function better with lots of background noise and others appreciate a more quiet setting. (Outside the second grade classroom there is an inviting bench with pillows, perfect for quiet reading, and there are other nooks and crannies for small group activities.) Throughout the lower school there is no tracking; collaborative units are used instead. Students might have a group lesson and then divide into smaller groups.

There is also recognition that children learn at different rates. Our tour guide told us: "They journey from first through fourth grades at their own rate, but by fourth grade they are all at the same place." The learning specialists at Town move into the classrooms, avoiding the stigma to certain children of being "pulled out" for remedial help. One parent with three children in the school said her children are having different experiences, "as if it were three different schools."

Students use the full-size gym, one of four playroofs or John Jay Park playground, a wonderful resource right across the street. From kindergarten through fourth grade coed cooperative games and skills are stressed. In fifth grade, intramural competition begins. There is a full-size gym, and upper schoolers have two double periods a week for sports at Randall's Island. They have a very fine basketball program. In the upper school the athletically inclined can participate in a variety of single-sex interscholastic sports. Parents say Town is a great place for girls who are interested in sports.

The upper school at Town is composed of fifth through eighth grades. As in the lower school, desks in the upper grades are grouped for collaborative learning. But fifth grade is an important transition year with new responsibilities and expectations. The fifth grade day is fully departmentalized and fifth graders begin to receive letter grades in the second trimester of the year. French is introduced in fifth grade; Latin instruction begins in seventh grade. Support is provided: A special study skills course is built into the fifth grade curriculum to help students acclimate to the upper school. Fifth through eight graders take a "Lifeskills" program taught by a team including the school nurse that covers AIDS, drugs and alcohol education.

The social studies curriculum in the upper school compares different cultures during the same time period or with the same theme. Fifth grade studies ancient Rome, Greece and China; sixth grade studies Medieval Europe and Japan. Seventh grade focuses on The Age of Discovery and Exploration and Pre-colonial America. The eighth grade studies the colonization of America through the Constitutional Convention.

Readings in English focus on the classics and are often related to the social studies curriculum within a spiral curriculum. Science continues to be experiential. The science lab is networked with the computer lab. Collaborative science projects require tremendous research and culminate in a science fair. Town School graduates place well in advanced science and math in the ongoing schools. Each year a number of students are accepted at Stuyvesant High School (one of the specialized New York City public high schools.)

Students have the opportunity to perform in class plays and in musicals. Fifth graders have an intensive trimester of art, music and dramatic arts. The eighth grade performs in a play as a graduation year culminating activity. Upper school students can work on the literary magazine, yearbook or newspaper. Student photographers help provide photographs for the yearbook.

Town students have the opportunity to assume positions of leadership. The student senate is an elected body with co-presidents, vice president and class representatives. The senate plans assemblies and organizes social events and community service activities. The Town School has a relationship with Yorkville Common Pantry, and food and clothing drives are often organized on its behalf. There is an in-house recycling program. Town also has a sister school, P.S. 92.

Eighth grade is an important and exciting year at The Town School. The eighth grade musical is the culmination of years of musical training and performance. Eighth graders spend a week in Boston. At graduation the William Lee Younger, Jr. Educational Award is given to "the student who flourished at Town [and] developed into an individual of fine character and dedication to excellence."

Discussion about ninth grade placement begins early in the year when recent Town graduates return to talk about their high schools. All eighth graders take a "Decisions" course and learn to recognize and articulate their own particular talents, strengths and interests. They discuss interviewing and essay writing.

A parent who has sent two children to Town (one is now at Trinity, the other attends an Ivy League college) says, "They care for each child as an individual and work with them until the children find something good in themselves. Kids admire kids with different strengths, and they cheer for each other. Although expectations for academic achievement are high, they care equally about the emotional and social development of each child." A parent says, "My child is known and understood as a whole person." Most Town School graduates choose to go on to the coed day schools. (We ran into Town grads at Trinity—the graduation speaker—and at Dalton—the Student Senate President.) A number also go to the specialized public high schools each year. The close-knit feeling at Town persists after graduation. Parents say: "There is a strong feeling of community. Students go back to school to visit their teachers."

Popular Secondary School Choices   Riverdale, Trinity, Columbia Prep, Fieldston, Dalton, Spence, Nightingale and Stuyvesant

Traditions   Fall Welcome Back Picnic, Book Fair, parent-faculty musical, Spring Benefit, parent education seminars, class trips for grades 3–8, 4th grade musical, annual 8th grade musical, alumni reunions

Publications   Alumni News: *Currents*
Annual report
Yearbook
Newspaper
The Town School Family News (monthly)
Literary magazine

Community Service Requirement   Community service begins in the nursery program. Every class has a buddy class in another division; student senate organizes community service projects, often in conjunction with the Yorkville Common Pantry; during winter trimester, 5th–8th graders participate in a community service period once a week, going to a nearby soup kitchen and serving lunch to the homeless and so on; 8th graders also work with third grade students at P.S. 92 every Friday after school.

Hangouts   Bagels & Co., John Jay Park, Little Robin's Pizza Parlor (on Friday afternoons)

Trevor Day School

Lower School
(Pre-K–5th Grade)
11 East 89th Street
New York, NY 10128
(212) 426-3355

Upper School
(6th–12th Grade)
1 West 88th Street
New York, NY 10024
(212) 426-3380 Admissions
web site: www.trevor.org
e-mail: go to website, select the faculty and staff button
and click on the e-mail link

Coed
Pre-nursery (2.9 year olds)–12th grade
Accessible (Both Campuses)

Dr. John H. Dexter, Headmaster
Ms. Deborah Ashe, Co-Director of Admissions, Lower School
Ms. Nancy Newman, Co-Director of Admissions, Lower School
Ms. Marcia Roesch, Director of Admissions, Grades 6–12

Uniform   None

Birthday Cutoff   Children entering kindergarten must be 5 by September 1

Enrollment   Total enrollment: 685
  Nursery places: 25
  Kindergarten places: 35
  Graduating class 1998: approx. 50

Grades   Semester system/trimester system in high school
  Extensive written reports twice a year, plus family conferences
  Letter grades begin in 9th grade
  Full departmentalization by 6th grade
  First final exam in 6th grade

Tuition Range 1998–1999 $8,950 to $19,350, pre-nursery–12th grade
Additional fees: for books (grade six and up) and Parents Association dues, technology fee (K–12), and yearbook: approximately $650

Financial Aid/Scholarship   Approximately 20% of the students receive some form of financial aid (allocation begins in Kindergarten)

Endowment $2.3 million

Diversity   Approximately 17.5 percent students of color
11 Prep for Prep students enrolled as of fall 1998

Homework   Kindergarten–2nd: parent/child reading for 30 minutes
3rd: approximately 45 minutes
4th: $1\frac{1}{2}$ hours
5th and 6th: $1\frac{1}{2}$–2 hours
6th–8th: 2–$2\frac{1}{2}$ hours
9th–12th: $2\frac{1}{2}$–3 hours
(An additional 30 minutes of reading is expected each night for all grades)

After-School Program   Enrollment usually limited to The Trevor Day School students: fees vary from program to program
Encore, Gymnastics Friday, and Friday Soccer: Nursery–grade 5, sports, arts, science, cooking, karate, a variety of clubs including book and chess
Athletics and Activities: Grades 6–12: sports (soccer, volleyball, baseball, girls gymnastics, softball, tennis, track and field) drama, Choreolab, driver's ed; intramural sports begin in grade 4
Athletic Program: grades 6–12, interscholastic team sports competition in various leagues
Music Conservatory: grades K–12, instrumental and voice study with professional artists

Summer Program   All programs require an additional payment
June sports program (ages 4–11)
Summer Day Camp: for 3–5 year olds; 5 weeks, 9 A.M.–3:00 P.M.

Trevor Day School was founded as a nursery school in 1930 under the aegis of the Church of the Heavenly Rest. In 1971, The Day School, having grown into a primary school, became independent of the church. The rector of the church continues to serve ex-officio on the board of trustees but Trevor Day School has no religious affiliation or instruction.

In 1991 Trevor Day School expanded further by purchasing the old Walden-Lincoln school building on West 88th Street and creating a high school division (grades nine through twelve). The school also expanded into a building on East 89th Street, renovated the lower school classrooms and connected the early childhood building to the middle school building by a bridge. Trevor Day School is divided into the Lower School and the Upper School. The Lower School has two divisions: prenursery through kindergarten (early childhood) and grades one through five (elementary school). The Upper School is comprised of the middle school (grades six through eight) and the high school (grades nine through twelve).

According to a spokesperson, the School recently changed its name from "The Day School" to "Trevor Day School" because the former name sounded too "generic." The school took the last name of long-standing board member, Paul Trevor, who had made many significant contributions to the school.

Trevor Day School offers an eclectic blend of the old and the new. There is an elegant marble staircase in the limestone lobby of the East Side building suggesting that this is a staid traditional school, but don't be misled. Trevor Day School has incorporated many innovative features into a curriculum that stresses active learning: common rooms, miniterms, family conferences and a policy of no letter grades until ninth grade. Although these can be considered elements of progressive education, Head of School John "Jack" Dexter says, "We do not categorize ourselves as progressive. We pay attention to a traditional curriculum in a somewhat untraditional educational setting."

Dexter has a definite philosophy about education and the development of young children. A parent told us: "Dexter is warm, articulate, with a great sense of humor. He's relaxed and in tune with the kids; it's hard to talk about Trevor Day School without mentioning him." At the upper school open house Dexter described Trevor Day School as a learning community, "a community that values diversity, in which each person is a natural resource." The school's mission statement emphasizes cooperation and collaboration rather than competition as a motivational device: "Students see the value of working hard and pursuing excellence; they see the usefulness of high achievement all around them."

Getting in: Trevor Day School offers information evenings and tours in the fall that parents may attend before they apply. Do call and ask for these dates. Once they have applied, parents come to the school twice, once for a parent tour and once with their child for a peer group interview time. Children are met in the lobby of the East Campus building and go upstairs to work at a table with age-appropriate materials, followed by a snack and free play. One parent who said that she barely survived the admissions process in general, commented that "Trevor was wonderful at handling the shy, quiet child, both through admissions and in the classroom."

On a separate date parents are taken on a tour of the school and then meet with a member of the admissions staff for about twenty minutes. Parent representatives lead the tour groups and they are very informative as well as candid. Recommendations are optional and there is a wait list.

Parents: Parents describe the parent body at Day as a "mixed but cohesive group of East Siders, West Siders, Jews, WASPs and families of color. But the parents, along with the students, teachers and administrators, all share a strong enthusiasm for the school." All types of parties are given during the year, including a new parents' cocktail party. Parent partners are assigned to new parents. Parents are automatically members of the Parents' Association. Meetings are held three times a year and parents are encouraged to attend. Other opportunities to become involved include the annual auction, the Fall Festival (a very popular event), parent workshops, clothing sale and Book Fair. Parents are also welcome to spend time at school and participate in the classroom.

Program: One division of lower school is pre-nursery through kindergarten. The kindergarten day at Trevor Day School is long, from 8:40 to 3:00 P.M., Monday through Thursday, and until 2:15 on Friday. There are four kindergartens, each with fifteen children, a head teacher and a co-teacher. Parents say that Day School students have the benefit of two teachers all the way through this lower school division. Our guide told us that "the homeroom is an extension of the home." The smallish square classrooms are neat, well-equipped, clean and carpeted and each has its own bathroom and a locker for each child. Classrooms are divided into zones for reading, science, big books, and so on. Foreign languages (French and Spanish) are introduced in pre-kindergarten. Kindergartners go out for library, art, gym and roof time (on the padded playroof), and there are specialists in music and art. Lower schoolers go to a well-equipped art room staffed by a full-time teacher and an assistant. Their expressive and very individual work is displayed on the bulletin boards in the hallways.

Parents say kindergarten at Trevor Day School is "academic" but nurturing and "takes into account the varying rates of development of the children." Along with traditional skills the children gain a sense of security. "The development of self-esteem is important," say parents. "They know each child is cut from a different cloth." The curriculum is structured but not too much so. In kindergarten the classes split into half groups for reading and math (The school uses very small groups for traditional academics). Kindergartners begin working with math manipulatives and math games, using big books, practicing letter sounds, writing in their journals using approximate spelling and learning D'Nealian handwriting.

We observed a group of focused children sitting in chairs in a row learning letter sounds, but parents say, "There is very little recitation or rote learning, it's not learn or else—it's learn at your own pace." Dexter says, "Kids should always be working on things they don't know. We want children to make conclusions rather than just remember the answers."

The other Lower School division consists of grades one through five. Hot lunch is offered starting in grade one. The Day School believes that children should feel free to make mistakes: "We'd rather have a child take chances, do something daring." In order to free children from the constraints of working for grades, there are no letter or number grades until ninth grade. Students in nursery through eighth grade receive narrative reports, sometimes as long as three to four typed pages, and also receive regular feedback from teachers. Family or cooperative conferences are a feature unique to Trevor Day School: The student participates in the parent-teacher conference, reinforcing the idea that the student is considered a participant in his or her education.

There are three homerooms in the first and second grades, but by third grade students are divided into four small homerooms adjacent to a common room. The common room at Trevor Day School is considered the nucleus of the learning community—a place where students can do homework, use the computers, play chess or learn independently with the guidance of faculty. Time-management and a cooperative teacher-student relationship are two themes central to The Day School's philosophy. Homework assignments begin in third grade. Assignments are usually posted by the teacher. Students can complete some of their homework in school during common room time, which is part of their daily schedule.

Parents say there is more social interaction with the entire grade during the early years because groups are mixed, not tracked. A mother told us that second graders are assigned buddies. Her child, who was new to the school, was led comfortably around the building. "He was so happy at Trevor Day School that he wanted to spend weekends there!"

Classroom life in this division is informal but the day is structured. Reading and math groups might be as small as four to eight children. Third grade uses chapter books and word processing as part of the writing experience while the children continue to practice their handwriting in workbooks. All of the classrooms have computers and second, third, and fourth grades have their own computer labs. During math we saw some of the class using Cuisenaire rods, some doing math with numbers on a blackboard and some sitting or lying on the floor working with manipulatives or math games. The students in all three groups were actively engaged.

There is a large science lab for the Lower School. The Investigation Colloquium Method is used, which emphasizes "child-directed exploration and interpretation." First graders study snails; second graders, life cycles; third graders, the solar system, rocks, minerals, plate tectonics. The computer program at The Day School begins in the nursery school in the classrooms; beginning in third grade students concentrate on word processing, data-base use in the common rooms and some desktop publishing. Beginning in the fall of 1996, Trevor Day School became the first private school in Manhattan to join the Microsoft/Toshiba Laptops for Learning program. All students in grades five through twelve use laptops for inquiry and learning. (Families purchased them outright; there is a payment plan.) Students are generally enthusiastic about the project although carrying the laptops, which weigh five pounds, along with heavy textbooks in their backpacks has resulted in additional business for local chiropractors! The goal of this program is for the computer to become a "transparent" tool, like paper and pencil. "I use the laptop in every class," said a seventh grader. "In English to write essays and take notes on classroom reading, in history, foreign language and science to take notes and do homework, in math for writing assignments and graphing."

Social studies topics begin with community and interdependency, and students learn early on an awareness and respect for difference. Topics broaden from a study of family history to units on immigration and ethnic diversity in New York City and the history of Manhattan Island. African-American history and environmental studies are included. As an outgrowth of a unit on the environment, the third grade sponsors a school-wide recycling program.

Music is an integral part of the curriculum. Study begins with the Orff, Kodaly and Dalcroze methods and students start learning to play recorders in third grade.

Grades four and five are partially departmentalized. The home-room teacher, who is also a subject teacher, serves as advisor to approximately twelve children. Students make use of a central common room with glass-fronted classrooms on the perimeter. There are three common room periods a week as well as a daily quiet reading period.

The "miniterm" is first introduced in grades four and five. This is a two-week period during which academic electives occupy the morning while afternoons are reserved for rehearsal for the musical, a production that relates to "the lives and experiences of the students, using material taken from various literary sources as well as the students' own work." Music and dance from other cultures are often incorporated. Throughout the year there are opportunities for students to gain confidence in public speaking and to participate in plays. A parent said, "Nobody is ever excluded. Everyone is in the plays, and no one is made to feel inferior."

Students leave their homerooms now to be taught by specialists in music, gym and art several times a week. The fourth grade studies the geography of the Caribbean region. Fifth graders begin a two-year sequence in American history.

Parents praise the art program, which stresses each child's individual expression, as well as the attainment of skills. According to the head of the Lower School art department, "Children need to be who they are. If one is an artist, he is given a lot of credit for becoming an artist." From an early age, Trevor Day School students learn to use and maintain a variety of art materials from a central supply area. By fourth grade they are working on projects in various media, including drawing, painting, collage, 3-D paper, ceramics and printmaking.

Students can do film and computer animation, and graphics and photography in the school darkroom.

The middle school is composed of grades six through eight. The middle school common room is the center of student and teacher activity. The homeroom/advisor system changes somewhat in the middle school. Eight to nine students share an advisor who acts as friend, counselor, advocate. They meet at the start of each day. In addition, each student meets individually each week with an academic advisor. There are still no grades in the middle school (not until ninth grade) but students do self-assessment and are continually receiving feedback from faculty.

The middle school has its own three-week-long miniterm, during which students take academic electives in the morning and rehearse for a gala musical in the afternoon, take short courses and participate in special arts offerings. Students are involved in all aspects of putting on this full-scale production. Miniterm reinforces community spirit at The Day School, with everyone working toward a common goal in different capacities. Health education is introduced during miniterm, which includes an AIDS curriculum.

The teaching of English in the middle school is literature based. Students write, edit and produce finished drafts. Much time is spent on the mechanics of grammar and vocabulary building. Group discussion and collaborative learning activities dominate the classroom experience. In sixth grade students are assigned "considerable homework in reading and writing." Seventh graders focus on essay writing, critical thinking and oral expression. Eighth graders engage in "formal literary analysis of classic adult literature" while continuing to improve their essay-writing skills. The first in-class timed essay tests are given in eighth grade.

Foreign language study continues in sixth grade with either French or Spanish.

The middle school history curriculum is a continuation of the fifth grade American history cycle. Seventh and eighth graders study ancient civilizations in depth.

Science in the middle school utilizes a laboratory format. Emphasis is on the scientific method. By the end of eighth grade, all students have covered the basics of biology, physical science and some chemistry. Students can do a project at the end, such as constructing a digital clock.

In mathematics, critical thinking, problem solving and competency are stressed. Eighth graders take "Algebra I" or a course to reinforce their pre-algebra skills.

Participation in the arts is not optional at Trevor Day School. All sixth graders take a rotational Arts Workshop series, sampling the arts available to seventh and eighth graders. Electives include "Video Workshop", "Designing for Illustration" and "Photography."

Middle schoolers may select from vocal or instrumental electives in music. There is a middle school chorus. Students interested in dance can participate in Choreolab, which meets after school and puts on an annual student dance concert.

Community service activities in the middle school are coordinated with the lower school. There are numerous food, toy and clothing drives and UNICEF collections. Trevor Day School has a relationship with two camps for homeless children and with The Association to Benefit Children. Seventh and eighth graders may volunteer to serve either in the Trevor Day School Community, using schoolday periods for that purpose, or outside of school. *Service Beat*, a monthly publication, and the Director of Community Service, keep students informed.

Middle schoolers go to a camp for a week of outdoor education.

Physical education is required three times a week. After school there is a range of intramural and interscholastic sports. Parents say that no child is ever cut from a team. If you show up and participate, then you are considered a member of the team. But a participant in the physical education programs says, "We deemphasize competition in gym until 3:00 P.M. and then we don't like to lose." The Day School also has a championship gymnastics team for grades six through twelve.

The high school is composed of grades nine through twelve. The high school building has a working theatre, music rooms, a dance studio, a full-size basketball court, darkrooms, ceramics studio and an audiovisual studio. The high school library has 15,000 volumes, microfiche and is computerized. The Day School added the student-faculty center (common room) where students and staff can meet and work in a relaxed and informal setting, and which continues to function as the nucleus of the school.

Twenty-two credits are required for graduation. This includes three math, three science, three language, four English, three history and nine trimesters of the Arts. Advanced courses in computer science, foreign language, mathematics, biology, physics and chemistry are offered. Letter grades are introduced in ninth grade and are sent home twice a year with written reports. All high school students are required to complete eighty hours of community service over their four years.

Highlights from the English curriculum include: Electives in Asian Literature, European Drama, The Romantic Imagination, Shakespeare: Poetry and Drama, Dostoevsky and Conrad, Myth as Literature, and Literature of the African Diaspora. History electives include: Native Americans, Utopias, Model U.N. and Philosophy-Ethics.

The in-house Learning Skills program helps students reinforce and polish skills in math, foreign language, history, reading comprehension, critical thinking and writing. Ninth graders have a first semester required course in academic foundations. Tenth graders have a required course in Ethical Foundations.

Trevor Day School students participate in their graduation, putting on a performance with slides, songs and tributes. The strong sense of community at Trevor Day School persists after graduation. A parent of two alumnae says, "There's a warmth among the children, a camaraderie that continues even though some go on to different schools. They're still friends."

Cynthia E. Bing, former president of the Board of Trustees, describes the school's unique approach: "There is an adult presence that is not obtrusive. Students are encouraged to take the initiative but there are plenty of adults around to help them make [wise] decisions." Parents and alumni say that the emphasis on independent learning and time management pays off in college.

Popular College Choices   Bard, Boston University, Brandeis, Brown, Connecticut College, Cornell, NYU, Penn, Tufts, University of Vermont, Wellesley, Wesleyan, Wisconsin

Traditions   Fall auction/dinner, head of school's fund-raising party, clothing sale, class parties, Fall Festival, parent workshops, Parent Partners, Friday assemblies, potluck dinners, Goodman Convocation, High School Conference Day, Career Day, Field Day, miniterm musical productions, workshop theatrical productions, Music Conservatory student recitals, family/faculty concerts, Choreolab production

Publications   Yearbook and newspaper
Magazine: *Trevor*

Two literary magazines
Grades 4 and 5 desktop publication: *The Friday Story*
Foreign language newsletters

Community Service Requirement   80 hours over four years in high school

Hangout   McDonald's on 91st and Columbus
Common Room and Center (open to 5:30)

Trinity School

139 West 91st Street
New York, NY 10024
(212) 873-1650
website: Trinity.nyc.ny.us

Coed
Kindergarten–12th grade
Not accessible

Mr. Henry C. Moses, Headmaster
Ms. Patricia Robbins, Director of Admissions 7–12
Ms. June Hilton, Director of Admissions K–6

Uniform   For boys, Trinity polo-style shirt or turtleneck, chinos or corduroy pants, walking shorts may be worn in warm weather, no jeans or gym shorts. Sweater or navy blazer, no sweatshirts. Tied shoes or sneakers

For girls, white uniform blouse, white or navy turtleneck, long or short sleeve Trinity polo-style shirt. Light blue cord or glen plaid uniform jumper. Tan or navy pants, Bermuda shorts may be worn in the warm weather, no jeans or gym shorts. Sweaters or navy blazer, no sweatshirts. Shoes or sneakers, appropriate legwear.

Dress code in 7th and 8th grades: no jeans, short skirts or shorts permitted; skirts or slacks and neat collared shirts are preferred; hats cannot be worn in class

Dress code in 9th and 10th grades: jeans and sneakers may be worn; clothing must be neat, clean and socially appropriate

Birthday Cutoff   Children entering kindergarten must be 5 by September 1

Enrollment   Total school enrollment: 970
   Kindergarten places: approximately 60
   Graduating class size: approximately 100

Grades   Semester system
   Kindergarten–5: detailed anecdotal reports and checklists
   Departmentalization begins in 5th grade

Letter grades begin in 6th grade
First final exam is offered in 7th grade

Tuition Range 1998–1999 $16,355 to $17,645, kindergarten–12th grade
Additional fees: approximately $1,460 for lunch, student deposit account
$300 for graduation expenses and senior retreat

Financial Aid/Scholarship   Approximately $1.7 million available
17% of the student body receives financial assistance

Endowment   Approximately $20 million

Diversity   56 Prep for Prep students enrolled as of fall 1998 (The Prep for Prep program was originally housed at Trinity School); 6 Albert G. Oliver Scholars; 10 Early Steps students
Trinity School has a Cultural Diversity Club, Asian Cultural Appreciation Club, Hispanic Affairs Club and a Middle East Club

Homework   Kindergarten: None
1st grade: minimal, beginning in second half of 1st grade
2nd: 15–20 minutes (some homework given Monday is due on Friday)
3rd: 20–30 minutes (spelling quizzes and tests)
4th: 45 minutes–1 hour
5th and 6th: 1–2 hours
7th and 8th: 2–3 hours
9th–12th: 40 minutes per subject, approximately 3–4 hours

After-School Program   K–6: After-school program for an additional fee, a variety of creative and recreational activities
Some clubs meet after school
Intramural sports for 7th and 8th graders
Interscholastic sports in the Ivy Preparatory League (boys) and the Independent School Athletic Association (girls)

Summer Program   June Program
Trinity Day Camp: a variety of creative and recreational activities, including swimming; Trinity students have priority in enroll-

ment and there is usually a wait list; an additional payment is required

———

Trinity School was founded in 1709 as the first public charity school in New York City. While Collegiate claims to be the oldest school, Trinity claims to be the oldest *continually operated* school in Manhattan, as it remained open throughout the British occupation of New York City during the Revolutionary War. Trinity was a coed school until the mid-nineteenth century, when the city withdrew its support from charity schools. According to the school's brochure, Trinity then reincorporated as a private boys' school, eventually moving uptown alongside the town houses of the well-to-do on Manhattan's Upper West Side. At this time Trinity modeled itself on the English public (private) schools like Harrow, Eton, Westminster and Winchester. Trinity was a single-sex traditional school until the sixties. One alumnus said that "the Kennedy days marked the fall of the 'preppie' era at Trinity." Beginning with the upper school in the seventies, Trinity School again became coed, and by the late eighties was coed throughout. Trinity is a traditional school with "West Side" style; this is the key to the school's growing popularity. Many dualities are present in Trinity: highly selective admissions but generous financial aid, a diverse student body, with an emphasis on classical education, all bound by a respect for Trinity's traditions and a Protestant ethos.

Headmaster Henry C. Moses, former dean of freshmen at Harvard, replaced Christopher Berrisford in 1991. Parents say Moses, who gives speeches at chapel and has been seen in school plays, is approachable and cares about the students. He teaches the upper school course: "Literature of Fact."

The headmaster and trustees are committed to diversity at Trinity. Trinity's annual report recently boasted that Trinity had enrolled a "truly diverse" kindergarten: "Our goal is a school population that reflects our city's, and we have taken a major step in that direction this year." The Parents Association has its own Diversity Committee to support this commitment, and meetings have been held with parents to discuss their concerns and also to encourage them to help with recruitment of children from diverse backgrounds.

Despite the name Trinity, compulsory weekly chapel and the presence of an Episcopalian chaplain, Trinity School strives to be inclusive; the school has recently become popular with Jewish families. Scheduled holidays include Rosh Hashanah, Yom Kippur,

Christmas, Passover and Good Friday. There is the traditional all-school Christmas chapel with a candlelit procession, a holiday fair and a lower school Christmas program, and also a Chanukah Chapel. Beginning in first grade all lower school students attend chapel once a week and often sing as a group in chapel. The program is interfaith, and one parent said the religious component is not as prominent as the ethical and moral aspects. For example, on Valentine's Day her child's class read their own work aloud, and one child read a story about being friends forever. Chapel speakers in the upper school might include a senior faculty member or a protester from Tiananmen Square. In the brochure, Headmaster Henry C. Moses says, "I hope the chapel will always be a place of quiet reflection for all." All students take introductory religion courses in fifth and sixth grade. Eleventh and twelfth graders can choose among seven electives, including "Morals and Ethics" and "Religion and Literature," to fulfill their one-semester religion requirement.

Getting in: There are three open houses in the Fall. Parents of kindergarten applicants are advised to send in their completed application along with the $50 application fee as soon as possible to be granted an interview at the school. A wait list for interviews has been maintained in recent years. Kindergarten tours and interviews are on separate days. Children do not tour. In our opinion, the gentle-mannered Director of Admissions, June Hilton is the best part of Trinity's admissions process. The child goes upstairs with the tester while you go into Ms. Hilton's office for a conversation. Your child will join you shortly so ask your important questions quickly. Your four-year-old may have questions of his/her own (most likely "Can we go home now?") but this is to be expected. The fact that the school asks your child to sit on the couch while the adults are speaking suggests that they are looking for the mature child. Don't send your child to Trinity to be coddled. A parent said, "Trinity is a tough, no-nonsense school, but they really care about the kids."

Trinity's application fee is $50, among the highest required by any independent school but it is waived for those requesting financial aid. They also request a recent photograph of your child, so have some good wallet-size pictures made. Do not cancel your interview appointment with Trinity unless your child really is ill. The demand for kindergarten places is high; you might not get another appointment time. According to one nursery school director, "They like to see both parents." Once admissions decisions have been made, Trinity has an active wait list, and there is a strong sibling policy.

Although occasionally places are available in grades two through six and eight, ten and eleven, the main entry points after kindergarten are grades seven and nine. Each family is interviewed individually and has a student guide for the tour of the upper school. Interviews begin in late September and end in mid-February. There are three receptions in the fall that include tours of the facilities, and throughout the process there are opportunities to meet and talk with faculty members. After a candidate has been accepted, he or she visits classes.

Parents: The style at Trinity is traditional but not formal. "It's a very relaxed atmosphere for a traditional school," a parent told us. There is no typical parent. This is definitely not a celebrity school. There is a multicultural mix along with a fair share of East and West Side powerhouses. Many East Side parents said the one thing they would change is that they would move Trinity to the East Side of Manhattan. One parent said the school is financially mixed. There is money, but "by and large it's low-key." School dinners are held in the Trinity cafeteria. Parents Association meetings are scheduled so that all parents can attend, and there are meetings between the Parents Association and the trustees. Parents of entering kindergarten students attend a May reception.

Separation is handled gently. The kindergarten schedule is staggered in the beginning, and parents walk children up the stairs to their classroom. After a few weeks parents say goodbye at the bottom of the steps and the students go up by themselves. They shake hands with the teacher at the end of the day. Lower School Principal Rosemary Milliman greets the children in the morning. Parents say Milliman is always asking parents for input on how to improve the school. Lower School parents are kept informed about school and classroom events by the LS newsletter, "The Tuesday Newsday."

Program: There are three kindergartens with two teachers each, approximately twenty students in each class. The children go out of their classrooms for music, gym, swimming (on the premises) and art. There is swimming, gym or turf time daily and a new play area for kindergarteners with age appropriate equipment. In first grade the three kindergartens split into four smaller classes with approximately fifteen children in each; each class has a head teacher and an assistant. Parents say that this is a great advantage academically: "Students receive a lot of individual attention—they are really focused on developing important reading and math skills early." The approach to teaching reading is eclectic, with a recent emphasis on the Whole Language approach. June Hilton says, "We use all approaches to accommodate different learning styles." The Writing Workshop includes creative writing and reading stories aloud. Trinity seeks to instill a love for reading with programs such as D.E.A.R. (Drop Everything and Read). Kindergartners deliver their own "Sunny Day Newspaper" weekly. The marvelous lower school library at Trinity is inhabited by larger-than-life stuffed figures from children's classics: Clifford the Big Red Dog and some of Maurice Sendak's "wild things."

By second grade, expectations are greater. One parent told us she was afraid to go out and leave her second grader with the babysitter because he wouldn't be able to do his homework. New material is never introduced in homework assignments. Reading and math groups are formed according to ability. Foreign language (French or Spanish) is introduced in the lower school. Formal computer instruction in the computer lab begins in second grade. Kindergarteners and first graders are taught in their classrooms. At many points in the lower school the curriculum is integrated. For example, second graders study Native Americans of the Eastern Woodlands in social studies, and in music they present a festival of Native American song, story and dance for parents.

There is support for different learning styles, and a staff of specialists works with the homeroom teachers. At Special Services Night parents meet the team of specialists who provide remedial instruction. As in many independent schools, some tutoring is initiated by the parents. At Trinity a breakfast was held with the school psychologist and parents to discuss academic pressure but a consensus was not reached. We were told "Some parents think there is too much pressure and some think there is too little, depending on how their child is doing." While academic achievement is appreciated in the lower school, one parent said, "You don't have to be brilliant to be happy at Trinity. There is a spectrum of intelligence." One mother whose daughter is struggling with the academics, but bubbling with enthusiasm for Trinity nonetheless, was told by her child, "I'm really learning a lot this year!"

One of the highlights of the applicant tour is the lower school science room, which looks like a Woods Hole laboratory with aquatic life tanks around the room and charts, specimens and waders hanging on the walls. Howard Warren, lower school science head, oversees a hands-on science program. Warren received a Governor's Environmental Study Citation for his memorable beach cleanup with third graders (who do a unit on the environment). Warren takes the fourth graders wading into Jamaica Bay to collect specimens, which they bring back and put into the tanks, study and release at the end of the school year.

Music is an area of strength at Trinity. Twice weekly, beginning in kindergarten, students use the Orff, Kodaly and Dalcroze methods to learn rhythm and singing skills. Every class performs music, ranging from psalms sung in chapel to rap songs about the fifty states. The Adventures in Strings Program gives fourth graders the option of studying violin or cello and continues through fifth and sixth grades. There is also a lower school orchestra.

Trinity recently reorganized and consolidated the lower middle (grades five and six) and upper middle schools (grades seven and eight) into one middle school serving grades five through eight. The middle school is housed in its own bright, newly renovated wing and features a middle school technology resource center. The school now has two full size gymnasiums. Departmentalization begins in middle school. Modern language instruction, begun in the lower school, continues in grades five through eight. Latin instruction begins in grade six. Students who need reinforcement take a study skills course in which they meet with a learning specialist in small groups. Middle schoolers participate in the Pythagorean Contest and in the middle school Science Fair. In athletics, middle schoolers choose between coed kickball and football on the Astro Turf and Sports Club (interscholastic or intramural sports competition). Required swimming classes continue through eighth grade. There are informal "chalk talks" born out of the Project Charlie anti-drug program in middle school. After sixth grade the uniform requirements relax.

The upper school at Trinity is composed of the ninth through twelfth grades. After the architectural grandeur of the lower school, Trinity's upper school (Hawley Wing) with its cinderblock walls and bustling corridors has the feeling of a suburban public school. There are no bells in the upper school. There is a school store where a student can charge supplies and sweat suits to his or her account. The upper school library has Proquest and Newsbank, and students can work in carrels or on computers. Computers will soon be networked throughout the school.

Approximately forty new students enter at the ninth grade. Trinity is a popular high school choice for students at the single-sex schools who want a city coed day school.

To ease the transition into high school and integration of new students into the class, ninth graders take an orientation trip to Frost Valley in the Catskills, with senior leaders and faculty, and continue to meet once a week during the school year with their Frost Valley groups.

Contact between students in the three divisions occurs formally at all-school events several times a year. Currently, twice a week, ten to fifteen seniors eat lunch with kindergarten students, other seniors help fourth graders put on plays about Greek myths, several juniors and seniors work with lower school students on math enrichment, and upper and middle school students meet in programs like Kids Helping Kids to discuss social issues.

The graduation requirements at Trinity are similar to those at the other rigorous high schools. Students take a minimum of five or six academic courses in grade nine. In grades ten through twelve, they must take a minimum of four, but almost all students take more. Seniors may choose from a variety of electives, including "Cultural Diversity in America," Modern Poetry," and "Literature about Growing Up." We did not see any interdisciplinary courses listed in the course guide. English is required but seniors choose from seven different options each semester. About seventy percent of the seniors are enrolled in advanced science.

Some classrooms are set up in traditional rows or seminar style with oak lectern desks, but in English, history, modern languages and religion, the desks are arranged in a circle or the tables in a rectangle to promote discussion.

Trinity maintains its traditional emphasis on the classics, the study of Latin and Greek. The school's course guide asserts that the classics are "a rigorous and significant part of the curriculum." "The best Latin program in the country," says one student. The study of DWAMS (Dead White Ancient Males) really comes alive at Trinity. Advanced reading in elegiac poetry and Ovid's *The Art of Love*, a provocative and satirical portrait of love in ancient Rome, is offered. Advanced students can participate in The Virgil Academy, in which students read a book of the *Aeneid* in tutorial and later take part in public examination by teachers from other schools and colleges. In addition to Latin and Greek, students can continue study in French, Spanish and German. The English department requires upper school students to read five books over the summer. Ninth graders begin the year with a six-week Writing Workshop to perfect their essay-writing skills. Eleventh and twelfth grade English electives offer multiethnic perspectives, including "Latin American Writers," "Politics in Literature" and "Women Writers of the Twentieth Century."

After a solid grounding in modern European and American history, seniors can choose from the following electives (these vary from year to year): "Prejudice in America" (women and nonwhite ethnic minorities), "The Postwar World, 1945–1965" and "U.S. History, 1965–1984," and Economics.

In keeping with the commitment to diversity at Trinity there has been much discussion about the need to incorporate more views of nonwhite ethnic minorities and women into the upper school curriculum. At the first alumni panel (with faculty), part of a Faculty Professional Day, the theme was "Perspectives in Multiculturalism and Education." Five recent Trinity graduates talked about the need to broaden the curriculum with more diverse viewpoints, and one student said that although they visited many cultural sites in New York City including, of course, the Metropolitan Museum, "We should have taken trips to the Schomburg Center along with the Guggenheim Museum."

Honors courses exist only in mathematics and modern languages. Although not all advanced courses follow the AP curriculum, AP Prep courses are offered to prepare students for the exam. Science requirements are biology plus one year of another laboratory science. Science electives include "Psychology," "Marine Biology," "Astronomy" and "Twentieth-Century Science and Technology." The computer science department offers courses in word processing, programming and applications of artificial intelligence plus one AP computer science course in which advanced programming in Apple Pascal is taught.

High school students can do advanced independent work in addition to the required four academic subjects. Advanced work is graded pass/fail and doesn't count as a credit toward graduation. Seniors, however, may enroll in an independent study in a specific discipline such as German literature, chemistry or studio art, but they must also take four other courses. Seniors receive a letter grade for their independent study program.

The arts and theatre programs at Trinity are extensive. Theatre at Trinity is exciting. Every year there is a major musical production and a Cabaret. We saw a rehearsal for *Fiddler on the Roof* in the chapel; another year it was *Carousel*. The Theater IV play production course allows students to direct any one-act play of their choice. These spring productions are very well attended.

Adjoining visual arts and ceramics studios are large and bright. High school students with artistic promise and interest can earn credits attending classes at the Art Students League and the National Academy of Art. Students make good use of New York City's museums. Students can take beginning through advanced photography for credit. There is room for individual initiative in the arts at Trinity. In fall of 1991 a small group of students with a keen interest in films and filmmaking organized the first New York National High School Film Festival and received 215 entries from across the country. Prizes were awarded. The Festival has become an exciting annual event.

When they're not studying, students can relax in the Swamp (a seating area off the main lobby) or in the Food Zone (another side of the lobby). There is no student lounge as such. There is a no-smoking zone around the school. Students can leave campus as early as the second half of freshman year.

Three representatives from each grade serve in the student senate (serving grades nine through twelve). The Senate recently voted to install a Snapple or soda-vending machine but this was not permitted. Homecoming, run by the student senate, takes place at a boys' varsity basketball game in the winter. At other times during the year the senate gives out hot chocolate.

There are numerous clubs. The most popular, we were told, is the "Free Tibet" club, with over 200 members.

There is no community service requirement, but most Trinity students participate in at least one community service activity. Often an entire grade will do a project together, for instance, clean an area of Riverside Park or give a variety show to make money for hurricane victims. The Student Volunteer Service Organization (SVSO), born in the sixties, continues to coordinate a range of student volunteer activities, such as Santa's helpers, the Thanksgiving program for senior citizens, You Gotta Have Park and the March of Dimes Walkathon.

In recent years, AIDS has been important issue on campus and there were numerous discussions at Trinity among parents and students about AIDS. "Although abstinence is preferred," said one mother, "we have to be realistic."

The athletic program at Trinity is wide ranging and strong. Some teams begin two-hour morning practice sessions at 6:00 A.M. Games are held after school and some are well attended. Soccer, lacrosse and swimming are a few of Trinity's best teams, but students say "this is definitely not a rah-rah school."

At graduation, awards are bestowed upon Trinity seniors, in recognition of excellence in nearly every area. The three students with the highest grade point averages in each grade receive the Hawley Prizes. On Prize Day in May, all academic departments announce the students in grades nine through twelve, who are recipients of endowed prizes, including four prizes that have been given annually since 1890—the Eaton Prize for Classics, the Alumni Prize in English, the Rector's Prize in Religion, and the Eaton Prize for Senior Mathematics. At a formal induction ceremony in the spring, students with outstanding academic records are elected to the Cum Laude Society, the high school equivalent of Phi Beta Kappa. There are some students who compete for these prizes, but the *real* source of competition, one alumnus told us, is college placement.

Graduation exercises, complete with academic gown, are held in a church at 96th and Central Park West. A Baccalaureate service, planned by the seniors, is held the night before graduation at Trinity Church, the original site of the school, near Wall Street. By tradition, the graduation speaker is the parent of a senior.

Popular College Choices   Yale, Harvard, Brown, Princeton, University of Pennsylvania, Cornell, Wesleyan, Stanford

Traditions   Holiday Fair, Spring Auction and Dinner, Virgil Academy, Reunion Weekend, Cabaret, Theater IV productions, senior Halloween Costume contest

Publications   Yearbook: *The Brun*
Literary magazine: *Columbus*
Newspaper: *Trinity Times*
Photography journal: *Malinconico*
Trinity School magazine: *Trinity Per Saecula* (Trinity through the Ages)

Hangouts   The Swamp (a small seating area in the rear of the upper school lobby), the Food Zone (seating in the lobby where students can eat), the McDonald's at 91st and Columbus

United Nations International School

24–50 Franklin D. Roosevelt Drive
New York, NY 10010
(212) 684-7400
website: www.unis.org
e-mail: admissions@mail.unis.org

Coed
Kindergarten–12th grade
Accessible

Dr. Kenneth Wrye, Director
Ms. Barbara Daelman, Director of Admissions

Uniform None

Birthday Cutoff Children entering kindergarten must be 5 by December 31

Enrollment Total enrollment: 1,502
Kindergarten places: 85–90
Graduating class size: 95–105

Grades Semester system
Number grades begin in 7th grade
Full departmentalization by 7th grade

Tuition Range 1998–1999 $11,200 to $13,100, kindergarten–12th grade
Additional fees total approximately $400

Financial Aid/Scholarship 13% of the student body receive some form of financial aid, $650,000 available

Endowment Approximately $14 million

Diversity Students at UNIS come from over 100 countries.

After-School Program Open to UNIS students only
A variety of creative and recreational activities from 3:00 P.M. until 6:00 P.M.; an additional payment is required
Varsity and junior varsity teams

Summer Program   The six-week UNIS summer program is open to children from UNIS as well as from the community, nursery through 12th grade; a variety of creative and recreational activities as well as English as a Second Language are offered; an additional payment is required

----

UNIS is housed in a modern, spacious building overlooking the East River. A large garden forms the tranquil core of the edifice. For younger students the school has a fully equipped, multi-level playground. UNIS was founded in 1947 by a group of United Nations parents to provide their children with an international curriculum and to inspire in its students the spirit and ideals of the UN. Today, UNIS is open to all New York City families. Students at UNIS represent over one hundred countries; the faculty represents over fifty different nationalities.

UNIS is organized into three schools: The junior school is for kindergarten through fourth grade students, the middle school is composed of fifth through eighth grade, and the high school (tutorial house) is for ninth through twelfth grade students. Each school has its principal and staff, who insure a smooth transition from school to school. After eleven years as Director, Dr. Blaney retired in 1998. Dr. Kenneth Wrye replaced him. Dr. Wrye is a U.S. Citizen and was formerly head of the Copenhagen International School.

Getting in: UNIS offers Spring and Fall tours (led by current parents) for prospective applicants; students in fifth grade and above are welcome to accompany their parents on the tour. Once an application has been filed, the school will contact parents to set up an interview date and parents can tour at this time. Children applying to kindergarten through fourth grade are observed in an informal play group of four or five. While the children are playing, their parents meet as a group (approximately twenty parents) for a Q. and A. session with the school principal and admissions staff. All English speaking students are required to submit results of ERB testing. Teacher recommendations are strongly recommended; personal recommendations are welcome but not required. The school is sensitive to applicants from other cultures and countries and they are familiar with all of the different national systems. UNIS has its own in-house assessment specialist who can test children (for placement purposes) who don't speak fluent English. Each year one or two places in each grade are held open for children of incoming U.N. diplomats. Forty-four per cent of students are affiliated with the U.N.

Program: The curriculum is designed to provide for direct interaction by the children with the world around them. The children are encouraged to think for themselves, while working cooperatively in small groups. Academics are stressed in an integrated International Baccalaureate Primary Years Program that includes, music, art, French, Spanish, science and computer science taught by specialists. Creativity is encouraged.

UNIS recognizes that the middle school years are critical ones for social, emotional and intellectual growth. The curriculum builds upon the basics learned in previous years, adding new subjects and additional language options. The IB middle years program is the focus of the curriculum. In English, middle school students read world poetry and explore works of literature from many countries and cultures. UNIS places high value on the teaching of foreign languages. French is offered from grade one. Nine languages are taught by native speakers and there are beginning, intermediate and advanced classes available. English as a Second Language is a separate course. At seventh grade level, electives, in addition to the regular curriculum, are offered in drama, art, computer, music and modern languages. Students are required to choose one of these electives for a two year period.

The curriculum of the "Tutorial House" (high school) balances electives and required subjects. In grade ten students can pursue a special talent or interest, whether it be math, science, languages, writing, the humanities, music or art. The program culminates in the International Baccalaureate Diploma Program (IB), study for which takes place during the last two years of high school. The vast majority of UNIS students take the full IB program. Students with high grades can sometimes receive up to one year of advanced standing at American universities. Eighty-five percent of graduates choose to attend colleges in North America.

UNIS has an articulated computer studies program. Technology is integrated into classroom instruction in many different subject areas. We saw computers in all of the classrooms and there are four computer labs. The school is networked, connecting all classrooms and bridging both campuses. The school is connected to the Internet through a T1 line.

There are numerous opportunities for leadership throughout the school. Students can be elected to Student Council as early as grade two. Members of the Student Councils of all three schools meet periodically with their principal and with the director to discuss issues of concern.

The UNIS athletic program includes twenty-six varsity and junior varsity teams.

The annual UNIS/UN conference is an exciting annual event. This conference is held in the UN's General Assembly Hall and requires months of planning and research by UNIS students and students from the more than fifty participating schools from around the world.

Popular College Choices   Brown, Columbia, Cornell, Harvard, MIT, Parsons School of Design, University of Michigan, NYU, Tufts, Vassar, Yale, McGill, London School of Economics

Traditions   United Nations Day, Winter and Spring Concerts, UNIS/UN Conference, Theater Workshop, English Writing Weekend at Bard College, Theory of Knowledge Weekend, Science Weekend, Math Weekend, Senior Trip, Sports Carnival, Sports Banquet, International Book and Craft Festival, World Outreach to Needy People.

Publications   Yearbook
Upper School Newspaper: *UNIS Verse*
Student Council Newsletter
Junior School Newsletter
3 Literary Magazines

Community Service Requirement   An important aspect of student life is community service, either in-house or at an approved public service agency in the metropolitan area.

Village Community School

272 West Tenth Street
New York, NY 10014
(212) 691-5146

Coed
5/6's (kindergarten)–8th grade
Not accessible

Ms. Eve Kleger, Director
Ms. Victoria Ruffolo, Director of Admissions

Birthday Cutoff   Children entering kindergarten must be 5 by December 31

Enrollment   Total enrollment: 300
5/6 (kindergarten) places: 35 to 40
Graduating class size: 25–30
6 Prep for Prep students enrolled as of September 1996

Grades   Semester system in the upper school
Lower and upper schools: detailed anecdotal reports and conferences twice a year
Full departmentalization begins in 6th Grade

Tuition Range 1998–1999 $13,500 to $14,200, 5/6's–12/13's
Additional fees: for books, approximately $400

Financial Aid/Scholarship   25% of the student body receive partial financial aid

Endowment   Currently, in the early stages; the school requires each family to make a non-interest-bearing loan to the school of $800 per child, returnable when the child leaves the school

After-School Program   After School at VCS: for children ages 5 and above; open to children from other schools; Monday–Friday 3:15 P.M. to 4:45 P.M.; activities include sports, arts and crafts,

music, theatre and dance; an additional payment is required
A play group is available until 5:30 P.M.

Summer Program VCS has a summer camp from mid-June through July open to students from other schools; an additional payment is required

---

Village Community School was founded in 1970. VCS's building, with its high ceilings and wide stairwells, was originally a public school one hundred years ago. VCS is governed by an elected Council which is composed of parents, faculty and administrators. Recent capital improvements include a new sky-lit library, two science centers, and an elevator. There is a full-sized air-conditioned gym on the premises in addition to two outdoor play spaces. No ERB testing is required for kindergarten admissions (it is required for second grade and above). There are two divisions: The lower school is composed of ages five through ten. The upper school is composed of grades six through eight. VCS has interage (flexible) class groupings until sixth grade. There is no uniform. VCS does not have a cafeteria and students must bring their own lunches.

VCS has a friendly, relaxed atmosphere but the curriculum is highly structured. Students address their teachers (as well as the director) by their first names. Parents say that in the lower school VCS is very nurturing; in the middle years the expectations are more demanding. Foreign language is introduced in sixth grade; in seventh grade students choose either French or Spanish. In 1998, VCS admitted four Prep for Prep students.

Most VCS graduates attend a variety of city high schools including the specialized public schools, NYC independent schools and boarding schools.

York Preparatory School
40 West 68th Street
New York, NY 10023
(212) 362-0400

Coed
Grades 6–12
Accessible (elevator)

Mr. Ronald P. Stewart, Headmaster
Ms. Randy Kleinman, Principal
Ms. Brinton Taylor Parson, Director of Admissions

Uniform   None, there is a dress code

Birthday Cutoff   None

Enrollment   Total enrollment: 250–275
6th grade places: 9–14
Average graduating class size: 40–50

Grades   Semester system
Letter grades begin in 6th grade
Departmentalization begins in 6th grade and is complete by 7th grade

Tuition Range 1998–1999 $16,200 to $16,900, 6th–12th grades
Additional fees: for books, activities, trips, graduation and Parents' Association dues are approximately $1,400

Financial Aid/Scholarship   Approximately 33% of the school receive some form of aid
$500,000 in financial aid was distributed in 1998–1999

Endowment   None

After-School Program   Varsity and junior varsity team competition in the Interschool League
An active intramural program
Academic clubs meet after school
All teachers remain after school for extra-help classes
Extracurricular activities include: horseback riding, golf, computer

animation, jewelry making, tennis, drama, literary magazine and newspaper, "mock trial" team, and swimming

Summer Program   An academic enrichment program is offered from mid-June–July for an additional charge; open to students from other schools

———

York Prep was founded in 1969 by its present Headmaster Ronald Stewart. In 1998 the school moved from its former location on East 85th Street into its current home on the Upper West Side, a handsome seven-story granite building formerly occupied by the Hebrew Union College. After completing a "boiler to roof" renovation, the school, crisply painted in white and blue, reflects the can-do optimism exuded by the Oxford-educated Headmaster, and his wife, Jayme Stewart, who has been Director of College Guidance since the school's inception.

York Prep is a proprietary (for-profit) school, owned and operated by the Headmaster. The school is run like a high class Mom and Pop organization: The Stewarts oversee every aspect of the school which operates free of the politics of a board of trustees. Liv Tyler and Kelly Klein are two of the school's glamorous grads; so is James de la Vega, a graffiti artist (recently profiled in *The New York Times*), who grew up in El Barrio, studied art at Cornell and now teaches at his alma mater, "occasionally taking his students on a tour of Harlem street art."

When you enter the school, a regulation sized basketball court serves as the backdrop to the reception desk. A uniformed security guard stands nearby, who on closer inspection turns out to be an effigy. York Prep values both athletics and a sense of humor, both of great advantage when managing adolescents, as the Stewarts, who have three grown children, know well. Participation in athletics and other extracurricular activities is encouraged here; a component of the school's philosophy is "putting children in situations of success." A parent told us: "It's a very nurturing school, the teachers are great; it's the perfect alternative to one of the real high-powered schools; an excellent private school education."

The schoolhouse has two modern science laboratories, a library/media center (with beautiful Shaker-style windows), computer room, performance and art studios, and a sprung hardwood floor gymnasium with weight and locker room facilities. The classrooms are light and airy, carpeted and climate controlled. The classrooms are wired with a T-1 line and students and staff have e-mail addresses. In addition, all classrooms are linked to the school's in-house television station, WYRK, over which daily announcements are read.

Getting In: Open Houses for Parents are offered regularly by the Headmaster. Upon request, parents can tour the school individually with the Director of Admissions, Ms. Brinton Taylor Parson, before filing an application. Applicants and their parents have an interview meeting and the applicant is invited to spend a day visiting the school. In 1998, York Prep admitted four Prep for Prep students.

Program: Stewart believes that a student must be offered a real opportunity for success, and that is a major factor in student motivation. York Prep's curriculum provides a strong foundation in the traditional core subjects of liberal arts education. For a small school, it offers an impressive range of courses with electives in most fields for qualified students and a growing number of AP courses in History, Math and foreign languages. Beginning in seventh grade each subject area is divided into at least three tracks (homogeneous ability groups). These tracks are fluid; students whose skills improve will move into the next track enabling students to experience success while always being challenged to work beyond their "comfort level." Each student's program is constantly evaluated for proper placement within the tracking system to ensure the right balance of challenge and support is maintained in all subject areas.

"York Prep's system of academic support has helped many students who've been 'over-faced' [at other schools] rediscover the thrill of learning," says Stewart. For gifted students, York Prep provides the challenge of its top track courses leading to AP courses. In addition to the tracking system and individual assistance given to students, the school uses a study skills and learning strategies program of its own design that is taught in every grade and every subject.

The school has always provided academic support and accommodation for students with different learning styles and educational needs. The *Jump Start* program is an individualized and intensive program that works to strengthen reading comprehension and writing skills. This program also imparts organizational and study skills. It was created to help students develop independence not only with day-to-day tasks but also with respect to long range goals. There is an additional fee for the *Jump Start* program. York Prep also offers an ESL program with daily English-language instruction and tutorial assistance.

Seniors and advanced eleventh graders who qualify may either take courses at Columbia, New York University, or Hunter College, or independent study and advanced placement courses.

Communication between parents and the school is frequent. "The teachers and staff have their fingers on everything that's going on; if my son was having a problem I could ask the principal to 'keep an eye on him today' and they will," said one parent.

Teachers take full advantage of the school's Lincoln Center location in addition to visiting museums, theaters and the Wall Street area.

A wide range of sports is offered at York and the full trophy cases are proof of their success. York Prep competes in the Independent School Leagues, the Private Schools Athletic Association and the Manhattan Independent Schools tennis and golf league. Students can choose from competitive or non-competitive basketball, softball, soccer, swimming, track, tennis, cross-country track, aerobics, gymnastic, golf and weight training. Horseback riding at the Claremont Stables is a feature of York Prep's extra-curricular program, as are ski weekends and trips to Europe and Washington, D.C. The range of clubs and activities changes each year according to student interest.

York Prep students volunteer their time at more than 150 non-profit organizations, including the American Red Cross, the ASPCA, the Legal Aid Society, and so on. Some students surpass the required hours of the Community Service Program.

Stewart says "Each child needs a feeling that he can do something well—whether it's athletics or origami. (Regarding origami, Stewart told us, 'One student got into Stanford because of it') "We tell them 'you pick it, we'll support you.' " This philosophy is carried all the way through to graduation. York Prep is very successful at college placement thanks to the expertise of Jayme Stewart, author of *How to get Into the College of Your Choice* (William Morrow & Co., 1991) Ms. Stewart encourages students to make realistic choices. Her thoroughness and tenacity as a student advocate pay off because more than 85% are accepted at their first choice school.

Popular College Choices   Barnard, Bowdoin, Brown, Colgate, Boston University, Cooper Union, Juilliard, George Washington, University of Michigan, Cornell, Penn

Publications   Literary Magazine: *Genesis*
Yearbook: *The Legend*
Newspaper

Community Service Requirement   90 hours

ADDITIONAL SCHOOLS:

Lyceum Kennedy
(French Bilingual Pre-Kindergarten–12th grade)
225 East 43rd Street
New York, N.Y. 10017
(212) 681-1877

Total enrollment: 160

Montessori School of New York, Inc.
(Nonsectarian 2 year olds–14 year olds)
347 East 55th Street
New York, N.Y. 10022
(212) 223-4630

Total enrollment: 100

RESOURCES FOR CHILDREN WITH LEARNING DISABILITIES

A complete listing of educational resources in the New York City area for children with learning disabilities can be obtained from:

The National Center for Learning Disabilities, 381 Park Avenue South, Suite 1041, New York, NY 10016, (212) 545-7510
NCLD is a voluntary, not-for-profit organization founded in 1977 by Carrie Rozelle. NCLD operates a national information and referral service and is the nation's only central, computerized resource clearinghouse committed solely to the issues of LD.

The Learning Disabilities Association of New York City Telephone Referral Service: Weekdays from 9 A.M. to 5 P.M., (212) 645-6730
This nonprofit organization is an affiliate of the Learning Disabilities Association of America. Trained counselors will explain how to recognize symptoms, and offer referrals to community based agencies in the New York City area. The Learning Disabilities Association also provides printed material and conducts workshops.

Other resources for information about LDs:

The New York Branch of the Orton Dyslexia Society, 71 West 23rd Street, Suite 514, New York, NY 10010, (212) 691-1930
This is the New York branch of the national nonprofit Orton Dyslexia Society, which uses a multisensory approach for teaching children with dyslexia. They offer a free telephone referral service to parents looking for information on testing, schools, trained remediators, psychologists and other professionals. The Orton Dyslexia Society also sponsors an annual three-day conference on a topic of interest to parents, a conference for teenagers and parent support groups. A yearly membership is available.

The Parents League of New York, Inc., 115 East 82nd Street, New York, NY 10028, (212) 737-7385
The Parents League sponsors a workshop and provides information and referrals about learning disabilities to member parents. Mrs. Alice Goldman, an adviser with the Parents League, is particularly knowledgeable about which schools specialize in which type of LD.

Resources for Children with Special Needs, 200 Park Avenue South, Suite 816, New York, NY 10003, (212) 677-4650
Resources for Children is a nonprofit information, referral, advocacy,

training and support center for programs and services for children (from birth to age twenty-one) with learning, developmental, emotional or physical disabilities. Resources for Children publishes a family support guide listing camps and summer programs for children with special needs.

The Churchill Center, 22 East 95th Street, New York, N.Y. 10128, Tel: (212) 722-7226, Fax: (212)410-3199
An outreach center for services and programs for children and adolescents with attention and/or learning problems.

Advocates for Children, 105 Court Street, Brooklyn, N.Y. 11201, (718) 624-8450
Advocates for Children works to protect and extend the rights of children with learning and/or developmental disabilities in public schools.

National Information Center for Children and Youth with Disabilities, P.O. Box 1492, Washington, D.C. 20013-1492, (1-800) 695-0285

The A.D.D. Resource Center, Inc., 215 West 75th Street, New York, N.Y. 10023, Tel: (212) 721-0049, Fax: (212) 724-4519
Seminars, courses, workshops and services for parents and children.

The Schools

The tuition for the schools listed below ranges from approximately $15,000 to $25,000, higher than the tuition range for other independent schools because of the specialized services provided to students, such as: a very small student-teacher ratio, speech and occupational therapists, psychologists and learning specialists. Financial aid is available.

1. **The Churchill School**
   22 East 95th Street
   New York, NY 10128
   (212) 722-0610
   Coed
   Ages 5–14
   Total enrollment: 150

2. **The Gateway School of New York**
   921 Madison Avenue
   New York, NY 10021
   (212) 628-3560

   Coed
   Ages 5–11
   Total enrollment: 52

3. **The Gillen Brewer School**
   1190 Park Avenue
   New York, NY 10128
   (212) 831-3667

   Coed
   Ages 3–8
   Total enrollment: 16
   The Gillen Brewer School opened in December 1993

4. **The Mary McDowell Center for Learning**
   110 Schermerhorn Street
   (corner Boerum Place)
   Brooklyn, New York 11201
   (718) 625-3939

   Coed
   Ages 5–11
   Total enrollment: 84

5. **The Parkside School**
   48 West 74th Street
   New York, NY 10023
   (212) 721-8888

   Coed
   Ages 5–10
   Total enrollment: 80

6. **Stephen Gaynor School**
   22 West 74th Street
   New York, NY 10023
   (212) 787-7070

   Coed
   Ages 5–13
   Total enrollment: 118

7. **West End Day School**
   255 West 71st Street
   New York, NY 10023
   (212) 873-5708

   Coed
   Ages 5–12
   Total enrollment: 38

8. **Windward School**
   Windward Avenue
   White Plains, NY 10605
   (914) 949-6968

   Coed
   1–12
   Total enrollment: 296

9. **Winston Preparatory School**
   4 West 76th Street
   New York, NY 10023
   (212) 496-8400

   Coed
   6th–12th grades
   Total enrollment: 80

The Dwight/Anglo-American International Schools Quest program: An in-house program for children with mild learning disabilities, discussed *supra* pages 207–209.

Columbia Grammar and Preparatory School: The school's in-house program for children with mild learning disabilities is discussed *supra* on page 167.

PUBLIC
SCHOOL
OPTIONS

Many parents agonize over the choice of public or private education for their children. If sending their children to private would be a tremendous financial burden on families already stretched to their limits, we feel it is very important not to add additional pressures. Parents should resist societal pressure and use common sense to make the right decisions for their family. Children might be better off with a parent who is accessible, rather than one who is working "twenty-four and seven" to make tuition payments. Select public schools offer a top-notch education at a rock bottom price and parents who get involved in their child's school can really make a difference.

The public schools are experiencing a revitalization as a result of a number of factors: More families are making the decision to raise their children in the city, there is a budget surplus as a result of the recent Wall Street boom, the cost of a private school education is well beyond the reach of most families. Parents also say they select public school as a values choice; they don't want to raise children who are "precocious," and "entitled."

Clara Hemphill's book *The Parents' Guide to the City's Best Public Elementary Schools* (Soho Press 1998) reassures parents that the best school for their child might be the one right around the corner. Community School District 2 in Manhattan, for example, is a pilot district for the New Standards Project and boasts schools with the highest reading and math scores in the city. Recent announcements of multi-million dollar gifts from alumni to Brooklyn Tech and Bronx Science ensure that the specialized high schools can compete with the independent schools in their ability to attract the best and the brightest students.

The New York City school system, the largest in the nation, offers a truly diverse student body, enrichment programs for gifted students, magnet/option programs°, bilingual immersion programs, collaborations with the city's major cultural institutions, corporate grants for computer and science curricula—whatever is new and exciting in education is happening in New York City's public schools. Be aware that

°Option or alternative schools are schools of choice that are at the forefront of the educational reform movement. They are small, director-managed schools with a clear guiding vision and specific philosophical, thematic and curricular commitments. Although they are located in regular school buildings, they are autonomous. Staff, parents and students elect to attend these schools. They are magnet (TAG) schools with a mandate for ethnically, socioeconomically and gender-balanced populations. Admission is by application, which can be obtained from the schools. Parents must contact each school since application requirements and notification dates vary from program to program.

...among individual schools in terms of magnet grants, enrichment programs, ...parent involvement. There are traditional 'option" schools. Parents need to see with ...public education can be.

...arents ask most often concern class size and ...mentary schools. For grades K–3 class size is limit... ...tudents but can go to twenty-eight. For grades 4–6 the maximu... ...s size is generally thirty-two, but can go beyond that. Student-teacher ratios vary from school to school because some schools have student teachers and parents often pay for extra para-professionals to staff classrooms. District superintendents say "there are fair, firm and consistent rules of discipline" in effect at all the elementary schools. Every elementary school has a guard in front who requests identification from visitors.

The standard time to preregister for the public school in your catchement area or zone (immediate neighborhood) is May of the same calendar year your child will be attending school (register in May of 1999 for fall of 1999). But be advised that many New York City public school gifted and talented programs require an application process that begins in the fall *prior* to the calendar year that a child would attend the school. Following the national trend toward a return to middle schools serving sixth through eighth grades, District 2 and 3 elementary schools now end after fifth grade.

How to Begin Finding Out About New York City Public Schools

1. **The Parents' Guide to New York City's Best Public Elementary Schools**, Clara Hemphill (Soho Press) and **Public Middle Schools: New York City's Best**, Clara Hemphill (Soho Press, September 1999)
Everything you need to know about the elementary and middle schools in your area.
2. **The Public Education Association (PEA)**, 39 West 32nd Street, New York, NY 10001, (212) 868-1640, Fax: (212) 268-7344, Judith Baum, Director of Information Services. e-mail: info@PEA-online.org
This one hundred year old organization is an advocate for highest quality schools for all of New York City's public school children. The PEA's Education Information Center, created in 1993, pro-

vides timely and useful information to parents and the public about schools, including how to find a good elementary school in your neighborhood and how to obtain a variance. The Education Information Center publishes a ~~Consumer's Guide to NYC Public High Schools~~ and the new ~~Consumer's Guide to Middle Schools~~. The PEA also publishes *The Parents' Guide to Mathematics, Science and Technology Education in NYC Public Schools*.

3. **The 92nd Street Y, the Parenting Center at the Center for Youth and Family**, 1395 Lexington Avenue, New York, NY 10128, ~~(212) 996-1100~~ (To Register) ~~"Public School Options in District 2"~~. The 92nd Street Y offers a very informative seminar on public school options in ~~October~~. Call the 92nd Street Y for reservations. ~~There is a $15 registration fee.~~ The evening features a panel discussion and Q. and A. *Mond. Oct. 4 8:15 – 9:45*
#15.00

4. **The Manhattan White Pages**
In the center of the telephone book is a section called the Blue Pages that contains a directory of New York City government offices. Under the heading Education, you will find a listing of all the Manhattan public schools, elementary through high schools.

Manhattan is composed of six community districts. (The Upper East Side is in District Two. The Upper West Side is in District Three.) Call your community school district office for general information on alternative/option schools in the district (these include gifted and talented programs).

Call the elementary school or middle school nearest you to request a tour. A representative of the Parents Association usually conducts these tours and can answer many of your preliminary questions. A school might have an excellent reputation but you should see the school with your own eyes and let the principal/teachers describe the school's philosophy to you. Some alternative/option schools *require* a parent tour before application.

Students who live within a zone (or "catchment") have first priority for enrollment in neighborhood elementary schools, followed by students who live outside the zone but within the district. A student may attend a school outside his zone only if there are "empty seats." Parents interested in sending a child to a school outside their zone or district need to obtain a variance. Children of a parent who works in another zone or district can receive a "working" variance so that they can attend a school near the parent's place of work. Contact the district office of the desired school for variance information.

449

Due to recent budget cuts, free busing on a Board of Education School bus to a school outside the student's zone is no longer provided; although busing *is* provided for students attending a gifted and talented school within the student's district. Students may obtain a bus pass for New York City buses.

PROGRAMS FOR GIFTED AND TALENTED STUDENTS

Tracking (ability grouping) within grades at the elementary level, an educational practice familiar to many baby boomers, has fallen out of favor these days. However, many parents still prefer their "bright" children to be with other children of similar ability. In the past, many middle-class families made financial sacrifices to send their children to prestigious private schools where they would receive an enriched educational program alongside the best and the brightest. The burgeoning gifted and talented programs (also known as talented and gifted or "TAG" programs) within the New York City public schools are an attempt to lure these parents back to public education and it is working. Getting a child into Hunter Elementary is as prestigious as gaining admission to the most selective independent school. Like the private (independent) schools, most of the TAG programs require parents to apply on behalf of their children one year prior to the year of enrollment. While some of the public TAG programs still have a "cutoff score" (they will only accept students who score above a certain percentile on an I.Q. test; the Stanford-Binet IV is the most commonly used test) in District 2, a screening process (which includes an interview with the child) has replaced I.Q. testing. New York City public school TAG programs fill up quickly and waiting lists are maintained. All of these programs are free of charge.

Many of the programs for talented and gifted students are contained within the public elementary and middle schools. A few programs are housed separately (The Laboratory School for Gifted Education, Hunter Elementary). Because the gifted and talented programs are not all alike—there are different models and different approaches—parents are advised to tour them.

Institute for the Academic Advancement of Youth (IAAY), Johns Hopkins University, 3400 N Charles Street, Baltimore, Mary-

450

land 21218, Phone (410) 516-0337, Fax (410) 516-0804, website: http://www.jhu.edu/~gifted (check out the "hot math sites"). Parents who are seeking enrichment programs for a gifted child need look no further. The Johns Hopkins University Talent Search identifies students with exceptional mathematical and/or verbal reasoning ability in grades 2–8. These students (who have scored above the 97th percentile on nationally normed standardized aptitude or achievement tests) take above-grade-level tests through the Talent Search to provide an accurate evaluation of advanced talents. Test-takers receive recognition, guidance materials, and, if qualified based on above-grade-level test scores, the opportunity to participate in academic programs. CTY (Center for Talented Youth) and CAA (Center for Academic Advancement) offer three-week summer residential programs (approximate cost, $2,000). The Center for Distance Education offers Math and Writing Tutorials year-round (approximate cost, $400–500). Schools can form a team and join the on-line Math Olympiad. Students apply in the Fall and most test in December or January at test centers nationwide. Contact the IAAY for an application and brochure which lists deadlines and instructions.

I.Q. Testing

Hunter Elementary and some of the gifted programs require I.Q. testing, and the Stanford-Binet IV is the most widely used test. Testing must usually be done after July 1 of the year of application at an approved testing site. The results are shared with the parents and sent to the program. The usual fee is $125 but "accommodation can be made for families who are in need" we were told.

A good source on I.Q. testing for the various TAG programs is Victor Toledo, director of the **National Training and Evaluation Center**, 15 West 84th Street, New York, NY 10024 (off Central Park West), (212) 877-4480.

Hunter Elementary provides a listing of approved testing agencies with the application.

The Programs

The programs highlighted below are only *a few* of the elementary programs for gifted and talented students available in Manhattan public

451

schools. For information on TAG or alternative programs in your zone, contact your district office. (Keep in mind that the birthdate cutoff for public schools is December 31.)

The Hunter College Campus Schools:
Hunter Elementary, 71 East 94th Street (94th and Park), New York, NY 10128
(212) 860-1262 (Elementary School admissions)

Hunter Elementary is administered through Hunter College of the City University of New York. The school is tuition free and serves as a laboratory for the study of education. Admissions to nursery and kindergarten are open only to Manhattan residents. At seventh grade they take applicants from all five boroughs. Nursery, kindergarten and seventh grades are the only points of entry. However, there is an active wait list for kindergarten applicants. You must apply for your child one year in advance of enrollment—apply to the nursery school the year that he is three, apply to kindergarten the year she is four. Applicants to seventh grade are tested in sixth grade. Parents are advised to call or write for an application in September of the year prior to the year of enrollment. Parents must then make a testing appointment for the Stanford Binet IV at an approved testing center. (The usual fee for the Stanford Binet is $125 but it can be waived.) Students are interviewed in a group at Hunter Elementary. One recent year the cutoff for the Stanford Binet was 98th percentile and above but this score varies from year to year.

Hunter High School, (212) 860-1259 admissions, (212) 860-1261 for certification information. Seventh grade is the *only* point of entry to Hunter High School. Entrance is based solely on performance on the Hunter entrance exam. Each year there are approximately 2,000 applicants for 240 places; there is a slightly lower cutoff for students of economically disadvantaged status and thirty places (of the 240) are reserved for these applicants. In order to sit for the January exam, students must have the principal of their school submit a certification package to Hunter High by the first week of November. To qualify, students must have scored in the 91st percentile or above in reading and in the 93rd percentile or above in math on *any* standardized test taken in fifth grade. There is a $40.00 fee.

452

The Anderson Program, at Public School 9, 100 West 84th Street (at Columbus Avenue), New York, NY 10024, (212) 595-7193
Alice Geismar, Coordinator

The Anderson Program accepts applications for kindergarten through fifth grade. There are two classes per grade. Applications must be submitted the year before entering. Interested parents will be sent an application and a brochure describing the application process in full (or can pick up an application at the school during school hours). Admission is based on "very superior performance on a test of cognitive ability, an interview and screening, teacher recommendation, school records and social maturity." Call the following number(s) in the fall to arrange for a group tour: (212) 678-2812 or 678-2813.

New York City Laboratory School for Gifted Education (Lower Lab), 1700 Third Avenue (between 95th and 96th Streets), New York, NY 10128, (212) 427-2798
Elizabeth Kasowitz, Director

The Lab School "operates on the premise that gifted education need not be elitist." The Lab School uses flexible or mixed-age class groupings serving ages four through nine/ten (kindergarten through fifth). There are generally two classes per grade: two K/first classes and two first/second classes and so on. Applications must be submitted one year prior to enrollment. The Lab School has open houses every fall—call for dates. Call in early October for a group tour appointment which is required before application is made. The tour is followed by an explanation of the school's philosophy and a question-and-answer session. Parents are then given an application. The application requires a skills checklist and a teacher evaluation. The school will accept any psychoeducational testing completed within a year of application. There is no cutoff score. When the file is complete, the child comes in for a thirty minute observation (open work time) within the classroom with four to six other applicants. Note: Students in Lower Lab must apply to the Upper Lab School as they would to any other gifted/option middle school program. Admission to Upper Lab is not automatic.

New York City Laboratory School for Collaborative Studies (Upper Lab School), 333 West 17th Street, New York, NY 10011 (212) 691-6119
Rob Menken, Sheila Breslaw, Co-directors

The Upper Lab consists of grades six through twelve. Total enrollment is approximately 650. The Upper Lab School is rigorous and academic, but non-traditional; emphasis is put on collaborative and interactive approaches to learning. The middle school has consistently scored #1 in reading and math scores in the city. The majority of students come from District 2, but a small number are accepted from out of the district. Applications should be filed by the first week of January of the year prior to enrollment. The largest point of entry is at sixth grade. Sixth and seventh graders are required to have an interview and to take a teacher-designed math problem solving test and a teacher-designed essay test; both are administered at the Upper Lab School. Ninth grade is the second largest point of entry. Applicants for ninth grade use the normal high school application process, but applicants must have a solid academic background and should have completed Sequential I Math and Spanish. "We look at grades and courses." College courses are offered in the eleventh and twelfth grades and internships are available in eleventh. Students can take college level courses at area universities including NYU, Borough of Manhattan Community College, Hunter and Parson's School of Design. The school has an overseas and foreign exchange program funded by the Lauder Foundation.

Community Districts Two and Three

District Two is composed of Manhattan below 59th Street, East and West Sides (excluding the Lower East Side (District One)) and most of the Upper East Side.

Community School District Two Office, 333 Seventh Avenue, 7th Floor, New York, NY 10001, (212) 330-9400
Call and ask for the brochure "Choosing a Public School in Community District Two."
District Two magnet program choice coordinator: Eileen Friedman, (212) 330-9407. Ms. Friedman will answer questions about the alternative programs, which include the gifted and magnet programs.
District Two Variance Coordinator: Beverly Herschkowitz, (212) 330-9406
Coordinator for Middle School Choice (212) 330-9407
There are six elementary gifted and talented programs in District

Two: P.S. 6, New York City Laboratory School for Gifted Education, P.S. 116, P.S. 11, P.S. 124, P.S. 130.

Community School District Three Office, 300 West 96th Street, New York, NY 10025, (212) 678-2800. District Three extends north from 59th Street to 122nd Street and east from the Hudson River to Central Park West.

District Three Gifted and Talented Programs, call Marilyn Carello at (212) 678-2896 for an application to Gifted Programs in District Three.

Office of Alternative Schools (Middle School information) (212) 330-9407

T.A.G. Programs in District 2

P.S. 6, 45 East 81st Street, New York, NY 10028, (212) 794-4772
Pam Fuchs, Liaison.
For a tour of P.S. 6 call the Parents Association in October at (212) 988-1029.

This popular East Side elementary school attracts many families who live in the zone.

A small number of children are also accepted into kindergarten from outside the zone but within the district. Acceptance is based on a performance-based screening and teacher recommendation. Siblings of children currently attending P.S. 6 are accepted automatically. No psychological testing is required. The deadline for kindergarten applications is mid-December before the year of enrollment. Parents are notified in late Spring. Children from other districts may apply to grades 1 through 5, if space is available. All classes at P.S. 6 are heterogeneously grouped. School tours start in October. Parents can get an application during the tour or from the front desk between 4:00 PM and 6:00 PM whenever school is in session.

P.S. 116, 210 East 33rd Street, New York, NY 10016 (212) 685-4366
Steve Zownir, Coordinator

The gifted and talented program at P.S. 116 serves kindergarten through fifth grades. Students are selected on the basis of a screening process. An interview and a teacher evaluation form from the child's current teacher are required for admission. There is usually one class per grade.

P.S. 124, 40 Division Street, New York, NY 10002, (212) 966-7237
Nancy Jung, Gifted and Talented Program Liasion
The gifted program at P.S. 124, located in Chinatown, serves kindergarten through fifth grades. There is one gifted class per grade. The deadline for applications is December 31st previous to the year of enrollment. Admissions decisions are based on a screening process. Tours are given the first Friday of every month. For a tour call the Parents Association at (212) 274-0263. Parents can send a self-addressed, stamped envelope for an application.

P.S. 11, West 21st Street, New York, NY 10011, (212) 929-1743
Brenda Steele, Principal
The Gifted and Talented Program at P.S. 11 serves kindergarten through fifth grades. There is one gifted section per grade. Prospetive applicants should call for a tour.

P.S. 130, 143 Baxter Street, New York, NY 10013, (212) 226-8072
Lily Woo, Principal
P.S. 130 is located between Little Italy and Chinatown. The gifted program, created in 1998, serves grades kindergarten and first grade and will add a grade each year through fifth grade. The schoolhouse recently received a $32 million facelift and boasts an art room with a kiln, a science room, and a media center in the library. Applicants are admitted based upon a screening process and interview.

T.A.G. Programs in District 3

Patricia Romandetto, Superintendent, (212) 678-2880
Marilyn Carella, Coordinator of Gifted Programs in District 3: (212) 678-2897 (Grades pre-K through five.)
Lizabeth Sostre, Coordinator of Alternative Programs, District 3: (212) 678-2885

P.S. 145: 150 West 105th Street
(212) 678-2858 contact: Leonore
One class per grade pre-kindergarten through fourth grade.
The Stanford-Binet IV is required for admission.
Tours are given beginning in mid-October.

P.S. 163: 163 West 97th Street
(212) 678-2854 general, (212) 678-2926 for tour dates, contact: Trish Eckert
Jorge Izquierdo, Principal
P.S. 163 has a dual language (Spanish) Talented and Gifted Program (TAG) for kindergarten through fourth grades. The Stanford-Binet IV is required for admission.

P.S. 9: 100 West 84th Street
(212) 678-2812 general
For Gifted Program contact Ms. Carella at the District 3 office, (212) 678-2897
P.S. 9's Program for Gifted and Talented students is a magnet program. After much controversy about moving the G & T program out of P.S. 9 to P.S. 166, in 1998 the program was reinstated. There is one class per grade, kindergarten through fourth grade. The Stanford-Binet IV is required and most students score above the 90th percentile. A teacher evaluation and scores from standardized tests in reading and math are required for admission to third and fourth grades.

P.S. 166, 132 West 89th Street, New York, NY 10024, (212) 678-2829
Iris Sutton, admissions coordinator
The gifted program at P.S. 166 was created in 1998 and serves prekindergarten through second grade, adding a grade each year through fourth grade. The program is very popular (especially in pre-K) so parents should call Marilyn Carella at the district office (678-2897) the first week of October for applications, which are first come, first served. The school prefers the Stanford-Binet but will also translate ERB scores. Check out the school's website which was set up by a P.S. 166 parent.

P.S. 185, 20 West 112th Street, New York, NY 10026, (212) 678-2841
Norma Genao, Principal
The G&T program at P.S. 185 serves kindergarten through second grade. One class (out of four) per grade is designated as "gifted." The test for admission is administered at the office of Community School District Three. P.S. 185 is a sister school to P.S. 208.

P.S. 208, 21 West 111th Street, New York, NY 10026, (212) 678-2882
Corine Pettey, Principal

The gifted program at P.S. 208 serves grades three through five. There is one gifted class per grade. P.S. 185 feeds into P.S. 208.

M.S. 54 The Delta Honors Program, 103 West 107th Street, New York, NY 10025, (212) 678-5855
Frederick La Senna, Director
Students can apply to this top-rated middle school at grades five or six. Entrance is based upon superior reading and math scores plus an interview. The school does not usually accept students from out of the district. Parents looking for a middle school should call the district office for the "middle school options book" in late October of the year prior to enrollment.

T.A.G. Programs in District 4

Community District Four Office: 319 East 117th Street
(212) 828-3500
Harvey Newman, Director of Option Programs, Coordinator of TAG/alternative programs in District 4: ext. 3516

P.S. 171, Patrick Henry Prep, 19 East 103rd Street
(212) 860-5801
Miss Dolores Greyez, Director of Gifted Program
The TAG program at P.S. 171 serves kindergarten through sixth grade.

The Bilingual, Bicultural Mini-School at P.S. 83, 219 East 109th Street, Room #300
(212) 860-6031 or 6032
Miss Lourdes Arroyo, Director
The dual language (Spanish) TAG program serves kindergarten through eighth grade.

J.H.S. 117, 240 East 109th Street
(212) 860-6003
Janette Cesar, Director
The TAG program is part of the alternative complex within Junior High School 117. The program serves children in kindergarten through eighth grade. Applicants are tested at the school.

T.A.G. Programs in District 6

The Discovery School, P.S. 98, 512 West 212th Street
(212) 927-7870
Ms. Maria Fraga, Coordinator
The Discovery School's dual language Program for Gifted and Talented Students within P.S. 98 serves kindergarten through fourth grade.

Mott Hall, 131st Street and Convent Avenue, (212) 927-9466
Dr. Miriam Acosta-Sing, Director
Mott Hall offers a very demanding academic program for grades four through eight. The program is over ten years old. Eighty percent of the students are bilingual in Spanish but only one of the classes is bilingual. Applications must be filed one year in advance of enrollment. Applicants must live in District 6 and score 85% and above on citywide reading and math tests; students are also tested at Mott Hall. Teacher recommendations and grades are also considered for admission.

THE PUBLIC HIGH SCHOOLS

General information can be obtained by calling the Division of High Schools, the Office of High School Admissions, (212) 481-7034
The board of education publishes a yearly *Directory of the Public High Schools*, which will be sent to you upon request, free of charge, if you call the Division of High Schools at (212) 481-7034 or (718) 935-3415. The directory provides detailed information on over 150 public high schools, including the thirty new "theme" schools that opened in 1994. The directory describes the admissions process and requirements for each school.
The Public Education Association (PEA) publishes a guide to city high schools consisting of statistical information and rankings.

The Specialized High Schools

There are four specialized high schools. These schools require an entrance examination or audition. *The Student Handbook for the*

Specialized High Schools (which describes the individual schools and their admissions process and includes two sample admissions examinations) can be obtained by calling or writing the New York City Public Schools Division of High Schools, 22 East 28th Street, New York, NY 10016, (212) 481-7034, or from the Office of Access and Compliance, 110 Livingston Street, Room 808, Brooklyn, NY 11201, (718) 935-3415.

Stuyvesant High School, Bronx High School of Science and Brooklyn Technical High School, known as "the science schools," emphasize mathematics and science studies. New York State Education Law requires a written examination for admission to the science schools. The three schools are different from one another so applicants must take the entrance exam at their first-choice science school. In addition, there is the Fiorello H. LaGuardia High School of Music and Art and the Performing Arts.

In 1998 Alumni of Brooklyn Tech pledged to create a $10 million endowment fund. Three months later, Leonard and Ronald Lauder, both Bronx Science alumni, pledged $1 million to launch a campaign seeking to raise $10 million for their alma mater.

Timetable for admissions to the specialized high schools:
September: Call for a handbook and application
November: Applications are due in early November
December: Exams are offered to students in either 8th or 9th grades one year *prior* to the year of enrollment. The exam is taken at the candidate's first-choice school.
March: Notification of acceptance

THE MATH/SCIENCE INSTITUTE
345 Chambers Street
New York, NY 10282
(212) 312-4816
Fax: (212) 312-4815
e-mail: ravageb@stuy.edu

Bruce Ravage, Director

In March 1995 former Public Schools Chancellor Ramon C. Cortines announced the creation of an 18-month preparatory program designed to groom able seventh graders from diverse backgrounds for admission to any one of the three specialized science high schools.

Participating students attend various parochial, public and independent schools. Originally housed at Stuyvesant High School, the program has expanded to four sites. Recommendation to the program must be made by the student's school principal. The Math/Science Institute has a post-grade six summer session, a Wednesday/Saturday grade seven school-year program, a post-grade seven summer session and a fall grade eight session. Over an 18-month period approximately 1,000 students participated. In addition to test preparation, students take courses in literature, writing, math, science and research skills.

Bronx High School of Science

75 West 205th Street, Bronx, New York, NY 10468, (718) 817-7700
Stanley Blumenstein, Principal

Total enrollment: 2,600 students. Students come to Bronx Science from every borough. The Bronx Science yellow school bus can be seen travelling up and down Manhattan's avenues. The school population is 40% Asian. Bronx Science students have opportunities for independent research. There is a Holocaust Study Center and Museum, nine foreign languages are offered, and there are partnerships with NASA, The Bronx Zoo, Rockefeller University, Stevens Technology and so on. The handbook says, "Bronx Science is the nation's all time leader in the Westinghouse Science Talent Search." The school has five alumni Nobel Laureates. Extracurricular activities include over 60 clubs, numerous school publications, orchestral and vocal music programs, and 30 athletic teams; a nationally acclaimed speech and debate team, Mock trial, and a full-scale theatrical production each year.

Brooklyn Technical High School

29 Fort Greene Place (South Elliot Place at DeKalb Avenue), Brooklyn, NY 11217, (718) 858-5150, Dr. Lee McCaskill, Principal

Total enrollment: 4,600 students. The student body is diverse. The brochure states that Brooklyn Tech excels in the areas of engineering, math and science and computer science. During 9th and 10th grades students take an academic core of studies and are introduced to engineering, computer science and lab science through hands-on experiences in well-equipped laboratories. At the end of sophomore year, students select a major area of concentration which they begin in 11th grade. All tech students are prepared to follow any course of study at the college level, but are particularly well versed in their major area. Brooklyn Tech has over 100 clubs and fields varsity and junior varsity teams in handball, fencing, football, swimming, baseball, soccer and basketball.

Stuyvesant High School

345 Chambers Street, New York, NY 10282, (212) 312-4800, Mrs. Jinx Perullo, Principal

Total enrollment: 3,028 students. Stuyvesant High School occupies a brand-new high-tech building in lower Manhattan. In addition to advanced courses in mathematics and the sciences, students can select from a wide range of electives. Advanced Placement classes in biology, chemistry, physics, foreign language, mathematics, English and social studies are offered. Stuyvesant's extracurricular offerings are broad. There are over 50 clubs, a symphony orchestra, dance band, choral and ensemble groups, thirty-two athletic teams, fifteen student publications and an active student government. The school has an Olympic-size swimming pool.

Fiorello H. LaGuardia High School of Music and Art and Performing Arts

100 Amsterdam Avenue, New York, NY 10023, (212) 496-0700, Dr. Paul R. Saronson, Principal

Total enrollment: 2,600. LaGuardia is the high school featured in the movie *Fame*. It is the only public high school in the world that offers a complete academic program along with professional-level training in the arts. Because of the dual nature of the program, LaGuardia students can expect to put in very long days. Admission to this high school is based on an individual audition in dance, drama, instrumental music, vocal music or art. Only New York City residents are eligible. The handbook describes what is needed for the audition.

AFTER-SCHOOL ATHLETIC
AND OTHER PROGRAMS

There are a number of organized after school athletic programs such as **Joe Espinoza**, **Cavaliers**, and so on, which feature quality coaching and team play and provide door to door bus transportation from your child's private or public school to the program and home. Your child's school probably has an established relationship with one of these programs. Both boys and girls are welcome to participate. Fees vary but since they provide transportation these programs are costly. As an alternative, we have listed below some of the most popular city athletic programs.

CYO Manhattan Youth Baseball: Bobby Hoffman, Coordinator, 118 East 93rd Street, #1D, New York, NY 10128, (212) 722-6383 for recorded registration information. CYO Baseball is the Manhattan version of suburban Little League. Priority is given to returning players and there is a wait list for new members. Call in early fall to register for spring.

Yorkville Youth Athletic Association: Arlene Virga, Director, (212) 876-4976. Yorkville Youth Athletic Association offers a Saturday basketball league that plays from December to March. Teams play at four East Side locations. Kindergarten through tenth grade, co-ed, girls' and boys' teams. Volleyball in September, Tennis December through April. Baseball (K–8) begins in March; played at Asphalt Green and Central Park. Fees are very reasonable ($75.00 for a season of play) and there is space for new players.

City Sports for Kids at Asphalt Green: Bob Glover, Shelley Lynn-Florence, Coordinators, (914) 366-4175. Track and field program, for a very reasonable fee.

Westside Soccer League: (212) 663-7660 to register. Website: WSSL.org. Open to children from around the city, ages 5-16.

Stanley Isaacs Neighborhood Center: 1792 First Avenue, (212) 360-7625, Girls' gym night: every Wednesday, basketball for 11–20 year olds. Softball leagues for 11–14 year olds and 14–18 year olds. All programs are free of charge.

The After School Workshop, 45 East 81st Street (at P.S. 6), New York, NY 10028, (212) 734-7620, Mrs. Sheila N. Bandman, founder and supervisor. Located in the "penthouse" at P.S. 6, the After School Workshop, now approaching its 20th year, is one of the best kept secrets on the East Side. In a relaxed and low-key atmosphere, children can choose from a variety of creative and recreational activities (crafts, dance, board games, sports, homework help, and computer). The attentive staff keeps things humming along. The workshop is open to children from other schools (a large contingent from Brearley attend) 3:00 to 6:00 P.M. weekdays and all day on vacation days. Children can attend from one to five days a week and regular Workshop children can bring a playdate free of charge.

Job !

OTHER RESOURCES

1. **The National Association of Independent Schools (NAIS)**, Office of Public Information, 1620 L. Street NW, Washington, D.C. 20036, (202) 973-9700, website: nais-schools.org. The website has a database of over 1,000 schools.

   NAIS is a voluntary organization to which accredited independent schools may apply for membership. The primary function of NAIS is to serve its over 1,100 member schools. NAIS does not accredit independent schools but does issue guidelines, chart trends, sponsor workshops and publish information on issues relevant to the independent school community from diversity to boarding schools. Many of these publications can be ordered by parents free of charge. NAIS recently published *Taking Measure: Perspectives on Curriculum and Change*, available from NAIS publications order department (203) 973-9749

   Also available from NAIS publications is JoAnn Deak's readable and informative book: *How Girls Thrive: An Essential Guide for Educators (and Parents).*

   Parents who are interested in learning more about boarding schools can call the Association of Boarding Schools Answer Line, (800) 541-5908, and speak with an experienced boarding school admissions counselor, Monday, Wednesday or Friday from 9 A.M. until 1 P.M., Tuesday or Thursday from 12 P.M. until 4 P.M.

2. **Educational Testing Service (ETS)**, P.O. Box 6657, Princeton N.J., 08541-6657, (609) 921-9000.

   The Educational Testing Service publishes informational pamphlets on many issues related to independent schools, including financial aid. **School and Student Services for Financial Aid** is administered by the ETS and their direct number is (609) 771-7770. The SSS processes financial aid applications.

3. **Reading Reform Foundation of New York**, 333 West 57th Street, Suite 1L, New York, NY 10019, (212) 307-7320, Fax (212) 307-0449, e-mail: ReadingReform.rrfny@mcimail.com.

   The Reading Reform Foundation of New York, founded in 1981 by a group of reading specialists and interested citizens, is a nonprofit literacy organization based on the belief that almost every child, regardless of social and economic background, can learn to read, write and spell if taught by effective methods (with an emphasis on the use of phonics). Reading Reform Foundation offers courses all year 'round in the teaching of reading, writing and spelling, holds an annual fall conference, conducts workshops for parents and sends skilled teaching consultants into public schools throughout the city to work with classroom teachers.

4. **The Council for Religion in Independent Schools**, 4405 East-West Highway, Suite 506, Bethesda, Maryland 20814, (301) 657-0912

The Council for Religion in Independent Schools (CRIS) is a nondenominational organization composed of 360 member schools the majority of which are secular coed day schools located in the Middle Atlantic states.

CRIS is independent of any religious body and does not impose any one point of view. According to the brochure "It is the only national, interfaith, professional organization meeting the moral and religious needs of independent schools." CRIS conducts workshops and directs conferences on values, ethics and religion education.

CRIS has been actively promoting community service in schools for many years and sponsors conferences that feature community service workshops. CRIS sponsors the National Community Service Network, which publishes a newsletter keeping member schools abreast of innovative, successful community service projects at various schools.

New York City Independent Schools That are Members of CRIS:

The Allen-Stevenson School
The Browning School
The Buckley School
The Caedmon School
The Cathedral School
Collegiate School
Convent of the Sacred Heart
Grace Church School
Horace Mann School
Marymount School of New York

The Nightingale-Bamford School
The Packer Collegiate Institute
Saint David's School
St. Hilda's & St. Hugh's School
St. Luke's School
The Spence School
The Town School
Trinity School

5. **The Catholic Center**, Office of Superintendent of Schools, Education Department, 1011 First Avenue (between 55th and 56th) (18th floor), New York, NY 10022, (212) 371-1000

   For $8, The Catholic Center will mail its complete directory of elementary and secondary schools. A list of Catholic high schools only will be mailed to you free of charge.

6. **The National Coalition of Girls' Schools**, Meg Milne Moulton or Whitney Ransome, Executive Directors, 228 Main Street, Concord, Massachusetts 01742, (978) 287-4485, Fax (978) 287-6014, website: ncgs.org

   The National Coalition of Girls' Schools has 79 member schools in North America (both public and private). Its members share a commitment to the values and advantages of an all-girl's school. They conduct research, gather data, and sponsor forums for leading girls' and womens' groups; The NCGS also provides guidance for choosing a girls' school. NCGS publications, including: *Choosing a Girls' School, Raising Confident, Competent Daughters*, and *What Every Girl in School Needs to Know*, and *Girls and Technology*, are available by mail order.

7. **American Association of University Women (AAUW)**, 1111 Sixteenth Street N.W., Washington, D.C. 20036-4873, 1(800)326-AAUW (membership information and to locate a local branch of AAUW), (202) 785-7788 (general) or 1(800)225-9998 (for a copy of *How Schools Shortchange Girls* and *Separated by Sex: A Critical Look at Single-Sex Education for Girls*). Members' Help Line (800)821-4364.

   In 1992 the AAUW Educational Foundation released the report *How Schools Shortchange Girls* which challenged myths about the education of girls in the public schools and uncovered disturbing evidence of new barriers to their learning. In March 1998 the AAUW released a report that finds separating by sex is *not* the solution to gender inequity. *Separated by Sex: A Critical Look at Single-Sex Education for Girls* is controversial and well worth reading. The AAUW has been working toward eliminating the educational, financial and legal barriers faced by women and girls for over 125 years. Parents can request free of charge useful guides for assessing gender bias in their children's schools—the *School Assessment Guide* and *Growing Smart: What Works for Girls in School*.

8. **The Association of Teachers in Independent Schools in New York City and Vicinity, Inc. (ATIS)**, P.O. Box 1385, Gracie Station, New York, NY 10028, (212) 472-3572

ATIS was found in 1914 to ensure that teachers in private schools were properly paid and protected. Today the incorporated, non-profit organization continues its support of educational professionalism and increased opportunities for private-school teachers. ATIS sponsors several workshops for teachers throughout the year as well as the annual conference—book exhibit. ATIS publishes *The Bulletin* twice a year, which reports news of schools represented by the association, and in the spring contains a list of school positions available. Yearly dues are $25.

9. **The Interschool Faculty Diversity Search**, (212) 758-5413, Fax: (212) 758-8931.

The Search is a newly created organization (1996) whose purpose is to enlarge the pool of talented candidates of color for faculty and administrative positions in participating schools. Although the Search is administered by Interschool (a consortium of eight Manhattan independent schools) many more schools (over 25) participate. Peter Clifton, who with his wife also runs Clifton Associates (a beginning teacher placement agency), is the Search's full-time recruiter.

10. **The Guild of New York Independent Schools**, Dr. Stephen M. Clement, III, Headmaster, The Browning School, President, 52 East 62nd Street, New York, NY 10021 (212) 838-6280

The guild is an informal association of approximately fifty-two heads of school (from schools located in all five boroughs) who meet three times a year at the Cosmopolitan Club to discuss common concerns within the independent-school community (such as medical benefits for faculty) and to coordinate their calendars (vacation schedules, opening and closing dates). They do *not* discuss tuitions. The guild does not provide information to parents about individual schools.

11. **NYC-Parents in Action Inc.**, P.O. Box 555, Lenox Hill Station, New York, NY 10021, (212) 987-9629

Rumors circulate that certain schools have more drug and/or alcohol abuse than others. The truth is that a portion of the student body at all the New York City independent high schools (and boarding schools) does experiment with alcohol, drugs and/or sex. NYC-Parents In Action, Inc. is a nonprofit, voluntary organization that was incorporated in 1979 as a response to growing alcohol, marijuana and other drug use among minors and their parents. In support of the belief that "Good parenting is substance abuse prevention," NYC-PIA provides information, parent education, seminars and workshops and provides trained facilitators for parent-organized discussion groups. The Parent Representative program provides a link to the parent body within the independent schools. NYC-PIA publishes *FOCUS* and a newsletter. In cooperation with the Parents' League, NYC-PIA sponsors the annual Teen Scene—a candid discussion of teen life in the city by a panel composed of students from various independent and boarding schools.

12. **State Education Office of Non-Public Schools**, New York State Education Department, Non-public School Services Team, Room 471 Education Building Annex, Washington Avenue, Albany, New York 12234, (518) 474-3879

   State Education Office of Non-Public Schools, Department of Instruction and Program Development, (a division of the State Education Office that compiles statistical information), Room 962 Education Building Annex, Albany, New York 12234, (518) 474-7965

   Upon request, the Department of Instruction and Program Development will send a statistical breakdown for each school based on an extensive questionnaire. Information includes the number and type of computers the school owns, which foreign languages are taught and the ethnic and religious composition of the student body and faculty. (Most of this information can be obtained more easily from the school's brochure or directly from the school.)

ACCREDITING ORGANIZATIONS

The New York State Board of Regents authorizes both the New York State Association of Independent Schools and the Middle States Association to accredit schools. According to the National Association of Independent Schools, "Accreditation is a process of peer evaluation that certifies that schools meet certain generally accepted standards of educational quality defined by an independent entity." Each of the independent schools sets forth its accreditation in its brochure. Tradition determines which organization accredits the school. NYSAIS deals primarily with the independent schools in New York State, whereas Middle States accredits many independent as well as public schools in the Middle Atlantic states. Note: NYSAIS and Middle States do not provide parents with information about specific schools—do not call them to find out which school is the best for your child.

How does it work? Both NYSAIS and Middle States evaluate a school based on its philosophy (or mission) and how well the school puts its philosophy into practice—is the school doing what it says it does? This evaluation process takes place every ten years or so. The first step in the reaccreditation process is a year-long self-study. Next, the school is evaluated by a team of recognized evaluators, which often includes heads of other independent schools. The evaluating team makes recommendations for improvement, and the school is requested to provide an action plan for implementing these changes. Accreditation is granted if the self-study, evaluation and planning reports reveal that the school meets the standards for accreditation. Accreditation is granted for a period of ten years. After approximately eight and a half years, the school begins another self-study and the cycle is renewed.

1. **New York State Association of Independent Schools (NYSAIS)**, 287 Pawling Avenue, Troy, NY 12180-5238, (518) 274-0184 website: www.nysais.org, Executive Director: Fred Calder

    NYSAIS is an accrediting organization for over 140 independent elementary and secondary schools in New York State. NYSAIS publishes a useful pamphlet entitled "Choosing a School: A Guide for Parents."

2. **The Middle States Association of Colleges and Schools (Middle States)**, 3624 Market Street, 2nd Floor Annex, Philadelphia, PA 19104, (215) 662-5600 or 5610

    Susannah S. Pierce, Associate Director for Nonpublic Schools
    John A. Stoops, Executive Director, Commission on Elementary Schools

    The Middle States Association established standards that are administered by the three accreditation authorities under the auspices of the Middle States Association: the Commission on Elementary Schools, the Commission on Secondary Schools and the

Commission on Higher Education. The Middle States Association is a nonprofit organization established in 1887 to set standards for American education. Middle States publishes information on school standards and the accreditation process.

Index of Schools and Programs